The Urban Fix

Resilient Cities in the W
Climate Change, Heat Islands and
Overpopulation

Doug Kelbaugh

[handwritten inscription: To President & Fellows of Clare Hall, from life member and fan of Cambridge. Cheers, Doug 10/9/22]

Routledge
Taylor & Francis Group

NEW YORK AND LONDON

First published 2019
by Routledge
52 Vanderbilt Avenue, New York, NY 10017

and by Routledge
2 Park Square, Milton Park, Abingdon, Oxon, OX14 4RN

Routledge is an imprint of the Taylor & Francis Group, an informa business

© 2019 Taylor & Francis

Library of Congress Cataloging-in-Publication Data
Names: Kelbaugh, Doug, author.
Title: The urban fix : resilient cities in the war against climate change, heat
    islands and overpopulation / Doug Kelbaugh.
Description: New York, NY : Routledge, 2019. | Includes bibliographical
    references and index.
Identifiers: LCCN 2018048899 (print) | LCCN 2018049971 (ebook) | ISBN
    9780429057441 (ebook) | ISBN 9780367175696 (hbk : alk. paper) |
    ISBN 9780367175702 (pbk : alk. paper) | ISBN 9780429057441 (ebk)
Subjects: LCSH: Urban ecology (Sociology) | Cities and towns—Growth. |
    City planning—Environmental aspects. | Urban heat island.
Classification: LCC HT241 (ebook) | LCC HT241 .K45 2019 (print) |
    DDC307.76—dc23
LC record available at https://lccn.loc.gov/2018048899

ISBN: 978-0-367-17569-6 (hbk)
ISBN: 978-0-367-17570-2 (pbk)
ISBN: 978-0-429-05744-1 (ebk)

Typeset in Sabon
by Swales & Willis Ltd, Exeter, Devon, UK

The Urban Fix

Cities are one of the most significant contributors to global climate change. The rapid speed at which urban centers use large amounts of resources adds to the global crisis and can lead to extreme local heat. *The Urban Fix* addresses how urban design, planning and policies can counter the threats of climate change, urban heat islands and overpopulation, helping cities take full advantage of their inherent advantages and new technologies to catalyze social, cultural and physical solutions to combat the epic, unprecedented challenges humanity faces.

The book fills a conspicuous void in the international dialogue on climate change and heat islands by examining both the environmental benefits in developed countries and the population benefit in developing countries. Urban heat islands can be addressed in incremental, manageable steps, such as planting trees and painting roofs white, which provide a more concrete and proactive sense of progress for policymakers and practitioners. This book is invaluable to anyone searching for a better understanding of the impact of resilient cities in the monumental and urgent fight against climate change, and provides the tools to do so.

Doug Kelbaugh FAIA FCNU, with two degrees from Princeton University, USA, has been an acclaimed educator and practitioner who has won over 20 design awards and competitions over the past four decades. He speaks internationally, publishes voluminously and teaches the largest elective offered by his college at the University of Michigan, USA, where he is a Professor and Dean Emeritus. He has authored and edited six books and many book chapters on livable, lovable and resilient architecture and cities. The AIA and ACSA awarded Professor Kelbaugh the 2016 Topaz Medallion for Excellence in Architectural Education, the highest award in the field, noting that he has bridged the fields of architecture, sustainability and urbanism as much as any member of his generation.

This longest book of my career is dedicated to my wife Kathleen, my children Casey Kelbaugh and Tess Kelbaugh MacDonald and her husband Michael, as well my two grandkids Ramsey and Nell MacDonald. May they find both respite from and meaning in the challenges ahead.

Contents

Foreword, by Peter Calthorpe   viii
Preface   xi

1 Connecting the Dots: Climate Change, Heat Islands,
   Overpopulation and Cities   1

2 Triple Threat: UHIs, CC and Overpopulation   39

3 Urban Albedo and Morphology   84

4 Waste Heat   106

5 Cool Micro-climates and Urban Trees   150

6 Policies and Case Studies   173

7 The Sharing Cosmopolis: Prosperity
   without Growth   198

8 Cities: Our Last, Best Hope   211

9 Time to Act   265

   Index   301

Foreword

I met Doug Kelbaugh four decades ago, as a fellow pioneer in the early passive solar movement. His famous Trombe Wall house in New Jersey was among the most publicized and influential passive solar buildings of the era. Little did we know it would lead to career-long collaboration, including a short-lived partnership, and lifelong friendship. It has been a close, fruitful relationship and collaboration that has included many essays and several books on architecture and urbanism that culminate in these pages.

He posits that cities are our last, best hope. That's a bold-faced claim. However, he builds the case brick by brick, like the talented architectural and urban designer he is. The foundation is the already well-understood climate crisis, which he elaborates in compelling and new ways, with a comprehensive and perceptive list of facts and figures.

The first course of bricks on top the foundation wall of climate change is the extreme heat that increasingly plagues most of the planet's cities. Urban Heat Islands and heat waves are making cities hotter twice as fast as their surrounding countryside and as the planet as a whole. Extreme heat and humidity are taking an ugly toll on health and livability. And as Doug points out, hotter temperatures can deter people from moving to cities and induce existing urban residents to leave for cooler places. Why is this important? Because cities have many benefits that are essential to human wellbeing and survival.

The second brick course supports a major benefit in the developed world: urban residents have smaller energy/carbon footprints than their suburban and rural counterparts. He aptly refers to this good, if counter-intuitive news as the "environmental paradox of cities."

The third course in this edifice is being laid in the developing world, where rural migrants to cities reduce their birth rates, sometimes drastically. Their smaller families mean smaller energy/carbon footprints per household and a smaller national footprint. The reduction in fertility rates helps compensate for their larger per capita footprints as higher incomes in the city encourage greater consumption.

The next layer is more good news: the ways to address climate change and urban heat islands are one and the same. That is, reducing local heat in cities also combats global climate change, often in equal amounts. So why make the distinction between local and worldwide climate change? Because very hot urban temperatures, especially with high humidity, make life miserable, and misery motivates people to act. Whereas climate change is a more remote, abstract, longer-term problem and does not rally people to act as urgently. And the science of local climate change is different from global climate change.

The fifth brick course consists of the actual strategies and tactics to mitigate and adapt to urban heat islands. Cities overheat for two reasons. Their dark rooftops and paved areas, both of which are vast in area, absorb solar radiation that can overheat the local environment. The second source is emissions from tailpipes, chimneys and air conditioners, which add heat as well as carbon to the air. Reducing tailpipe emissions – something we're both working on currently – is a larger scale issue. It requires getting people out of cars onto transit, bikes and their feet, which is a more systemic challenge, but it is a battle that is starting to be won. As for heat spewed into the city by air conditioners, passive solar cooling techniques can reduce their use, as we both learned four decades ago.

The last brick course is an arch – the self-supporting array of benefits of cities that go beyond the mitigation of and adaption to climate change. As Doug writes of urbanism, "the environmental-social synergies and the potential for shared economies, are harnessed, along with cities' productivity, creative ferment, social tolerance and cultural richness, not to mention their economic-political efficiencies and successes."

The arch brings up a dimension that is not typical in books on climate change – esthetics, which the author calls the 4th E of sustainability. Although the book is not about design and beauty per se, it does point out that unless the built environment is pleasing, it will not be loved and therefore not sustained over time. Doug would know, having won so many design competitions and design awards – no doubt more than anyone from the passive solar movement.

All this started with that movement, which was triggered by the 1972 Oil Embargo and responded to both energy shortages and environmental degradation. It led to site-specific architecture that honored local climate, terrain and building culture, and used the building itself rather than solar hardware to collect, store and release solar energy. It spawned an interest in "critical regionalism" that celebrated the local over the universal and in turn ultimately led to the regional planning that frames much of this book, and is still a primary interest of ours.

Our mutual early and ongoing commitment to New Urbanism has led us around the world – literally. We have worked together on projects throughout Asia, the Middle East, Africa, Russia and Europe for a large and progressive development company headquartered in Dubai, collaborating on massive projects that were walkable, mixed-use and transit-oriented. Indeed, we long ago collaborated on a design charrette at the University of Washington that produced *The Pedestrian Pocket Book*. This short book helped popularize what is now known as TOD, or Transit-Oriented-Development – a term now familiar to planning officials around the world.

All in all, his book gathers a remarkable array of facts, figures, concepts, knowledge and insights that only a long lifetime of searching inquiry can assemble and integrate. The author personally knows of what he writes, and when he wades into new waters or offers up-to-date news, he's careful to cite credible sources.

Doug Kelbaugh's accomplishments and honors – some of the highest in the field – underlie the excellence and value of this book: the Association of Collegiate Schools of Architecture and the AIA awarded him the Topaz Medallion, the highest award in the field, and his college gave him a collegiate professorship. His life of teaching and professional practice has allowed him to deepen the book's content. *The Urban Fix* is arguably the most comprehensive and definitive book on how cities combat climate change, urban heat islands and overpopulation.

Peter Calthorpe, Berkeley, California, 2018

Preface

Our species has enjoyed almost perfect climatic and ecological conditions to survive and prosper during the last 12,000 years of the relatively tranquil Holocene Age. We've benefited from a miraculously even-tempered climate, the most stable period of the past 650,000 years.[1] We have come to take a benign climate for granted; civilization has never experienced anything else. These gentle conditions for the last 400 generations have allowed us to develop farming and cities, which in turn have spurred and sponsored very complex, advanced societies. Indeed, we have taken great advantage of this Eden of hospitable and bountiful conditions. We are an intelligent, adaptable and fecund species that has burgeoned and prospered during a fortuitous epoch that our carbon-based civilization has now turned into the Anthropocene Age.

This book attempts to advance a comprehensive, definitive case for the positive and essential role that cities continue to play in our evolution. As long ago as ancient Greece, Plato wrote "By far the greatest and most admirable form of wisdom is that needed to plan and beautify cities and human communities." It is now as essential as it is admirable in the current rush of imperatives and opportunities at the dawn of the Anthropocene Age. The most urgent threat is climate change (hereafter CC). Mark Childs writes in *Sharing Cities*: "That you can't fix the planet without fixing our cities is obvious, but less obvious is that cities can fix the planet."[2] In this era of incessant sound bites and revelations, the long-term challenges are forever being eclipsed by the sensational short-term issues that carry the day. In the meantime, our extraordinarily successful species flirts with its downfall, possibly its collective suicide. In spite of the climate change skeptics, most humans now realize that the climate is changing. Global warming is upon us, with accelerating and profound changes to our civilization and our lives. And most of us accept the world's scientists' near-unanimous verdict – climate change appears to be primarily if not exclusively caused by humans.

In addition to CC, we face resource depletion, ecological destruction and environmental pollution. Social unrest and violence may likely crest before these natural crises, as the psychological impacts are hitting sooner and harder. There has already been more CC than we realize, much less address.

We need to respond to the challenges as interconnected problems, not silo by silo.[3] Climate change is our biggest single challenge. It's mother to a mosaic of existential problems and opportunities that range from environmental, economic and social to spiritual (right up to the peak of Maslow's famous pyramid). More specifically, it's the offspring of CC – the everyday weather, the ubiquitous storms, the nagging narrative – that are overtaking us, while the abstract mega-story fails to mobilize us into action.

Another mega-narrative lurking in the background is global population growth, that other hockey-stick curve of the last several centuries. It is of course connected to CC, because total energy use tracks the number of humans. Our population is expected to peak and level off this century, and then decline, but whether it will be a smooth transition is far from certain. We know both of these two unprecedented challenges won't be pain- or violence-free; evolutionary and revolutionary change never is. Whether the collective response of humankind will be robust enough, soon enough and peaceful enough is up to us. This book presents how we can ease and possibly prevent much of the pain and damage.

A quick preview of what's to come in this wide-ranging, no-stone-unturned, something-for-everybody, encyclopedic book about heat, health and habitat in the Anthropocene. For starters, average annual temperatures in the United States (U.S.) will continue to increase, making recent record-setting years commonplace in the near future. Increases of 5 to 7.5°F (2.8 to 4.8°C) are projected by the late century, depending on the level of future carbon emissions.[4] The five warmest summers in Europe since 1500 have all occurred since 2002, and soon, a U.N. panel of experts warns, "simply being outdoors that time of year will be unhealthy for much of the globe. Even if we meet the Paris goals of limiting the planet to 2°C of warming, cities like Karachi and Kolkata will become close to uninhabitable, annually encountering deadly heat waves like those that crippled them in 2015. At 4°C, the deadly European heat wave of 2003, which killed as many as 2,000 people a day, would be a normal summer . . . The scale of . . . economic devastation is hard to comprehend . . . with an economy half as big, which would produce only half as much value, generating only half as much to offer the workers of the world."[5] The World Health Organization forecasts that by 2030 there will be some 92,000 deaths per year from heat waves, with that figure expected to rise in 2050 to 255,000 deaths annually unless cities reduce and adapt to the threat.[6]

"Fossil fuels accounted for 81% of the world's energy consumption in 1987. Thirty years later it's still 81%."[7] If we don't reduce carbon emissions, imagine this scenario by the end of the century:

> a Hurricane Sandy-level flood inundating Long Island, N.Y. every two weeks, Dust Bowl-intensity drought in the Southwest that persists for decades, Miami largely abandoned and under water, and

Missouri as hot as Arizona is now, with 46–115 days above 95°F each year. Such catastrophic scenarios are not hyperbole, but probable consequences of inaction. Indeed, if there is a fault in climatological findings as a whole, it is that scientists have tended to underplay the threats . . . By 2100, rising oceans could force as many as two billion residents of coastal areas worldwide to migrate to higher ground . . . Unrest will increase across the globe, as it did in drought-ridden Syria, in part because heat makes people agitated, and in part because deteriorating conditions will simply make people desperate.[8]

Worse yet, if humans stopped emitting greenhouse gases tomorrow, we would still have a problem: In 2017, the concentration of CO_2 in the air was 410 parts per million, higher than at any time since the mastodons roamed North America and humans-as-we-know-them didn't exist.[9] The compounding impacts of CC are agonizingly easy to imagine.

A 2°C temperature change may not sound like much: After all, the temperature in most places swings far more during the annual seasons, even during a single afternoon. However, when the average for an entire planet swings a few degrees, the impacts are immense. For instance, the Arctic icecap and mountain glaciers will all but disappear with a 3–5°C (5–9°F) warming.[10] To put it in more theatrical terms, a 5°C (9°F) rise in temperature since the last Ice Age was enough to melt an ice sheet roughly a kilometer thick that covered Michigan. That's equal to the possible rise in temperature by 2100 with business as usual. To put it in perspective, the volume of the vast East Antarctic ice sheet (up to 3 miles thick) is over 1,000 times that of the Great Lakes, and over 100 times the Greenland ice sheet. Although not imminent, the melting of these two ice sheets would respectively raise sea level about 65 m and about 6.6 m. If we don't reduce Greenhouse Gas (GHG), emissions by 2100 the frequency of 100-year floods could increase 3,500-fold.[11] A recent study of New York City found that a flood depth of more than seven feet – which took place only once every 500 years or so before 1800 – would occur every five years or so.[12] Even if these estimates are off by a sizeable factor, the impacts on human mortality and the ability to support the world population of some 8 billion or more are obviously profound.

Speaking of ice and flooding, the U.S. Geological Survey study estimates that the lower 48 states will lose all their glaciers by 2050, with noticeable impacts on seasonal runoff from glaciers, streams, ecological systems and biodiversity. The planet has been through many cycles of warming and cooling, with glaciers having advanced over continents like North America, retreated and disappeared. It has gone from "volcanic blob to iceball to tropical steam to desert, back to another kind of iceball – several times – to its present state."[13] The planet itself will do fine; it is species like ours that will suffer from the heat and ice-melt. Most ecosystems, plants and animals will adapt to the new conditions, as they always have. The critical takeaway is that significant adaptation will be required of *humans*.[14] But homo sapiens also need to better respect other species and the earth. As the Dalai Lama has written, "Every day, we drive 150 species of plants and animals to extinction, expand the deserts by 50,000 hectares, and spew 150 million metric tons of greenhouse gases into the air. Essentially, we are fighting a World War Three against nature."[15]

The stakes for humans have never been higher. In the almost poetic words of a graduate architecture student, the challenge is immense:

> It is an agglomeration of problems across every discipline.
>
> It encompasses consequences that span well beyond the lifetime of a single individual.
>
> It does not respect any human borders.
>
> It is a phenomenon of unprecedented scale.[16]

Needless to say, every generation fears that there's some crisis brewing or catastrophe looming, and that civilization must pull back from the proverbial precipice . . . from biblical Armageddon to medieval plague to the modern nuclear apocalypse. But we now have less space, resources and time to negotiate crises, because our species has come to so overwhelm the environment and planet. It will surely get wilder and more precipitous as we speed up civilization to what might even be the hypothetical *singularity* – that hard-to-fathom moment when artificial intelligence (AI) and other technologies have become so fast and powerful that humanity undergoes some sort of hyperbolic climax and irreversible change. Whether an implosion or explosion, reality would fall off a cliff or reach the top of many hockey-stick graphs, or both – simultaneously. Hopefully it won't go that far, because human evolution has been full of natural checks, balances and course corrections. On the other hand, science tells us that we *are* close to irreversible tipping points into an unknown climate of the Anthropocene.

When I think of tipping points, Ernest Hemingway's novel *The Sun Also Rises* comes to mind: "How did you go bankrupt," one character asks another, who responds: "Two ways. Gradually, then suddenly." This may uncannily apply to CC. Yes, the future has always been unknown and the stakes have always been precipitously high, but the scale has never been so grand. Whatever happens, there are far more humans to experience the effects. As our species has come to so dominate its natural systems, the earth will forgive us fewer mistakes. In a sense, it's time to become grown-ups, an adult race, to think and act in more mature ways that focus on a bigger, longer-term picture. And not to think and hope that some techno-breakthrough, good luck or divine intervention will suddenly rescue us.

Enough bad news! We can look at the last few centuries for some very good news, as our world has never improved so fast. We have significantly, even spectacularly reduced poverty. Extreme global poverty has been reduced over the last 200 years from 90 percent to 10 percent today.[17] Every day, the number of people around the world living in extreme poverty (less than about $2 a day, adjusted for inflation) goes down by over 200,000. Every day, an additional 325,000 people gain access to electricity, and 300,000 more gain access to clean drinking water. Before the 1960s, the majority of humans had always been illiterate and lived in extreme poverty. Less than 15 percent are illiterate now, and fewer than 10 percent live in extreme poverty.[18] Between 1990 and 2015, the number of children dying before the age of 5 fell to 6 million from 12.7 million.[19] Human-on-human violence is way down when compared to either World War, or more strikingly to our prehistoric tribal days, when archeologists claim that up to a quarter of all hunter-gatherers were killed by fellow human beings.[20] Murder rates in the Middle Ages were about 35 times higher than today in Europe! Warfare deaths have come down 20-fold since 1945, and domestic violence is down, as is child abuse.[21] Despite all the international hot spots and conflicts, fewer people died in 2017 from human violence than from obesity or car accidents or suicides.[22]

Despite the recent rise of plutocracy in the West, there has been an increase in global equity. Many of the developing countries of the Global South have substantially closed the economic gap with the developed countries of the industrialized Global North, while growth rates have boomed in both (but with a dramatically increasing gap between rich and poor *within* both poor and rich countries). The abolition of slavery, the fall of colonialism, the education and suffrage of women, and the decrease in disease are a big part of this growing equality, as is science and technology.[23] Despite this moral and technical progress, inequality *within* most countries has increased, often with a plutocratic surge of ostentatious wealth, while the middle class has been growing in developing countries and declining in developed countries. And as Economics Nobel Laureate Joseph Stiglitz argues, increased equity leads to greater economic wealth, not just a greater sense of social stability and civic solidarity.[24]

We're in the midst of a golden era for cities, as unannounced and unappreciated as it is. They are exploding with social vibrancy and cultural richness, while growing with residents, visitors, commerce and economic opportunity. Urban density, done well, has all kinds of benefits: On average, people who live in dense, walkable areas tend to be physically healthier, happier and more productive. Per capita local governments spend less on infrastructure to support urbanites than they do to support suburbanites, and energy consumption is lower in cities than in suburbs. Long unrecognized but now becoming more evident and appreciated are several positive urban trends – "paradoxes of the city." Stay tuned for these four urban paradoxes, with antidotes, reasons and mechanisms behind them, as well as other ways in which cities enrich our lives.

Cities are on the right side of many other equations, making our society more productive, more livable, more diverse, culturally richer and wealthier. Urbanization provides an important opportunity for the developed and developing world alike. As the director of the Indian Institute for Human Settlements Aromar Revi puts it,

> Urban areas constitute over three-fourths of the current global economy, house more than half of the global population and an increasing proportion of the poor and vulnerable, and concentrate over 75% of the world's climate and economic risks. They also provide the economic, institutional and innovation basis for much of the incremental national employment, savings, investment and growth potential of the next few decades.[25]

The historical gains of humanity and positive benefits of urbanism are impressive. But they are all put at risk by the simple arithmetic of too many people consuming too many resources too fast, and producing too much pollution and waste for the earth to handle. Its transforming atmosphere is altering the planet's climate and ecosystems, with compounding effects. On the one hand, the impacts are happening too fast for many species to deal with but too slowly to alarm the human species into decisive action. As we run out of ecological time, we need to choose wisely and quickly our collective moves as a civilization. It's a task made all the more difficult by its sheer size and geopolitical complexity, but all the easier by our technical abilities to understand, communicate and address pressing issues. *This book is not so much about new or radical ideas, strategies or techniques, as it is about how to connect, balance and deploy effective antidotes as soon as possible.* The question that remains is whether we can soon enough summon the will and fortitude in a way that tackles the many interlocking challenges.

If asked to be more specific about the objectives of the book, I would say there are three:

1 Wake up and shake up urban planners and design professionals, teachers, students, government officials, community leaders, developers, as well as interested, responsible members of the general public, by explaining and connecting well-known and not-so-well-known concepts, with a multitude of compelling facts and data.

2 Expand and deepen the understanding and agency of those who are already knowledgeable about the topics. Likewise, encourage more university faculty, students and professionals to study and take leadership in urban design and planning. This commitment includes communicating with colleagues, friends, family and neighbors about not only the problems, but also the benefits of the antidotes, especially success stories. The public – forever distracted by quotidian

problems – needs "more movies, more TV, more music . . . We have
to touch people's hearts."[26]

3   Elicit common cause and incentivize positive action on the personal,
social, political and policy level and in the marketplace, because
deeds mean more than words, intentions, motivations or beliefs. We
need to act now or forever hold our peace.

In pursuing these objectives, the book tries to illuminate a constellation
of three problems that threaten to irreparably tip the balance against our
species and the remarkable civilization it has slowly developed – namely
climate change, extreme heat and *overpopulation*. How can we address
them? What role can cities play? How can the design, planning and policies of the built environment help address these epic challenges? I hope
my 125,000 words of text will help to clarify, illustrate and facilitate a
way forward. The cluster of problems is simply too important for our
species to kick down the road.

Truth in advertising: I've tried to write this and previous books with an
academic's mind, a professional practitioner's experience and a teacher's
heart. I am not a scientist or an engineer, nor a policy wonk or a schol-
arly monk. I am a designer and an academician, but not just a pedagogue
and an author but someone on a personal journey. And I'm fed up with
our profligate consumption of resources, the sheer waste in our daily
lives, our quickly designed and shabbily constructed built environment,
and our political inaction in the face of CC – so disheartened that I've
kept at the endless effort to unravel the giant hairball through teaching,
traveling and writing. I've been involved in energy issues since the 1973
Oil Embargo prompted me to design, general contract and live in one of
the early passive solar homes of the modern era. Many years later, I am
still trying to address what has slowly expanded from an energy shortage
to an era of environmental consciousness and now to the current climate
crisis of existential dimensions. My quarter-century involvement with
sustainable cities, urban design, New Urbanism and now Lean Urbanism
has been a gradual but bracing process of transformation, as it has mor-
phed into an increasingly pointed assault on CC.

Although a part-time academic for a decade and a full-time one for
the past three decades, at heart I'm not so much a scholar as a journalist. The sentences may be long and some of the vocabulary arcane or
pedantic, but the prose attempts to clearly convey and interpret a lot of
information to a broad audience. As such it is situated within the "scholarship of interpretation and of application" rather than the "scholarship
of discovery." Accordingly, the text sometimes surveys and sometimes
dives deep, but is rife with lateral and vertical connections, allusions,
digressions and tangents, with a few anecdotal ambles. I repeat key
points for two reasons: Readers' attention spans are shorter and more
interrupted than ever, and the pedagogic value of repetition has been

lost in contemporary education. For some readers, it may be a call to action, for professionals a guide, for students a textbook, a reference book for academicians or simply an eye-opener for lay readers.

As a designer, I am someone who is totally turned on, motivated, sometimes transfixed by architectural aesthetics and urban beauty, but this book is not about that important matter. There are no beautiful photos of stunning architecture, no seductive images. But this verbiage is about addressing underlying design and planning issues – getting the right platform for architects, interior designers, landscape architects and urban designers to do their magic. And I do mean magic, as aesthetics can be pure, sublime and transcendent. I see it not only as an end in and of itself, needing no justification, but also as attaching value and affection that encourages the built environment be loved, maintained and sustained. Like love, it can move people to act and exalt in life. Beauty can also help to engender a more just world. As Elaine Scarry beautifully writes in *On Beauty and Being*, beauty motivates the slackening of self-interest from which justice springs.[27] I've barely touched this important dimension of design not because it's unimportant, but because it's too important to shortchange.

As someone who studies and falteringly attempts to practice Buddhism, I have found it relatively easy to accept and embrace the interdependence and interconnectedness of everything in the known world and universe. Buddhism's emphasis on generosity, compassion and discipline fits well with caring for our planet and the present and future generations of homo sapiens and other species. In a sense, any civilization develops its own karma, as its actions speak louder than words. In Buddhism, there is no deity to save us; only ourselves, which means we need to individually and collectively face our challenges and act. As Thich Nhat Hanh, the Vietnamese Buddhist monk turned famous international teacher says:

> The Earth is out of balance; as a species, we have not given back to the Earth as much as we have taken from it. We have exploited the Earth's natural resources and polluted her environment. When we upset the balance of Mother Earth, it leads to a lot of suffering.[28]

Suffering may prove an understatement. A research team tried to quantify the suffering that would be avoided if the planet were kept below 1.5°C of warming, rather than meet the 2° goal of the Paris Climate Accord – in other words, how much additional suffering would result from that additional half-degree of warming. Their answer: Some 150 million more people would die over the next 40 years from air pollution alone in a 2°-warmer world than in a 1.5°-warmer one. The extra half-degree would result in more than a million deaths in just the metro areas of Asia and Africa.[29] The math is speculative, of course, and some may disagree with the paper's methodology. Numbers of this magnitude are hard to grasp, but 150 million deaths are equivalent to 25 Holocausts and almost three times the death toll of World War II.

> Three-degree warming is a prescription for short-term disaster: forests in the Arctic and the loss of most coastal cities. Robert Watson, a former director of the United Nations Intergovernmental Panel on Climate Change (IPCC), has argued that three-degree warming is the realistic minimum. Four degrees: Europe in permanent drought; vast areas of China, India and Bangladesh claimed by desert; Polynesia swallowed by the sea; the Colorado River thinned to a trickle; the American Southwest largely uninhabitable. The prospect of a five-degree warming has prompted some of the world's leading climate scientists to warn of the end of human civilization.[30]

One English journalist has penned a scary scenario that suggests a very wild ride for the next generations:

> Even if all the world's countries meet their Paris agreement targets (which is very unlikely, since the targets are non-binding), if we do nothing else we'll still be hurtling toward more than 3°C of global warming, and possibly as high as 4.4°C. Way over the threshold. What might our planet look like if it warms by 4°C? No one can say for certain, but projections show that this level of warming is likely to bring about heatwaves not seen on earth for 5M years. Southern Europe could dry up into a desert. Sea levels could rise by 1.2 meters before the century is out, drowning cities like Amsterdam and New York. Furthermore, 40% of species will be at risk of extinction. Most of our rainforests will wither away. Crop yields could collapse by 35%, destabilising the world's food system and triggering widespread famine. In short, a 4°C world looks very bleak indeed . . . We face a stark choice: either we act now, right-sizing our economy and managing the transition in a careful and controlled way, or climate change will do it for us. If we wait for the latter option, it will be unimaginably destructive and chaotic.[31]

My generation has experienced several dramatic shifts in consciousness and attitude, although nothing remotely close to the magnitude of changes currently required. The environmental movement started with two great female authors – the nature writer Rachel Carson exposed the toxic ugliness of pollution and the need for *conservation*, while Jane Jacobs brilliantly jumpstarted the slow revival of our dying cities. The *historic preservation* movement hit its stride in most communities, but we young architects were pretty much oblivious to it in our zeal to design a brave, new world with Modernist architecture (much to our later chagrin, as we came to appreciate that the preservation and adaptive reuse of existing buildings is a key component of sustainable cities). This period was followed by long lines at gas stations during the Oil Embargo, as the *energy crisis* raised its head for the first time. Then came *sustainability*, with development that meets the needs of today without compromising the ability of future generations to meet their own needs. Sustainability is still with us, but it has also evolved into *resilience*, as CC, the biggest game-changer yet, has taken center stage. With increasing UHIs, *urban resilience* is now foregrounded. In retrospect, it seems a fast ride, but nothing like what upcoming generations will experience. Indeed, these young people need to quickly become leaders. As Al Gore says, "Every great morally based movement that has advanced the prospects for humanity has been led in significant measure by young people. I see this climate movement in the context of these previous movements, [such as the] abolition of slavery . . ."[32]

The book has been shaped by many years of study, reading, teaching and professional practice, as well as by traveling much of the world. The carbon footprint of these trips, alas, are a glaring weakness of mine; I must keep reminding myself that the energy consumed when you're moving is 20 times per minute more than stationery time spent at home,[33] and that every round-trip flight between New York and London melts three more square meters of Arctic ice.[34] The conferences and speaking engagements have taken me to scores of interesting places, including some 70 architecture schools; I always try to link and consolidate these trips. We are as blessed with inexpensive air travel, as our offspring are cursed and burdened by its carbon consequences. Technological advances now allow frequent travel, the consumption of imported goods, and the ability to use faraway places as playgrounds. Historically unprecedented income levels have enabled a global elite to enjoy lifestyles more lavish than the royalty of yore, living in more thermal comfort and traveling further afar.

Everywhere that I visit humbly reminds me of how astoundingly complex and interconnected the world is. Many things are going wrong all the time, as has always been the case with human society, but I'm frequently amazed, given the hyper-complexity, how *little* goes awry and how much somehow goes right, whether seamlessly or muddled through. The background level of socio-political friction and geopolitical unrest suggests there would be constant, widespread war. Yes, there is too much inequality and poverty, but there are also billions of people living comfortably in democratic societies. The other big takeaway from globetrotting is just how many people there are on the planet. On a gut level, after a half-century of travel, it seems evermore clear that there are simply too many of us. As everyone who has flown into a large city knows, the metro areas are vast. But our brains are not good at understanding numbers as large as the seven and a half billion fellow humans who live on earth. It would be like flying over 75,000 different stadia, each filled with 100,000 people. It's not hard to imagine how our species is overextending its welcome on the planet. To put it bluntly, as the earth continues to find new points of equilibrium, pandemics, wars, physical strife, drought, floods, famine cannot be avoided.

There will doubtlessly be momentous and painful resets, or chains of them, as we hit tipping points and slowly continue to foul our atmosphere and over-consume nature's bounty. Controversy will roil about why and how disasters, death and devastation are happening, with endless finger-pointing and blame. Some will blame lackluster and cowardly leaders, or their God or gods, short-term thinking, poor karma or just plain bad luck. Others will say it's endless entropy and/or the unavoidable combination of human failings and fallacies. The media and pundits will, as always, tend to be preoccupied with the immediate bad CC news – from disruptions, disasters and violence to the scandals of corrupt politicians, greedy kleptocrats and amoral corporations. We humans so easily lean toward sensationalism, I-told-you-so voyeurism and jealousy. Despite the less frequent feel-good stories and occasional "specials" on the vulnerability and future of humanity, the media is by nature less focused on long-term issues. Fortunately, periodicals like *The New York Times* and *The Economist*, which I frequently cite, are doing their best to focus on the long haul.

Through all the noise, the signals will often be blurry, but the smart money will be on CC, as the science is tight and the results demonstrable, if politically muddied at times. Those who care to dig deeper will see that climate has been the alpha driver in the history of civilization, and that it continues to be the litmus test for everything from agriculture to zoology. Unarguably, members of upcoming generations will be piqued by previous generations for not acting when they knew CC and its deleterious impacts were upon them. They will be especially angry at government leaders, corporate bosses, scientists and others who knew better, but blundered selfishly or blindly on. Our offspring may look upon current leaders as many now look on slave traders and owners, probably erasing hallowed names and institutions who knowingly and self-righteously hid or blindly perpetuated selfish and wrong beliefs and practices. But vested interests known to be on the wrong side of the ledger will be too large a category to revisit. It will be a sad and often bitter trail of tears.

On a more positive note, during a recent overseas trip I was poignantly and powerfully reminded of nature's complex yet simple economy and elegance. In the arid stretches of Namibia, Africa, one morning our small band saw bushes that turn silvery white to reflect the hot summer sunshine and revert back to green in the winter to absorb it. That afternoon, we observed desert zebras whose black stripes stop short of their bellies to better reflect the heat from the hot sands beneath. A day's drive away, the plains zebra grazing the cooler grasslands sport stripes that continue under their bodies. In both cases, every zebra's black-and-white pattern is slightly different from the next, a variation on a common theme that merges together and blurs the herd in the keen eyes of the lion that hunts them. This reminds me of another nugget of wisdom in a Kenyan proverb: "If you want to travel fast, travel alone. If you want to travel far, travel together."

This book applies the same thermal principles learned designing many passive solar buildings in the 1970s and '80s, but at a much larger scale – that of the city and metropolitan region. Teaching courses on sustainable architecture and urbanism has forced me to keep up with the latest developments and with simpler ways to explain the many issues of sustainability. After eight years of harvesting the growing bounty of new information for my courses, four large and important dots have emerged for me as ones that have not been sufficiently understood or connected to date. Trying to understand, amplify and connect them has inspired and motivated me to write this book. I know from authoring and editing a half-dozen books, that after the exhilaration of figuring out the theme, the researching and writing is a slog, which I once heard aptly described as rowing across the Pacific Ocean. Tom Hanks, after authoring his first book, described writing as pounding out "one damn thing after another."[35]

I didn't set out to write a book with so many numbers, statistics and citations. However, the subjects in this book are fast-changing and often technical, necessitating the citation of specialist experts with fast-changing figures. The absolute values of some of these numbers – like a 14-digit global population total or a 17-digit estimate of the global value of fossil fuel reserves – are often overwhelmingly, unimaginatively large. Accordingly, there are many "per capita" and percentage metrics. There are also many books, articles, websites and videos referenced in over 750 endnotes. The news kept coming in over the bow or the stern at a heart-stopping rate, demanding to be read on a daily basis in the attempt to leave no stone unturned. If you don't like statistics and numeric descriptions of the world, this may not be the book for you. And if you don't want to follow a long and sometimes twisty narrative, occasionally interrupted with short side trips, you may find it too detailed.

I've never liked the bibliographies at the end of books, which are much too long to be a useful reading list. And at the rate new books, as well as the firehose of media coverage, are being published on CC, urban, population and environmental issues, a list of books seems a somewhat futile exercise. Nonetheless, here are the key books recommended to read and/or reference, in no particular order: Ronald Wright's *A Short History of Progress*, Clair Brown's *Buddhist Economics*, Brian Stone's *The City and the Coming Climate*, Naomi Klein's *This Changes Everything: Capitalism vs. the Climate*, Paul Hawken's *Drawdown*, Benjamin Barber's *Cool Cities: Urban Sovereignty and the Fix for Global Warming*, Jonathan Rose's *The Well-Tempered City*, Stewart Brand's *Whole Earth Discipline: Edward Glaeser's Triumph of the*

City, Tim Jackson's *Prosperity without Growth*, Cynthia Rosenzweig et al.'s *Climate Change and Cities: Second Assessment Report of the Urban Climate Change Research Network* and Roy Scranton's *Learning to Die in the Anthropocene*, as well as Jane Jacobs' classic *The Life and Death of Great American Cities*. In alphabetical order, books by Stewart Brand, Peter Calthorpe, Vishaan Chakrabarti, Ellen Dunham-Jones, Douglas Farr, Harrison Fraker, Jeremy Rifkin, Jeff Speck and June Williamson have also been influential. For those who want more sources, there are many other good references lurking in the endnotes.

This brings me to giving credit and thanks – first, to institutions that have directly and indirectly supported and generously helped me. My academic life has been long, rich and meaningful. I count myself lucky to have received my undergrad and graduate degrees from Princeton University, which honored me with the opportunity to give a talk on this book to my undergraduate class on the occasion of its 50th reunion. After a dozen years of professional practice, chairing the Architecture Department at the University of Washington was my first full-time academic experience, after some years of part-time teaching at the New Jersey Institute of Technology and University of Pennsylvania. Deaning for a decade, and then teaching for another decade at the University of Michigan's Taubman College of Architecture and Urban Planning has been a fulfilling culmination to my academic life. All these wonderful opportunities allowed me to win the Topaz Medallion for Excellence in Architectural Education, the first time that any member of these two faculties was awarded this highest honor in the field and the biggest of my life. And being selected at the Emil Lorch Collegiate Professor by my college was icing on the cake. Last, I was able to concentrate on writing this book, thanks to a Visiting Fellowship at Clare Hall at the University of Cambridge, another wonderful institution and place to live, to think and to grow. What a rare opportunity to have a half-year away on a sabbatical to focus on research and writing – a privilege exceeded only by my 40 years in part-time and full-time academia. Indeed, what a privilege it has been to live such a blessed and fortunate life. But there's more to be done. As Wes Jackson, cofounder of Land Institute, says: "If your life's work can be accomplished in your lifetime, you're not thinking big enough."[36]

These pages would not be possible without the confluence and help of many fellow humans and institutions. Starting with my family and friends, there's my wife Kathleen Nolan, who has stood by and supported me for over 25 years, and been my lover, closest friend, housemate, soul mate and confidant, as well as my best editor. My supportive, loyal and influential parents helped by living on in my memory. My adult children Casey and Tess, noted in the Dedication, have inspired me with their lives and careers in idealistic social and creative cultural arts. They have added meaning and pride to my life, as have our first two grandchildren, Ramsey and Nell, a gift of Tess and son-in-law Mike MacDonald. A shout-out to their generation for the courage and stamina they will need as they rally to steer through the wild and crazy ride ahead.

Many people have directly contributed to this book – fellow Dean Emeritus and half-century friend and colleague Harrison Fraker, old friend and former professional partner Peter Calthorpe, and countless other colleagues, friends and compatriots. I will mention but a handful of them, in random order – Brian Stone, Michael Mehaffy, Ellen Dunham-Jones, Paul Murrain, Andres Duany, Edward Ng, Scott Bernstein, Robinson Brown, Karl Petit, Larry Serra, Lance Jay Brown, Dan Solomon, Jonathan Rose, Kit and Malcolm McCullough, Patrick Condon, Jonathan Levine and the members of various New Urbanism listservs, including Bruce Donnelly, Paul Crabtree, Steve Mouzon, Ann Daigle, Sandy Sorlien, Robert Orr, Sara Hines, Steve Coyle, Lynn Richards and the many others I am forced by space to leave out. And special thanks to the late Hank Dittmar, an important New Urbanist colleague who co-authored a book chapter on Lean Urbanism, who was sadly lost to cancer in 2018. With suggested readings and comments from many of these folks, it seemed at times like a collaborative team project. On a very different axis, I want to thank my upbeat golf partner Professor Peter Allen and my two spinning instructors, who have helped keep me physically active during the relentless slog of researching and writing – Elmo and Susan Morales, the latter of whom we also sadly lost to cancer in 2018. My assistant, the late Mary Anne Drew, made me a better dean, and person. Jane Heron, a former summer neighbor, did a voluntary, close edit of every sentence and suggested better prose and sequencing. And graduate student Leslie Infanger was indispensable in obtaining permission for all the figures, as well as redrawing some of them. Fellow student Qi Zhang helped with the final push. Kathryn Schell, Alexis O'Brien and the rest of the team at Routledge, without whom this project would only be fumes. And last but not least, Sonnie Wills of Swales & Willis, who was very accommodating in the production phase.

What joy and good luck to benefit from all these wonderful people and institutions, to whom I owe more gratitude than can be expressed in words. I ask for understanding and forgiveness for any mistakes, oversights or flaws.

Doug Kelbaugh, Ann Arbor, Michigan,
January, 2019

Notes

1 Roy Scranton, *Learning to Die in the Anthropocene*, City Lights Books, 2015, p. 38
2 Mike Childs, Foreword, *Sharing Cities*, MIT Press, 2015
3 Michael Mehaffy, personal email, 10/8/17
4 Lisa Friedman, "Scientists fear Trump will dismiss blunt climate report," *The New York Times*, 8/7/17

5 David Wallace Wells, "Climate change will make Earth too hot for humans," *New York Magazine*, 7/9/17

6 "Chilling prospects: providing sustainable cooling for all," www.SEforALL.org, 2018

7 Amy Harder, "The world needs clean coal but can't get it," Harder Line, *Axios*, 7/24/2017

8 Ned Kramer, "The climate is changing, so must architecture," *Architect*, October, 2017, p. 140

9 Adele Peters, "Can we suck enough CO2 from the air to save the climate?" *Fast Company*, 12/22/17

10 Roy Scranton, *Learning to Die in the Anthropocene*, p. 36

11 Ned Kramer, "The climate is changing," pp. 168, 178

12 Andra Garner et al., "Impact of climate change on New York City's coastal flood hazard: increasing flood heights from the preindustrial to 2300 CE," *PNAS*, 10/24/17

13 Bruce Donnelly, personal email, 12/21/17

14 Trevor Nace, "Glacier National Park may need to be renamed: will soon have no glaciers," *Forbes*, 5/17/17

15 Dalai Lama and Franz Alt, *An Appeal to the World*, HarperCollins, 2017

16 Jingjiang Zhing, M. Arch student, University of Michigan, October, 2017

17 Philip Galanes, "The mind meld of Bill Gates and Steven Pinker," *The New York Times*, 1/28/18

18 Nicholas Kristof, "Why 2017 was the best year in human history," *The New York Times*, 1/6/18

19 Douglas Farr, *Sustainable Nation*, as reviewed by Phil Langdon, *Public Square*, 6/12/18

20 Charles Mann, "State of the species," *Orion*, November/December, 2012

21 Philip Galanes, "The mind meld of Bill Gates and Steven Pinker"

22 Yuval Noah Harari, "Nationalism in the 21st century," YouTube, 2018

23 Charles Mann, "State of the species"

24 Joseph Stiglitz, *The Price of Inequality*, W.W. Norton, 2012

25 Aromar Revi, "Next month, a key opportunity to re-imagine the global response to an urban world," *citiscope*, 8/22/17

26 Melena Ryzik, quoting Prof. Andy Hoffman, "Can Hollywood movies about climate change make a difference?" *The New York Times*, 10/2/18

27 Elaine Scarry, *On Beauty and Being Just*, Princeton University Press, 1999, pp. 86–93

28 Thich Nhat Hanh, *Love Letter to the Earth*, Parallax Press, 2013.

29 Drew Shindell et al. "Quantified, localized health benefits of accelerated CO_2 emissions reductions," *Nature: Climate Change*, 3/19/18

30 Nathaniel Rich, "Losing Earth: the decade we almost stopped climate change," *The New York Times Magazine*, 8/1/18

31 Jason Hickel, "The Paris Climate Deal won't save us: our future depends on de-growth," *The Guardian*, 7/3/17

32 Al Gore, interview in *Axios*, 4/24/18

33 Kendra Pierre-Lewis, "Americans are staying home more: that's saving energy," *The New York Times*, 1/29/17

34 David Wallace Wells, "Climate change will make Earth too hot for humans"

35 Tom Hanks, *The Morning Show*, 10/15/17

36 Wes Jackson, personal communication, 2018

1 Connecting the Dots

Climate Change, Heat Islands, Overpopulation and Cities

Every hour of every day there is mention in the media of the planet's changing climate.

> Mind-boggling combinations of heat and humidity continued to emerge in cities near the Persian Gulf . . . sending feels-like temperatures toward the 160-degree mark . . . as relentless heat continued to broil much of the region . . . The searing heat led to an impromptu, mandatory four-day holiday in Iraq.[1]

There has also been a great deal of ink spilled on the topic. So why add another book to the chorus? Because climate change (CC) is by far the biggest challenge facing humanity, arguably the biggest since the start of civilization over 5,000 years ago. There are under-appreciated and mis-understood ways to address it. And the impacts of CC are also coming on faster and bolder than expected. In the words of CC chief warrior Bill McKibben:

> If we don't win very quickly on climate change, then we will never win . . . It's what makes it different from every other problem our political systems have faced . . . It won't stand still . . . the decisions we make in 2025 will matter much less than the ones we make in the next few years.[2]

CC is categorically new and qualitatively different from the chronic challenges that humanity has always faced – war, poverty, injustice, disease, hunger, oligopoly, crime, corruption, bankruptcy, ignorance, etc. It is also becoming quantitatively bigger as it exacerbates these perennial problems on top of dire environmental threats. "Climate change is a threat multiplier," states the U.S. Department of Defense at the Pentagon.[3] As it compounds and cascades, the future looks discouraging, even hopeless. There remain too many practices, policies and initiatives that are feeble or in the too-little-too-late category, the huge garbage bin of the many fallen civilizations that have doubled down on existing practices rather than adopt new ones.

Humans have enjoyed almost perfect environmental conditions to flourish for the ten to twelve millennia of the just-ended Holocene Age. As we start the Anthropocene, the warming atmosphere and oceans are triggering changes in the earth's ecosystems that directly threaten civilization. It is also increasingly clear that the causes of CC are primarily, if not overwhelmingly, anthropogenic. There is effectively unanimous agreement in the scientific community that it is the unprecedented high level of greenhouse gases (GHGs) in the atmosphere that is raising the earth's temperature. There are local variations in these temperature changes, with some examples of cooling, but the overall trend is warmer, with global temperatures annually setting records. For instance, May 2018 was over 5°F warmer than the average May since 1910 in the U.S.

Our degrading environment and ecosystems are threatening not only human civilization, but also many plant and animal species on which it depends. *CC is simply too fast for many species to adapt to, yet too slow to sufficiently motivate humans to act decisively.* Our comfortable, beneficent thermal commons is at severe risk, especially in cities. It's a battle of epic proportions that demands rapid, decisive and integrated mitigation and adaptation – individually and collectively, bottom-up and top-down, short-term and long-term. Although cities have huge eco-footprints and are warming faster than their hinterlands, for many reasons presented in this book, they are ironically the best hope for the foreseeable future.

Classifying things into recognizable patterns seems to be one of the most basic of human instincts and quests: making sense of the world, and searching for meaning in life. Naming and listing things is a way of collecting, even owning them. Humanity needs to connect several major dots in new ways, to better wrap its minds and hearts around disastrous future scenarios. It needs not only to focus on CC, but also to shine a spotlight on urban heat islands (UHIs), a relative unknown in the unfolding crisis. Another dot to be connected is extreme population growth, which is quickly leading to global challenges. Because the mix of problems is new to human beings and to the planet, connecting the dots in a fresh way offers surprising findings including some refreshing hope. But this is not a war that we will "win" or "lose." Rather it is a challenge we meet, well or badly.[4] It is both a global war against CC, and a local battle against extreme heat, both of which can be directly and effectively fought by cities, as well as good practices and policies. Slight mutations in pattern can trigger evolution, in the Darwinian sense. That is what is happening with three variables – changes in the atmosphere, urban temperatures and population. They interact, add up, cascade down and compound to make big changes, even tipping points that are difficult if not impossible to reverse. Climate is a major determinant of our survival, as well as of health and comfort, which in turn determine our population level – co-dependent dots in a bigger pattern.

Dot 1 is CC itself, with special focus on the deleterious role that the sprawling built environment plays in this *global* phenomenon.

Dot 2 is the UHI, a lesser known and misunderstood *local* phenomenon, which is heating up most cities twice as fast as their surrounding countryside or as the planet as a whole. Coupled with CC, many cities suffer *extreme heat*. The UHI has been surprisingly underplayed in the climate literature and public discourse about CC, and to date it has remained unclaimed by any environmental group as their clarion call.

Dot 3 is excessive, unsustainable *population growth* in developing countries, combined with excessive *consumption* and *carbon footprints* in developed countries.

The first three dots are challenges. Dot 4 is *the city itself*, which is a solution, or at least a strategy that offers very effective social and structural ways to address the challenges represented by the first three dots. Cities have experienced a stunning turnaround, one in which they are no longer seen as a problem, as they were a half century ago. As *The New York Times* architecture critic Michael Kimmelman wrote after attending U.N. Habitat III,

> Cities are being recognized increasingly as opportunities for economic and social progress, density as a response to environmental threats; the automobile as a big problem; slums as not just a blight but a potential template for organic urbanism. Young generations around the world, entering the tech economy and bound by the internet, are embracing urban ideals, including the common ground of public spaces, mass transit, streets and sidewalks.[5]

Indeed, cities enhance productivity, creativity, collaboration, wealth, arts and culture, often taking full advantage of new technologies.

How these four dots intersect raises several questions: What do the dots exactly mean and why are they so important? How can we simultaneously address the first two dots – CC and UHI? Why is reducing the UHI so timely? What, if anything, is the synergy and promise of connecting these dots? How do we frame the challenges to motivate and inspire individuals and societies to change behaviors that are counterproductive in the war against CC?

Connecting the Four Dots

What Is the Meaning and Importance of the Dots?

The first dot of climate change is a long-term, game-changing, Hydra-headed challenge that requires a longer explanation. A normal climate has always sponsored mercurial, unpredictable weather, but now its diurnal and weekly patterns swing up and down in bolder cycles and at faster tempos. *Mitigation* seeks to reduce the root *causes* of CC, primarily by reducing the emission of carbon, or GHGs, but also by sequestering carbon and by reflecting more solar radiation. *Adaptation* addresses the *impacts* of CC, by preparing for its effects, while lowering their risks and consequences. Both approaches are as costly as they are essential and urgent now and for the foreseeable future: If carbon emissions were radically decreased or even magically eliminated tomorrow, adaptation would still be needed to deal with the lingering effects of GHGs already baked into the system with their long half-lives.

First, it should be acknowledged that without *climate science* little would be known about the *existence* and *causes* of CC. It's invisible, inaudible, odorless, tasteless and untouchable. Thankfully scientists have studied it and alerted us to its dangers. Second, CC's early impacts – more extreme hurricanes, floods, storm surges, droughts and wildfires, plus higher sea levels – are increasingly obvious to everyone. And annual temperatures have slowly risen: over the contiguous U.S., the ambient temperature increased by 1°C (1.8°F) for the period 1901–2016, and the trend is accelerating. Third, its primary cause is established: too many GHGs clogging our atmosphere, so that more solar heat absorbed and more heat produced by combustion on the earth's surface is trapped by the atmosphere and doesn't escape to outer space. Fourth, it is very likely that annual average temperatures will rise by another 2.5°F in the U.S., relative to the last quarter of the twentieth century under all plausible future climate scenarios.[6] While this change may not seem that danger- ous, it is sobering to realize that a 5°C rise was enough to melt an ice sheet over a kilometer thick over much of the northern U.S. And fifth, it is clear what has to be done to address it: reduce GHG emissions through less combustion of fossil fuels and sequester, capture and store excess carbon already in the atmosphere. In short, we would be hapless and helpless without climate science.

Second, the term "climate change" needs more precise explanation. It's not ideal terminology, as the climate has always changed, is changing now, and always will change. But the term has overtaken "global warm- ing" as more heavily used, because not all of the earth's climate is getting warmer. In many ways, a term like "climate preparedness" is more use- ful, as it is more constructive and less laden with political baggage. Paul Hawken and his team of over 200 researchers and consultants decided to use "drawdown" as the operative term and title of their timely book, because it focuses on the solution rather than the problem.[7] But for bet- ter or worse, "climate change," like "sustainability," is likely to be the proverbial, everyday term.

On one level, the CC challenge is simple. There are only six basic strategies to address it: consume less, consume things that embody less energy, use energy sources that have lower carbon footprints, naturally sequester carbon, capture and store carbon, and give birth to fewer people.

The effective weight given to each of these strategies depends on whether it is for developed or developing countries. In developed countries, there is the need to reduce consumption, but in less developed countries, consumption is understandably on the rise as more and more people are born and more of them move up to middle-class lifestyles. In both cases, consumers will need to choose products, services and activities that have lower carbon emissions. And the choices need to be encouraged by public policy – by taxing, subsidizing, trading, rationing carbon with a downward-tapering ceiling and properly pricing it so the market can help.

On another level – scientific verification – the CC challenge is far from simple. The underlying scientific principles may be understandable, but collecting sufficient data to accurately model and predict CC is extremely elaborate and painstakingly intricate. To date, "modeling studies suggest that temperatures rise by about 2.5°C for every doubling of CO_2 . . . fixed by feedback mechanisms balancing input and removal of CO_2."[8] The oceans, it is agreed, are the major buffering reservoir; they are thought to contain over 50 times as much CO_2 as the atmosphere, and about 15 times as much as all living plants and soil, but these are ballpark numbers and fluctuate in ever-changing equilibria. Climate models try to represent and predict the dynamic interactions of the earth's atmosphere, ocean, ice, land and biogeochemical cycles under a broad range of scenarios, but not all the necessary data are currently available. For instance, there is a need to know more about marine feedback loops, some of which have a warming effect – a.k.a. *positive* feedback – and others of which have a cooling effect, which is ironically called *negative* feedback.

There are obvious examples of positive feedback that are already forcing CC. The melting of the Arctic icecap decreases the reflection of solar radiation back out through the atmosphere and raises the surrounding air and water temperatures, which in turn melt more of the icecap. The thawing of the Arctic tundra is an extremely worrisome example, given that it contains methane equivalent to 2.3 times all the carbon dioxide humanity has emitted since the 1800s![9] The feedback loop of dark algae on ice is a bigger issue than scientists previously realized: "On the Greenland ice sheet, the second-largest in the world, 'algal darkening' is responsible for 5% to 10% of its melting each summer."[10] It dilutes the salt water, which is likely to alter the Gulf Stream that keeps Europe warmer than its latitude warrants. An additional climatic impact of melting ice is the release of water vapor from the runoff. Whether in lower latitudes or in Arctic or Antarctic latitudes, ice stores water vapor in the form of frozen water. In the case of temperate climates, it could be claimed that winter ice and frozen snow both retain and detain water and water vapor – much like a retention or detention pond holds storm water – and releases it slowly if and when it thaws. (Unless an excessive buildup of snow and ice thaws quickly, causing local flooding, or if the local climate is subject to heavy spring rains that tend to flood in any case.) The delayed or slower melting of ice and snow is positive in two ways: locally it reduces winter flash flooding and globally it reduces the amount of heat-trapping water vapor in the atmosphere. Additionally, the increase in albedo helps combat CC globally.

The natural carbon cycle is essential to life, as well as an understanding of CC. CO_2 in the atmosphere keeps us from living at far below freezing temperatures.[11] Two terms need to be explained: "decarbonization," a word that describes part of the challenge, but not all of it, and "recarbonization," a seemingly contradictory part of the challenge. The planet has five major pools of carbon: the atmosphere, which is already overloaded with CO_2; the oceans, which are turning more acidic as they become saturated with carbon; underground fossil fuels that are being constantly consumed; forests; and soil. That leaves plants and soil as the largest potential repository for carbon, and they are gaining significant interest. Sometimes called carbon farming, its major promise is that if how we treat this land is reformed, huge areas of the earth's surface could be turned into a carbon sponge.[12]

Plants remove carbon from the atmosphere, require no additional power and grow essentially free. Through photosynthesis they harness the sun's energy to make sugars, while emitting oxygen. Lest we forget, the fossil fuels that now power civilization contain carbon removed from the air during photosynthesis millions of years ago. Every spring, as the Northern Hemisphere greens, the concentration of carbon dioxide in the atmosphere dips, before rising again the following autumn and winter as foliage dies. Some pundits describe this fluctuation as the earth breathing.

> Nearly all the carbon that enters the biosphere is captured during photosynthesis, and as it moves through life's web, every organism takes a cut for its own energy needs, releasing carbon dioxide as exhaust. This circular voyage is the short-term carbon cycle. Carbon farming seeks to interfere with this cycle, slowing the release of carbon back into the atmosphere.[13]

One such strategy utilizes biochar (powdered charcoal made from biomass), a commonplace substance with under-sung potential that is taken for granted. Scientists are documenting how sequestering carbon in soil can produce a double dividend: It reduces CC by extracting carbon from the atmosphere, and it restores the health of degraded soil and increases agricultural yields. Many scientists and farmers believe the emerging understanding of soil's role in climate stability and agricultural productivity will prompt a paradigm shift in agriculture, triggering the abandonment of conventional practices like tillage, crop residue removal, mono-cropping, excessive grazing and blanket use of chemical fertilizer and pesticide. Even cattle, usually considered CC culprits because they belch at least 25 gallons of methane a day, are being studied as a potential part of the CC solution because of their role in naturally fertilizing soil and cycling nutrients. Instead of overcoming nature, this approach reinforces it, promoting the propagation of plant life to return carbon to the soil that was there in the first place – until destructive agricultural practices prompted its release into the atmosphere as carbon dioxide. That process started with the advent of agriculture ten or twelve millennia ago and accelerated over the last century as industrial farming and ranching has rapidly expanded.

There are other interventions into natural phenomena that can be encouraged or expedited to act as negative feedback. Carbon capture and sequestration/storage (CCS) is the generic category for removing CO_2 from the atmosphere. Removing a significant amount would involve moving huge volumes of air through many thousands of capture machines, and powering those machines for decades. The need is great, but the science is young, the commercial incentives weak, and carbon sinks and negative emissions technologies (NETS) are very expensive. One estimate of money spent on all low-carbon technologies "puts the figure at $65B a year until 2050, four times the sum that renewables, batteries and the like attract today . . . a chunk of that would obviously need to go to NETS, which currently get next to nothing."[14] There is a tax credit in the U.S. for CCS, both at the source of the carbon emissions and directly from the air. A market for CO_2 would provide an additional incentive to mine this GHG from the air, but its commercial uses are still limited. And governments need to be careful about rewarding or subsidizing the extraction and storage or reuse of a byproduct like CO_2, as it could incentivize its production – in what some call the "cobra effect."[15] In other words, if it's profitable enough, some enterprising companies would likely forego the public good and produce more carbon.

The U.N.'s IPCC, a preeminent player in understanding and combatting CC, highlights one NETS in particular, sometimes called BECCS (bio-energy with carbon capture and storage).

> Basically, the idea is to develop enormous tree plantations that will suck carbon out of the atmosphere. Then they are harvested, turned into pellets and shipped around the world to power stations to be burned for energy, capturing the carbon emissions and storing the gases deep under the ground, where they won't have any impact on the climate.[16]

A senior researcher at the Center for International Climate Research in Oslo, says: "BECCS is unique in that it removes carbon and produces energy . . . So the more you consume the more you remove. In a sense, it's a dream technology. It's solving one problem while solving the other problem."[17] But some scientists think it is too costly and ambitious in terms of the extensive land required – one-third or more of the earth's arable land. And it's too late in any case to avert tipping points.

Other scientists are pursuing carbon capture from point sources, such as power plants, or more ambitiously from a dispersed source,[18] like the atmosphere itself. One of these potential game-changers is called direct air capture, which consists of machines that work like a tree does,

> sucking CO_2 out from the air, but on steroids – capturing thousands of times more carbon in the same amount of time, and, hopefully, ensuring we don't suffer climate catastrophe . . . to date, all estimates suggest direct air capture would be exorbitantly expensive to deploy . . . if direct air capture can be made cheap enough for there to be commercial interest, then carbon capture at point-sources (like power plants) will likely work, too. And if nothing else, the existence of direct air capture gives humanity a high-premium insurance policy against what would surely be a much more expensive disaster.[19]

Another process, called carbon mineralization, if applied inexpensively on a huge scale – admittedly a very big "if" – could help fight CC. One energy company is currently injecting modest amounts of carbon dioxide into volcanic rock, where it becomes mineralized. Dutch researchers have suggested spreading a green-tinted mineral called olivine as gravel along coastlines to capture CO_2. And scientists in Canada and South Africa are studying ways to use mine wastes, called tailings, to do the same thing.

To give yet another example, ocean phytoplankton's role in CC and ocean acidification is poorly understood and may have more negative feedback that helps to cool the earth than realized. This single-celled form of algae produces a type of sulfur called DMS (dimethyl sulfide) that, among other impacts, evaporates and forms clouds that are longer-lived and more reflective of sunlight than normal clouds, thereby bouncing more unwanted solar rays back through the atmosphere into space. Another possible ocean benefit could result from seeding the large parts of the ocean that have minimal life in them. Adding iron can increase growth of marine plant life that can absorb CO_2 by photosynthesis and then sink to the ocean floor when it dies, taking the carbon with it. But pouring metal into the sea remains a questionable technique. "Ocean kelp may offer promise: more flourishing than bamboo, it is the fastest growing plant to absorb GHGs."[20] However, the geopolitical questions inherent in trying to co-manage the reflectivity of the planet or its ocean bio-chemistry are at best thorny, at worst peace-shattering. And the stakes are exceedingly high, given the possibility of backsliding and/or backfiring.

Unfortunately, many of these processes are nonlinear. It's also possible that these negative feedback loops may turn positive, and warm the oceans and the atmosphere. The overall impacts are still unknown, perhaps unknowable, as is the total capacity of the oceans as carbon sinks. Always lurking below the surface are other possible global cataclysms. Literally under the surface, there is a supervolcano beneath Yellowstone National Park that is far more powerful than the average volcano that lies there. If it were to erupt, it "could blanket most of the United States in a thick layer of ash and even plunge the Earth into a volcanic winter . . . And it's not the only buried supervolcano. Scientists suspect that a super-eruption scars the planet every 100,000 years."[21] Apparently the one under Yellowstone is technically "due" to explode, in the sense that 600,000 years have elapsed since it last blew, which was the span of time before the previous eruption. There is also the possibility that shrinking glaciers may mean more volcanic activity, the logic being that lighter ice sheets compress the crust and mantle less, allowing more eruptions.[22] There are other potential factors in feedback loops, such as long-term variations in the earth's orbit that may help to limit or even reverse the rise in global temperatures.

These examples of negative and positive feedback in no way negate or erase the overall trend of a warming planet, but they may provide either CC respite or intensification. And at the moment, science cannot answer all these questions until more specific, long-term data on climate are obtained. It is comforting to know that astronomers may be able to confidently predict years in advance the exact minute of a solar eclipse, but it's humbling that meteorologists can't predict tomorrow's weather with anything close to that level of precision. Nonetheless, it's necessary to soldier on, collecting data and modeling climate, remembering that predicting the climatic future, like so many things in life, will never be fully accurate.

In any case, the evidence now asserts that *fully eliminating GHG emissions is not enough; they have to be sequestered or captured and stored.* Indeed, unless countries take negative emissions seriously, the Paris Climate Accord "will ring evermore hollow."[23] An important consideration is not just capturing and storing carbon, but using the emissions uptake in the manufacture of marketable and environmentally safe products, including concrete, biofuel – even food. Indeed, reusing the waste is far superior to burying it.

Before moving on, a brief dissection of the terms "tipping point" and "positive feedback" is instructive. Tipping point is usually associated with catastrophic collapse or change, often in slow-moving phenomena, like a stock market crash, a demographic shift in a neighborhood, or a landslide. In everyday scientific discourse, "tipping points" involve various types of abrupt changes in state, such as when water boils and turns to steam. Malcolm Gladwell popularized the term "tipping point" in a 1996 *New Yorker* article and later in his book *The Tipping Point*. He summarized the characteristics of tipping points as (1) being contagious and (2) involving a large change that (a) results from small changes and (b) occurs quickly.

The examples Gladwell provided of tipping points – epidemics of disease, crime, consumption or behavior – all exhibit rapid shifts between states, specifically from a state in which an infection or behavior is rare to one in which it is widespread. The scale and speed of the shifts result from positive feedbacks, particularly those related to network effects; the abundance of a contagious element increases the rate at which it spreads, which further increases its abundance . . . a tipping point is a critical threshold at which "a small change in forcing triggers a strongly nonlinear response in the internal dynamics of part of the climate system, qualitatively changing its future state."[24]

Tipping point is a useful term for describing a large sudden shift that tends to be extremely difficult to stop or reverse, whereas positive feedback describes self-reinforcing change that can be gradual or fast.

As noted in the Foreword, humans have enjoyed almost perfect environmental conditions throughout the just-ended Holocene Age. The warmer and warmer atmosphere is triggering changes in the earth's ecological systems, not to mention human habitat. There are local variations in these temperature changes, including cooling temperatures in many places and even a few (reportedly a total of two) growing glaciers, but the overall trend is hotter, most especially in the polar regions. The nearly unanimous agreement in the scientific community about how GHGs increase the earth's temperature is based on multiple independent lines of evidence that have been affirmed by thousands of independent scientists and many scientific institutions around the world. However, there is a wide range of estimates about the severity and rate of CC.

In the unlikely event that CC skeptics ultimately prove to have valid points or to be generally correct, the stakes are far too high to gamble on. If anything, there seems to be an "optimism bias" in studies, reports and media coverage that underplays the crisis. Extreme weather events are hitting cities harder and sooner than scientists have predicted.[25] The environmental benefits of fighting CC – clean air and water, habitat preservation, renewable energy, resilient institutional and physical infrastructure, etc. – are in any case a happy outcome that is good for the planet and our species. Not addressing CC is like not taking out fire insurance on your home, which is on average very unlikely to burn down. The risk is low, but the stakes are high. The risks are surely higher with CC, and the stakes are immensely higher. One wonders why CC skeptics and deniers are willing to buy fire insurance for their home and offices, but not willing to invest in mitigation and adaptation, even if they see the climatic risk as low.

Needless to say, climate science opens profound, scary questions: Is the long halcyon springtime ending, and are we in for the first cataclysmic climate shock and disruption in ten millennia? Is the changing climate and biosphere threatening unavoidable pandemics? Are we in an evolutionary race with an unknown superbug – one we could lose – given the speed with which we can now spread new infectious diseases? Moreover, is climate, the alpha driver of human history, starting to reach tipping points that will dramatically bring on a long, unbearably hot summer? If so, we know the physical planet itself will do well. It has no need to bargain with the likes of humans, as it has been through far more drastic changes, such as a 400-foot sea level rise since the end of the last Ice Age only 20,000 years ago, which may be a drop in the bucket in geologic time, but a long time in the history of civilization. Much less than a meter of sea level rise is the difference between a city built in the Napoleonic Age, the Jazz Age or the Digital Age. Some scientists tell us that in North America mile-thick sheets of ice slid southward 17 times during the last two million years. Each time the climate warmed the ice melted, then it returned when the climate cooled. Warm periods lasted about 15,000 to 20,000 years and cold periods lasted about 100,000 years, forming the Ice Ages. While no one can predict precisely when and how much, it is certain that the earth's climate will forever be in flux.

If the planet has repeatedly done well in extreme climatic shifts and will no doubt do so again, the question is whether our species will continue to grow in number and dominion, or will it decline and even collapse? Will the planet yawn and move on, as if the human species was an interesting experiment that simply didn't work out in the end? Will the newly emerging Anthropocene Age be a short-lived historical footnote, as the comfortable thermal regime of the Holocene Age gives way to profligate human activity as the dominant influence on climate and environment? Or, as the historian Yuval Noah Harari speculates, will "the boundaries between animals, machines and social systems dissolve: all these will come to be seen as algorithmic information-processing systems . . . what God once was, omnipresent and omniscient, wise and all powerful."[26] Prediction is hard, especially of the future, as the cliché goes.

The second dot is urban heat islands, with extreme heat and heat waves, which affects most large urbanized areas. Heat thrives in cities. All the dark roofs, walls, roads and other surfaces absorb and retain heat during the day. Waste heat, emitted from air conditioners and vehicles, concentrates in cities too. At night, the temperature differences widen. Cities may be as much as 12°C hotter than surrounding areas in the evening hours, because their buildings release heat absorbed during the day. UHI is the term that describes this concentration of higher air and surface temperatures in cities compared to their surrounding territory. UHIs are brought on by dark surfaces overheated by the sun and "waste heat," i.e., hot emissions from tailpipes, chimneys and air conditioners (AC). The UHI typically extends beyond the urbanized area, tapering off with distance. Because it occurs on top of warming from CC, these islands of heat and related heat waves are making many cities less and less hospitable for human occupation, even dangerous to the health of their residents. The U.S. Global Change Research Program stated with high confidence in 2017 that UHIs will strengthen in the future as the structure and spatial extent as well as population density of urban areas change and grow.[27]

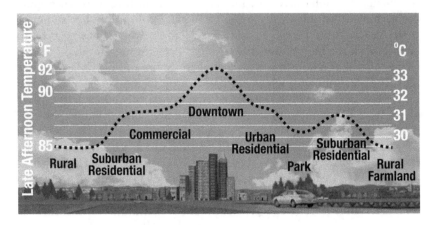

Figure 1.1 Cities are heating up twice as fast as their surrounding countryside and as the planet as a whole. The rural to urban temperature gradient is typically from 2°F up to 18°F (2°C to 10°C),[1] depending on the size, density, color and impermeability of the city. The difference can double in extreme heat waves. (Source: Heat Island Group, Lawrence Berkeley National Laboratory)

1 J. Raven et al., "Urban planning and urban design," in C. Rosenzweig et al. (eds), *Climate Change and Cities: Second Assessment Report of the Urban Climate Change Research Network*, Cambridge University Press, 2018, p. 146

The UHI is easily conflated and confused with CC. Although both are anthropogenic, they have different physical causes in terms of their physics and chemistry. CC is a far greater threat to humanity. Its science has been understood much longer, since it was first described in 1854, and is more widely followed by the scientific community. As noted earlier, CC results from changes in the composition of the earth's atmosphere, specifically more GHGs, directly or indirectly released by human activity. Currently some 25 percent of carbon molecules in the atmosphere are man-made CO_2, added since the Industrial Revolution and spiking since globalization started in the 1980s. In 2013 its accumulation reached 400 parts per million (ppm), which is higher than at any time in the last 3–5 million years.[28] Short-wave solar radiation easily passes through our atmosphere and hits the earth (unless it is intercepted by and reflected back by clouds) and is absorbed by the earth's surface. Increased GHGs, most notably CO_2, in the earth's upper atmosphere trap more of the solar heat that bounces back – re-radiates at a longer wavelength to be more precise – from the earth's surface. Like the glass in a garden greenhouse, GHGs are transparent to the incoming shorter wave radiation from the sun, but they absorb the longer wave radiation that is radiated back from the land or water. Hence the name "greenhouse effect."

Projected Days Over 100° F

Recent Past, 1961-1979

Lower Emissions Scenario, 2080-2099

Higher Emissions Scenario, 2080-2099

Number of Days

| <10 | 20 | 30 | 45 | 60 | 75 | 90 | 105 | >120 |

Figure 1.2 These maps show in the past and future the average number of days per year of very hot weather – with temperatures exceeding 100°F. In the higher emissions future, parts of Texas that experienced 10 to 20 days of 100°F weather per year in recent decades may experience more than 100 such days by the end of the century. (Sources: Climate.gov and U.S. Global Change Research Program)

Because the earth cannot bounce as much heat back to space through an atmosphere ever thicker with GHGs, its surface and air temperatures are slowly getting warmer.

Although compounded by the *global* phenomenon CC, the UHI is a *local* phenomenon. It has not measurably raised the earth's temperature, whereas CC is raising the average global temperature and disrupting the climate. Climatologists tend to see local weather as "contamination" of global CC. The increase in local temperatures, as previously noted, is more from a local increase in *sensible heat*. Sensible heat can be felt, as opposed to latent heat, which is held in a material, and can't be felt until it is released in phase changes, from vapor to liquid to solid. As also noted, this palpable heat has two basic causes: The first is *heat from dark surfaces*, such as dark-colored rooftops, streets and parking lots that have absorbed solar radiation. This heat results in more radiation, conduction and convection of heat, like dark sand on a sunny beach, which burns by conduction, warms by radiation and heats the air by convection. The second is *waste heat* from internal and external combustion of fossil fuels or discharged as hot air from air conditioners. It in turn induces more air conditioning, which spews more waste heat and consumes more electricity from power plants, whose emissions in turn add to CC. It's a self-reinforcing negative cycle, a non-virtuous spiral that is overtaking many urban climates.

These anthropogenic heat sources boost urban temperatures higher than the surrounding countryside, which has fewer tailpipes, chimneys, dark surfaces and air conditioners per acre, not to mention the lack of narrow urban street canyons that further entrap heat. "Because of the 'urban heat island' effect, cities of a million or more people can be 1.8–5.4°F (1–3°C) warmer on average – and as much as 22°F (12°C) warmer in the evening – than the surrounding area, according to the U.S. Environmental Protection Agency."[29] The relative contribution of waste heat and of heat from dark surfaces and street canyons varies from city to city. UHIs are strongest during calm and sunny weather, when extreme heat is more likely to cause discomfort, sickness and, in the case of severe heat waves, death.

The third dot of excessive population growth is a challenge in developing countries. Both a larger and a more consumptive populace demands more of the earth's finite supply of land, natural resources and energy, which in turn carbonizes our atmosphere. Addressing CC is about both decreasing footprints per capita and limiting the total number of capita. Population control is about the denominator, rather than the numerator, in this all-important ratio of energy use and GHG production. Obviously, we need to address both the numerator and denominator in this ratio. *Indeed, a central thesis of this book is that both total and per capita carbon footprints can be addressed simultaneously with the right kind of urbanism.*

We need to tailor different strategies for the developed and developing worlds. In the former, the prevailing high-consumption lifestyles require dramatic *per capita* carbon reductions. In developing countries, per capita consumption is much lower, but birth rates, a.k.a. fertility rates or replacement rates, are much higher. Thus, *reducing birth rates* is more effective than reducing the already low, sometimes distressingly low, personal consumption rates. Of the world's megacities with over ten million residents, most of the 35 largest ones are now located in developing countries. In these teeming, often hot cities with up to 35 million official and unofficial inhabitants, children tend to be an economic liability rather than the asset they typically are in the agricultural countryside, where they can help with farming chores. This added burden, including more expensive education and housing, results in a voluntary reduction in birth rates, without socio-cultural coercion or government interference. It also results in a rise in the percentage of the population over 65 years old, with the concomitant cost of more special housing, health-care and transportation services. With fewer young workers to support the elderly, robots are stepping in to perform the jobs of aging and missing middle-aged workers in some countries. And the deteriorating ratio of workers to retirees forces governments to adopt unpopular policies, such as lower pensions, cutting health care and admitting more immigrants. This dropping ratio is already a major challenge, especially in Asia, Europe and North America.

Birth rates have been declining in the developed world for over 200 years. For instance, the U.S. fertility rate in 1810 was approximately seven births per woman, and by 1850 the rate had dropped dramatically to 4.5 births per woman. During that 40 years, farm employment dropped from 80 percent to 50 percent of all Americans. The precipitous drop in fertility rates correlates with the rapid migration from farm to city, and is an early example of the phenomenon that continues today in the developing world. A notable if temporary exception was the post World War II "baby boom," when the U.S. birth rate jumped from 2.2 in the 1930s to 3.8 in the early 1960s, the peak of the baby boom and the rapid expansion of metropolitan areas that sprawled across farm fields. The boom was short-lived, however, with fertility rates returning to their longer-term decline, in line with continued urbanization, by the 1970s. In 1975 the U.S. fertility rate went below the replacement rate of 2.1 births per woman for the first time and in 2018 it was slightly above 1.7. Canadian rates were lower at 1.6, with European rates even lower at 1.4.[30]

Because each birth in developed countries tends to represent a large new carbon footprint, lower birth rates play a large role in combating CC. A growing number of city-dwelling European and American women are having fewer babies, having them later in life, or choosing to remain childless.

In many rich countries, between 15% and 20% of women, and a slightly higher percentage of men, will not have children. The share is rising . . . Childlessness is becoming more common in countries like Italy and Spain . . . Japan's childless rate has shot up from 11% for women born in 1953 to 27% for women born in 1970 . . . Almost everywhere, the most educated women are the least likely to have children.[31]

In the U.S. the percentage of 35-year-old females that were childless doubled between the World War II era and 1980, while it tripled for 30 year olds. And most of these women will remain childless, as child-bearing is postponed until it's biologically too late.[32]

The decline in urban birth rates within most developing countries seems so statistically robust and consistent as to be much more causation than correlation. Africa, with a current rate of 2.8, is rife with examples. The Union of South Africa's birth rate more than halved from over six to 2.4 births per woman[33] as the country became 65 percent urbanized between 1960 and 2010; the decline slowed when its urbanization rate dropped to 1.6 percent between 2010 and 2015.[34] The rural north of Nigeria has a fertility rate of seven to nine children per woman, while in the capital city of Lagos, the rate averages around four children.[35] In Bangladesh, "women have relatively high fertility rates in the poorer rural communities, however birth rates in the towns and cities have plummeted to less than two children per woman."[36] In South Korea, which in 2018 had the world's lowest national birth rate of 1.05, residents of Seoul had a rate of just 0.84.[37] The most precipitous national drop was no doubt in Iran, where the birth rate fell 400 percent from seven to 1.7 in just two decades. South America was not far behind, dropping from nearly six to 2.1 births per female between 1960 and 2015.[38] The benefits of this trend cannot be over-estimated in a world in which there currently are 140 million births per year versus about 60 million deaths.[39] That's over four births and less than two deaths per second. In fact, urbanization is the main reason given by the U.N. for its predicted leveling off and subsequent decline in world population later this century.

It is worth explaining why population does not stabilize the same year that births hit the replacement birth rate of 2.1, using India as an example.

Even though India's fertility rate is at or close to the replacement rate, India's population is not expected to stabilize, according to the U.N. until 2060. This is because there is a very long lag time before a gradually declining fertility rate is reflected in population reductions. Remembering that even low birth rates add to population rather than subtract, low birth rates have to be more than balanced by high death rates. As developing countries modernize and urbanize, mortality rates also tend to decline, i.e. people live longer . . . But until this now longer-living cohort of elderly do die they won't be subtracted from population counts. Thus, it can take decades for sub replacement rate births to result in total population declines . . . While birth rates in India's populous rural areas have indeed declined, apparently due to largely non-coercive policy supports such as government supported education and free birth control, the fertility rates in rural areas are still much higher than in urban areas. While the average fertility rate in all of India is now 2.3 births per woman, the rate in cities is much lower – less than even Sweden – at 1.8 births per woman.[40]

Migrating from rural farms and villages to the city usually means improved education, rights and self-determination for females, as well as more jobs, higher incomes and better access to family planning information and services. There is also less abortion and infanticide of female offspring, because "urban women grow more independent and more valuable to their parents."[41] Greater gender equity and balance is promoted by democratic cities, with both greater numerical and social parity between females and males. In general, the smaller families in cities make urbanization the most effective way to reduce high birth rates.

By 2060 . . . the population of Asia, Europe, North America, South America, and North Africa, will start to shrink – all except Africa. In the rest of the world we have, collectively, 40 years to get the city right. Immigration from rural to urban areas will continue to accelerate the growth of cities for those decades. Lower mortality rates will also mask the population reducing effect of lower fertility rates during those same decades. Unless any of these trends change, cities will, on average, stop growing by 2060 – excepting, possibly, in Africa.[42]

With the surging rural to urban migration and the long lag time before lower birth rates markedly reduce global population, the implications and questions are both large and ironic: Will cities and their nations be able to handle a relatively fast reversal in population? Or will it be a welcome relief after hyper-growth?

It is important to underline on the less promising side of the population equation in developing countries that migrants to the city typically end up with larger carbon footprints per capita as their income and consumption increase. So, the question remains whether the increased per capita footprint outstrips the decrease in birth rate, or vice versa. The fulcrum is different from country to country and time to time. Rural migrants to African cities don't necessarily increase their footprints, because they often are as poor or poorer in the city. Even if their per capita income and footprint rise, their total family footprint does not necessarily grow; with a lower birth rate, it may remain the same or even decrease. Many individuals and families in India who move to urban slums are also slow to climb out of their rural poverty and expand their consumption levels and carbon footprints. However, in China and most of Asia, the net effect is currently increasing CC. Although there's been no definitive study of this factor per se, the overall trend in developing countries currently seems to be toward both greater per capita and total carbon emissions.

How Can We Simultaneously Address CC and UHIs?

There are four basic ways to mitigate and adapt to them. The first is reducing *waste heat* from tailpipes with more walkable, bike-able and transit-oriented development, while reducing hot fumes from residential, commercial and industrial chimneys, as well as hot air from air conditioners. Second, lightening the color of roofs and pavements to absorb less solar radiation and reflect more of it back to outer space. Third is reducing deep, dark canyons created by tall buildings on narrow streets. And fourth is creating cool micro-climates, primarily by planting trees. The added good news is that most of these practices have collateral benefits beyond cooling UHIs and addressing CC: they reduce pollution, congestion and crime, not to mention improve safety, amenities and beauty.

Why Is the UHI So Timely?

Fortuitously, the local ways to mitigate and adapt to UHIs are essentially identical to ways to address global CC. And *because they're a shorter, perhaps a 10-year challenge, rather than a 100-year challenge, UHIs can more immediately and effectively rally individuals and societies to change their behavior.* As highlighted earlier, they are local, more in-your-face and more manageable, with actionable steps that give quicker feedback. Because UHIs beget quick, concrete attention, addressing them tends to feel more proactive and satisfying than trying to deal with longer-term, more uncertain climatic trends and impacts, such as very gradually rising sea levels or slowly declining agricultural yields. Since uncomfortably and sometimes dangerously hotter temperatures tend to be inescapable in the city, urban cooling initiatives can galvanize public action from a broad socio-economic cross-section of the city, among poor constituencies that are preoccupied with basic survival and among wealthy elites who can't fully escape heat in their air-conditioned lifestyles. Because the UHI threatens individual health and life expectancy, it is a *personal* stimulant to act. And as an urban phenomenon, it aligns well with municipal governance, which has been and promises to continue to be the most proactive level of government in combatting CC.[43]

To reinforce this point: three out of the four strategies to cool the *local* thermal commons simultaneously address the *global* thermal commons. Because the causes are more tangible and obvious than with CC, there is the added benefit of defusing partisan or sectarian skepticism and denialism in politically and religiously conservative communities about both the human-centric causes and the urgency of global CC. *Everyone* can feel in real time the heat radiating off hot, dark surfaces and coming out of tailpipes and air conditioners. City-goers and urban dwellers of all persuasions and cohorts can be overheated in narrow streets edged with tall buildings that trap hot air and reduce natural air flow. They appreciate the shade from trees and welcome cooling breezes. There's no esoteric science about invisible gases trapping infrared heat in the upper atmosphere and reradiating it back to earth. And there's less concern about apocalyptic tipping points with UHIs. There's also little if any excuse for pushback from skeptical or weak-kneed politicians. It provides a way to fight CC without even using the term. In summary, UHIs, often highlighted by heat waves, are more immediate, understandable and less controversial. And the manifestations and consequences of extreme heat in cities are getting demonstrably worse faster than CC.

What's Synergistic and Timely about These Dots?

This question brings us to one of the book's bedrock issues and new contentions: why it is beneficial and opportune in climate and other terms for more people to live in cities. Compared to their suburban and rural counterparts, urban residents in developed countries tend to have smaller ecological footprints. (Ecological footprint, or "eco-footprint," is the metric that measures the equivalent land area needed to provide the resources consumed and to absorb the wastes.) Typically, the eco-footprint closely aligns with the energy and carbon footprints, whether the scale is the home, community, region, nation or world. Urbanites walk, bike and use transit more than auto-dependent suburban and rural residents, as New Urbanists Scott Bernstein, Hank Dittmar and Jackie Grimshaw first pointed out with striking maps of Chicago in the early 2000s. Additionally, the more compact, party-wall/multi-floor housing in cities takes less energy to mechanically heat and cool, as do the larger buildings in which urbanites usually work. Their smaller homes, very often in multi-family buildings, tend to encourage less acquisition of material possessions, compared to suburban McMansions, with their larger rooms, extra bedrooms, attics, garages and lawns. A Canadian study of Ontario housing reported that "nearly two-thirds of the province's households live in homes that are bigger than what they need, with more than 400,000 homes that count three or more empty bedrooms."[44] (On the other hand, it is no doubt true that wealthy urbanites often consume more energy on air travel, fashion and luxury items, as well as larger apartment and condominium units.)

All of these benefits constitute the surprising, important and welcome *environmental paradox of cities*, a central theme of the book. It can be summarized as *urban residents on average have smaller footprints than their suburban and rural counterparts.* The suburbs may look green with their verdant leafiness and landscaped lawns, but in fact they are environmentally gray.

A second paradox – *the population paradox of cities* – applies to developing countries in an equally important but different way. As outlined earlier: *when rural residents move to cities, their birth rate drops.* Sometimes the reduction in birth rate is dramatic, by half or more. However, the smaller family and household sizes that result from the lower birth rate are offset by urban dwellers' larger footprints per capita as their incomes rise. It's paradoxical because the greater wealth of urban dwellers would suggest that larger families are more easily afforded than in the poorer, sometimes destitute countryside. It might be more logical to predict that family size would grow with household income and wealth. But the cost and complications of raising children are much higher in the city than "on the farm," where young family members are able to work and to help raise younger siblings.

The dampening of population growth is of great importance in the many developing countries that already are, or are rapidly becoming,

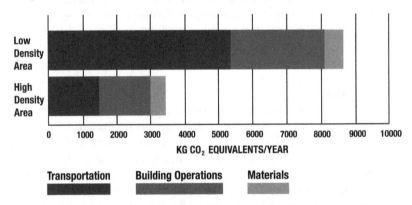

Impact of Urban Form on CO$_2$ Emissions Per Person

Figure 1.3 High density areas in the U.S. have considerably smaller carbon footprints per capita than low density areas, with transportation (in black) and building operations (heating, cooling, lighting, equipment in dark gray) constituting most of the difference. With Toronto as an example, North America epitomizes this *environmental paradox of cities,* but it also obtains in most cities in developed countries that have auto-dependent suburbs with freestanding houses. And it is found more and more in the megacities of the developing world that are decanting more residents to their mushrooming peripheries. (Heather L. MacLean, University of Toronto)

too populous for their natural resource base, land area and ecosystems. The wealthy countries' seemingly worrisome population loss due to low birth rates may well prove economically beneficial and politically positive. Meanwhile continuing media focus on global CC makes excessive lifestyles and carbon footprints more painfully obvious to both the culprits and the observers. Lower birth rates may soon become not only politically acceptable within developed countries but also applauded by developing countries, as the relatively huge footprints of most Americans and many Europeans are increasingly viewed by the rest of the world as both a glaring inequity and a CC liability.

How can we frame the growing problem in a way that will motivate and inspire individuals and societies to change their behaviors and act on the long-term, abstract and complex problem of CC, which seems so psychologically remote and even hopeless?

Much has been written on what makes people change the way they behave and act. How can mortals negotiate and address such an unwieldy, complex, amorphous and relatively slow-moving challenge? The extreme heat that people experience first-hand in cities is a basic motivator, focusing them on heat as the cause of discomfort and threat to health. People are hard-wired to deal with more acute, pressing problems, especially ones with personal, experiential immediacy. For instance, a daily assault on the senses, such as seeing and smelling pollution, trash and garbage, can be more motivating than being presented with objective facts on sanitation. We need to motivate homo sapiens in more immediate and palpable ways if we want to accelerate the reduction in their footprints. Because dealing with insufferable heat from UHIs also addresses global CC, it can help people deal with a longer-term problem.

Emotions are particularly powerful inducements to change behavior and to act. Arguably, *love* is the most powerful and positive emotional motivator, even stronger than self-preservation, as when someone lays down their life for someone else or some cause. As New Urbanist architect and author Steve Mouzon points out,[45] pleasure and beauty delight and satisfy us, while love and compassion *move us to act*. Accordingly, it could be argued that love of family, friends, community, country and nature are the most potent motivators to act on CC. We also know that competition, status-seeking, emulation and peer pressure, including the fear of failure and consequent guilt and shame, make us act. Perhaps nothing lubricates behavior change more smoothly than shared fun and humor, including the ability to laugh at ourselves. All humans are subject to these universal instincts and genetic hardwiring, in different ways and at different times. Love of one's home, of one's community and of one's city – all central to Dot 4 and enhanced by beauty, delight, humor and fun with our fellow humans – can be a potent incentive to act in our highest collective interests.

In any case, action requires that long-term threats are made threateningly real, and ways to act are present and clear. Many, many reasons to act are precipitated by the public disruptions of thermal and environmental events and crises – from urban congestion, overpopulation, air and water pollution to health problems, social unrest and infrastructure failure, not to mention the more direct CC phenomena of sea level rise, extreme weather, storm water flooding, drought, famine, climate refugees, etc. The particular cocktail of concerns varies from climate to climate, culture to culture and economy to economy. For many urbanized places, especially those in hot climates, rising urban temperatures are already stirring up trouble. Indeed, the loss of air conditioning in a Middle-Eastern city during a 2015 summer heat wave is reputed to have triggered civil unrest that was more intense than the civil war raging in the area, made all the more violent because state officials were spared the hardship.

Worldwide, heat waves kill more people than any other type of natural disaster, including hurricanes, tornadoes, earthquakes and floods.[46] "Heat kills ten times more people in the U.S. than tornadoes or other extreme weather events."[47] It should be mentioned that the young, the sick, the elderly and those without social networks are typically more affected by the dangers of heat waves, whereas other more violent natural disasters injure and kill more indiscriminately. Poverty makes extreme heat harder to handle.

> Excess mortality rates during extreme heat events are likely to be higher in the hottest neighborhoods; vulnerability and susceptibility in these areas are enhanced by poor socio-economic status, as expressed through poor housing quality, reduced air conditioning prevalence, and low household income levels.[48]

If the elderly poor can't afford air conditioners, much less to run them 24/7 during a heat wave, they are in danger of getting sick or dying. Although the poverty-stricken usually suffer the most in heat waves, there are examples of poor neighborhoods where healthy social infrastructure has proven to make a dramatic difference in how quickly and effectively these neighborhoods respond and recover. This difference was famously and positively shown in adjoining poor communities in a devastating Chicago heat wave, where healthy social integration fostered highly effective communication that helped one neighborhood react and rebound with astonishing higher speed.[49]

Outdoor urban heat is often so intense in hot, humid places like South Asia, that it can be physically sickening in the short term, including leading to heat stroke. And it can lower productivity in outdoor jobs and social interaction in the long term. UHIs tend to discourage outdoor activities, even in the evening, which is a traditional time for outdoor socializing and cultural events. But slum residents in cities like Dhaka – almost half Bangladesh's population – are reportedly too preoccupied and stricken with poverty to be aware of, much less understand and be concerned about CC. They are aware of extreme heat and regularly suffer its toll on their health, productivity and out-door socializing.

> One study in Bangladesh showed that extreme heat is more likely to drive migration than flooding is . . . Future sea level rise gets far more attention and study than increases in extreme heat, which may actually have a larger impact a lot sooner.[50]

The people of South Asia make up nearly a fourth of humanity, and so what happens to them stands to have inevitable global repercussions on everything from migration to conflict.

Although much of the new urban commercial space is air conditioned in developing countries, when there is power loss or load-shedding, these buildings become suffocatingly hot because their large floorplates, party walls and lack of operable windows make it difficult to naturally ventilate. The fairly frequent blackouts result in discomfort, reduced productivity, and physical and mental stress. In passing, it is worth noting that the advent and worldwide spread of air conditioning and flores-cent lighting, and now even cooler LED bulbs, have enabled commercial buildings with much bigger floor plates than traditional buildings, which needed daylight and operable windows relatively close to occupants. Today's fatter buildings, which would be too hot if lit with incandescent bulbs, are difficult to naturally ventilate, because much of the floor space is too far from windows, which often are not operable anyway in the ubiquitous sealed glass boxes of modern architecture. It could be said that the cooler florescent and LED lights have enlarged the horizontal dimension of architecture much as the elevator famously heightened its vertical dimension.

UHIs can extend well beyond the city, especially in the direction of the prevailing wind. When air flows over the hotter urban surfaces, a layer develops that "deepens with distance from the upwind edge. This envelope may be 1–2 kilometers thick by mid-afternoon and is distin-guishable as a warm and turbulent atmosphere that is enriched with contaminants, including GHGs."[51] This extensive layer means that higher temperatures and heat waves can impact wealthy areas of the metropolis, even though these neighborhoods are often more open to breezes and have more shade from foliage. UHIs can be dodged to a limited extent by the wealthy citizenry, but the combination of UHIs and CC is ultimately too pervasive for them to escape if they want to live within a metropolitan area, especially in one of its centers. In the short run, the rich can move to cooler climes and have the space and where-withal to stock supplies, but systemic breakdowns and geopolitical strife caused by a disruptive climate are inescapable. Among other hindrances, it will be the little things – such routine matters as getting spare parts for luxury paraphernalia – that will become more and more difficult.

The cooler countries of northern Europe have carbon footprints per capita significantly lower than other developed countries, because they have found effective ways *other* than polluted air and/or extreme heat to rally their citizens, institutions and corporations. Public policy, incentives and education have been effective. Whatever the prevailing motivator or wherever, policies and actions must be democratically prioritized and coordinated, with bottom-up input from citizens, as well as advice from experts. Prioritizing is critically important, because *there is neither enough money to solve civilization's problems all at once, nor enough time to solve them one at a time.* For instance, given the triple threat of CC, overpopulation and budget constraints, the economic and political reality is that infrastructure projects now have to serve multiple purposes. Synergies, efficiencies and co-benefits are essential, even in the wealthiest countries, which can sometimes be the sloppiest and most wasteful on both a total and per capita basis. Co-benefits of reducing UHIs and CC include less air pollution and smog, more jobs, healthier and more livable cities, longer lifespans of building materials, cleaner and cooler water for drinking and industrial uses, and less electricity consumption for air conditioning. Electricity for AC in cities increases 2–4 percent for each 1.8°F or 1°C increase in temperature, and it is fast becoming a major share of worldwide energy consumption.[52] Whatever the motivator or the reason to act, climatologists tell us we have no time to waste.

This brings us to related paradoxes of the city. The third one is the *thermal paradox of cities*. It is simply the flip side or cognate of the environmental paradox of cities: *Although living in the city can increase the* local *temperature, it can simultaneously help cool the* planet's *temperature.* In other words, as the city gets hotter, urban dwellers may nonetheless have a positive effect on *global* CC, due to smaller average footprints than their suburban and rural counterparts. Their thermal suffering is not in vain. Yet another way of stating it is that even though cities are getting hotter faster than the local countryside by concentrating heat in urban islands, cities exercise an overall cooling impact on the global climate. Unlike the first two paradoxes, which are causative, this paradox is only correlative, i.e., hotter cities don't actually combat CC, but they tend to accompany it. However, if the four strategies to fight UHIs presented in upcoming chapters are followed, the tendency toward hotter cities can be diminished, even eliminated. And the consequences of the first three of these four urban paradoxes cannot be overstated or underestimated, as they hold the key to the very positive role that cities can play in the long, slow war against CC.

Nevertheless, UHIs can give cities a bad name for being hotter than suburbia and the countryside at precisely the time when it's important to encourage people to move to and remain in urban places. In developed countries, UHIs could jeopardize the attendant climatic benefits. Suburban and rural developers can advertise cooler environments. Indeed, if the thermal differential between core and periphery is allowed to become severe enough, it could even trigger migration out of central cities. This reversal would tend to aggravate CC for two reasons. First, the carbon footprints per capita would increase in developed countries and, second, family size and the total number of people would increase in developing countries, since suburban and rural families tend to be larger. These possible outcomes underscore why *UHIs need to be aggressively addressed immediately*, with as little fanfare as possible about hotter city temperatures.

Related Urban Challenges and Opportunities

Higher air temperatures have other deleterious impacts. Stifling hot cities are more prone to disease, civil unrest and ultimately violence. Several quantitative studies have been compiled on the general relationship between heat and violence.

> Overall, the results show remarkable consistency in finding that hotter time periods (days, seasons, years) are associated with higher levels of violence, even when other relevant variables (e.g., poverty) are statistically controlled. Anderson and DeLisi studied US crime rates over 55 years and found that a 1°C increase in average annual temperature leads to over 7.5 more assaults and homicides per 100,000 population. Similarly, hotter summers yield larger summer increases in violent crime than cooler summers.[53]

And this increase doesn't assume any rise in collective unrest and mob violence, which would be likely to arise in many cities in already hot climates that get hotter. Indeed, another study found that "Each 1°C change in climate toward warmer temperatures or more extreme rainfall increases the frequency of interpersonal violence by 4% and intergroup conflict by 14%."[54]

Writing about Mexico City, Michael Kimmelman quotes a Columbia University report that found "where rainfall declines, 'the risk of a low-level conflict escalating to a full-scale civil war approximately doubles the following year.' And nowhere does this apply more obviously than in cities."[55] On the relationship between temperature and large-scale violence, researchers say that

> for every half-degree of warming, societies will see between a 10 and 20% increase in the likelihood of armed conflict. In climate science, nothing is simple, but the arithmetic is harrowing: A planet five degrees warmer would have at least half again as many wars as we do today. Overall, social conflict could more than double this century.[56]

The question hanging over these findings is whether human societies can both reduce extreme heat and learn to better cope with it.

Cities, with their many, many moving parts and complex systems, can also lack resiliency in times of disaster and panic, including heat waves. Nonetheless, if cities in developed countries are to play the positive, synergistic and catalytic role that they can naturally assume in the ongoing fight against CC, there is *no choice* but to retrofit them to be cool enough for human health, comfort, productivity and civility. Similarly, new and expanding cities in developing countries must be planned and built to prevent, mitigate and adapt to the UHIs from the outset. The issue has to be *framed* in an honest but positive light and in affirmative ways to motivate the public. It should be presented as an opportunity to protect and increase the pleasure and comfort of living in cities, both in developing and developed countries.

No antidote to UHIs is more universally beloved than trees. Having slowly evolved on the forest edge of the African savannah under sunlight dappled by foliage, we humans have come to like trees and see them as beautiful. They are cooked into our genes. Planting these multi-taskers in cities is a win in so many ways to mitigate and adapt to both CC and UHIs that a whole chapter is devoted to urban trees. It is an appealing, low-tech, time-tested practice that sequesters CO_2 and reduces air pollution, soil erosion and storm water runoff, not to mention providing oxygen, habitat for small animals, shade in the summer and more. And urban street trees are not as burdensome to maintain as the more numerous and more ornamental trees of suburbia. A clever if corny slogan of mine is "Plant a TREE on your sTREEt."

The benefits of trees are bumper-sticker simple, which is important in framing their numerous benefits. They can be sold as improving the quality of life by increasing safety and health, while reducing congestion and pollution. Their planting and maintenance can be implemented as private, neighborhood or governmental initiatives. Indeed, tree-planting programs can be civic, even patriotic campaigns, such as the nineteenth-century planting of American Elms that made scruffy towns beautiful in the Midwest and Northeast. Affectionately described as "cathedrals of shade," these iconic trees came to symbolize leafy American streets and college campuses. Installing green roofs can provide similar aesthetic and ecological benefits, but plants growing on terra firma have inherent advantages, especially in terms of installation, replacement and maintenance costs.

Reducing waste heat by converting our urban transportation system from cars to transit, shared vehicles, bicycles and walking will require a stronger framing effort. It's a bigger and costlier sea change than tree planting. Organizations like the Congress for the New Urbanism (CNU) and Smart Growth America have successfully promoted transit-oriented development, a.k.a. TOD, a term now familiar around the world. Countless conferences have been convened, and a torrent of books and articles have been published about the benefits of less automobile dependency. They are part of an effort to replace suburban sprawl with settlement patterns that are more mixed-use, mixed-income, connected, accessible, compact and denser – all of which promote walking, biking and transit.

Because urban cooling emphasizes adaptation over mitigation, its more immediate and concrete initiatives provide a proactive sense of progress against the vagaries and uncertainties of unfurling CC. And if cities fail to attract more residents, and/or to keep their current residents from migrating to their relatively cooler suburbs and countryside, their larger carbon footprints will eventually make *both* cities and suburbs hotter by exacerbating CC. It is about managing public perception, as well as mobilizing to respond to a costly and accelerating physical imperative. Cooling the local urban thermal commons, like addressing CC, sits on the right side of multiple equations. And there can be few if any regrets about mitigating UHIs, as the benefits of less extreme heat – from comfort to health to social life – are good for the world in any case. In short, UHIs are a great reason and a great motivator to address both local extreme heat and global CC.

The other good news is that cities also offer opportunities for people on all rungs of the socio-economic ladder. While not surprising or paradoxical for the upper economic classes of most societies, for poor residents, it could be considered the fourth paradox of cities – the *urban poverty paradox*. First observed by Harvard Professor Edward Glaeser, it posits cities don't make people poor, but attract them in large numbers because they offer economic opportunity. He goes on to point out that cities that don't attract and have many poor people are not as healthy as ones that do. Rust-belt and other shrinking cities don't offer as much promise of upward mobility to the poor from impoverished rural areas or other poor cities. For instance, Detroit has a very high poverty rate, but until its recent resurgence in places like its Mexicantown, it did not attract many poor migrants from other countries.

While fostering creativity, productivity, commerce, community, arts, culture and entertainment, cities also benefit from what economists call the economies of agglomeration, a term that captures the many efficiencies and synergies of cities. As denser communities, they more easily enable the sharing of assets, both physical and social. Cities offer intellectual stimulation and many educational opportunities; their schools, universities, institutes, libraries and museums are major shared assets. Arguably, urbanites exposed to these institutions can better deal with complexity and new technologies, such as automation and AI, which promise endless innovations while also threatening jobs. As cellphones give way to virtual reality and possibly direct bridges to the brain, a human–machine fusion could change, and either deeply challenge or enhance our social fabric. For instance, Elon Musk predicted in 2017 that a meaningful partial brain interface is only four or five years away.[57]

These innovations will accelerate, but it remains to be seen if they are up to the equally fast impacts of CC.

As society faces the widespread impacts of ubiquitous automation, the size of its cities is of relevance. A study by MIT's Media Lab posited that the smaller the city, the greater the disruption. Bigger cities, it reports, have a

> disproportionately large number of jobs for people who do cognitive and analytical tasks, such as software developers and financial analysts—occupations that are less likely to be disrupted by automation. Smaller cities (under 100,000 population) have a disproportionate amount of routine clerical work, such as cashier and food service jobs, which are more susceptible.[58]

New York City's economy is oriented toward financial markets, which are low-energy-consuming, white collar jobs. It also contained about 6 percent of the U.S. population in 2014, but consumed only 1 percent of the country's industrial energy.[59]

Cities also tend to develop and embrace new ideas more quickly than rural areas. There have been rural utopian communities that have embraced new ideas, but they have tended to be more rigid and shorter-lived. Cities cultivate social connectivity and tolerance of strangers better than small communities and homogeneous enclaves, where residents experience a smaller cross-section of the human condition. Riding urban public transit may have its monotonous or crowded moments, but it can be a humanizing and democratic experience compared to the internet or residential compounds, with their echo chambers of self-selecting groups of like-minded people. When cities are a traditional melting pot, or more contemporary salad bowl, they promote wider observation of and interaction with "the unfamiliar, the diverse and the complex."[60] As a result, urbanites tend to develop more open, cosmopolitan attitudes than residents of smaller and sectarian communities. What could be timelier in this era of pushback on immigrants by nationalists, nativists and white supremacists?

This openness to strangers can be an especially delicate and problematic issue in Europe, where cities struggle to heal the unrest and violence that can be triggered by the ongoing in-migration of foreigners. Immigration has become a lightning rod in more than one electoral upset there and in the U.S. The rural–urban and rich–poor divides in these polarized societies have brought new spatial meaning to politics. In the 2016 U.S. presidential election,

> 49 of the 50 highest density counties voted for Hillary Clinton, and 48 of the 50 lowest density counties chose Donald Trump (nearly the same split as for Barack Obama and Mitt Romney four years

earlier) . . . There are reasons for this trend that go beyond identity politics. Urban density has social and economic advantages that make cities attractive to liberals and that *also* condition and perpetuate liberal values. Living among diverse neighbors can reduce fear and resentment, as everyday interactions break down stereotypes and misconceptions of "the other." (which is not to ignore that cities have their own problems with racial and economic segregation) . . . In counties that voted overwhelming for Clinton, households are 215 feet apart on average; in strong Trump territory, they are nearly a half mile distant.[61]

A Pew Research Center poll on partisanship found

> 75% of conservatives want to live where "houses are larger and farther apart, but schools, stores, and restaurants are several miles away." 75% of liberals want to live where "houses are smaller and closer to each other, but schools, stores, and restaurants are within walking distance."[62]

Cities are also vexed with their share of problems – from congestion, noise and air pollution to higher crime rates, civic unrest, gentrification, racially segregated slums, excessive food waste and mountains of garbage. Many cities in industrialized regions in developed countries have been visited by five "D"s – de-industrialization, decay, disinvestment, depopulation and drugs. Fortunately, some of them have recuperated in recent years, although some linger in the doldrums. There's been plenty of cultural warfare resulting from competing value systems and inequities of opportunity. Living in dense, diverse cities requires "polycultural navigation,"[63] which balances mutual trust and access to common resources at the personal, community, national and global scale. It's about nurturing collective values and behavior, but without homogenizing and over-simplifying culture.

Gentrification, with its displacement of poor residents because of sharply climbing housing costs and local property taxes, has been a growing problem in an alarming number of cities throughout the world. Displacement is its signature misfortune in the otherwise welcome new investment and jobs. In the U.S., only 20 percent of families that are poor enough to qualify for a housing subsidy actually receive one. A quarter of all renters pay more than half their income in rent, which is well above an acceptable rate and affordable rent.[64] These families are forced to make painful choices between rent and food, doctor's visits and education costs. In their search for what public housing had promised as a "decent, safe and sanitary home," the poor have been pushed farther from the economic activity and opportunities of city centers. This trend threatens society's ability to nurture growing, mixed-income, sustainable cities the world over.

Urban gentrification is a chronic and age-old problem, having plagued cities since they became desirable and advantageous places to live millennia ago. It is not necessarily a zero-sum game – heads I win, tails you lose. And in some disinvested cities, it is better than no gentrification. Squelching private investment that creates new jobs in reviving cities like Detroit is the wrong solution to the wrong problem. It will only serve to ensure that unemployment will linger, and that lower-income, middle-income and upper-income people will continue to live in separate and unequal neighborhoods, making social and economic conditions in poor urban neighborhoods even worse. And if there is physical space made available by the abandonment and foreclosure of buildings and land, there can be new development and redevelopment without displacement of existing residents and businesses. There are many such vacant sites in hollowed-out American "legacy cities," like Detroit, Baltimore and St. Louis, as well as in "shrinking cities" in Europe.

Displacement has gotten notoriously worse of late in American cities like San Francisco, Los Angeles, Seattle and New York, as well as London, Mumbai, Dubai and other cities in both developing and developed countries, as well as the BRIC (Brail, Russia, India, China) countries in between. It's magnified by global economic trends such as increasing economic inequality, and by local trends such as the rise of high-tech companies that easily attract investment and pay very high salaries. For example, in 2018 "San Francisco is the world's #1 destination for venture capital: Two downtown neighborhoods each attracted more than $1 billion in venture capital funding in 2013 – more than most other *nations.*"[65] This extreme influx of money rapidly drives up housing and other costs of living, not only displacing renters with lower incomes, but also making it impossible for anyone but the wealthy to move in. The same displacement dynamic applies to retail and wholesale businesses, as well as institutions.

An international challenge, gentrification stretches from Jakarta and Johannesburg to San Jose and San Miguel de Allende, to name just four abutting names in the alphabet of expanding cities. A chronically hard problem to mitigate, it must be addressed by aggressive policies, subsidies and interventions. In our neoliberal world of the glorified marketplace, the availability of government housing subsidies has been in decline for decades, even in the social welfare countries of Europe. Never strong in the U.S., subsidies and assistance programs have been slowly gutted by the political groups that are suspicious of all such government interventions in the market, or are downright racist. Pressed with new fiscal challenges, these public programs are likely to continue their slide, because of a heavier bottom line: the accumulating obsolescence of housing stock, the added expense of replacing fossil fuel with renewable energy systems, and more emergency response brought on directly and obliquely by CC. Public–private partnerships, which are usually more private than public investment, tax incentives and land trusts can help fill the gap, but other things are needed, from relaxed codes and regulations to smaller units and more shared living arrangements.

There is a miscellany of other urban challenges that are less-discussed but non-trivial, such as ambient noise. Noise pollution from cars, trucks, trains and heavy machinery is harmful and unhealthy not only to human residents, but also to birds, bats, mammals and mollusks in cities and their harbors.[66]

> Experts are concerned that noise is quickly becoming the next great public health crisis ... Data collected by the United Nations estimates that by 2100, 84% of the world's 10.8 billion citizens will live in cities, surrounded by a smorgasbord of sound.[67]

Another less-recognized urban problem is the surprising link between air pollution and crime.

> A long-term analysis of pollution and crime statistics along with three experiments suggest that anxiety caused by exposure to pollution makes people more prone to cheating and unethical behavior. And that can be a driver behind the higher crime rates in high-pollution areas.[68]

On another front, University of Chicago researchers found there is a connection in some of the city's neighborhoods between repeated exposure to violent crime and elevated blood pressure and obesity. Using police data and patient health records, they found that living in areas with high rates of violent crime increases the odds of hypertension by 25 percent and of being obese by 53 percent.[69] Yet another problem is that factories and manufacturing facilities engulfed by urban development are challenged by lack of space to expand and by greater logistical complexity, both of which compromise productivity and require new types of urban factories.

While losing ground in some of these social and environmental battles, as already noted municipal and metropolitan levels of government are not only fighting on the front lines of CC but also have the best record of proactive commitment, goals and initiatives. Indeed, over 500 cities worldwide measure GHG emissions, often with ambitious reduction targets, including some that have declared a goal of zero emissions by mid-century. Hong Kong has been studying and trying to better handle its UHIs for years. Louisville, Kentucky, which seems especially hard hit by them, is actively putting many new initiatives in place designed to fight UHIs. New York City and Chicago and some northern European cities, have been increasingly aggressive in CC mitigation/adaptation policies, with agile, on-the-ground efforts. But exactly how to achieve the cuts is an open question. By mid-2018, only three U.S. cities had said how they plan to meet their goals. New York City passed the first Paris Agreement-compliant climate plan in the country, proposing specific measures to tackle emissions, including ones outlined in this book.[70] Cities have a wide range of strategies and policies from which to choose: street trees, urban reforestation, urban agriculture, recycling, electrical energy and heating from garbage incineration, fracking bans, rooftop wind turbines and high-rise buildings built of timber rather than more energy-intensive steel or concrete.[71]

As ambitious as their goals may be, municipal finance can be a major barrier. Organizing and harnessing both municipal and private wealth is essential for initiatives and projects. Only about 5 percent of cities worldwide have unilateral power to raise money and have established credit-worthiness in international finance markets, which makes it difficult to raise funds for sustainable infrastructure and to deliver on their climate commitments.[72] So, cities typically float municipal bonds, some $3.8 trillion worth in the U.S. alone. Municipal green bonds are now being offered, and some cities are starting to use crowdsourcing to raise funds for civic sustainability projects.[73] There are structural issues: On the one hand, "public balance sheets struggle to keep up with ongoing liabilities and therefore are constrained in terms of fiscal capacity. And on the other hand, private capital is largely place agnostic, flowing toward predictable, risk-adjusted returns."[74] The UN's New Urban Agenda is seeking to find funding and promote feasible financial borrowing to make sure its initiatives and programs are more than platitudes and spineless plans. Cities that don't adopt resilience plans risk credit downgrades that can significantly increase the cost of borrowing funds. A 2017 report by a major investment service company on the burgeoning risk to city and state credit ratings underscores that there "will be a growing negative credit factor for issuers without sufficient adaptation and mitigation strategies."[75]

In some instances, the legal power to pursue green policies and practices is delegated from above. In other cases, it is asserted from below, but in either case local and global politics are paramount. Some cities simply act on their own, even with other, distant countries. As Anne-Marie Slaughter writes in her 2017 book *The Chessboard and the Web*, "many city officials are essentially practicing urban foreign policy, working with their counterparts in other cities across borders."[76] As for the municipal policies and politics of CC, the late Benjamin Barber writes in his final book *Cool Cities: Urban Sovereignty and the Fix for Global Warming*,

> The problem isn't the science. The merchants of doubt who claim there is a climate science that is open to scientific debate are not *scientific* adversaries at all. They are political adversaries, mostly bought and paid for. It is in the realm of politics that the struggle

for sustainability must be fought and won . . . the fate of the campaign against climate change and other existential threats depends on democratic politics within and among cities . . . Today it is cities that look forward, speaking to global common goods, while fearful nations look back . . . The world is getting too hot. Science makes it clear that sustainability is both necessary and possible . . . Cities are poised to make it happen.[77]

As he pithily also pens in the same book, "politicians pay few costs for doing nothing, and receive little credit for acting aggressively." Amazingly, CC was not mentioned a single time at the 2016 Republican National Convention, and candidates were not asked a single question about it in their last three debates.

Seven Summarizing Propositions

1   CC is an existential threat to civilization that is as immense as it is unprecedented. It urgently needs to be addressed, including both mitigation and adaptation. However, as a long-term and abstract threat, it is difficult to sufficiently rally society, which is always faced with more immediate and direct threats.

2   The *environmental paradox of cities* – In developed countries, cities that are mixed-use, walkable, transit-served with compact, multi-unit buildings have lower carbon footprints per person than their suburbs or hinterland. The bigger and denser the city, the more pronounced this counterintuitive phenomenon is. Urban dwellers also tend to have smaller families because of the higher costs of housing and child-rearing expenses, as well as higher rates of female employment. And many infrastructure costs per capita tend to be minimized with density. The UHI is the one exception: the relative thermal comfort associated with low-density development comes at too high an environmental cost. In short, suburbia may be thermally more comfortable than cities, but its per capita contribution to CC is prohibitively high.

3   The *population paradox of cities* – In developing countries, migration to the city typically raises household carbon footprints, but it also tends to lower family size. This reduction in the birth rate dampens and sometimes decreases a nation's *total* carbon footprint. The paradox currently applies more in Africa, where birth rates sometimes drop from eight children to four or less per family, with little if any increase in income and carbon footprints per capita in the city. However, in China birth rates are already low, and incomes rise more, resulting in larger per capita footprints from increased consumption. In other *developing* countries, the net effect on household, city and national footprints is currently counter-productive

in CC terms, because the impact of higher consumption in the city outweigh the decrease in birth rate. And both per capita and total national carbon footprints increase when major cities mushroom into more energy-intensive patterns of sprawl.

4   UHIs are making cities hotter twice as fast as surrounding suburbs and countryside, or as the planet as a whole. Accordingly, UHIs can deter people from moving to or staying in cities, forcing them to never leave or to return to the countryside or suburbs, where their carbon footprints will be higher. And hotter urban temperatures trigger more reliance on air conditioners, with both their high carbon and waste heat emissions.

5   Addressing UHIs simultaneously addresses CC, usually in equal measure.

6   Because UHIs are more of an immediate, palpable, in-your-face but manageable problem than CC, they can better motivate people in most cities of the world to act – wittingly or unwittingly – on CC with a greater sense of urgency, agency and progress. Addressing UHIs is by no means a complete antidote to CC, but the scale of the strategy is aligned well with city and metropolitan governments, which to date have been quicker and nimbler to mitigate and adapt than larger political units. Indeed, the bureaucratic agility and civic resolve to address CC exhibited to date by cities have usually produced a better track record than nation-states, many of which have been slow or faltering in their attempts to act unilaterally and/or multi-laterally on sustainability policies and initiatives.[78]

7   As a result, the environmental-social-economic synergies, creative ferment, diversity and cultural richness of cities and their potential to address CC are harnessed. If well planned and well built, cities may be civilization's last, best hope as it moves into a future made all the more uncertain by CC.

These are urgent propositions that ask for the professional abilities and commitment of architects, engineers, landscape architects, urban designers, planners and developers, as well as policy makers, elected or appointed public officials, academicians, students and citizens. Understanding and connecting these dots boosts their agency and confidence to act more decisively, as well as to help reduce pessimism. It's also intellectually fruitful to understand *why* and *how* the dots interconnect as new ones emerge. And, as it happily turns out, most of the relevant concepts, policies and practices are neither difficult to understand nor daunting to implement.

Municipal and metropolitan levels of government are not only fighting on the front lines of CC but, as previously noted, also have the best record of proactive commitment, goals and initiatives. Over 500 cities worldwide now measure GHG emissions, often with ambitious reduction targets, including some that have declared a goal of zero emissions by mid-century. Hong Kong has been studying and trying to more effectively cool its UHI for years. Louisville, Kentucky, in the U.S. is especially hard hit, and is actively putting many initiatives in place designed to fight it. New York City and Chicago, like many northern European cities, have been increasingly proactive with on-the-ground CC mitigation/adaptation policies and initiatives. Many cities have a wide range of strategies and policies: street trees, urban reforestation, urban agriculture, recycling, electrical energy and heating from garbage incineration, fracking bans, rooftop wind turbines and high-rise buildings built of timber rather than more energy-intensive steel or concrete.[79]

Cities have long played a central role in our survival and evolution and will continue to do so as we combat CC. *If the populous city is a major citadel in this war, then the UHI is the Trojan Horse – sneaking behind enemy lines to change behavior and to win immediate battles, as opposed to the long frontal assault needed in the larger campaign against CC.* Even though cities occupy less than 3 percent[80] of the planet's land area, CC is like an ongoing land war, and UHIs with urban heat waves are more like terrorism, in that they typically come on suddenly in cities. As an activating catalyst in the grand challenge of CC and global overpopulation, they can mobilize a broad socio-political spectrum to act quickly in the many over-heating cities of the world.

Cities and smaller communities not only enhance our chances of survival, they also offer meaning in our lives: they can inspire loyalty to and love of place and of home – topophilia and oikophilia. Cities that are livable and lovable – attributes inspired by subjective, ineffable qualities like beauty and balance – have always played and will always play a role in the happiness and flourishing of humans. The city offers a confluence and synergy of personal, societal, environmental and climatic benefits. Rarely do so many positive things fall on the positive side of the ledger, which is why CC, UHIs and global overpopulation in cities beg to be addressed with more vigor and resolve.

Notes

1 Nick Wiltgen, *The Weather Channel*, 9/14/15
2 Bill McKibben, "Winning slowly is the same as losing," *Rolling Stone*, 12/1/17
3 M. Kimmelman, "Mexico City, parched and sinking, faces a water crisis," *The New York Times*, 2/17/17
4 Michael Mehaffy, personal email, 3/28/17
5 Michael Kimmelman, "The kind of thinking cities need," *The New York Times*, 10/28/16
6 *Climate Science Special Report*, U.S. Global Change Research Program, NOAA, June, 2017
7 Paul Hawken, webinar on Drawdown, The Security and Sustainability Forum, 10/4/17

8 Michael Bender, *Paleoclimate*, Princeton University Press, 2013

9 "The methane mystery," *The Economist*, 4/28/18, pp. 71–72

10 Zoe Schlanger, "Algae, thrilled about a warming climate, is making Greenland melt faster," *Quartz*, 12/23/17

11 Akshat Rathi, "Turbine redesign," *Quartz*, 12/5/17

12 Moises Velasquez-Manoff, "Can dirt save the earth?" *The New York Times Magazine*, 4/18/18

13 Ibid.

14 "Sucking up carbon," *The Economist*, 11/18/17

15 Letter by Iziah Thompson, "Letters," *The Economist*, 12/9/17

16 Jason Hickel, "The Paris Climate Deal won't save us: our future depends on de-growth," *The Guardian*, 7/3/17

17 Elizabeth Kolbert, "Going negative," *The New Yorker*, 11/20/17, p. 71

18 Shannon Hall, "A surprise from the supervolcano under Yellowstone," *The New York Times*, 10/10/17

19 Akshat Rathi, "The world's first 'negative emissions' plant has begun operation – turning carbon dioxide into stone," *Quartz*, 10/12/17

20 Paul Hawken, webinar on Drawdown

21 "Less ice, more fire," *The Economist*, 12/2/17

22 Ibid.

23 "What they don't tell you," *The Economist*, 11/18/17

24 Robert Kopp et al., "Tipping elements and climate-economic shocks: pathways toward an integrated assessment," *Earth's Future*, 8/25/16

25 Sophie Hares, "Climate change pushing weather extremes 'off the scale,' says global cities group," *place*, 2/27/18

26 Yuval Noah Harari, *Homo Deus: A Brief History of Tomorrow*, HarperCollins, 2017

27 *Climate Science Special Report*, U.S. Global Change Research Program, NOAA, June, 2017

28 Rob Monroe, "What does 400 ppm look like?" Scripps Institution of Oceanography, 12/3/13

29 Sarah Zielinski, "Why the city is (usually) hotter than the countryside," @SmithsonianMag on Twitter smithsonian.com, 7/9/14

30 Prof. Patrick Condon's manuscript for *Three Great Waves That Will Reshape Cities*, sent on 1/4/18, informed the whole paragraph

31 "The rise of childlessness," *The Economist*, 7/20/17

32 Ibid.

33 World Bank, *Public Data*, Google, 2014

34 *The World Fact Book*, C.I.A. website, www.cia.gov/library/publications/the-world-factbook/fields/2212.html

35 Peter Donaldson, "What world cities have the highest birthrates?" *Quora*, 5/31/17

36 Ibid.

37 "Procreative struggle, *The Economist*, 6/30/18

38 Condon, manuscript for *Three Great Waves That Will Reshape Cities*

39 *Wofram Alpha Viewer*, Wofram/Alpha Research, UK, 2017

40 Condon, manuscript for *Three Great Waves That Will Reshape Cities*

41 "Boy trouble," *The Economist*, 1/21/17, p. 50

42 Condon, manuscript for *Three Great Waves That Will Reshape Cities*

43 Bejamin Barber, *Cool Cities: Urban Sovereignty and the Fix for Climate Change*, Yale University Press, 2017

44 Ashifa Kassam, "Canada's 'us and them cities': data shows that most homes are too small – or too big," *The Guardian*, 5/27/17

45 Steve Mouzon, *Original Green*, website/blog 7/31/09

46 Several sources make this claim, but some claim that heat waves only are the number one killer among natural disasters
47 Steven Leahy, "By 2100, deadly heat may threaten majority of humankind," *National Geographic*, 6/19/17
48 Joyce Rosenthal, "Evaluating the impact of the urban heat island on public health: spatial and social determinants of heat-related mortality in New York City," Ph.D. dissertation, Columbia University, 2010
49 Eric Klinenberg, *Heat Wave: A Social Autopsy of Disaster in Chicago*, University of Chicago Press, 2002
50 Steven Leahy, "Parts of Asia may be too hot for people by 2100," *National Geographic*, 8/2/17
51 J. Raven et al., "Urban planning and urban design," in C. Rosenzweig et al. (eds), *Climate Change and Cities: Second Assessment Report of the Urban Climate Change Research Network*, Cambridge University Press, 2018, p. 145
52 Karen Seto and Shobhakar Dhakal, "Human settlements, infrastructure and spatial planning," *IPCC 2014 Mitigation*, p. 927
53 C. A. Anderson, "Climate change and violence," *The Encyclopedia of Peace Psychology*, Wiley-Blackwell, 2012, pp. 128–132
54 S. M. Hsiang et al., "Quantifying the influence of climate on human conflict," *Science*, 7/13/13
55 M. Kimmelman, "Mexico City, parched and sinking, faces a water crisis"
56 David Wallace Wells, "Climate change will make earth too hot for humans," *New York Magazine*, 7/9/17
57 Sarah Marquart, "Get ready: Elon Musk is releasing details on his plan to unite our brains with AI," *Futurism*, 4/17/17
58 Elizabeth Woyke, "In these small cities, AI advances could be costly," *MIT Technology Review*, 10/23/17
59 Brad Plumer, "Just how far can California possibly go on climate?" *The New York Times*, 7/26/17
60 Richard Sennett, "Shaping cities," Venice Biennale, 2016 (as reported by Brunella Angeli in *The Plan Journal*, No. 1, 2016)
61 Neeraj Bhatia, "Environment as politics," *Places Journal*, April, 2017
62 Mike Allen, "1 big thing: how American politics went batshit crazy," *Axios AM*, 11/14/17
63 James Chaffers, *SpaceSpirit*, unpublished booklet, April, 2018
64 Ben Austen, "The towers came down, and with them the promise of public housing," *The New York Times*, 2/6/18
65 Richard Florida, "Tech cities made too expensive: here's how to fix it," *Wired*, 4/26/17
66 Neel V. Pateel, "Noise is the next great public health crisis," *Futurism*, 12/19/17
67 Kristin Houser and Patrick Caughlin, "10 things children born in 2018 will probably never experience," *Futurism*, 1/3/18
68 Terry Kosdrosky, "Research suggests air pollution linked to unethical behavior, crime," *The University Record* (University of Michigan), 2/12/18
69 Ese Olumhense, *Chicago Tribune*, 7/10/18
70 Brendan Gibbons, "In greenhouse gas inventory, San Antonio measures its carbon footprint," *Rivard Report*, 7/9/18
71 Benjamin Barber, *Cool Cities*
72 Gregory Scruggs, Interview with Nick Godfrey, *citiscope*, 5/16/17
73 Leena Rao, "This startup wants to modernize public finance," *Fortune*, 5/16/17
74 Bruce Katz, "How impact capitalism re-discovers place," thenewlocalism.com, 5/15/18

75 Rachel Dovey, "Here's how much money green design could save cities," *Next City*, 2/14/18
76 Anne-Marie Slaughter, *The Chessboard and the Web*, Yale University Press, 2017
77 Benjamin Barber, "How to fix climate change: put cities in charge," *The Guardian*, 5/7/17
78 Benjamin Barber, *Cool Cities*
79 Ibid.
80 J. Raven et al., "Urban planning and urban design," p. 145

2 Triple Threat
UHIs, CC and Overpopulation

By now, almost everyone on the planet views CC as real and sees human activity as the main cause. A higher and higher fraction agree that urgent action is needed, and many feel institutions and governments are not moving quickly enough to prevent the unfurling of an epic tragedy.

> Changes must be planned and executed decades in advance of the usual signals of crisis, but that's like asking healthy, happy sixteen-year-olds to write living wills . . . In the name of nature, we are asking human beings to do something deeply unnatural, something no other species has ever done or could ever do: constrain its own growth . . . Now we are asking *Homo sapiens* to fence itself in.[1]

Despite ever-mounting evidence that CC is perhaps the greatest crisis ever to face humanity, it is difficult to rapidly change people, institutions and governments.

Our intellect tells us that this invisible threat is quantitatively and qualitatively different from the chronic problems that have plagued humans since our beginnings. Common sense tells us that its ultimate impacts will be massive, with unraveling consequences that are hard to fathom, much less predict and address. Our hearts tell us that the worst-case scenario will be devastatingly painful for many generations to come, with widespread suffering by humans and other animals. There may be a major die-off of our species, as some species are already experiencing, especially those with large body size, often the ones we most cherish. An exhibition at New York University estimates that one species goes extinct every seven minutes and this rate may be 1,000 times faster than evolutionary norms.[2] The situation has been described as the sixth major extinction – the biggest in the last 65 million years[3] – by eminent scientists, including Richard Leakey and E.O. Wilson, respectively called the father of sociobiology and biodiversity. Elizabeth Kolbert, author of *The Sixth Extinction: An Unnatural History*, estimates that at least a quarter of extant animal species are at risk of extinction in the near term, and that long term as many as half could vanish.[4] Because it is human-caused, Wilson says "This is the folly our descendants are least likely to forgive us."[5]

The insightful author Charles Mann writes:

> Ten thousand years ago, most demographers believe, we numbered
> barely 5 million, about one human being for every hundred square
> kilometers of the earth's land surface . . . a scarcely noticeable dust-
> ing on the surface of a planet dominated by microbes. Nevertheless,
> at about this time – 10,000 years ago, give or take a millennium –
> humankind finally began to approach the first inflection point. Our
> species was inventing agriculture.[6]

A stable climate has been with us from the start of civilization, with few
perturbations, which has allowed both agriculture and cities to flourish.
However, our recent fossil fuel use, industrial agriculture and forestry
have deeply disturbed this steady climate. Humans are directly altering
the earth's atmospheric, geologic, hydrologic, biospheric systems and
cycles at an alarming rate, enough to name the Anthropocene. And the
natural biodiversity of the world that supports us is equally endangered.
It's going to be a wild ride, one that could easily veer out of control for
our children and grandchildren.

However, nature is not like democratic politics, which has been
famously described as "the art of the possible." It doesn't negotiate or
announce in advance of its tipping points. It ultimately dictates. Natural
organisms and systems may be the best possible alpha drive or even dic-
tator, but they have an utterly non-partisan, long-term goal: survival.
Nature does bet on horses, and it has its favorites – not the strongest or
fastest, but the fittest. It also has demonstrated a welcome inclination
toward creating things and places that homo sapiens find livable, bountiful, beautiful and even sublime.

Questions burgeon into dilemmas, even unresolvable Greek trag-
edies: Are we victims of our own success as a species? Are the endless
little gasoline bangs in hundreds of millions of internal-combustion
engines around the world disabling us in what is effectively a giant,
slow-motion explosion? Will we drown in our own garbage, and for
the first time succumb to our gaseous waste? Are we – as civilizations
have classically done in previous terminal crises – doubling down
on producing goods, depleting resources, borrowing more from the
future, fighting extended wars, showing off with ever-taller buildings
and bingeing on evermore spectacular extravaganzas? Are we stutter-
stepping, or even sleep-walking, into a catastrophic endgame? Is the
upward migration of wealth demoralizing us, while vested interests
promote go-slow CC strategies and denial? Can other species and their
habitats migrate as quickly as the climate changes?

As Stewart Brand writes in *Whole Earth Discipline*, "If we fail to stabilize climate, our civilization will either be gone or unrecognizable."[7]
The problem is how can we mortals wrap our minds and arms around

such an unwieldy, complex, amorphous and relatively slow-moving challenge? According to 2016 data, most Americans believe climate change is happening. The majority of them agree it is harming people, but most don't believe it will harm them. Although people in other countries seem more aware of and unnerved by CC, under-perceiving risk and the difference between apparent and real danger is a universal issue. Global warming is precisely the kind of threat that humans are terrible at dealing with: a problem with enormous long-term consequences, but little harm that is clearly visible on a personal level in the short term. *Humans are hard-wired for quick fight-or-flight reactions in the face of an imminent threat, but not highly motivated to act against slower-moving and more abstract problems, even if the challenges that they pose are ultimately dire.*[8]

Challenge #1: Climate Change and Its Impacts

Carbon dioxide was "discovered" in 1754 by a Scottish physician named Joseph Black. A decade later, another Scotsman, James Watt, invented a more efficient steam engine, ushering in what is now called the age of industrialization, but which future generations could dub the age of emissions. It is likely that by the end of the nineteenth century human activity had raised the average temperature of the earth by a tenth of a degree Celsius. As the world warmed, it started to change, first gradually and then suddenly. By now, the globe is at least 1°C (1.8°F) warmer than it was in Black's day, and the consequences are becoming ever more apparent.[9] Although CC was first described as a scientific phenomenon in 1854, the first prediction that the planet would warm as humans released more CO_2 was made in 1896. Now scientists contend that "Humanity's fossil-fuel use, if unabated, risks taking us, by the middle of the twenty-first century, to values of CO_2 not seen since the early Eocene (50 million years ago)."[10]

More carbon has been released into the atmosphere since 1988 than had been released in the entire history of civilization before that![11] "Fossil fuels accounted for 81% of the world's energy consumption in 1987. Thirty years later it's still 81%."[12] Carbon emissions have increased 43 percent above the pre-industrial level so far, and the earth has warmed by roughly the amount that scientists predicted it would. There is essentially unanimous agreement in the scientific community about *how* GHGs interact to increase the earth's temperature. Less than 5 percent of scientists believe that CC is not anthropogenic, or that it is an insignificant or coincidental factor. These skeptics focus more on the connection of CC to cycles in the earth's orbit, tilt and the wobble as the earth rotates. Some scientists contend that there may be yet other causes – such as variations in sunspots or in long orbital cycles – that might increase or slow, even reverse, the trend. But scientists who study the earth's history say the current warming is extremely rapid on the geologic time scale, and no other factor can explain it as certainly as human emissions of GHGs.

If CC is driven by GHGs, it would be good to review the sources of these atmospheric gases. In 2010, CO_2 accounted for about three-fourths of GHGs, with about two-thirds of them coming from burning coal, oil and natural gas, and another one-tenth from rotting organic matter resulting from deforestation and land use. Since then coal use has been dropping every year: In 2017, Britain enjoyed its first coal-free day since igniting the Industrial Revolution. The primary human activities causing carbon emissions globally are: (a) energy generation of electricity and heat, which accounts for 35%; (b) 25% from agriculture, including live-stock (6% from beef alone), rice cultivation, fertilizer use, deforestation and the burning of fields; (c) 21% from industry (a quarter of which is cement production), excluding electricity use; plus (d) 14% from trans-portation and (e) 6% from non-electrical uses in buildings.[13] Methane, from agriculture, landfill sites and natural gas now accounts for two-and-a-half times as much as before the Industrial Revolution. Jumping up recently, methane accounted for 16% of GHGs, with the last 6% emitted by nitrous oxide from fertilizer and the burning of biomass. The global total would be higher, but for the carbon removed from the atmosphere by forest ecosystems and oceans.

There are different ways to slice the pie, but buildings, transportation and industry are commonly cited as the big three, with percentages vary-ing between and within different countries. For instance, CO_2 emissions from transportation are highest in the U.S., recently having overtaken electricity generation as the top source of GHGs.[14] Wringing CO_2 out of transportation is hard, in contrast to the encouraging progress underway in electricity. A Columbia University Center on Global Energy Policy study suggests that

> Taxing U.S. carbon emissions with an escalating levy that starts as high as $73/ton would have a pretty small effect on carbon emissions from the transportation sector . . . if achieving deep economy-wide GHG reductions is one of the policy goals for a carbon tax, then either a much higher carbon tax rate or policy interventions targeting transportation demand, vehicle technology, and decarbonization of fuels may be necessary.[15]

Industry has a problem with methane, which is the main component of natural gas. According to a half-decade national study, the U.S. oil and gas industry annually emits nearly 60 percent more than thought. The leak rate is 2.3 percent, which represents enough natural gas to fuel 10 million homes and save an estimated $2 billion. One of the study's co-authors states,

Scientists have uncovered a huge problem, but also an enormous opportunity. Reducing methane emissions from the oil and gas sector is the fastest, most cost-effective way we have to slow the rate of warming today, even as the larger transition to lower-carbon energy continues.[16]

The human impacts of these gases on the environment, starting with the more obvious, include the difficult-to-ignore extreme weather events of late. The huge typhoon that ripped through the Philippines in 2013 and Hurricane Maria in Puerto Rico in 2017 caused many months of power outages, the two longest in recorded history, on top of all the casualties (over 6,000 deaths in the former, over 4,000 in the latter) and physical and socio-economic mayhem. The rise in temperature is increasingly seen by climatologists to drive these events, evaporating more water into the atmosphere, which leads to more precipitation and catastrophic storms. The ultimate nightmare scenario is a widespread blackout during a heat wave that leaves millions of people without electricity for their fans or air conditioners. The economic costs are mounting: In the U.S.,

> According to the National Climatic Data Center, since 1980 there have been 151 weather or climate disasters for which costs were at least $1 billion (adjusted to 2013 dollars). The total estimated cost is over $1 trillion. Seven of these events took place in 2013.[17]

Superstorm Sandy alone accounted for over $50 billion of federal recovery assistance. To put its magnitude into context, it cost the national treasury more than the entire first year of revenue from the income tax increase that averted the infamous "fiscal cliff" that came so close to shutting down the government at the end of 2012. Hurricane Harvey dwarfed Sandy, with an estimated cost of almost $200 billion.[18] It would be an understatement to say that extreme weather events incur extreme and rising monetary costs, atop the immeasurable personal losses.

Certain types of weather events lend themselves to analysis better than others. Researchers have higher confidence when investigating heat waves, droughts or heavy precipitation than hurricanes and other more complex phenomena.

> Some scientists hope to eventually launch a kind of standardized extreme event attribution service, similar to a weather forecasting service, that would release immediate analyses – with uniform methods used for each one – for every extreme event that occurs. It's still unclear what such a service might look like, but one could imagine receiving an email or smartphone notification each time an extreme heat wave or flood rolls through, explaining its connection to climate change.[19]

It will no doubt become used in attributing causes and assigning responsibility and blame for damages in legal cases arising from extreme weather.

As CC becomes more pronounced and better understood, its relationship to the more violent weather events will become more precise and predictable. Current evidence suggests that hurricanes and cyclones will be more intense, and that tornadoes and severe thunderstorms will be more frequent. Tornado paths tend to avoid cities and are either amplified or dissipated by them as they veer away. Although exact predictability remains difficult, it seems clearer that extreme weather is intensified by CC, and is on an upward trajectory. (Skeptics and deniers should simply confer with the property insurance companies.) Weather and climate intensification work both ways, with some areas experiencing greater flooding and some drought. Flooding has been the nemesis of cities and drought has plagued agriculture for millennia, creating famine that has famously contributed to the decline and even collapse of a number of civilizations.[20] It remains to be seen if our increasingly populated and globalized civilization will be able to adequately feed itself with increased droughts and hotter weather (and more expensive chemical fertilizers and insecticides with rising fossil fuel costs). For a specific example, "scientists have found that corn and soybean yields in the United States plummet precipitously when temperatures rise above 84°F (29°C)."[21]

In both cases, water is the first medium through which CC is becoming most impactful. At the core of many of its extreme risks, sea level rise is already putting pressure on cities and societies to act

> lest their entire system collapse and leave many victims in its wake. Water is essential for social and cultural well-being. Its quality defines economic and social prosperity, and its quantity – whether too much or too little – defines social vulnerability . . . [A] World Economic Forum Global Risks Report identifies the impact of water crisis as the number one global risk for the next decade. Two billion people will be devastated by 2050 if the world continues with its current practices. Of all worldwide disasters, 90% are water-related.[22]

Half the world's population – approaching 4 billion people – is already struggling to cope without adequate water supplies for at least part of the year, as water demand rises faster than population. In short, civilization is already living in the age of water stress.

The earth's growing human population is using fresh water faster than it can be replenished. Rivers, streams and lakes usually are fed by snowmelt or rainfall, and in dry parts of the world, those sources are in decline as droughts strike harder and more regularly. Because the supply of water is finite, water engineers need to rethink the traditional approach to water infrastructure. It may mean installing cisterns in backyards to harvest the rain, or doing as astronauts have always done – drinking recycled urine.

Since 2003, Singapore has been treating sewage to potable water standards. About 40 percent of the island nation's total water needs are currently met by "toilet-to-tap," significantly reducing their dependence on rainwater, desalinated seawater and imports. As it improves to its 2060 target of 55 percent, no doubt other nations will follow its example.[23]

An imperfect, dynamic equilibrium may be the best outcome we can achieve at this point. The current popularity of "resilience" recognizes this ongoing volatility of natural and human systems, as opposed to more static equilibria. The National Academy of Sciences defines resilience as

> the ability to prepare and plan for, absorb, recover from and more suc-cessfully adapt to adverse events . . . Enhanced resilience allows better anticipation of disasters and better planning to reduce disaster losses – rather than waiting for an event to occur and paying for it afterward.[24]

The use of the term reflects a slowly growing shift in thinking about CC, from prevention to response. Implicit in this shift is a tacit acknowledg-ment that CC is now inevitable, even though the types and magnitude of its impacts are uncertain. It's a new level of risk management that requires us to anticipate and then act decisively in a time of uncertain change – not our species' strong suit.

There is a panoply of serious impacts already unfolding: sea level rise and the dislocation of coastal residents and physical assets; the expo-nential increase in climate refugees; more air pollution, from particulate matter to ozone; loss of biodiversity and habitat for other plant and ani-mal species on which humans rely; acidification of the oceans and loss of life-filled coral reefs; economic disruption and institutional instability; and breakdowns in social norms and civic culture. Even if these chal-lenges came at us one at a time, they would be formidable challenges, but they will tend to happen simultaneously, concatenating themselves into new complex, more ominous configurations. Yes, there will be many scientific and technical breakthroughs that help us to mitigate and adapt, but like all technologies, they will also have unintended negative conse-quences. Let us hope the list of problems is overstated and that numerous major technological advances will arrive in time. But let us be prepared for the worst. Win or lose, the city will play a pivotal role.

> [A]ny existing city that can meet what will be new stringent measures for survival – food, water, safety from rising sea levels or tempera-ture extremes – will be a better bet, because there will be buildings and some form of infrastructure in place.[25]

On top of these global challenges, there is a local one that is rapidly sneaking up on and threatening us, but could ironically help us in the war on climate change. UHIs figure prominently in this book and are its single largest focus, primarily because they have received too little attention in government, industry, academia and the press. Global overpopulation is also a key focal point, even though it gets more media attention. However, in the end, CC is the central lens through which all the issues should be viewed. It is the bottom line.

Challenge #2: Urban Heat Islands – a Trojan Horse in the Battle against Extreme Heat?

In *The City and the Coming Climate*, Brian Stone writes:

> [L]arge cities in the U.S. are warming at more than twice the rate of the planet as a whole . . . global estimates of climate change are likely to underestimate rates of warming in the very places where most of the global population now resides: cities.[26]

This important book focuses on U.S. cities, but it's safe to assume other cities are heating up as fast. To reach his conclusion, he left out 14 of the 50 cities in his statistical sample. If the coastal cities, which are cooled by sea breezes, are included, the full sample was found to be warming at 1.5 times the average rate of the planet. The temperature increases in rural areas and on the planet as a whole are typically happening at the same rate. The Arctic region, which lacks cities, is also heating up at twice the average global rate, but for different reasons.[27] The New York State Energy Research and Development Authority reported more extreme results for New York City: local temperatures recently rose by 2.4 percent over a span of 40 years, which is more than two times the average for global temperatures.

Ironically, UHIs are usually more pronounced in winter than summer when they are less noticeable and less problematic. The extra heat in winter brings benefits – fewer weather-related deaths, lower heating costs, more outdoor comfort, fewer travel hazards, such as less ice on walking and driving surfaces. In fact, far more people annually die in the U.S. from weather-related vehicle accidents (annual average of 6,000) than from tornado, hurricane, lightning, flood or extreme heat events (average annual total of 375).[28] And moderating cold is generally more favorable for plant and animal life. Regardless of how welcome the extra warmth and resulting drop in cold-related deaths may be in winter, UHIs have become a pressing problem in summer. In the cities that are currently hot, which are home to the majority of the world's urban dwellers, they are rapidly making them more dangerous than the surrounding countryside, especially when there are heat waves. A useful term for the combination of UHIs and heat waves is "extreme heat." It is here that we start the tale of how cities combat CC.

The urban heat island effect (UHIE) is the full technical term, coined in the 1940s, to describe the higher air and surface temperatures in cities compared to their hinterland. These "reverse oases" have been observed for two centuries, with the first documentation done in a seminal if amateur study of London's climate in 1818, followed by studies in Paris later that century. Systematic study of heat islands in the U.S. commenced in the mid-twentieth century, before CC was the high-priority concern that it is now.

> Until the 1980s, this effect was considered to have relatively little practical significance. In fact, given that most studies were done in cities with cold winter climates, a warmer temperature was seen as a potential benefit, because it reduced the need for heating.[29]

Since then, concern about UHIs has emerged and escalated, along with ways to minimize them.

Whether writ large or small, in warm or cold areas, UHIs happen in almost all urban areas.[30] Despite their physical and climatological variety, research on UHIs has suffered from a relatively vague and simple distinction between urban and rural areas. In 2012, two Canadian geographers developed a more precise classification system, with 17 Local Climate Zones. The ten "built types" range from Compact and Open High-rise, Mid-rise and Low-rise to Lightweight (wood single-family houses) and Open Low-rise (e.g., office parks), plus Heavy Industry. The seven "land cover types" include Dense and Scattered Trees, Bush/Scrub, Low Plants (grassland, agricultural farmland and pasture), Bare Rock or Paved, Sand and Water. The many combinations of built and land cover types, not to mention ephemeral conditions like snow, foliage and wetness, make the system suitable for UHI researchers, as well as urban planners, landscape ecologists and CC investigators, but too detailed for this book.

The five causes of UHIs:

1 Greater absorption, caused by the low urban albedo (solar reflectivity) of dark surfaces and the entrapping geometries of buildings and the spaces between them;
2 Greater retention, due to less openness to the sky and less natural ventilating in street canyons;
3 Greater absorption and delayed release of solar heat by buildings and paved surfaces;
4 Greater proportion of absorbed solar radiation converted to sensible heat, which we can feel, rather than latent heat, which we can't feel. (Pavements and roofs do not absorb as much heat as plants and moist soils, which go through a phase change that takes up additional heat without raising its temperature);
5 Greater release of heat from combustion of fuels for transportation, industrial processes and space heating and cooling, summarized as "waste heat" in this book.

Figure 2.1 Air and especially surface temperatures are higher in the central city than surrounding suburban and rural areas. This melted asphalt is in an Indian city, where pedestrians crossing the street have been known to lose their shoes to the melted, sticky road surface. (Photo by Harish Tyagi/Epa/REX/Shutterstock (7978897g))

The UHI is easily conflated and often confused with global CC, as noted earlier. One way to illustrate the difference is to examine the thermal behavior of a common automobile. We're all familiar with heat that is produced by combustion in the engine, much of which is released from the tailpipe in the form of hot gases. These hot fumes – *waste heat* – elevate the nearby air temperature. Then there's the solar radiation absorbed by the body of the car, which heats the steel shell to a temperature exceeding the ambient air temperature. The darker the paint color, the hotter the surface. This hotter surface warms nearby air by convection currents and nearby objects and people by heat radiation – or by conduction if they happen to touch or lean against the car. These three modes of heat transfer, plus waste heat are responsible for UHIs.

Then there's the overheating of the car's interior, which is a function of the exterior and interior colors and the window configuration. A recent study found that after parking in the sun for an hour, a silver car had a cabin air temperature about 9–11°F lower than an otherwise identical black car.[31] The amount of glass and the color of the upholstery play a much bigger role – one that is uncannily equivalent

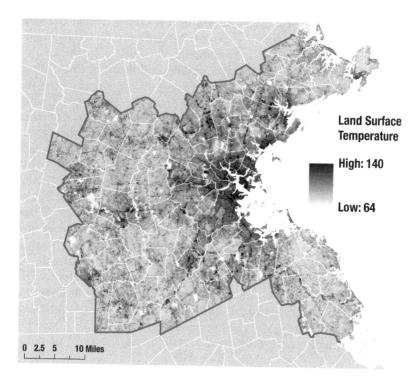

Figure 2.2 The map of land surface temperatures depicts metropolitan Boston
in late August, when the average surface temperature during the
day is as much as 76°F higher than the average air temperature.
"Temperatures of dark, dry surfaces in direct sunlight can reach up
to 190°F (88°C), while vegetated surfaces with moist soil under the
same conditions might reach only 70°F (18°C). Anthropogenic heat,
slower wind speeds and air pollution in urban areas contribute to
the formation of UHIs."[1] (MAPC, MassGIS)

1 T.R. Oke and I.D. Stewart, "Local climate zones," *Bulletin of American Meteorology
Society*, 93, 2012, p. 6

to global warming. The temperature in a closed, sunlit car can increase
20°F in only 10 minutes, and 33°F in 20 minutes.[32] Seats soak up the
solar radiation that comes through the windows, which are transparent
to short wave radiation that makes up most of the sun's energy (only
half of which is visible to the human eye). The seats get hot, especially
dark-colored ones, and re-radiate the heat, but at a longer wavelength
(invisible infra-red radiation as opposed to visible light or short wave
radiation). The longer radiation waves that hit the glass are absorbed.
Half is re-radiated outwards and half back into the car's interior, *trapping half the solar heat inside the car*. This same physics happens with

the greenhouse effect at the planetary scale; the earth's atmosphere acts in the same way as the car's windows. But it is GHGs, rather than the window glass of the car (or in a garden "greenhouse," GHG's namesake) that trap the infra-red heat radiating upward from the earth's surface. Like anyone with dark automobile upholstery knows, it's a potent effect.

Since the advent of modern agricultural practices, another GHG has come to the fore: nitrous oxide (N_2O). The earth's nitrogen cycle is more complex than the carbon cycle, and beyond the scope of this book. Suffice it to say that it also contributes GHGs, most notably N_2O, which is about 300 times more potent than CO_2 in radiative "forcing" (the technical term for increasing the greenhouse effect). Why is N_2O a contemporary climate problem? Nitrogen has become an essential fertilizer in the many parts of the world where soils are nitrogen deficient. When these fertilized crops are eaten by livestock, their belching, flatulence and manure adds nitrous oxides that combine with air to form the intense GHG methane. Bovine emissions are a significant global problem, as the total body weight of cattle exceeds the total weight of human beings.[33] If we combine our collective weight, or biomass, with that of our domestic animals, the total makes up 90 percent of all mammal biomass, up from 2 percent a millennium ago![34] The enormous number of cattle raised for meat-eating humans is not only an unsustainable agricultural practice, but its inefficiency is an immense contributor to CC. "Already 35% of the world's grain harvest is used to feed livestock. The process is terribly inefficient: between seven and ten kilograms of grain are required to produce one kilogram of beef."[35] And much more water is required to grow the feed for beef and lamb than for pork and chicken, the preferred environmental choices for meat eaters.

In short, the increase in GHGs, most significantly CO_2, in the earth's upper atmosphere causes it to trap more of the solar heat re-radiating from the earth's surface. To refine this important point, GHGs are selective permeable filters that are transparent to the incoming shorter wave radiation from the sun but absorb out-going longer wave radiation. The warmer atmosphere in turn triggers changes in land, air and ocean temperatures, with ensuing impacts on everything from biodiversity and ecosystems to human civilization. Hence the term "global warming" has given way to "climate change" to reflect the fact that not all parts of the planet are getting warmer, and that some areas are getting cooler.

Before moving on to health impacts, some detail on ecosystems: Scientific research has moved toward a more organic model of open-endedness, flexibility and adaptation, rather than a mechanistic model of stability and control. Now understood as open systems that are self-organizing and to some extent unpredictable, ecosystems are characterized in part by uncertainty and dynamism. Coupled with added uncertainty around CC, it is necessary to realize that our species cannot manage whole ecosystems; rather, it can manage *itself* and its activities. This realization has major implications for the way we design buildings and cities, as Chris Reed and Nina-Marie Lister wrote in 2014.[36]

Human Health

Because N_2O also forms an air pollutant when there's ozone in the air, it also contributes to respiratory health problems.

> Nitrogen dioxide and particulate matter from road traffic and sulphur dioxide, from the burning of fossil fuels have been linked to suppressed lung growth in children, asthma, heart disease and the onset of Type 2 Diabetes. The exposure of pregnant women to air pollution has also been found to affect fetal brain growth.[37]

This is yet another reason why the continued heavy dependence on fossil fuels, in this case for manufactured fertilizer, is unwise.

This health hazard brings us to the first of many physiological impacts of extreme heat. Humans are endotherms, which means that various mechanisms keep our core body temperature within a normal range of 97.7–99.5°F (36.5–37.5°C). This thermoregulation is controlled by the hypothalamus, a part of the brain that acts like a biological thermostat connected to temperature-sensing nerve cells. As temperature increases – depending on age, time of day and level of activity and emotions – the body attempts to cool down.

> One way to do that is by secreting water with dissolved ions – sweat. Water absorbs heat so as sweats evaporates it liberates heat by evaporation, that's why sweat cools people down . . . The problem with heatwaves is that excessive heat can put humans under a lot of physiological stress. Because sweating is the most effective mechanism, during hot weather the people who are most vulnerable are the ones whose sweating mechanism is, for various possible reasons, subpar – the elderly, the chronically ill and children, as well as pets.[38]

As Gregory Wellenius, an epidemiologist at Brown University, says "There's a point where the human body can't cool itself, which means you are either in an air-conditioned space or you're having serious health problems."[39]

> Humans, like all mammals, are heat engines; surviving means having to continually cool off, like panting dogs. For that, the temperature needs to be low enough for the air to act as a kind of refrigerant, drawing heat off the skin so the engine can keep pumping . . . that would become impossible for large portions of the planet's equatorial band, and especially the tropics, where humidity adds to the

problem; in the jungles of Costa Rica, for instance, where it routinely tops 90%, simply moving around outside when it's over 105°F would be lethal. And the effect would be fast: Within a few hours, a human body would be cooked to death from both inside and out.[40]

Human discomfort typically starts above 100°F; life threatening conditions arise at 104°F and get more and more serious with temperatures above 106°F, with brain damage and death normally occurring above 109°F and certain death at 111°F or higher. When the body temperature is in or near the normal range, comfort depends on several factors – the temperature of the air and surrounding surfaces, the humidity and the air speed. The psychrometric chart combines these and other variables (dry and wet bulb temperatures, dew point, relative humidity, enthalpy, air density or pressure, but not air speed or temperatures surrounding surfaces) to provide a window of comfort. Ventilation, dehumidification or air conditioning by natural or mechanical means is highly desirable, even necessary for survival, when warmer or more humid conditions prevail.

This is a list of possible health problems and medical maladies:

- *Heat rash* occurs when the sweat glands become blocked, trapping perspiration under the skin and causing a red, itchy rash. It is more common among babies and young children, and usually does not require medical attention.
- *Heat cramps* are muscle spasms that happen during heavy exercise in hot weather, with medical treatment rarely needed.
- *Heat exhaustion* is brought on when evaporative cooling from perspiring skin begins to fail. Profuse sweating and dehydration set in, often accompanied by dizziness, faintness, weakness or excessive fatigue, as well as weak pulse and low blood pressure. Rehydration is essential, and worsening symptoms require immediate medical treatment.
- *Heat stroke*, also called hyperthermia, happens when the body can no longer regulate its core temperature, causing lethargy, confusion, delirium, loss of consciousness and, in the worst case, seizures. It requires an immediate ambulance trip to the emergency room. Failure to act quickly can lead to unconsciousness, irreversible damage to the brain, or death.[41]

In addition to children, the elderly and the chronically ill, others at risk include the obese and those with existing medical conditions such as diabetes and heart disease, as well as the socially isolated, and the poor. These maladies are more frequent outdoors than indoors, especially if there is air conditioning. While thermally more comfortable and generally healthier, air conditioning does not come without its unintended health consequences. Their filters remove particulate pollutants from outside, but it's not clear if they decrease indoor pollutants overall.

For reasons that are not well understood, air conditioning is associated with increases in acute health symptoms often called sick building syndrome (SBS) symptoms, and also with asthma symptoms. SBS symptoms include irritation of eye, nose, and throat, headache, and fatigue, and sometimes other effects.[42]

These afflictions will no doubt become more widespread as mechanical cooling spreads globally.

While it is obvious that heat-related ailments will increase with warmer climates, the link to infectious diseases is more complex, but just as credible and alarming. Warmer weather helps food-borne organisms like salmonella multiply more quickly, and warmer seas foster bacteria like vibrio that make shellfish such as oysters unsafe to eat.

Spikes in heat and humidity have less visible effects, too, changing the numbers and distribution of the insect intermediaries that carry diseases to people. When former Vice President Al Gore spoke (in 2017) at a meeting on climate and health, he chose to start his talk not with a starving polar bear or a glacier falling into the sea, but with images of mosquitoes and ticks. "Climate change is tilting the balance, disrupting natural ecosystems and giving more of an advantage to microbes," Gore said, standing in front of a giant image of . . . the mosquito species that transmits yellow fever and dengue, and now the Zika virus as well. "Changing climate conditions change the areas in which these diseases can take root and become endemic."[43]

A new scientific specialty called *disease ecology* has arisen to study the interaction of climate and disease carriers, with serious implications for public health. Diseases carried by insects are affected by the impacts of CC, especially flooding and more frequent and extreme precipitation. As Gore points out, controlling the notorious mosquito becomes all the more important, because various strains of this pesky arthropod can also spread West Nile Fever, not to mention the age-old scourge of malaria. Most of these are tropical diseases, but their geographic range will tend to expand on a warmer, wetter planet. And drought and famine will aggravate their effects by weakening human resistance, especially in poor rural and urban areas.

Environmental problems have been likened to human disease. University of Michigan Professor Scott Campbell, offers a telling analogy: environmental problems in the 1970s and '80s were thought to be akin to an acute illness or infectious disease that can be cured outright, but we have now come to see them more like chronic, degenerative diseases that are more systemic and not easily cured. Adaptation to CC might even be compared to long and careful palliative care for cancer, rather than remission.

We will likely not know, in the long run of history, whether human life is intrinsically unsustainable or whether mass urban society can live "in harmony" with nature. Planning's contribution is to carve out habitat niches that support life, in a volatile world, for a diverse array of populations with a minimum of misery and disparity. One can't "cure" unsustainability. But one can treat it as a chronic, increasingly manageable disease: to incrementally transform a once fatal environmental deterioration into a tolerable condition.[44]

Heat Waves

"Meeting fast-rising cooling demand with today's high global warming potential . . . is creating an environmental disaster – a veritable carbon time bomb."[45] Professor Edward Ng of the Chinese University of Hong Kong has been studying urban climate in his city since 2003. His research finds that waste heat from anthropogenic sources such as vehicles, factories and air conditioners contributes about 1°C to Hong Kong's heat island on average. There is minimal waste heat from vehicles: Hong Kong had the top 2017 world ranking for sustainable mobility, with inexpensive transit handling 90 percent of all daily trips, the highest rate in the world.[46] The big UHI contributors are several: the low albedo of dark surfaces, the thermal absorption and retention of heat by large amounts of building mass, the notoriously dense urban configurations that trap heat and block ventilation of outdoor space, and the lack of vegetation. These factors add on average about 7°F (raising the air from 28° to 32°C) in the summer daytime, which is the most critical time for human comfort and health, and about 11°F (from 24° to 30°C) in the summer night, making sleeping difficult without air conditioning.[47]

If global emissions are allowed to continue at a high level,

> additional nights of sleeplessness can be expected . . . the poor, who are less likely to have air-conditioning or be able to run it, as well as the elderly, who have more difficulty regulating their body temperature, would be hit hard.[48]

Professor Ng likes to point out that Hong Kong's thermal map closely aligns with the residents' economic status, with the poor living in the most uncomfortable areas and the affluent in verdant areas. In Indian cities, "templates of segregation are being remapped . . . and how class- and caste-based exclusions are being reimagined."[49] Indeed, the question of social equity within and between countries is underscored by UHIs. Of the 1.1 billion people who face "cooling access risks," it is estimated that 630 million are located in hot, poor slums with little or no cooling to protect them against extreme heat.[50] Within the U.S., people of color are up to 52 percent more likely to live in UHIs than white people, according to a University of California, Berkeley report on 2000 census data.[51]

UHIs are also harmful in hot arid climates. For instance, most of the American Southwest may be facing a deadly mega-drought worse than anything seen during the last 2,000 years. Scientists, including a group at NASA, think it's "a near certainty sometime not long after 2050 if carbon emissions continue along their current trajectory. Big cities in Texas, Florida and Southern California are projected by 2050 to wither under 105°F days for about a third of the year."[52] In these and other arid climates with less vegetation, the UHI is strongest during dry periods, when the weather is calm and skies are clear.

> These conditions accentuate the differences between urban and rural landscapes. Cities are distinguished from natural landscapes by . . . the extent of the urban land cover, the construction materials used, and the geometry of buildings and streets. All of these factors affect the exchanges of natural energy at ground level.[53]

Professor Stone has written that hot, humid American cities like Atlanta have experienced more climatic modification from its local UHI than from global CC.[54] He suggests that hotter temperatures amplified by the UHIE will soon make outdoor activities for more than a few hours a day too uncomfortable for most of its citizens. The authors of *American Climate Prospectus*

> have predicted that residents of the Southeast are likely to experience between 56 and 123 days, or almost one-third of the year, when temperatures exceed 95°F . . . The temperature of 95°F is not chosen arbitrarily . . . When the relative humidity is 100% this is the maximum temperature at which a normal, resting, well-ventilated individual can maintain a normal body temperature by the evaporation of sweat."[55]

A 2018 global study

> projects that in coming decades the effects of high humidity in many areas will dramatically increase. At times, they may surpass humans' ability to work or, in some cases, even survive . . . population exposure to wet bulb temperatures that exceed recent deadly heat waves may increase by a factor of five to ten, with 150–750 million person-days of exposure to wet bulb temperatures above those seen in today's most severe heat waves by 2070–2080 . . . exposure to wet bulb temperatures above 35°C – the theoretical limit for human tolerance – could exceed a million person-days per year by 2080. In the coming

decades heat stress may prove to be one of the most widely experienced and directly dangerous aspects of CC, posing a severe threat to human health, energy infrastructure, and outdoor activities ranging from agricultural production to military training.[56]

Indeed, heat extremes threaten large economic losses as temperature maximums limit outdoor activity and labor productivity. For outdoor laborers, such as those at construction sites, models of "work capacity losses" by 2050 for Southeast Asia during hot weather for moderate work in the shade at the height of the day are expected to be as high as 40–50 percent, increasing to 60–70 percent in the sun.[57] In the Southeast U.S., some roofing companies provide personal canopies for their roofers, as working in direct sun light is already too dangerous. These kinds of "personal micro-climates" may be needed more widely and more often, as temperature and humidity conspire to make outdoor work exceedingly difficult, if not impossible. Extreme heat is making outdoor workers less productive and less healthy.

Heat waves are overtaking their bigger, more dangerous cousin CC as the more immediate problem. In most large American cities, there is an increasing need for "cooling centers" that are open to people whose homes are without air conditioners and dangerously hot. These air-conditioned sanctuaries are typically in institutional buildings open to the public, like municipal libraries and schools, where citizens can find relief, including extended stays if necessary. Evidence suggests that as annual deaths from heat waves increase,[58] more of these centers will be needed to cope with hotter and longer episodes of extreme heat. Health officials report that getting people to cooling centers can be a challenge: some residents simply don't know about them or are reluctant to leave their homes. In Philadelphia, PA, designated block captains check on older residents during heat waves. And cooling centers can be difficult to access by public transit.[59] A poignant example is in Phoenix, where homeless people rode the air-conditioned light rail to cooling centers to avoid 2017 heat so brutal that it killed 155 people in the city and surrounding areas.[60] The city is expected to "spend 2/3rds of the typical year in heat of more than 100°F (37°C) by the time today's preschoolers are drawing a pension . . . a climate change and planning professor . . . states 'The fact is, there's not going to be enough refuge for everybody.'"[61]

"If communities do not take preventative measures, the projected increase in heat-related deaths by the end of this century would be roughly equivalent to the number of Americans killed annually in auto accidents."[62] To be more specific, "During 2006–2010, about 2,000 U.S. residents died each year from weather-related causes. About 31% of these deaths were attributed to exposure to excessive natural heat, heat stroke, sun stroke . . . 6% were attributed to floods, storms, or lightning."[63] It must be observed that *cold* weather was indirectly responsible for 63 percent of weather-related deaths, but in this case the hypothermic effect is less often a specific event, such as a cold wave. These winter deaths are actually diminished by UHIs, which is perhaps their only direct benefit, along with more comfortable winter temperatures.[64]

Even though mortality from heat is highly episodic, heat waves already kill an estimated 12,000 people annually across the world.[65]

> The July–August 2010 heat wave in western Russia killed about 54,000 people . . . from 1981 to 2010, the average American experienced about four dangerously hot and humid days, with wet-bulb temperatures exceeding 80°F. By 2030, that level is expected to more than double, to about 10 days per summer.[66]

In 1995, the American Midwest was hit by a monstrous heat wave that ruined crops and killed over 700 people in roasting cities, which was seven times more than would later die in New York and New Jersey as a result of Superstorm Sandy. Excruciatingly hot summers – the kind that were rare in the 1950s – have become commonplace. The famous climatologist Dr. James Hansen and two colleagues have compared actual summer temperatures for each decade since the 1980s to a fixed baseline average:

> During the base period, 1951 to 1980, about a third of local summer temperatures across the Northern Hemisphere were in what they called a "near average" or normal range. A third were considered cold; a third were hot . . . Between 2005 and 2015, two-thirds of values were in the hot category, and nearly 15% were in a new category: extremely hot. Practically, that means most summers are now either hot or extremely hot compared with the mid-20th century.[67]

Cities in hot, humid tropical climates are being increasingly hard hit with the sickening and deadly combination of higher temperatures and more humidity.

> Those facing the greatest risk live in the wet tropics, where only slight increases in average temperatures or humidity can result in deaths. However, heat can be deadly even at moderate temperatures of less than 86°F (30°C) if it's combined with very high humidity.[68]

South Asia, where one in five of the world's people dwell, could face summer heat waves that are impossible to survive without protection. Hardest hit regions are likely to be in northern India, Bangladesh and southern Pakistan, with a combined population of 1.5 billion people, many of whom are very poor. Many are dependent on subsistence farming that requires long hours of hard outdoor labor.

A 2015 heat wave that killed at least 3,500 in India and Pakistan saw wet-bulb temperatures around 122°F (45°C). A similar wet-bulb temperature was reached during the 1995 Chicago heat wave. Currently about 2% of the Indian population gets exposed to extremes of 32°C wet-bulb temperatures. According to (one) study, without carbon emissions cuts that will increase to about 70 percent of the population by 2100.[69]

The Middle East is a hot, arid region that is also very vulnerable to extreme heat. Some towns on the coast of the Persian Gulf have already experienced temperatures of 150°F (65°C)! They are on their way to becoming uninhabitable. The average water temperature in the Gulf itself is now 90°F. For comparison, the Caribbean Sea, one of the hottest parts of the Atlantic Ocean, averages 82°F (28°C). The Middle East is getting even more arid, and with less rainfall predicted, the average yield on a number of grain crops is predicted to drop by about 30 percent by 2050.[70] CC has already played a destabilizing role, with a three-year drought in Syria sending farmers to its cities, where insufficient jobs resulted in political unrest and ultimately contributed to the long civil war. The number of Middle Easterners seeking refuge in Europe is sure to mount ever higher as CC drives more farm families from their parched and strife-ridden land.

More information on heat waves has been recorded, researched and written about than on UHIs. The overlap is clearer and the literature is getting more alarming. The web portal Carbon Brief identified 138 peer-reviewed papers, covering 144 weather events. "Of 48 heatwaves, 41 contained humankind's imprint on the data."[71] The heat waves that swept America in the summer of 2018 put 100 million people under official heat warnings. "It caused power cuts in California where temperatures in places such as Palm Springs approached 122°F (50°C) and resulted in deaths from New York to the Mexican border."[72] The 2018 heat waves set many records: maximum temperatures were recorded in Norway, Sweden, Japan, California and Montreal, Canada, to name some examples. As Delhi, India is expected to grow by 10 million to a metro population of over 36 million by 2030,[73] it will get even more extreme heat.

> Heat waves in the North China Plain – China's breadbasket – are predicted to become so severe, they would "limit habitability in the most populous region of the most populous country on Earth . . ." The big picture: Such heat waves could both threaten lives and dampen economic output in the region, where 400 million people live.[74]

The flip side of this grim issue is that air conditioning can be an essential adaptation tactic, and arguably a human right in very hot, humid climates, especially in mosquito-infested places where natural ventilation tends to be problematic. In countries without widespread mechanical cooling, deaths rise more sharply during the hottest days. "One study estimated that heat deaths in India increase by 3.2 percent for every 1.8° above 68°F (every 1° above 20°C). Energy use in many countries may rise sharply as people struggle to adapt to a hotter climate."[75] This increased use of energy will only serve to aggravate extreme heat.

Climatologists state that estimating the probability of the recurrence of heat waves is possible. One group of climate scientists

> concluded that human activity has more than doubled the probability of experiencing an even worse heat wave than the one that gripped Europe in 2003 . . . Another group . . . concluded that the probability was greater than 95% that a 2003-like heat wave has "more than doubled . . . in spring and autumn, while for summer it is extremely likely the probability has at least quadrupled."[76]

The final death toll in the 2003 Europe-wide heat wave is thought to be around 70,000, a sobering reminder of the health challenge of combined UHIs and CC. Temperatures that used to be seen as outliers – like those in the summer of 2003 – will become "the norm for summer" after 2060, said Jean Jouzel, former Vice Chairman of the IPCC in 2007 when it won the Nobel Prize. Occasional heat waves could push temperatures in Europe toward 120°F unless there is a substantial slowdown in global-warming trends, he said.[77]

> [Another] team of researchers examined 1,949 deadly heat waves from around the world since 1980 to look for trends, define when heat is so severe it kills, and forecast the future. They found that nearly one in three people now experience 20 days a year when the heat reaches deadly levels. But the study predicts that up to three in four people worldwide will endure that kind of heat by the end of the century.[78]

A 2016 Columbia University study projected that by 2080, up to 3,300 New Yorkers could die each year from intense heat made worse by climate change.[79]

Not all UHIs are the same. For starters, the bigger and denser the city the more intense the differential between city and rural air and surface temperatures. UHIs depend on the local climate and vegetative cover. Much of the focus of this book is on cities in the Global North, with their relatively temperate climates and considerable tree coverage. In all cases the focus is on air temperatures and humidity more than surface temperatures, because the former two factors tend to be a better indicator of discomfort and debilitating heat waves. In these cities, the UHIs peak during the late summer afternoon or evening – primarily because there is less shading and evapotranspiration from vegetation in the city center than in the countryside, as well as more vehicles driving about spewing heat from their tailpipes during the day than later at night. Even though they can be more severe in the evening and night, in most cities air temperatures are still cooler at night than during the day. With the gradual increase in global overheating caused by CC, it suggests more daytime activities are likely to be shifted to after sunset. And the lunch-time siesta may move further north and south of the equator as an effective way to deal with mid-day heat.

Summer nights in the U.S. have warmed at nearly twice the rate of days.[80] In Mexico City research indicates that arid cities can have UHIs that peak late at night.[81] There can even be "urban cool islands" during the day and evening. The reason for this reversal is that these cities have more trees and vegetation than the surrounding desert or semi-desert. These plants during the day provide shade and cool the air temperature though evaporation of moisture from their leaves. But these cities stay warmer because the heat absorbed by unshaded buildings and pavements during the sunny day is carried into the night, like a giant thermal flywheel. This thermal momentum can actually be a benefit in arid climates, if the nights are cool and clear, with little water vapor in the air. This combination allows warm urban mass to radiate its heat through the more transparent atmosphere, cooling its buildings and occupants during the night more quickly and fully than in climates with warmer and more humid nights. In addition to this radiative cooling, there can be cooling night breezes that ventilate the buildings.

The centers of metro areas can also be hotter at night because of night-time inversions that dramatically lower air temperatures near the ground in the surrounding countryside (even creating frost in early spring). Inversions are produced in cities by UHI plumes of warmer air over cities that trap cooler air near the ground at night, especially when the air is calm. They affect the time of day or night that UHIs hit their peak intensity. These temperature inversions are weakened by buildings and vehicular traffic, which tend to create more air turbulence within cities. Local weather also has an effect, with more intensity during clear weather that allows greater solar heat gain. Weaker UHIs happen when there is cloud cover, and when wind removes heat more quickly from the city. It is clear that heat islands are complicated by the differing sizes, morphologies, altitudes, terrains and weather patterns of urban areas, as well as the multitude of ways these factors can interact during the annual cycles. An unusual example is San Jose, CA, where another University of California, Berkeley study has shown downtown San Jose is in fact cooler than its first ring suburb of strip malls and shopping centers, with their parking lots.[82] While UHIs tend to display similar characteristics, ultimately each metropolitan area finds its own unique and dynamic balance points and scenarios.

Current research on UHIs focuses primarily on temperate climates in developed countries, despite the fact that almost half of the world's population lives in the tropics. Few studies have focused on tropical climates and even fewer examples exist. The urban context and settlement patterns in cities of the developing world are substantially unlike those found in the usually colder Western countries. Therefore, the strategies applied to cool their cities are not necessarily appropriate for use in tropical cities. Research identifies

> urban geometry as one of the most important factors governing outdoor microclimatic conditions in a high-density, tropical climate. Due to rapid urbanization and limited resources for managing the urban planning, many parts of the case-study city Dhaka have grown spontaneously. These...areas, mainly residential, with irregular plot sizes and building heights, were found to have relatively better microclimatic conditions than the contemporary, formal built areas with more uniform building heights and sizes. Significant variation is identified in terms of air temperature, mean radiant temperature and wind speed between the two areas.[83]

This research is based on analysis of urban geometry, Computational Fluid Dynamics simulations, statistical analysis of thermal comfort surveys and building energy performance – more of which is needed to link urban design and planning with urban climatology.

As already noted, UHIs are economically costly. A 2017 analysis of almost 1,700 cities

> shows that the total economic costs of climate change for cities this century could be 2.6 times higher when heat island effects are taken into account . . . For the worst-off city, losses could reach 10.9% of GDP by the end of the century, compared with a global average of 5.6%. (For comparison's sake, that's almost double New York City's 2017 budget, and more than China has been recently spending on national defense.) This effect is expected to add a further two degrees to global warming estimates for the most populated cities by 2050.[84]

Hotter temperatures hurt an economy in several ways: more energy is used for electric fans and especially for air conditioners, air is more polluted, water quality suffers and workers are less productive. The research team carried out a cost–benefit analysis of various local UHI strategies, such as cool pavements, cool roofs and green roofs, and expanding vegetation in cities. The cheapest measure turned out to be a moderate-scale installation of lighter-colored pavements and roofs. Changing 20 percent of a city's roofs and half of its pavements to brighter surfaces could save up to 12 times as much as they cost to install and maintain, while reducing air temperatures by about 0.8°C.[85] This is a high return for almost any type of investment, especially in buildings and infrastructure. A paper by MIT scholars offers some other encouraging news on both the economic and health front: China will largely or even fully offset the costs of its climate initiatives with avoided mortality.[86]

There is another longer-term cost – a combination of health and socio-economic issues. A growing body of research concludes that rising global temperatures not only increase the risk of heat stress and stroke, but that they affect children's health to the extent that it decreases their economic prospects as adults. A study by Stanford, the University of California, Berkeley, and the U.S. Department of the Treasury suggests that even short periods of extreme heat can carry long-term consequences for children and their financial future. "Fetuses and infants are 'especially sensitive to hot temperatures because their thermoregulatory and sympathetic nervous systems are not fully developed.'"[87] Accordingly, heat waves during an individual's early childhood, including the period before birth, can affect his or her earnings three decades later. Exposure to just 23 days of temperatures above 90°F (32°C) before their first 21 months is estimated to cut a $50,000 salary in later life by almost 5 percent. And unchecked CC could reduce average global income by around 23 percent in 2100, and as much as 75 percent in the poorest countries.[88] While these estimates may seem overly precise and tentative, the overall trend is not.

Geoengineering

Geoengineering, a.k.a. climate engineering, climate intervention or solar radiation management (SRM), is risky, serious business – again explained by comparing it to the common car. Changes in the chemical composition of the earth's atmosphere, like the transparency of a car's windshield (or a greenhouse's glazing), trap more or less of the warmth of the sun. Many car windows are tinted to reduce the incoming solar radiation. That tinting is analogous to solar geoengineering, where humans intentionally alter the atmosphere to reflect back more of the sun's energy by cloud seeding and the like. There are several techniques under consideration to raise the planet's albedo to reflect more incoming solar radiation: giant space reflectors, releasing sulfate aerosols in the stratosphere from an extremely large number of balloons, shooting canons at an absurdly high rate, or changing the reflectivity of naturally-forming clouds by seeding them with salt.[89] With these approaches, it is technically tricky to prevent unintended collateral effects that are counter-productive, if not outright dangerous. The second type of geoengineering is GHG removal, a.k.a. negative emissions, which was discussed in Chapter 1. This capture and storage of carbon naturally sequestered in the soil, oceans and plants is not known to be dangerous, like the large-scale human interventions into nature mentioned above.

Policymakers need to recognize the perils and acknowledge that the large-scale geoengineering techniques are freighted with uncertainty. They are neither developed, nor are their side-effects well understood; they're terribly fraught with political and moral dilemmas, such as who decides when and how to deploy techniques that will inevitably help some regions and countries and hurt others. The problem of ocean acidification would continue unabated in any case, because enhancing albedo does not reduce the production of the GHGs that acidify the seas. The world's inland waters could also be endangered as CO_2 is absorbed and aquatic life is threatened.[90] Last, there'd be an immediate, sudden increase in CC if and when these interventions were discontinued, because high levels of GHG production would very likely have continued, perhaps even increased, during the period that geoengineering was deployed. The effects of those increases would hit the world suddenly, like a bucket of hot water. On the other hand, these capabilities could buy valuable time to develop more and better mitigation, adaptation and negative emissions strategies and techniques.

As the issue of geoengineering is gathering momentum. Akshat Rathi, a frequent and informative writer on CC, feels strongly about the pitfalls:

> CCS and even removing carbon dioxide from the atmosphere is not geoengineering. There are plenty of people who don't want to keep them separate and make a pig's breakfast of it. But they are radically different things. Interestingly, the Paris agreement threw down the gauntlet for geoengineering. The goal isn't to keep the world's CO_2 levels below a certain threshold. The goal is to keep global average temperatures below 2°C. And it's looking like we won't hit that goal. So, in a way, the Paris agreement has forced the geoengineering question: If we aren't going to hit our temperature targets by managing emissions, then we have to meet our targets through geoengineering, such as solar-radiation management. It has accelerated the timeline for policymakers to study and make decisions, including ones about governance, economics and social ramifications. The fundamental challenges around geoengineering have not changed. First, global governance is a mess. Second, the technology keeps getting cheaper and easier, which means someone's going to try it at some point . . . I think about geoengineering the way I think about gastric bypass surgery. In an extreme case, it may be necessary. But also, I'm glad doctors did research on it before trying.[91]

More on the Environmental Paradox of Cities

Cities are greener than they look. To emphasize a key point, this is because urbanites walk, bike and use transit more than auto-dependent suburbanites and rural residents, and their more compact, party-wall/multi-floor buildings takes less energy to mechanically heat and cool.

The environmental paradox of cities applies most conspicuously to North America, where an average low-density area, as shown in Figure 1.3, can produce up to two-and-a-half times as much carbon emissions per capita as an average high-density area. This is a very significant differential that also obtains in other developed countries of the Global North and in Australia, where suburban lifestyles are also highly auto-dependent, energy- and resource-consumptive and waste-producing. And as cities in the developing world continue to expand with low-density suburbs, the paradox increasingly applies to them as well.

Density, which can also be called compactness, is fundamental to the paradox, and needs some elaboration for the less initiated readers. How is it measured? How much is needed to be urban as opposed to suburban? It is typically measured in dwelling units per acre (du/acre), or per hectare, although people per acre is the key factor (sometimes measured in beds/acre). Another metric is Floor-Area-Ratio (F.A.R.), which measures the habitable floor area in relation to the land area of the parcel. At the urban scale, the distinction between net and gross density is also very important: the former includes only the land parcel on which the building sits, whereas the latter includes adjacent sidewalks, streets, roads and other parts of the public realm. Gross density is often the more useful term, as it better deals with overall density of a community, whether urban or suburban. And F.A.R. is helpful because it includes all land and building uses, not just residential.

How dense or compact must the built environment be to be considered urban? The answer of course varies from culture to culture, country to country and is not a hard and fast number. In the U.S., the main difference is usually measured by F.A.R. When they are similar, the *configuration and morphology* of the built environment can be the determining factor. One could argue that suburbia has a F.A.R. of less than 0.5, or a density of less than 8–12 du/acre, and that it consists primarily of freestanding single-family dwellings, with some townhouses and garden apartments. Retail commercial is typically in one-story strip development on arterial roads with parking out front. Larger, multi-story office and institutional buildings are located in campus-like settings surrounded by lawns and parking lots. There are exceptions, like "edge cities," which are considerably denser than conventional sprawl but often not considered genuinely urban. The variables in the developing world's suburbs can differ significantly.

Fewer vehicular miles travelled (VMT) per capita is arguably the biggest environmental benefit of cities. U.S. highway statistics show that rural residents drive about twice as many miles per year as urban residents – in 2012, the former drove roughly 14,000 miles and the latter about 7,000 miles.[92] Automobiles are a crazy system: They take up 20 times as much space and weigh 20 times as much as a human body, and like to go 70 mph on freeways that penetrate and chop up the city center. Stronger urban policies that curtail car usage and ownership are needed in both

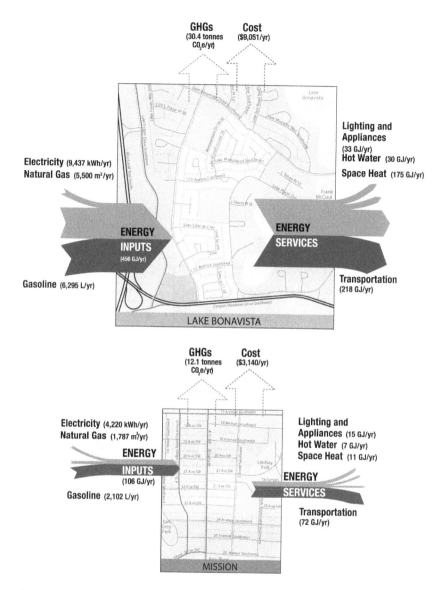

GHGs (30.4 tonnes CO₂e/yr)

Cost ($9,051/yr)

Electricity (9,437 kWh/yr)
Natural Gas (5,500 m³/yr)

Lighting and Appliances (33 GJ/yr)
Hot Water (30 GJ/yr)
Space Heat (175 GJ/yr)

ENERGY INPUTS (456 GJ/yr)

ENERGY SERVICES

Gasoline (6,295 L/yr)

Transportation (218 GJ/yr)

LAKE BONAVISTA

GHGs (12.1 tonnes CO₂e/yr)

Cost ($3,140/yr)

Electricity (4,220 kWh/yr)
Natural Gas (1,787 m³/yr)

Lighting and Appliances (15 GJ/yr)
Hot Water (7 GJ/yr)
Space Heat (11 GJ/yr)

ENERGY INPUTS (106 GJ/yr)

ENERGY SERVICES

Gasoline (2,102 L/yr)

Transportation (72 GJ/yr)

MISSION

Figure 2.3 These two diagrams of communities in Canada illustrate the environmental paradox of cities by showing energy inputs and outputs per house. In the sprawl example, the large suburban house spends roughly three times as much money on transportation and space heating, hot water, lighting and appliances as the small urban house, while producing 2.5 times as many tons of GHGs. (Her Majesty the Queen in Right of Canada, as represented by the Minister of Natural Resources, 2018)

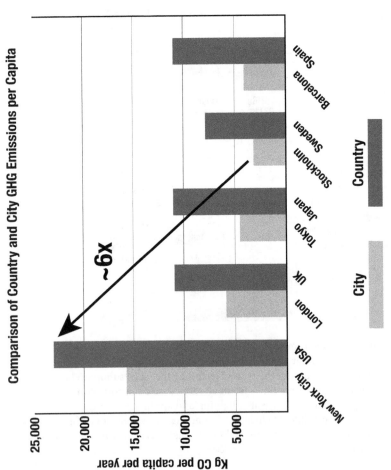

Figure 2.4 The comparison of U.S. carbon emissions per capita with other developed countries is dramatic, even embarrassing. Here the U.S.'s national average is shown to be over twice the U.K.'s or Japan's. It is six times greater than the city of Stockholm. (Courtesy of Michael Mehaffy, based on 2015 UNFCC inventory data, via chart by World Bank and McKinsey Co., 2015) (Source: Mehaffy, M. W. (2015). Urban Form and Greenhouse Gas Emissions: Findings, Strategies, and Design Decision Support Technologies. Delft: A+ BE: Architecture and the Built Environment)

Atlanta and Barcelona Have Similar Populations but Very Different Carbon Emissions

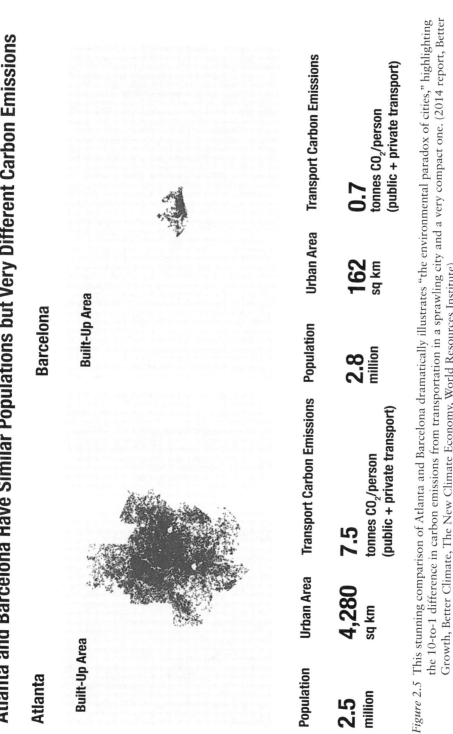

Atlanta

Built-Up Area

Barcelona

Built-Up Area

	Population	Urban Area	Transport Carbon Emissions
Atlanta	**2.5** million	**4,280** sq km	**7.5** tonnes CO$_2$/person (public + private transport)
Barcelona	**2.8** million	**162** sq km	**0.7** tonnes CO$_2$/person (public + private transport)

Figure 2.5 This stunning comparison of Atlanta and Barcelona dramatically illustrates "the environmental paradox of cities," highlighting the 10-to-1 difference in carbon emissions from transportation in a sprawling city and a very compact one. (2014 report, Better Growth, Better Climate, The New Climate Economy, World Resources Institute)

cities and suburbs – policies to remove parking spaces, enhance bicycle usage, calm traffic speeds, impose congestion charges on cars as they enter heavily congested urban cores, and ban vehicles from more streets. That's in addition to expanding the ubiquity of personal and shared bicycles, scooters, shared cars, station cars, golf carts, buses, Bus Rapid Transit (BRTs), trams and rail or metro lines, many of which will become electric and/or autonomous. Anything that gets people on their feet, on bicycles or onto transit can dramatically reduce both emissions and congestion.

It is important to note that density alone is not enough for the environmental paradox to obtain. Monocultural cities with densely packed residential towers can be *high-rise sprawl* if they lack mixed uses. This dense sprawl is lazy density in that it is easy to stamp out repetitive housing, with little mixing of uses. Many Asian cities, from Dubai to China, have large clusters of exclusively residential towers. They have neither the compactness nor mix of uses to prompt walking nor the comfortable, safe network for circulation by foot or bicycle. The superblocks and wide arterials are not conducive to walking, and the grain of transit is often too coarse to provide service within convenient walking distances. They are simply dense sprawl, with heavy VMT. Monotonous, single-use developments – at high or low density – do not get people out of their cars. Designing density around cars is a recipe for failure: Beijing has more transit than Dubai, but the wide streets and generous parking are inviting to vehicles and inhospitable to pedestrians. Dubai has created a number of special economic zones that are narrow and specialized in focus: Internet City, Design City, Media City, Academic City, Health Care City. Unlike mixed-use "innovation districts," these single-use zones are another manifestation of un-walkable, auto-dependent, dense sprawl. High-rise sprawl is one of the main reasons that Dubai has the world's highest carbon footprint per capita. The other reasons are the extravagant size of residential and commercial buildings, and the prodigious, ongoing rate of energy-intensive construction.

Challenge #3: Overpopulation – Exploding Megacities

The third big challenge is global population growth, another topic that unavoidably entails a numerical onslaught. In 1900, there were only one billion people living on the earth, with only 13 percent in cities. Since then, the growth has been staggering. Now there are over 7.6 billion earthlings, and some 55 percent live in urbanized areas.

> [E]ach week the global urban population increases by 1.3 million. Today there are nearly 1000 urban agglomerations with populations of 500,000 or greater; by 2050, the global urban population is expected to increase by 2.5 to 3 billion, corresponding to 64% to 69% of the world population.[93]

Five million more people every month live in the cities of the developing world, mostly in the sprawling cities and slums of Africa and Asia. The U.N. estimates the total may peak at nine or ten billion, maybe more, toward the end of this century, with as many as 75 percent living in urbanized areas.

Of the world's 31 megacities in 2016, six were in China and five in India, and by 2030 each will have at least seven megacities.[94] None of the world's ten largest cities are in Europe. Africa is coming on strong:

> UNICEF's Generation 2030 Africa reports that a current one billion-plus population will double within 35 years and the 18-and-younger cohort will increase to almost one billion. During the same time period, over 50% of Africans will be living in cities, overtaxing infrastructure and natural resources. From 1950 to 2016, Africans moving to cities increased from 14% to 40 percent, with 50% projected mid-2030s.[95]

Africa is currently home to "16% of the world's population and by 2050 it will probably be about 30%."[96] This represents a remarkable change in the world's demographics, as well as its geopolitics.

Too few Sub-Saharan African countries have had aggressive birth control and family planning programs, but it may

> muddle its way to a lower birth rate faster than the forecasters estimate, even without help from governments. The region's cities have been growing at a terrific clip of about 4% a year. The growth is often unplanned and messy, and the cities are seldom terribly productive. But urban living is likely to suppress birth rates all the same. Whereas farmers can put even young children to work pulling weeds and minding goats, city-dwellers find their offspring add little to household output and, moreover, require expensive schooling. As a result, they seek to have fewer children.[97]

Nonetheless, current and future urbanization trends are significantly different from the last two centuries. According to the U.N.'s IPCC,

> urbanization is taking place at lower levels of economic development and the majority of future urban population growth will take place in small- to medium-sized urban areas in developing countries. Expansion of urban areas is on average twice as fast as overall urban population growth, and the expected increase in urban land cover during the first three decades of the 21st century will be greater than the cumulative urban expansion in all of human history . . . Overall, urbanization has led to the growth of cities of all sizes. Although megacities (those with 10 million or more residents) receive a lot

Figure 2.6 Slums are staggeringly abundant: about 25 percent of the world's urban population lives in slums. Since 1990, over 200 million slum dwellers have been added to the global population, like these in Nairobi, Kenya. Over half of Africa's urban population lives in slums, and by 2050, the number is expected by some pundits to increase from 400 million to 1.2 billion. (Photos by author)

of attention in the literature, urban growth has been dominated by cities of smaller sizes. About one-third of the growth (1.16 billion) between 1950 and 2010 occurred in settlements with populations fewer than 100 thousand.[98]

Global Urbanism has increasingly taken shape as vast, distended city-regions, where urbanizing landscapes are increasingly fragmented into discontinuous assemblages of enclosed enclaves characterized by global connectivity and concentrated wealth, on the one side, and distressed zones of neglect and impoverishment, on the other.[99]

Slums, a.k.a. informal or squatter settlements, have absorbed much of the urban poor. Like the late nineteenth-century settlement houses in Chicago slums or their Victorian equivalents in England, they are places with formal and informal social services that poor rural migrants to the city need and rely on. Moreover, slums often replicate the physical patterns of village, town and city, including the lively, walkable, mixed-use street that predates the superblock and the wide arterial. They persist despite governmental action to raze them and relocate their residents primarily "because of the existence and resilience of social and economic networks, and the continuation of loose and close ties and affiliations. Relocation is resisted because it disrupts these useful networks."[100]

Many cities in the Global South are at breaking point.

Soon, one third of humanity will live in a slum. Over 90% of urbanisation this century will be due to the growth of slums. By the end of this century, the top megacities will no longer be London and Tokyo; they will almost all be in Asia and Africa, and they will be far bigger than the metropolises of today. Lagos is projected to have a population of 88 million. Dhaka: 76 million. Kinshasa: 63 million.[101]

Although these population counts lack accuracy, these numbers would have been unthinkable a generation ago. However, there are compelling arguments that these dense, informal settlements could become model "micro-cities" of the future. Their density allows the adoption of district energy systems, independent but also connected to the regional utility electrical grid. WiFi connectivity, Blockchain, AI and micro-loans can streamline access to services with local hubs that cluster schools, clinics, community kitchens and shared bikes and shared cars, AVs and shuttles.

Local governance can experiment with more direct forms of democracy, which is more immediately and directly connected to individual voters with electronic systems. The World Economic Forum has started a micro-city . . . partnership . . . in hopes of seeding a global network in one hundred cities in Asia, Africa and South America.[102]

UN statistics also suggest that just three countries – China, India and Nigeria – may account for 40 percent of global growth over the next decade and many of the five million more people who move every month to the cities in the developing world. "Africa is the world's fastest urbanizing continent. In 1950, sub-Saharan African had no cities with populations of more than 1M; today it has around 50. By 2030 half of the continent's population will live in cities."[103] In absolute terms, the biggest move to cities is happening in Asia. "In 2030, China's cities will be home to close to 1 billion people or 70% of the population."[104] The number of people China currently plans to move from farm to city in the next 12 years (post 2016) is 250 million, which is equivalent to some two dozen of the world's largest urban areas. The numbers are staggering, as are the size of new administrative urban areas. Jingjinji, which includes Beijing, Tianjin and Hebei, is expected to grow to 130 million residents, more than Japan and six times the current population of metro New York City. The Yangtze River Delta has approximately the same number of people, and the Pearl River Delta is also one of the largest conurbations in the world.

The planet's dozen densest cities are in Asia – from Hanoi and Bangalore to Hong Kong and Mumbai, with upwards of one thousand residents per acre.[105] One wonders if the density in these and other megalopolitan regions is sustainable and whether there might be some changes in migration patterns. For instance, there could be more migrants moving from rural areas to small cities, or from large cities to small cities, and ultimately from cities back to rural towns or even the countryside. And many will decamp to sprawling suburbs. While reverse migration to rural areas might seem to undermine one of the main theses of the book, it would no doubt be selective and limited in total scope by the availability of jobs. "The area of urbanized land could triple globally from 2000 to 2030. This is equivalent to adding an area bigger than Manhattan every day."[106]

As noted, secondary cities are often the fastest growing urban areas in Asia and Africa. In China, some secondary cities have populations of over five million, the size of a major metropolis in America. Secondary metro areas in the U.S. – Tucson, Nashville, Oklahoma City, Charleston, SC, etc. – are about a tenth that size. Rahul Mehrotra, Harvard professor and noted Indian architect/urban designer, believes the secondary cities of India now offer the most opportunity for sensible growth and livability, an idea that may very well apply elsewhere in Asia, Africa and beyond. They might soon prove to be the next generation of rapid urbanization, offering fewer problems, greater resilience in times of crisis, and healthier, more livable lifestyles. It's not clear, however, that smaller cities will fare so well in the U.S. To quote the Nobel-winning economist Paul Krugman,

[O]nce upon a time dispersed agriculture ensured that small cities serving rural hinterlands would survive. But for generations we have lived in an economy in which smaller cities have nothing going for them except historical luck, which eventually tends to run out.[107]

On the other hand, many towns seem to be enjoying a resurgence in America.

Urban sociologists like Saskia Sassen argue that giant first-tier cities – New York, London, Shanghai, Mumbai, Tokyo, etc. – need other major urban economies of their size and type more than they need the standard smaller cities in their hinterlands that have traditionally been part of their physical supply chain.[108] In other words, New York needs London more than, say, Bethlehem, PA, which used to supply it steel. The megacities and some of their corporate residents have become untethered from the suppliers in the small cities within their country. Where San Francisco Bay and Baltimore shipyards once drew timber and engine parts from rural towns and manufacturing cities across the U.S., today's Silicon Valley companies are much more likely to deal with Japanese investors, Chinese regulators and European lawyers. Google digital products don't depend on a physical supply chain; Facebook doesn't have manufacturers dispersed around the country and Apple manufactures overseas. This new dynamic has social and political ramifications, as smaller cities feel alienated and resentful of the "elite" cities that seem untouched by the forces that are hollowing them out. Small cities understandably feel left out of the prosperity enjoyed by these major metro areas.

The explosive growth of megacities threatens the social fabric and the environment as much as climate change. As Sassen writes

[R]ather than functioning as spaces for people from diverse backgrounds and cultures, the global cities of today are expelling people and diversity. Their owners, mostly part-time inhabitants, are very international, but that does not mean that they represent diverse cultures and traditions: they represent the new global culture of the successful, which is astoundingly homogeneous no matter how diverse its countries of birth and languages.[109]

Not all density is diverse; some forms of density actually serve to de-urbanize cities, as privatization has been losing the ownership of public buildings and spaces to large corporations. Density, as exemplified in Dubai, is not enough to have a true city. Nor is a city of jet-setters going to reduce either per capita or the total carbon footprint of humans.

The explosion also puts devilish demands on our finite supply of natural resources and pumps more pollutants into the atmosphere and water. It will exacerbate an already massive mismatch between urban population and infrastructure, while threatening socio-cultural cohesion and global geopolitical stability.

If the global population increases to 9.3 billion by 2050 and developing countries expand their built environment and infrastructure to current global average levels using available technology of today, the production of infrastructure materials alone would generate approximately 470Gt of CO_2 emissions. Currently, average per capita CO_2 emissions embodied in the infrastructure of industrialized countries is five times larger than those in developing countries. The continued expansion of fossil fuel-based infrastructure would produce cumulative emissions of 3,000–7,500GtCO_2 during the remainder of the 21st century.[110]

We cannot continue to count on limiting global emissions with the small footprints of a huge number of poor people! Addressing the gaping mismatch between the developed countries and the Global South is an urgent and just agenda.

The convergence of overpopulation and CC are an overwhelming challenge for the Global South. African countries like Niger, Nigeria and Senegal have

> rampant poverty and poor access to contraception, Niger has one the highest birth rates in the world: 7.6 children per woman. I met a man there who boasted of 17 kids. Neighboring Nigeria is growing so fast it will replace the U.S. as the third-most-populous country in the world by 2050. Nigeria is a third bigger than Texas. Meanwhile, climate change in the region is so severe that nearby Senegal's national weather bureau says that from 1950 to 2015, the average temperature there rose 2°C and the average annual rainfall declined by about two inches and . . . In other words, parts of sub-Saharan Africa are already at heat levels that Paris was supposed to prevent *by the end of the century* – and the region is heading for a four-degree rise, which will lead to the collapse of even more small farms and lead to a mad scramble of refugees toward Europe, competition for food and more unemployed males.[111]

The benefits of this rapid urbanization in the developing world should not be overlooked or forgotten. "In the last three decades, hundreds of millions in China, India, and other formerly poor places have lifted themselves from destitution – arguably the most important, and certainly the most heartening, accomplishment of our time."[112] Informal settlements over time show signs of self-organization into distinct components analogous to organs of the body. Could they be on their way to slowly evolving into the patterns of the once-poor and now much-loved urban towns and cities of Tuscany, Italy or Provence, France? Indeed, "Given the pace and scale of urbanization . . . It may be that the developing world is the best hope for a sustainable world, and it may be that the cities of the developing world that hold the greatest promise."[113] And if this urbanization continues to curtail birth rates, it can reduce world population by as many as several billion people, which would mitigate CC considerably and make it easier to adapt to.

A deeper dive into overpopulation in the developing world is worthwhile. This study published by the International Institute for Environment and Development in London reinforces earlier ones:

> education, infant and child mortality reduction, women's empowerment, wage labour, women's participation in the labour force, increased consumption aspirations and social mobility – are among the main factors that motivate people to regulate their natural fertility . . . Urbanization . . . has long been touted by analysts as a main factor in fertility decline. It is almost universally acknowledged that urban fertility is lower than rural fertility, except in the very poorest urban slum areas. On the surface, this would appear to be attributable to the fact that urban populations, across the world, enjoy advantages over rural populations in relation to all those factors that affect fertility levels, including education and employment of women, gender equality and better access to all types of services. Guo et al. (2011) observe that not only was urbanization important in China's fertility decline but that it will become the primary factor in future fertility decline, allowing it to relax its One Child Policy. The relevance of urbanization in fertility decline has been highlighted in other studies on developing countries. As repeatedly demonstrated in the literature, reductions in infant mortality are a precondition for the reduction of fertility rates. Urbanization has a direct effect on mortality, especially on infant mortality, given the aggregate advantages of cities in terms of basic sanitation (clean water, sewerage and garbage collection), of health services that help reduce fetal deaths through prenatal care, of paediatric care and of better coverage through vaccination campaigns. Moreover, urbanization is correlated with greater access to better sexual and reproductive health services that allow effective regulation of fertility . . . surveys on the 83 countries having available data for the latest year presented, shows that in every country, without exception, rural fertility is systematically higher than urban fertility. The un-weighted average difference is 1.5 more children in rural areas. In 30 per cent of the countries surveyed, the rural–urban difference was more than 2 children . . . urban areas provide conditions that stimulate lower fertility while also making it easier to provide people with at least some of the advantages of modernization and some of the components of citizenship that allow them to take somewhat better control of their lives, including in the reproductive domain."[114]

The planet itself doesn't know the difference between individual and collective footprints; it is impacted by the *total* eco-footprint. Even though carbon emissions per capita have fallen marginally since 1968, the total global carbon emissions have roughly tripled.[115]Again, *we need to address both the total number of people and their individual footprints, placing more emphasis on per capita improvements in the wealthy, developed countries with declining populations, and more emphasis on reducing explosive population growth in the developing countries, where per capita consumption is growing. The good news, in a nutshell, is that cities can cut birthrates in half in developing countries and cut carbon footprints in half in developed countries.* It is essential to address the combination of per capita and total carbon emissions: the simple arithmetic of individual emissions multiplied by the number of individuals on earth is what ultimately counts in the war against CC. Conversely, the more humans there are, the less planet there is per person, not to mention per animal and per plant.

More on the Population Paradox of Cities

This urban environmental paradox only applies to *some* developing countries, but the population paradox applies to most of them. To repeat: rural migrants to cities reduce their birth rates, that is, a nation's population growth tends to slow as it urbanizes. However, if the individual footprints of the new urban residents grow due to higher income, the paradox diminishes or disappears. In other words, the urban dividend obtains only when the lower urban birth rate more than compensates for the increased consumption of urban dwellers. Unfortunately, in many developing countries, the trade-off doesn't occur when the rural poor move to cities.[116] Regions that have seen extreme reductions in poverty, specifically East Asia and the Pacific and South Asia, have increased their carbon emissions by over 200 percent in the last third of a century.[117] For instance, Professor Ng's research on Hong Kong and mainland China, has found that the per capita energy/carbon footprint roughly triples when people move from poor rural areas to the much more consumptive lifestyles of the city, while the birth rate drops by a quarter to a third. Fortunately, megacities like Beijing and Shanghai have ultra-low birth rates of less than 1.0, which has the country's leaders worried. China's birth rate has actually dropped since 2017, when it substituted a Two Child for a One Child Policy, which had lowered family size for many years in both rural and urban areas. Overall, the increase in consumption has resulted in about a two-fold net increase in the country's total footprint, which means that sometimes urbanization does *not* directly combat CC. As negative as this trend is, if these very poor migrants had moved to, or later relocated to *suburbs* of these cities as they became wealthier, there would be an even larger net increase in both their personal footprints and the national footprint.

Fortunately, birth rates have fallen in other Asian countries, especially Southeast Asia, and in Africa, where it has been the most dramatic. Nonetheless, this environmental penalty of urbanization in developing countries is a very significant issue for the world, and if left unchecked, could prove disastrous. It has major political ramifications: U.N. accords and programs have typically expected the richer countries of the developed world to shoulder more than their per capita share of the costs of addressing CC. It's a reasonable expectation, given the wealthy countries not only have greater economic capacity, but also are responsible for putting most of the carbon in the atmosphere in the first place. The divide between rich and poor, donor and recipient countries is increasingly complicated:

> The International Energy Agency (IEA) expects that 89% of the CO_2 emissions growth in cities between 2006 and 2030 will come from non-OECD countries . . . a formidable challenge to global change and its governance . . . (as) the majority of future population growth for the remainder of this century is reported to occur in urban areas of low- and middle-income nations. Asia alone added a billion urban dwellers in the 30 years between 1980–2010, more than the population of Western Europe and USA combined, and it is expected to add another billion in the next 30 years. Africa is expected to urbanize rapidly in the next 20 years, adding another 500 million to its cities . . . *the so-called global "North–South" economic divide is actually an "Urban–Rural" spatial disparity in the making.*[118]

It is likely to further devolve into a more local but complex dynamic, as the developing world faces the double challenge of rapid urbanization and CC.

On the other hand, it should also be pointed out again that in some African countries, such as Liberia and Madagascar, migrating from farms to large cities, can lower income and consumption. "African cities are crowded, but not necessarily economically dense . . . they are undergoing an urbanization of people, not capital."[119] The decrease in the absolute level of consumption and carbon production per urban resident means *the environmental paradox does* apply outright in cities of some developing countries. And the population paradox is reasonably robust: according to World Bank statistics, the birth rate in sub-Saharan Africa dropped from about seven births per woman to about five between 1980 and 2013. It is still the highest rate in the world, as the countries of South Asia have seen a more dramatic drop, from 5 to almost 2.5 births per mother, exceeded only by China's even more precipitous drop from about five to almost one under its One Child Policy.[120] The carbon penalty and population dividend is not as clear in the cities of India, which is fast becoming the most populous country on earth. The footprints of agrarian villagers are extremely small and ultimately increase after moving to the city. However, most of them initially move to informal squatter settlements, where their incomes remain roughly the same as average villagers, and the birth rate drops about a quarter from about 2.7 to about 2.0.[121] Although the overall trend appears to be positive, more research is needed to calculate the population paradox in these and other developing countries.

Each country, region and city needs its own formula for decreasing the triple threat of UHIs, CC and overpopulation. For instance, as its birth rate declines, the Indian subcontinent is reducing waste heat from its power plants, while pursuing an ambitious solar strategy. "A signatory of the Paris Agreement, India is forecast to meet its renewable energy commitments three years early and exceed them by nearly half. The country is aiming to generate nearly 60% of its electricity from non-fossil sources by 2027."[122] The country's leadership has committed to building 60 solar cities, and has already installed the world's largest photovoltaic (PV) array – some 2.5 million panels and 6,000km of cables, enough to power 150,000 homes.[123] India is also improving the efficiency of it air conditioners, which is critical because their use has been growing

> rapidly at a rate of 20% on average per year over the last ten years and is likely to be a major contributor to the need for new power plants in India. In 2010, the room AC saturation amongst urban households was only 3%, compared to 100% in China. With rising incomes and urbanization, falling AC prices and a hot climate, it is expected that the AC ownership is going to rapidly increase in India . . . Meeting this demand requires construction of nearly 300 new coal fired power plants of 500MW each . . . efficient ACs can lead to reduction of the AC demand by more than 40% cost effectively; this translates to avoiding building more than 100 new power plants.[124]

Alternately, China has committed to reducing its monumental consumption of coal; at the end of 2017 they laid off 1.8 million workers in the coal and steel industry (compared to a national total of less than 200,000 workers in those fields in the U.S.).[125] In the same year, it also instituted a carbon exchange to indirectly tax and lower the use of coal and to encourage the use of renewables in its huge state-run power industry, which accounts for half the country's electricity production.

The environmental penalty of urbanization in the countries of Asia could be reduced if and when the differential in wealth between the countryside and the city diminishes. Indeed, the current differential in developing countries is exacerbated by the extreme poverty in the countryside. Rural poverty may lessen as urban migration leaves the countryside less populated, allowing remaining farmers to shift from subsistence farming on marginal land to higher-yielding cash crops on more fertile land. Poverty, of course, should never be used as a means to keep down the total global eco-footprint. *We emphatically should not depend on billions of the global poor to compensate for the much larger footprints of the wealthy. We need to find and promote ways for the global poor to ascend to higher living standards without aggravating CC, while reducing the already excessive footprints of the rich.* Achieving prosperity and well-being without economic growth is surely one of humanity's greatest challenges in the twenty-first century and beyond. This is especially true in wealthy, highly developed countries like the U.S. – if and when we own up to the disgraceful fact that the average American eco-footprint is about four or five times that of an average Indian or African.

Sadly, not a single country currently meets the basic needs of its citizens in a way that is globally sustainable. According to data on the quality of life and resource consumption from some 150 countries, either the basics of a good life are not provided to all, or they are provided with excessive resources, or they fail at both.

> Physical needs such as nutrition, sanitation, access to electricity and the elimination of extreme poverty could likely be met for all people without transgressing planetary boundaries. However, the universal achievement of more qualitative goals, such as high life satisfaction, would require a level of resource use that is 2–6 times the sustainable level.[126]

The task of more efficiently balancing human needs and equity with our planet's available resources remains as elusive as it is essential.

Notes

1 Charles Mann, "State of the species," *Orion*, 2012
2 "Collapse: climate change, cities and culture," Global Design, New York University, summer 2018
3 Richard Leakey and Roger Lewin, *The Sixth Extinction*, Doubleday, 1995
4 Elizabeth Kolbert, The Sixth Extinction: An Unnatural History, Bloomsbury, 2014
5 E.O. Wilson, *The Future of Life*, Little, Brown, 2002
6 Charles Mann, "State of the species"
7 Stewart Brand, *Whole Earth Discipline*, Viking, 2009, p. 20
8 "Yale Climate Opinion Maps – U.S.," Yale Program on Climate Change, 2016
9 Elizabeth Kolbert, The Sixth Extinction: An Unnatural History
10 Gavin L. Foster, Dana L. Royer and Daniel J. Lunt, "Future climate forcing potentially without precedent in the last 420 million years," *Nature: Communications*, 8, 4/4/17
11 Nathaniel Rich, "Losing earth: the decade we almost stopped climate change," *The New York Times*, 8/2/18
12 Amy Harder, "The world needs clean coal but can't get it," Harder Line, *Axios*, 7/24/17

13 Clair Brown, *Buddhist Economics*, Bloomsbury, 2017, p. 52
14 "Transportation is the biggest source of U.S. emissions," *Climatecentral.org*, 11/21/17
15 Ben Geman, "1 big thing: transportation emissions are stubborn," Generate, *Axios*, 7/19/18
16 Ramon A. Alvarez et al., "Assessment of methane emissions from the U.S. oil and gas supply chain," *Science*, 6/21/18
17 Alan H. Lockwood, *Heat Advisory*, MIT Press, 2016, pp. 51–52
18 NOAA and the Ball State University for Business and Economic Research, 2017
19 Chelsea Harvey, "Scientists can now blame individual natural disasters on climate change," E&E News, *Scientific American*, 1/2/18
20 Ronald Wright, *A Short History of Progress*, House of Anansi Press, 2004
21 B. Plumer and N. Popovich, "95-degree days: how extreme heat could spread across the world," *The New York Times*, 6/22/17
22 Richard Sennett et al., *The Quito Papers and the New Urban Agenda*, Routledge, 2018, pp. 32–33
23 Zoe Schlanger, "Dams and reservoirs can't save us: this is the new future of water infrastructure," *Quartz*, 8/22/18
24 *Disaster Resilience: A National Imperative*, Committee on Increasing National Resilience to Hazards and Disasters, Committee on Science, Engineering, and Public Policy, National Academy of Sciences, National Academies Press, 2012
25 Sara Hines, personal email, 5/3/18
26 Brian Stone, Jason Vargo and Dana Habeeb, "Managing climate change in cities: Will climate action plans work?" *Landscape and Urban Planning*, 107, 2012, pp. 263–271
27 Confirmed in email exchanges with Brian Stone in mid-April, 2017
28 *The Weather Channel*, 12/9/17
29 Gerald Mills, "Explainer: why are cities warmer than the countryside," *citiscope*, 1/26/16
30 T.R. Oke and I.D. Stewart, "Local climate zones," *Bulletin of American Meteorology Society*, 93, 2012
31 Cool Cars, Heat Island Group, Berkeley Labs, https://heatisland.lbl.gov/coolscience/cool-cars
32 "Q and A, hot cars," *The New York Times*, 11/8/17
33 V. Smil, "Planet of the cows," *IEEE Spectrum*, 54, April, 2017, p. 24
34 Diane Ackerman, *The Human Age: The World Shaped by Us*, Headline, 2012
35 Charles Mann, "State of the species"
36 Chris Reed and Nina-Marie Lister, "Ecology and design: parallel genealogies," *Places*, 2014
37 Paul Tinker and Tom Levitt, "How air pollution affects your health," *The Guardian*, 7/5/16
38 Joao Medeiros, "The science of why heatwaves are so dangerous to human health," *Wired*, 7/22/18
39 Oliver Milman, "'It can't get much hotter . . . can it?' How heat became a national US problem," *The Guardian*, 7/14/18
40 David Wallace Wells, "Climate change will make Earth too hot for humans," *New York Magazine*, 7/9/17
41 Ibid., paraphrasing from pp. 40–42
42 "Increased use of air conditioning," Indoor Air Quality, Berkeley Lab website
43 Marilyn McKenna, "Why the menace of mosquitoes will only get worse," *The New York Times Magazine*, 4/20/17

44 Scott Campbell, "Unsustainability as a chronic, manageable disease? Alternatives to sustainability-as-equilibrium," ACSA Conference, October, 2015

45 Dan Hamza-Goodacre, Kigali, Rwanda Cooling Efficiency Program

46 Niall McCarthy, "The world's top cities for sustainable public transport," *Forbes*, 10/30/17

47 Based on conversation and email exchanges with Professor Edward Ng, Chinese University of Hong Kong, February, 2017

48 Justin Gillis, "An effect of climate change that you could really lose sleep over," *The New York Times*, 5/26/17

49 Dana Nuccitella, "Switching to electric cars is key to fixing America's 'critically insufficient' climate policies," *The Guardian*, 1/22/18

50 Andrew Freedman, "The huge challenge of cooling a warming world," *Axios*, 7/16/18

51 Justine Calma, "Heat check," *Grist*, 7/11/18

52 Ted C. Fishman, "The shape of water," *Chicago Magazine*, April, 2018

53 Gerald Mills, "Explainer: why are cities warmer than the countryside"

54 Brian Stone, *The City and the Coming Climate*, Cambridge University Press, 2012, pp. 93–95

55 Alan H. Lockwood, *Heat Advisory*, p. 46

56 Ethan D. Coffel et al., "Temperature and humidity based projections of a rapid rise in global heat stress exposure during the 21st century," *IOP Science*, 12/22/17

57 "Chilling prospects: providing sustainable cooling for all," www.SEforALL.org, 2018

58 Ibid., pp. 1–15

59 Brad Plumer, "Really big ideas to beat the heat," *The New York Times*, 8/9/18

60 Anita Snow, "'Urban island effect' compounds Phoenix's sweltering heat," *Chicago Tribune*, 7/30/18

61 Oliver Milman, "'It can't get much hotter . . . can it?' How heat became a national US problem"

62 B. Plumer and N. Popovich, "As climate changes, southern states will suffer more than others," *The New York Times*, 6/29/17

63 Jeffrey Berko et al., "Deaths attributed to heat, cold, and other weather events in the United States, 2006–2010," *National Health Statistical Reports*, 7/30/14

64 "Beware: winter is coming," *The New York Times*, 12/20/16

65 "Chilling prospects: providing sustainable cooling for all"

66 *The New York Times*, 6/6/15

67 Nadja Popovich and Adam Pearce, "It's not your imagination: summers are getting hotter," *The New York Times*, 7/28/17

68 Steven Leahy, "By 2100, deadly heat may threaten majority of humankind," *National Geographic*, 6/19/17

69 Steven Leahy, "Parts of Asia may be too hot for people by 2100," *National Geographic*, 8/2/17

70 Juan Cole, Professor of History, University of Michigan, talk at Science Cafe, Ann Arbor, Michigan, 10/4/17

71 "Heat is causing problems across the world," *The Economist*, 7/28/18

72 Oliver Milman, "'It can't get much hotter . . . can it?' How heat became a national US problem"

73 Susan Goldberg, "A talk with Michael Bloomberg," *National Geographic*, February, 2018

74 Andrew Freeman, "China may be most at risk for deadly, extreme heat waves," *Axios*, 8/2/18

75 B. Plumer and N. Popovich, "95-degree days: how extreme heat could spread across the world"

76 Alan H. Lockwood, *Heat Advisory*, pp. 48–49

77 Alissa J. Rubin, "Europe gets a scorching preview of how climate change will affect the continent," *Seattle Times*, 8/4/18

78 "DoE head displays willful ignorance while killer heat waves broil the southwest," *DarkSide*, 6/24/17

79 Justine Calma, "Heat check"

80 K. Pierre-Louis and N. Popovich, "Nights are warming faster than days. here's why that's dangerous," *The New York Times*, 6/11/18

81 Yu Yan Cui and Benjamin de Foy, "Seasonal variations of the urban heat island at the surface and the near-surface and reductions due to urban vegetation in Mexico City," *Journal of Applied Meteorology*, May, 2012

82 Professor Harrison Fraker, personal conversation prior to the report's publication, 8/4/18

83 Tania Sharmin, "Urban form and microclimate: impacts on outdoor thermal comfort and building energy performance in a high-density tropical context," Department of Architecture, Cambridge University, April, 2017

84 "'Heat island' effect could double climate change costs for world's cities," www.sussex.ac.uk/broadcast/read/40429, 5/29/17

85 Ibid.

86 "Research: China's CO2 push will pay for itself, *Axios*, 4/25/18

87 James Temple, "Global warming may harm children for life," *MIT Technology Review*, 12/4/17

88 Ibid.

89 Perry Samson, North Campus Sustainability Hour lecture, University of Michigan, 10/30/17

90 Carl Zimmer, "Climate change is altering lakes and streams, study suggests," *The New York Times*, 1/11/18

91 Akshat Rathi, "The compelling case for capturing carbon emissions and burying them underground," *Quartz*, 12/13/17

92 Richard Florida, "What drove the driving downturn," *City Lab*, 4/6/17

93 "Human settlements, infrastructure and spatial planning," Chapter 12, *Climate Change 2012: Migration of Climate Change*, Working Group III, Fifth Assessment Report, IPPC, p. 926

94 Mike Allen, "The global megacity boom," *Axios*, 10/8/17

95 Steve Coyle, "Lean Urbanism in Central Africa," in Mahyar Arefi and Conrad Kickert (eds), *The Palgrave Handbook on Bottom-Up Urbanism*, to be published in 2018

96 Daniel Yamamoto, interviewed by Joshua Johnson, "1A," NPR, 1/2/18

97 "Generation games," *The Economist*, September 16–22, 2017

98 *Climate Change 2012: Migration of Climate Change*, p. 927

99 Martin Murray, *The Urbanism of Exception*, Cambridge University Press, 2018

100 S. Doshi, "The politics of the evicted: redevelopment, subjectivity, and difference in Mumbai's slum frontier," *Antipode*, 45, 2013, pp. 844–865

101 Jonathan Hursh, "How slums can inspire the microcities of the future," World Economic Forum, Annual Meeting, 1/26/18

102 Ibid.

103 "Left behind," *The Economist*, September 17–23, 2016

104 *New Climate Economy*, World Resources Institute (WRI), 2014

105 Alain Bertaud, Stern Urbanization Project, New York University

106 *New Climate Economy*, WRI, 2014

107 Paul Krugman, "The gambler's ruin of small cities (wonkish)," *The New York Times*, 12/30/17

108 Emily Badger, "The megacity untethered," *The New York Times*, 12/24/17

109 Richard Sennett et al., *The Quito Papers and the New Urban Agenda*, p. 29

110 Seto and Dhakal, "Human settlements, infrastructure and spatial planning," *IPCC 2014 Mitigation*, p. 927

111 Thomas Friedman, "Trump, Niger and connecting the dots," *The New York Times*, 11/1/17

112 Charles C. Mann, "State of the species"

113 Paulo Ferrao and John Fernandez, *Sustainable Urban Metabolism*, MIT Press, 2013

114 George Martine, Jose Eustaquio Alves and Suzana Cavenaghi, "Urbanization and fertility decline: cashing in on structural change," IIED, December 2013

115 "Key data trends since our founding as ZPG," *Population Connection*, June 2018

116 "Ups and downs," *The Economist*, September 17–23, 2017

117 Adam Goldstein, "What is the link between carbon emissions and poverty," World Economic Forum, 12/15/15

118 Mahendra Sethi and Jose Puppim de Oliveira, "From Global North–South to local urban–rural," *Urban Climate*, December, 2015, pp. 529–543

119 mgrafrica.com, citing World Bank statistics, 4/18/16

120 Ibid.

121 Edward Ng, email exchanges, February, 2017

122 "India just broke the world record with its new solar farm," *Futurism* (blog), February 18–24, 2017

123 "India shows it's serious about solar with giant power plant," *Nation.com*, 1/26/17

124 A. Phadke, N. Abhyankar, N. Shah, "Avoiding 100 new power plants by increasing efficiency of room air conditioners in India: opportunities and challenges," Lawrence Berkeley National Laboratory, 2017

125 Steve LeVine, "The big layoff in China," *Axios*, 11/22/17

126 Daniel W. O'Neil et al., "A good life for all within planetary boundaries," *Nature: Sustainability*, February, 2018

3   Urban Albedo and Morphology

Atop ongoing CC, UHIs also have major implications for the planning and design of cities. There are four primary ways to mitigate and adapt to extreme heat in cities: brightening albedo, ventilating urban canyons, reducing waste heat and creating cool micro-climates. The first two strategies will be discussed in this chapter, and the third and fourth in the next two chapters respectively. It is important to note at the outset that these strategies are neither new techniques nor technically arcane. They are in fact well established and tested, but not as understood or deployed as widely or effectively as they could and should be in the Anthropocene.

The four UHI prevention and reduction strategies:

1   *Raise albedo with lighter-colored roofs, pavements and walls.*
2   *Open up tight street canyons to ventilating breezes and winds.*
3   *Reduce waste heat from tailpipes, chimneys and air conditioners.*
4   *Provide cool micro-climates with more trees and other vegetation to cool the air, sequester CO_2 and shade streets and buildings.*

Brightening Albedo

The sun drives both CC and UHIs.

> [It] shines so fiercely that it dazzles the eyes and makes the skin sting in summertime. And that's after almost all of its output simply radiates off into the void: for every one unit of solar energy that impacts the Earth, 1.6B units do not. Life on Earth depends on the sun's table scraps.[1]

Our sun may be 93,000,000 miles away, but it provides 99.9 percent of all energy on earth. Its shorter rays are visible as light to the human eye, and its longer, invisible waves can be felt as heat. The full spectrum of rays contains energy, which take multiple forms. The first is direct radiation in the form of natural light and heat, which keep us from living in near-total darkness at absolute zero degrees. A second form is wind power, as it drives the local and global currents of air. The sun also lifts moisture into the air, forming clouds, which release rain that eventually provides hydropower. Solar energy powers photosynthesis, producing biofuels and the carbohydrates that fuel the bodies and minds of humans and animals. The sun is what is powering your breathing and your eyes as you read this. Last, it is the original source of the fossil fuels that humans burn so profusely for every imaginable purpose. Only tidal power is driven by the moon rather than the sun. In many ways, the sun is the source of life, and one can easily see why some prehistoric and ancient cultures worshipped it.

The earth's atmosphere selectively filters this solar bounty of radiation, both incoming waves and outgoing waves that are reflected back from the earth's surface. Albedo is the percentage of radiation reflected back as given by the Solar Reflectivity Index (SRI) or solar reflectance (SR). This metric is thermally very significant, because most of the solar radiation that hits light-colored surfaces is reflected directly back into space *before it gives up any of its heat*. Technically, the solar energy bounces back before it makes the photo-thermal conversion, that is, before it changes from shorter wave to longer wave radiation, just as it does inside an automobile. Both the reflected visible and invisible rays pass back through the atmosphere's filters as easily as they arrived. Accordingly, white and light-colored surfaces – primarily roofs and pavement with a high SRI – increase albedo, thereby reducing the temperature of the earth's surface and the air above it. Conversely, dark surfaces reradiate the thermal energy as longer wave, infrared radiation, which is trapped by GHGs in the atmosphere and raises its temperature. This additional heat is what drives CC.

Rooftops

Much of the urban landscape is made of hard, dark-colored materials and is devoid of vegetation. So, most of the incoming solar energy is absorbed by the surface layers of buildings and pavements. Building and paving materials are dense and impervious to water; most of them – particularly dark-colored ones – have a high uptake of solar radiation. Urban rooftops, which tend to be flat and dark in color with low SRIs of about 5%, are particularly fat targets for the high summer sun. For comparison, bare soil has a SRI of about 30%, and vegetation is about 50%; gray concrete averages 35% and white concrete 75%, while snow reflects 80% of the incoming radiation.[2] These and other SRIs tend to lower with age and the accumulation of dirt. Hence, there has been increasing interest in cooling roof surfaces, either with light-colored "cool roofs," or with "green roofs," a.k.a. "garden roofs" that have plant materials.

By converting half a city's rooftops to green roofs, it is estimated that air temperatures in the immediate vicinity can sometimes be diminished by up to 3.5°F.[3] Planted green roofs offer other environmental benefits, such as storm water retention and detention, habitats for birds, small mammals and insects, as well as the biophilic beauty and evapotranspiration. They are particularly enjoyable when they can be easily accessed by the building's occupants, and/or seen from windows and balconies above. New York City's Javits Center has a green roof of over 6 acres, and is home to many birds, bees and insects. On the other hand, with limited soil depth roof plantings can be subject to wholesale die-off. Green roofs function well in wet, cool climates, but don't work well in hot arid climates, because the soil is usually too shallow – for structural reasons – to retain sufficient moisture.

In Hamburg, Germany, building owners can receive subsidies of 30–60 percent of its installation costs, and from 2020, green roofs will be mandatory for all new, large-scale buildings. City University of New York researchers assembled images taken by a LIDAR-enabled (Light Detection and Ranging) aircraft, that showed some two-thirds of the city's buildings had roof space suitable for commercial photovoltaic installations. They also estimated that, even with New York City's changeable weather, rooftop installations could meet close to 14 percent of the city's annual electricity consumption. São Paulo has announced that future low-income housing developments should include rooftop photovoltaics. Of course, these examples are very site-specific. There is no universal solution to make urban roofs more sustainable.[4]

A recent study suggests that simple white roofs are more effective at reflecting solar radiation than green roofs.[5] They can increase the SRI from 20 percent up to 80 percent. The study compared three types of roofs – green, black and white – and concluded that white roofs have measurable economic benefits and are three times more effective than the other two roof types at fighting CC.[6] Light-colored roofs are less problematic than pavements of similar reflectivity, because they convect less heat into the air at the pedestrian level. Through its CoolRoofs Initiative, New York City had painted more than 5 million square feet of its roofs with reflective coating by 2018. However, in hot humid places like Florida, reflective materials have less impact and could potentially reduce local rainfall.[7] A cool roofs initiative in a town of 15,000 in one of the hottest parts of South Africa found that the cool coatings had the potential to reduce temperatures by 20 percent and reduce energy used on cooling by up to 15 percent. Residents immediately noticed the temperature difference and improvement in comfort, which led to a bigger roll out on about 500 residential rooftops by 2018.[8]

Also, roofs are easier to keep clean than streets and parking lots, which get marred by car tires, oil drips and the dirt that tends to find its way to the lowest available horizontal surface. The National Center for Atmospheric Research (NOAA) looked at what might happen if every roof in large cities around the world were painted white, raising their reflectivity from a typical 32 percent to 90 percent. They found that it

Figure 3.1 Painting a roof white. New York City's CoolRoofs program has
brightened some 6 million square feet of rooftops on over 600
buildings. Manhattan is often 7°F warmer due to the heat island effect.[1]
On the other side of the globe in Ahmedabad, India (Figure 6.3), there
are initiatives to replace black tar roofs with white tiles or have citizen
volunteers paint them with white coatings. (Ken Cavanagh, Alamy
Stock Photo C1RR55.) Fluorescent Roby Red and Egyptian Blue[2] are
two colors that have been found to be almost as reflective as white,
which is not often appropriate for sloped roofs that can be seen from
the street

1 *Cool Cities, Good Practice Guide*, C40 Cities Climate Leadership Group, February, 2016
2 Julie Chao, "Ancient pigment can boost energy efficiency," Berkeley Lab News Center,
10/9/18

would decrease the UHIs by a third – enough to reduce the maximum
daytime temperatures by an average of 1°F (0.6°C), and more in hot
sunny regions such as the Arabian Peninsula and Brazil. Other studies
suggest even greater benefits in the U.S.: cutting temperatures by up to
1.5°C in California and 1.8°C in cities such as Washington D.C. On the
other hand, another study concluded that changing albedo in cities (or
on farmland) would not likely mitigate global CC.[9] Time will tell which
scenario is true, as we wade deeper into UHIs and CC.

In the U.S., about a quarter of a city's surface is typically roofs, and
over a third is pavement, including many of the estimated 800 million
non-residential parking spaces.[10] Roofs and pavements provide a broad

target for solar energy. Together they absorb and convert into heat about 80 percent of the sunlight that hits them.[11] New products allow pitched roofs to have high albedo, with special optical coatings that don't require light or bright colors. Roofs and paved parking lots can also be covered in whole or in part with photovoltaic (PV) panels, which have low albedos of roughly 10 percent. Covering these urban surfaces with horizontal or tilted PV panels not only shades and cools them, but also the cooler faces of the panels do not heat up the air as much. And the layer of space between the panel and the roof or pavement helps to air-cool them, increasing their efficiency. Solar thermal collectors for heating domestic hot water are more efficient at converting solar energy into hot water than PV panels are at converting it into electricity – 60 percent for solar thermal, and currently 5–20 percent for PVs, projected to soon be 30 percent. Solar thermal systems also contribute less to UHIs, despite a slightly higher albedo (11–16 percent), because the circulating water takes more heat away from the collector panels.

A scenario of a large but realistic deployment of solar panels in the Paris metropolitan area was simulated and showed that, by shading the roofs, they slightly increase the need for winter heating by 3 percent, but reduce the energy needed for air conditioning by 12 percent, as well as slightly reduce the UHI by 0.36°F (0.2°C) by day and up to 0.54°F (0.3°C) at night. More dramatically, "the thermal solar panels would produce approximately . . . an equivalent of 28% of the energy consumption for domestic heating and air-conditioning."[12] A study in Australia found that in Sydney, a city-wide array of solar panels could reduce summer maximum temperatures by up to 1°C.[13] These fortuitous combinations of albedo enhancement and renewable energy production represent an important way that cities can simultaneously address both global CC and local UHIs.

> Cooling systems consume 15% of electricity generated globally and account for 10% of global greenhouse gas emissions . . . And the demand for cooling is expected to grow tenfold by 2050 as the planet gets warmer and more people can afford air-conditioning and refrigeration.[14]

Stanford University researchers have developed a panel technology to reduce cooling costs by 20 percent through rooftop albedo enhancement. The panel is a solar water *cooler* rather than the conventional solar water heater. It's made of a plastic layer covered with an ultrathin metal coating that absorbs all incoming sunlight, keeping the panel from heating up. The surface radiates back at a longer wavelength that passes through the earth's atmosphere and escapes into space, cooling the water pumped through it by 5–8°F (3–5°C) below the ambient air temperature. These panels can save electricity by cooling the air conditioner's condenser or by absorbing heat from the occupied space below. And they can occupy parts of a roof that are in shade and thereby work efficiently with rooftop solar panels. Because the plastic materials are commercially available in large quantities, the system has the potential to scale up economically. This and other cooling technologies will surely grow as both the market and temperatures rev up.

Paul Hawken's *Drawdown* lists rooftop solar as offering the tenth largest potential impact of all possible strategies for reducing GHGs in the global atmosphere. Moreover, it means less land is needed for solar arrays, which, along with wind farms, could potentially result in the "conversion of 20% of the planet's remaining natural land."[15] Other studies suggest much less land coverage, especially as PVs and wind machines become more efficient.[16] Onshore wind and solar farms (as opposed to rooftop solar) are respectively #2 and #8 on the *Drawdown* list, which suggests extensive use of these systems and underscores that land consumption will be a major challenge with renewable energy. One promising approach to ground-mounted solar farms is to integrate agriculture with it. Minnesota has been testing pollinator-friendly habitat, including beehives, and fruit and vegetable crops around solar arrays. The National Renewable Energy Lab predicts 3 million acres will be devoted to solar farms by 2030, and 6 million by 2050.[17] If deployed heedlessly the quantities of PV panels needed to prevent CC tipping points could result in "solar sprawl," underscoring the need for urban installations and appropriate public policies. Solar power expert Varun Sivaram warns that absent major innovations in technology, finance models and policy, PVs' current boom will be limited to far below its potential to fight CC and to provide one-third of global electricity demand.[18]

Surface temperature reductions, as well as the monetary savings of cool roofs, can be high and the payback periods very short.

> Industry analyses of these materials have found that the surface temperature of roofing materials can be reduced by as much as 50°F during periods of intense solar gain . . . Cool roofing treatments can be applied to low-sloping roofs for a cost premium that raises the cost of a 1000 square foot roofing project by as little as $100. Balanced against this low initial cost are annual energy savings estimated by the U.S. Environmental Protection Agency (EPA) to be about $0.50 per square foot.[19]

These savings depend to a large extent on how heavy the insulation is below the roofing membrane, but in any case, they can almost be instantaneous. White "cool roofs" cost as little as 3 percent as much per square foot as planted "green roofs," and their rate of return on investment is about 2.5 times greater in terms of energy consumption, storm water retention, health and CC. But they do not detain storm water, which is the biggest return on investment for planted roofs. After crunching numbers in three cities – Washington D.C., Philadelphia and El Paso – one study concluded that investing in "smart surface technologies" could deliver them roughly half a trillion dollars in net financial benefits.[20] A cautionary note about these and other huge savings: As encouraging as the math of these systems is, the "economization and financialization of nature" by market capitalism is ultimately a slippery slope. For instance, the economic value of the planet's healthy ecosystems to humanity has been roughly estimated at $33 trillion.[21] This is an appropriately gargantuan amount, but in the end, is it possible to put a value on the ecological health of the earth?

A negative issue with high albedo roofs and paving emerged in a 2017 Stanford University study of southern California. It found that, while reducing UHIs, the higher UV reflectance can have deleterious effects on ozone and other pollutants.

> Although the other benefits of cool roofs could outweigh small air-quality penalties, UV reflectance standards for cool roofing materials could mitigate these negative consequences. Results of this study motivate the careful consideration of future rooftop and pavement solar reflectance modification policies.[22]

Because cool roofs on most new, non-residential buildings are now required in California, the State is working with the Cool Roof Rating Council to try to ensure that new roofs have the temperature-reducing benefits without adding to pollution. Roofing and paving products will no doubt evolve to address this challenge.

A common misunderstanding is that the solar gain absorbed by dark roofs helps *heat* buildings in cold weather. This is only true if there is little or no roof insulation below the roof surface. With the heavy roof insulation now mandated in most cold climates, the color of the roof membrane or shingles has negligible effect on the heating load and thermal performance of the building in winter. In other words, a dark roof contributes to the urban heat island around the building in the hot season, but does little if anything to help heat the interior of the building in the cold season. (This effect of heavily insulated white roofs in the cooling mode is also negligible.) A *horizontal* roof is exposed to less solar radiation in winter, because both the day is shorter and the sun's angle of incidence is lower. In other words, the roof "sees" less sunshine, further reducing thermal impact on spaces below. And when there is snow cover on the roof, the albedo is increased in any case. The angle and orientation of a *sloped* roof matters more: A south-sloping roof is exposed to more winter insolation, and it reflects some of the incoming radiation back to the sky, adding to CC. The impact of both the roof angle and building's orientation depends on the latitude, and it is easily calculated on solar charts. Not only horizontal and sloped roofs, but also light-colored walls of buildings can help reduce UHIs, as the sun's radiation bounces between buildings, warming the local environment.

Flat urban rooftops should never default to leftover, purposeless spaces. There are at least four options: usable by people; covered with solar thermal and/or photovoltaic collectors; planted to grow edible and ornamental plants and retain storm water; or brightly colored to reflect solar radiation. Often a combination of these functions is desirable. In arid environments, new technology allows a fifth option: nets to catch and extract large amounts of water from dew and fog, as is done in Morocco and planned for Dubai.[23] As a building's fifth façade – often a horizontal one that is always open to the environment – the flat roof should get as much attention as the four vertical sides.

Pavement

Obviously, the infrastructure for motorized vehicles is also a fat target for albedo enhancement. Along with the onslaught of the motorcar in the early twentieth century came paved surfaces (although ironically, it was bicyclists that first protested for street paving in the U.S.). Streets, roads, bridges and parking lots tend to be paved with dark asphalt, which absorbs more solar radiation than vegetation and heats the surrounding air to a higher temperature. Asphalt and other mineral-based materials also hold heat for longer than less dense materials, making for hotter nighttime air and surface temperatures. Paving has another thermal penalty: Because one of its primary purposes, like roofs, is to be impervious to water, less moisture is retained in heavily paved urban areas, which in turn means less cooling of the air by evaporation. "Rainwater – instead of being sucked up by plants, evaporating, or filtering through the ground back to rivers and lakes – (is) forced to slide over pavements and roads into drains, pipes and sewers."[24]

The surface area devoted to vehicles in motion is immense, as are the paved parking areas for vehicles at rest, which is 95 percent of the time.[25] "Parking is the single biggest land use in most cities; there's more land devoted to parking than there is to housing or industry or commerce or offices," says parking guru Donald Shoup.[26] Municipally mandated parking "minimums" have been around since the 1920s in America, and have spread across the country. Recently some cities have heavily reduced or dropped parking requirements altogether, notably London in 2004. And on-street parking is notoriously expensive. London's tallest building, the 98-story "Shard" office building designed by Renzo Piano, has only 48 parking spaces. On the other hand, Apple's new circular space-station-of-a-headquarters in sunny suburban California has 11,000 spaces, some of it in surface lots. Overall, it has slightly more space for parking than the over 3 million square feet of offices and laboratories.[27] Even though the stalls in its parking structures are shaded from the sun, the immense amount of costly land and building devoted exclusively to cars is on the scale of parking at major airports.

Parking can seem a humdrum matter in urban planning.

> Even planners, who thrill to things like zoning and floor-area ratios, find it unglamorous. But parking powerfully influences the way cities work, and how people travel around them. Many cities try to make themselves more appealing by building cycle paths and tram lines or erecting swaggering buildings by famous architects. If they don't also change their parking policies, such efforts amount to little more than window-dressing. There is a one-word answer to why the streets of Los Angeles look so different from those of London, and why neither city resembles Tokyo: parking.[28]

In some cities, the combination of streets and surface parking lots – call it "motorized space" – is a ridiculously high percentage of the land area. In downtown Detroit, this open paved space recently constituted about 60 percent of the land area. These surfaces could be lightened up with white paint, made all the more feasible by recent technical and cost breakthroughs in durable pavement coatings. So-called "cool pavement" not only lowers the temperature of the paved surface and surrounding air, but it also reduces the volume and temperature of storm water run-off, and even improves nighttime visibility in the city.

Los Angeles has been testing a light gray coating on streets.

> Mayor Eric Garcetti has predicted that the city could reduce its so-called UHI effect – caused by dark surfaces, lack of vegetation and discharges from traffic and industry – by three degrees over the next 20 years . . . The City's chief sustainability officer, said test applications . . . had shown a 10-degree reduction in heat gain . . . Weeks later, residents told *The Los Angeles Daily News* that they could already feel the difference.[29]

The gains of course have to be weighed against the GHG emissions in the manufacture and application of the coating. The City now requires that new or replaced roofs for homes and other residential buildings have an SRI of at least 75 percent for flatter roofs and 16 percent for steeper ones. Through a provision in California's building energy efficiency code, cities throughout California have been converting flat, commercial roofs, like those on big-box stores, to light-colored cool roofs when a new roof membrane is needed.[30]

As important as surface reflectivity is, thermal performance is deeper than the skin. To get beneath the outer skin of buildings and pavements, we need to discuss energy balance, heat storage, radiation, convection and

MOTORIZED SPACE

Motorized Space
15,038,961 sq. ft. (499 acres)

60%
of Land

Non-Motorized Space
20,738,166 sq. ft. (298 acres)

36%
of Land

Open Green Space
1,650,994 sq. ft. (37 acres)

4%
of Land

Figure 3.2 In downtown Detroit, Michigan, the streets, surface parking lots and empty sites make for "motorized space" of about 60 percent, well above the American norm, which is estimated by some experts to be roughly 40–50 percent (by the author, University of Michigan Design Charrette, 2007)

Figure 3.3 In cities that have been visited by less decline, the percentage is
         lower, but still surprisingly high. This widely-published photo of
         parking lots in downtown Houston, Texas purportedly embarrassed
         the City into building several public venues and arenas in the area,
         where the pavement shown exceeds 50 percent by an alarming
         margin. De-paving and planting can be an even more effective
         technique. (Alex S. MacLean / Landslides Aerial Photography)

evaporation. Energy balance is about the First Law of Thermodynamics,
which states that energy is never gained or lost. This means that all the
solar energy and anthropogenic heat that is absorbed by surfaces in the
city or countryside has to go somewhere. Either it warms the surrounding air, evaporates or raises the temperature of physical materials, which
store heat. Heat storage is a function of two properties of materials:
thermal conductivity and heat capacity. High conductivity means the
material can quickly absorb heat into its mass, as well as discharge it;
heat capacity measures how much heat can be stored in a given amount
of a material. Together these two parameters are called thermal diffusivity, which can be thought of as thermal stubbornness, i.e., the ability
of a material to soak up and hold heat with a relatively small rise in its
temperature. Many materials commonly used in the built environment
have relatively high thermal diffusivity: concrete, stone, brick and asphalt
can store heat during the day without getting too hot to touch. And they
release it relatively slowly at night – a phenomenon previously referred
to as a thermal flywheel, which slows the movement of heat over time.

Figure 3.4 The reflectivity of roof and pavement surfaces is very sensitive to color, the lighter the better for reducing both UHIs and CC by a factor of up to four. (Heat Island Group, Lawrence Berkeley National Laboratory)

This flywheel effect can be put to good use during heating seasons, with passively heated dark masonry floors and Trombe Walls, which carry the heat of the day into the night and radiate it to occupants.

The SRI, permeability and thermal diffusivity of paving and building materials are important in the energy balance of a place, far different than the soil and vegetation they displace. These three characteristics make cities' surface and air temperatures warmer at night than surrounding rural areas, which have fewer buildings and less pavement, as well as benefit from evaporative cooling provided by more trees. As noted, hot pavement and rooftops can heat storm water runoff: Pavements that are 100°F (38°C) can heat initial rainwater from roughly 70°F (21°C) to over 95°F (35°C). This heated storm water generally becomes runoff, which drains into storm sewers and raises water temperatures as it is released into streams, rivers, ponds and lakes. These hotter waters, with decreased concentrations of dissolved oxygen, affect all aspects of aquatic life, especially their metabolism and reproduction. Rapid thermal changes in aquatic ecosystems resulting from warm runoff can be particularly stressful, even fatal to aquatic life.[31] This is yet another thermal challenge facing cities.

Urbanization has other impacts on local hydrological processes and water quality. Impervious surfaces reduce the rate of infiltration to the underlying soil, thus limiting the storage and cleansing of ground water. While sewers and channelized rivers improve the efficiency of drainage systems, the net effect is to increase flooding by increasing the volume and intensity of runoff. Traditional drainage of storm water was designed to rapidly convey rainwater from where it has fallen to a soaking area, detention pond or watercourse. This old method increases the risks of flooding, environmental damage and water pollution, as runoff usually carries contaminants including oils, heavy metals, pesticides, fertilizers, chemicals and other organic matter. The implementation of sustainable drainage systems (SUDS) is now widely demanded by authorities as a prerequisite for planning approvals, from early site evaluations to design and environmental-impact assessments. In the last decade, American municipalities have been slowing runoff with detention and retention ponds, in a repudiation of the long-standing Army Corps of Engineers efforts to speed up the flow of runoff. Slow is better, especially in cities with combined sanitary and storm water systems (SROs), where heavy storms overwhelm the sewerage treatment plants, and unsanitary sewerage is discharged into streams, rivers and lakes.

Last, there is the thermal impact and resilience of other parts of the physical infrastructure. Transportation planners and engineers can also design or retrofit roads, bridges and other structures to heat up less and to be less affected by extreme heat. This is especially helpful in lessening electrical power outages during heat waves. Generally, concrete is a better infrastructure material than steel. Although there is more embodied energy in concrete, which is produced in one of the most energy-intensive manufacturing processes, it incorporates materials that are more heat-tolerant and resilient. Concrete helps physical infrastructure withstand higher temperatures and reduce service disruptions.

In summary, there are three basic strategies to cool urban surfaces: green, white and solar. Green includes living roofs and walls, as well as greening parking lots, plazas and other paved surfaces; white includes painting and otherwise brightening vertical and horizontal surfaces, especially roofs; and solar is installing solar electric and solar thermal panels on roofs and above outdoor urban spaces, such as parking lots. Obviously, which strategy or combination of strategies is most sensible and cost-effective depends on local conditions, such as the micro-climate, economy, building practices, codes, etc. There is no clear preference among the three options, and professional judgment is needed. Nonetheless more general and geographically focused research is needed to analyze and compare these strategies.

Ventilating Urban Canyons

This strategy applies to the three-dimensional configuration of cities, especially the confinement of outdoor space by buildings. The issue is the entrapment of heat in "urban canyons." The shape, color, height, positioning and orientation of buildings, and the pattern and width of streets, determine the degree to which both hot air and radiant heat are trapped and concentrated. Because heat radiates from surfaces evenly in all directions, some of the heat emitted by a horizontal surface like a street or parking lot is lost to the sky. Some of the radiated heat is absorbed by the walls of adjacent buildings. Buildings facing each other – especially ones that are in direct sunlight for a significant part of the day – absorb heat and reradiate it to each other. The darker the surfaces exposed to direct solar radiation, the hotter they get, and more heat builds up because less radiant heat is lost to the sky. And if the buildings are made of heavy mass, such as stone, brick, asphalt and concrete, they carry more of the day's UHI into the evening and night. The buildings also curtail air movement, especially when streets are narrow and buildings are tall. It's a recipe for hotter, unhealthier, cost-lier UHIs. In the state of Florida, for instance, UHIs cause an estimated $400 million in additional air conditioning costs.[32]

The geometry of street networks and buildings makes a surprisingly big difference in how heat builds up, as a 2018 MIT study shows. Cities, such as New York and Chicago, are precisely laid out on a rectilinear grid, like the atoms in a crystal, while others such as Boston or London are arranged more organically, like the disordered atoms in a liquid. The researchers found that the crystalline-like cities had a greater build-up of heat than did the more chaotically configured ones. The study of 47 cities in the

U.S. and other countries used mathematical models that led to a relatively simple formula to describe how urban design influences UHIs. Using city maps and algorithms developed to determine the temperature difference between a city and its surrounding countryside, they found that the cities differed by a factor of 1 to 1.8. Because building façades in a gridded city face each other orthogonally, the heat build-up can be considerably greater than in irregular street patterns. Accordingly, rectilinear grids are less appropriate in hot climates, although they can provide welcome winter warmth in cold climates. These dramatic findings suggest that more geometrically irregular networks of streets, as well as lighter-colored building skins, are increasingly appropriate in warm climates getting warmer.

Cities sometimes have a characteristic hue given by the buildings. Those largely built of brick, like London and Boston, tend to darker shades of browns, reds and yellows, depending on the local clay color. Many European cities with stucco façades traditionally have a yellowish or pinkish palette, depending on whether there were brass or copper additives. Some cities have more blatant colors due to deliberate choices: Caribbean buildings often have bright, saturated shades of primary colors; Catania in Sicily is black, courtesy of the volcanic rock used to build many of its buildings; and an area of Rabat in Morocco is blue due to the belief that the color wards off mosquitos. In the Indian state of Rajasthan, Jodhpur is known as the blue city, Jaisalmer is known for its golden palette, and Jaipur for its pink buildings. Greek towns on Aegean islands have white walls to reflect the bright sunlight, as do the walls of Tel Aviv and the roofs of Bermuda. The regional distinctions enrich the world with their individuality, but darker-colored walls will need to be lightened as cities grow unhealthily hot. The lighter the hue and the lower its saturation, the more appropriate it is for cooling cities.

The more dramatic changes in temperature occur below roof levels, where access to sunlight is restricted, wind is slowed and diverted, and radiant energy is continuously exchanged between buildings. The spatial variety in the urban landscape creates a myriad of micro-climates associated with the relative placement of buildings, other superstructures, streets, parks, etc. Urbanites are exposed to a great variety of indoor and outdoor urban climates. This urban zone of intense human occupation is where buildings are heated and cooled, as well as where emissions of waste heat and pollution from traffic are concentrated. It's where most of the energy is consumed, literally where the rubber meets the road. Indeed, "meeting urban energy demand accounts for up to three-quarters of CO_2 emissions from global energy use and thus represents a significant driver of global climate change."[33] CC and UHIs meet and mingle in this bottom layer of the city in ways that are not conducive to sustainable human habitat.

Deep urban canyons curtail air movement more than low-rise buildings in suburbs.

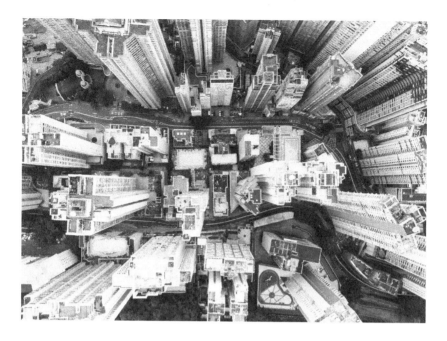

Figure 3.5 Very dense cities like Hong Kong have tightly packed tall buildings that both trap radiant heat and hamper natural airflows that cool both interior and exterior spaces. Lighter-colored surfaces tend to bounce the heat out of deep canyons, like the ones in this photo. And matte exterior finishes diffuse light to reduce the visual glare. (Marc Dalmulder @mdalmuld via Flickr)

Buildings in urban and suburban areas act as windbreaks, slowing wind speeds by up to 60%. However, in some instances wind speeds can increase around the bases of high-rise buildings. Winds can be funneled down the sides of buildings to the street under certain conditions. Heat Islands have also been found to create their own breezes. Hot air tends to rise above the city, drawing cooler air in from the surroundings. Two coastal cities – Houston, Texas, and Tokyo, Japan – have been found to pull cool air in from the sea as they heat up during the day.[34]

Despite these exceptions, urban canyons typically create hotter, more stagnant conditions. They are less of a problem in hot arid areas, because unlike humid air, still air is more comfortable than when it is moving. And, unlike waste heat from emissions and dark albedo, urban canyons don't contribute much to CC, although brightening vertical surfaces does reflect more solar radiation back through the atmosphere into outer space.

A quantitative study has been done on the impact of covering building walls and roofs with vegetation in urban canyons. Not surprisingly, the wider the canyon the lower the thermal penalty, i.e., the temperature

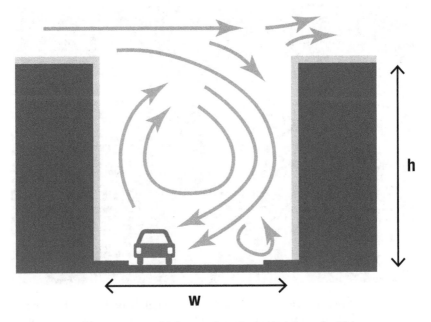

Figure 3.6 Urban canyons, which are a function of height and width, entrap radiant heat and slow cooling winds. If wider and lined with lighter-colored surfaces and/or vertical plantings, the canyons are cooler. And lighter-colored and planted roofs also cool air and surface temperatures in the vicinity. (Drawing by author)

increase was smaller. For all nine climates studied, green walls inside the canyon had more impact than green roofs. However, at the scale of the whole city, green roofs had the greater cooling effect. The combination of green walls and green roofs was better yet. "If applied to the whole city scale, they could mitigate raised urban temperatures, and, especially in hot climates, bring temperatures down to more 'human-friendly' levels and achieve energy savings . . . of 32% to 100%."[35] The benefits can be dramatic, especially in hot, arid cities like Riyadh, Saudi Arabia, where daytime temperatures inside street canyons are cut on average about 18°F (10°C).

Even in hot, humid Hong Kong, temperatures can drop by up to 16°F (8°C). Orientation and wind direction are not as important a factor as the amount and geometry of the vegetation, with sunny surfaces benefitting the most from vegetation.[36] Tall and wall-like slab buildings (Figure 3.4) in the high-rise clusters block the incoming wind and sea breezes, increasing UHI temperatures. Over the past ten years, the number of very hot days, with highs greater than 94°F (33°C) and very hot nights with highs above 84°F (28°C) has increased. The mean wind speeds have decreased, intensifying discomfort, sleeplessness, heat stress and related health problems, and increasing energy consumption.[37]

It is worth noting again that green roofs and walls are considerably more expensive to install and maintain than light-colored roofs and walls. White membrane roofing is easily installed, maintained and repaired; it is now cost-competitive with bitumen or tar roofs, which remain widely used because they are inexpensive. And white roofs can be three times more effective at countering climate change than green roofs.[38] They also lend themselves to being more readily drained into cisterns, with runoff to be recycled as gray water to flush toilets and/or irrigate plants, or to be filtered into potable water. Compared to black roofs,

> white roofs provide a 50-year net savings of $25/m² ($2.40/ft²) and green roofs have a negative net savings of $71/m² ($6.60/ft²). Despite lasting at least twice as long as white or black roofs, green roofs cannot overcome their installation cost premium. However, (the) annual difference is sufficiently small that the choice between a white and green roof should be based on preferences of the building owner.[39]

Those who want to fight CC and UHIs should select white roofs, while those more concerned with local ecology and landscape design might choose a green roof. In any case, dark-colored roofs should be quickly phased out in warm and temperate climates.

Particulate air pollution – emitted by diesel cars and trucks, coal-fired power plants, factories, rudimentary cook stoves and the burning of forests – is a related problem that affects urban temperatures, in two opposing ways. First, air-borne particles block radiation during the day, reflecting radiation from both the sun and the earth. The unhealthy pall of smog that blankets many cities and regions, particularly in the developing world, temporarily cools the planet. An international team of scientists has quantified that cooling effect, calculating that the earth would be 0.9–2.0°F (0.5–1.1°C) warmer if that pollution were to suddenly disappear. In this case, pollution is actually slowing down global warming.[40] Second, the particulate smog also absorbs solar radiation, raising the air temperature and increasing the amount of energy the particles radiate to the city below. And the deeper the street canyon, the more concentrated the particulates are. Beijing, famously plagued by particulate air pollution, is considering a radical strategy to address its urban heat canyons and dirty and hot air: tearing down existing high-rise buildings to encourage more natural ventilation at the urban scale. The plan is to restore urban breezes and winds that have been slowly choked by the construction of tall buildings, which extend to the horizon in cities like Beijing. Just as they have always been concerned with natural light, architects and urban designers need to consider the geometry of natural ventilation at the urban scale. They need to more fully consider the breadth, height and placement of buildings in order to absorb less heat and to stifle less air movement in dense cities.

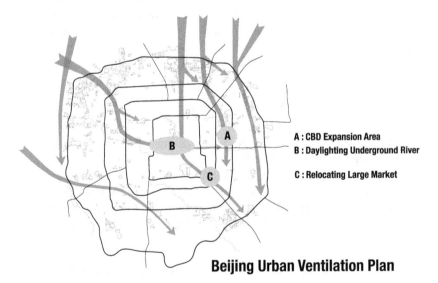

A : CBD Expansion Area
B : Daylighting Underground River
C : Relocating Large Market

Beijing Urban Ventilation Plan

Figure 3.7 Beijing is considering tearing down tall buildings to open up wind corridors to better flush out polluted air, a policy that will also reduce the build-up of stagnant heat in street canyons. It is already controlling building height and density, while strategically placing parks or lakes instead of buildings along key pathways. The location, spatial packing and the height of new clusters of high-rise buildings need rethinking in all large, dense cities. (Drawing by author, based on City of Beijing chart)

According to several recent studies, changing weather patterns linked to CC have diminished the wind across northern stretches of China, "exacerbating a wave of severe pollution that has been blamed for millions of premature deaths. Wind usually helps blow away smog, but changes in weather patterns in recent decades have left many of China's most populous cities poorly ventilated."[41] With all the more reason to improve the location and the massing of buildings to increase wind speed and duration, polluted cities like Beijing are clearing their air of pollution, thereby mitigating UHIs and CC as a co-benefit. Other global cities may need to consider such strategies, such as heavily-polluted New Delhi. It is reassuring to know that fighting air pollution usually fights CC, but as noted, ventilating urban canyons is a UHI antidote that offers little help in this larger war.

University of California, Berkeley Professor Harrison Fraker has written about the importance of poetics in resilient, sustainable urban design. He emphasizes the latent aesthetic potential of the "urban section" – the slice through the vertical fronts of buildings and the horizontal streets, plazas, sidewalks, parks and rooftops. Indeed, the canyon can be turned from adversity to advantage with designs that have wider streets and shorter structures. This includes not only lightening the surfaces to reflect more heat out of the canyon, but also greening them with plant materials on both horizontal and vertical surfaces for shade and evapotranspiration. Codes can require a minimum albedo for all surfaces, a minimum percentage of living surfaces, and a minimum shading coefficient on ground-level surfaces. On the other hand, the more elusive poetic dimension of architecture and urban design is beyond the prescriptive scope of codes, even the power of words per se. Fraker's research has demonstrated the potential environmental advantages of the urban section. However, he argues that the enriched sensory experience has greater impact and meaning for the urban public. Designing the sensorial experience requires the ineffable touch and imagination of talented designers and planners.

Notes

1 *The Atlantic*, January–February, 2012
2 Roger Colton, "Evaluating glare from roof-mounted PV arrays," *Solar Pro*, March–April, 2015
3 Brian Stone, *The City and the Coming Climate*, Cambridge University Press, 2012, p. 107
4 Laurie Winkless, "The rise of the urban rooftop," *Forbes*, 8/10/18
5 James Bartolacci, "Why white roofs are better than green roofs for fighting climate change," *Architizer*, 3/28/17
6 Sproule et al., "Economic comparison of white, green, and black flat roofs in the United States," *Energy and Buildings*, 71, March, 2014, pp. 20–27
7 Brad Plumer, "Really big ideas to beat the heat," *The New York Times*, 8/9/18

8 "Chilling prospects: providing sustainable cooling for all," www.SEforALL. org, 2018

9 Fred Pearce, "Urban heat: can white roofs help cool world's warming cities?" *Yale Environment 360*, 3/8/18

10 Amara Holstein, "Parking as canvas: Q&A with Eran Ben-Joseph, author of ReThinking a Lot," *Build a Better Burb*, 8/16/17

11 *Cool Cities, Good Practice Guide*, C40 Cities Climate Leadership Group, February, 2016

12 Valery Masson, et al., "Solar panels reduce both global warming and urban heat island," *Frontiers in Environmental Science*, 6/4/14, https://doi.org/10.3389/fenvs.2014.00014

13 Fred Pearce, "Urban heat: can white roofs help cool world's warming cities?"

14 Prachi Patel, "New cooling method literally sends heat out of this world," *Anthropocene*, 9/7/17

15 Justin Adams, "Opinion: renewables are taking off, but we still have to plan them sustainably," *Devex Newswire*, 7/10/17

16 Dan Smith, "Solar collectors covering 0.3 percent of the Sahara could power all of Europe," *Science*, 6/22/09

17 Frank Jossi, "Putting the 'farm' back in solar farms: study to test ag potential at PV sites," *MidWest Energy News*, 1/22/18

18 Amy Harder, "A few big things with solar expert Varun Sivaram," *Axios*, 3/5/18

19 J. Raven et al., "Urban planning and urban design," in C. Rosenzweig et al. (eds), *Climate Change and Cities: Second Assessment Report of the Urban Climate Change Research Network*, Cambridge University Press, 2018, p. 154

20 Rachel Dovey, "Here's how much money green design could save cities," *Next City*, 2/14/18

21 Johannes Foufopoulos, Professor of Natural Resources, speaker at Science Cafe, Ann Arbor, MI, 2/21/18

22 Scott A. Epstein et al., "Air-quality implications of widespread adoption of cool roofs on ozone and particulate matter in southern California," *PNAS*, 7/5/17

23 Adela Suliman, "Five ways to make parched cities cooler," *place*, 3/20/18

24 Sophie Knight, "What would an entirely flood-proof city look like?" *The Guardian*, 9/25/17

25 "How not to create traffic jams, pollution and sprawl," *The Economist*, 4/8/17

26 Stan Paul, "UCLA parking guru releases follow-up to groundbreaking book," *UCLA News Room*, 4/17/18

27 Ibid.

28 "Sacred spaces," *The Economist*, April 8–14, 2017

29 Mike McPhate. "California today: a plan to cool down L.A.," *The New York Times*, 7/7/17

30 Aimee Cunningham, "Overwhelmed: heat waves are on the rise, putting city dwellers in danger," *Science News*, 4/3/18

31 "Heat Island Impacts," *Environmental Topics*, website of the U.S. Environmental Protection Agency, April, 2017

32 David L. Chandler, "Urban heat island effects depend on a city's layout," *MIT News*, 2/22/18

33 J. Raven et al., "Urban planning and urban design," p. 148

34 Lisa Gartland, *Heat Islands*, Earthscan, 2008, p. 21

35 E. Alexandri and P. Jones, "Temperature decreases in an urban canyon due to green walls and green roofs in diverse climates," *Building and Environment*, April, 2008, pp. 480–493

36 Ibid.
37 J. Raven et al., "Urban planning and urban design," p. 158
38 Lawrence Berkeley Laboratories report, January, 2014
39 Sproule et al., "Economic comparison of white, green, and black flat roofs in the United States"
40 Richard Shiffman, "How air pollution has put a brake on global warming," *Yale Environment 360*, 3/8/18
41 "Climate change may be intensifying China's smog crisis," *The New York Times*, 3/24/17

4   Waste Heat

The third major cause of UHIs has very different science than CC, and is a local rather than a global phenomenon. It has less to do with the color and morphology of the city, and more about its systems of transportation and of heating and cooling buildings. Efficiency is paramount, as suggested in the famous sayings of one of the greatest architects of the twentieth century and of one of the fast-emerging "starchitects" of the twenty-first century. Mies van der Rohe's immortal words were "Less is more." Bjarke Ingels has followed on with "more with less." Both phrases conjure up frugality, in this case of waste heat from vehicles and from heating, ventilating and air-conditioning equipment.

Reducing Waste Heat

In many ways, the history of life and civilization is the history of *fire*. Every warm-blooded animal leaves the earth a tiny bit warmer, by converting food into energy. Humans convert fuel into work, with heat as a byproduct. We have gotten ever more efficient at burning fuel, especially hydrocarbons, but the amount of combustion has increased with the size and progress of civilization. And when we converted from steam to internal combustion engines, the contained explosions provided more power to accomplish more work, all the while dissipating *waste heat* into the air. Waste heat is not a product of inefficient or incomplete combustion, but rather it is the combusted gases themselves that are exhausted into the environment. Urbanized areas are associated with this form of heat – from motorized vehicles, heated buildings, power plants, air conditioners and industrial processes. Waste heat in a city is the sum of anthropogenic heat dumped from these sources into its air shed. In the nineteenth century, waste heat was thought to be more organic: the bodies of humans and animals were considered to be a major factor in making cities warmer than the countryside, but now we know the major contributor is heat from burning fossil fuels. Waste energy increases linearly with energy use. It is simple arithmetic to see why CC and UHIs have intensified in cities. A study has shown that in "some U.S. cities, waste heat from energy consumption has been estimated to account for one-third of the UHI effect."[1] It can be the equivalent of a large fraction of the incoming solar gain, which is a vast amount of energy. An extreme example: "Tokyo's overall daily energy (use) . . . is equal to about 40% of the incoming solar energy in summer and 100% of the winter solar energy."[2]

Transportation Strategies

Objects in motion are more typically associated with the expenditure of energy than objects at rest, namely buildings and infrastructure. Recently surpassing power plants, transportation now accounts for a third of GHG emissions in the U.S., where stricter federal mileage standards have often been offset by longer and more frequent auto trips. The transport of goods and people is bedeviled by the internal combustion engine, which has so overtaken our culture. The waste heat from these guzzlers of gasoline must be significantly cut. The combustion of hydrocarbon fuels in motor vehicles in America creates more waste heat than either power plants or industry. Compact, walkable, bike-able, transit-oriented urbanism, plus cleaner vehicles to deliver goods to and within cities, is the most effective way to reduce this major cause of UHIs.

   In a 2010 report to Congress, the Department of Transportation concluded that land-use strategies relying on compact, walkable, TODs could reduce U.S. GHG emissions by 28–84 million metric tons of carbon dioxide equivalent (CO_2E) by the year 2030. Benefits would grow over time to possibly double that amount annually in 2050.[3] The primary reduction is from decreasing total VMT. "Developing parcels for lower-income households in *location-efficient* areas is likely to lead to higher reductions in VMT than developing those parcels for higher-income populations . . . because they live more compactly in location-efficient areas – allowing each parcel to yield more VMT reduction."[4] More recent analysis indicates that living in TOD locations reduces average household vehicle travel 37 percent for high-income households and 50 percent for extremely low-income households, and reduces car ownership rates at least 30 percent, with particularly large reductions by extremely low-income households. A walkable and transit-rich neighborhood allows households to annually save $5,000 or more compared to automobile-dependent sprawl. Studies emphasize the importance of providing affordable housing in TODs in order to maximize social equity, including improved economic opportunity and affordability.[5] Less auto-dependence, coupled with smaller dwellings in walkable settings, once again prove to be strong crowbars in the CC toolbox.

   The growing chorus arguing for greater emphasis on *accessibility* – essentially travel time – as opposed to *mobility* – essentially travel speed – is directly germane to this strategy. Transportation engineers, originally at the behest of New Urbanists, have finally, made this long overdue paradigm shift, perhaps with their tail between their legs. They now care about reducing travel times by increasing network connectivity, rather than speed. Connectivity is a function of how fine or coarse the street and road network is, with the more intersections the better. As the number of blocks increase, the choice of routes rises dramatically: Portland, OR has 37 times more routes than in an equivalent area in Ithaca, NY, and 3,300 times as many as in the same acreage in Irvine, CA![6] Urban planners have embraced finer grids, which not only have greater vehicle accessibility, but also are better for walking and biking. Traffic engineers have tended to jettison their erstwhile practice of automatically adding more vehicular lanes to arterials, which tends to induce more travel demand in a spiraling escalation of VMT. And over-sized, free parking for vehicles at rest also induces trips, adding "waste land" to the "waste heat" exhausted by the vehicles in motion.

Conventional suburban development (CSD) in America does not compare well to compact, walkable, mixed-use and transit-oriented neighborhoods, which reduce travel distances, miles driven and fuel burned. A large study prepared by the National Renewable Energy Laboratory and Cambridge Systematics in 2013, notes that residents of compact, walkable neighborhoods drive about 20–40 percent fewer miles on average than residents of less-dense neighborhoods. Other studies have found a doubling of residential densities in American cities is associated with up to a 30 percent reduction in VMT.[7] And rural residents sometimes pile up even more miles per year than suburbanites. (There are unanswered questions about whether urban residents rack up more miles from air travel, especially wealthy people that tend more and more to live in central cities.) Driving is not the whole story: daily diets, such as eating fast food with high red meat content at drive-in restaurants; buying a bigger house because it's possible to "drive until you qualify" for a bigger mortgage; and filling the bigger house and often a rental storage unit with ever more possessions.

To reduce waste heat from vehicles, Americans need to better connect land use and transportation. VMT per capita is much higher than in other developed countries. The endless smear of sprawl across the landscape sponsors endless automobile trips, in some cases every trip a household takes. Movements like New Urbanism and Smart Growth have worked hard to promote less auto-dependent settlement patterns and lifestyles. There has been significant progress, especially as young adults have rejected the suburban lifestyles of their parents in favor of urban living. They have opted for shared vehicles and bicycles in their embrace of urbanity. And if and when young families might elect to move to a less urban lifestyle, they now tend to move to older suburbs that are often on a streetcar or rail line and have a traditional Main Street, as opposed to cul-de-sac sprawl. Unfortunately, there's not enough good cities and suburban towns to go around. So, suburbs continue to be built in the U.S., albeit at a moderately slower rate.

Suburban "grayfield" malls, as opposed to "greenfield" developments on open land or "brownfield" redevelopments on contaminated sites, are more frequently being transformed into walkable urban centers that add housing, offices and institutional uses to the usual retail mix. Retrofitting and densifying curvy, cul-de-sac subdivisions will be a much bigger challenge, as this vast wall-to-wall carpet of infrastructure, lawns and buildings represents immense sunk costs. For the Atlanta region to have the density of Key West, a relatively dense, low-rise city of about 5,000 people per square mile, it would need a population of 40 million. To equal New Orleans' dense Garden District would require a metro population of about 74 million. The Atlanta region has just under 6 million people today.[8] Many people, including planners and designers, underestimate just how sprawling American metro areas are.

All of CSD must be re-imagined, not only with grayfield redevelopment and subdivision densification, but also with much denser apartment/condo complexes with less parking, accessory dwelling units (ADUs), more local retail and narrower streets for smaller vehicles. TODs with net densities of 40–60 units/acre can be inserted into sprawl in locations that can be served by rubber-tire or steel-wheel public transit. In more remote areas, complexes of half those densities can be served by driverless, or automated vehicles (AVs), and TaaS or MaaS ("Mobility as a Service" and "Transport as a Service," sometimes called the "New Mobility"). On the other hand, "Retrofitting TODs can carry land and building costs penalties that make the prescription too expensive, and awkward configurations for climate adaptive housing to convert enough of our 130 million (U.S.) units to make a difference."[9] It is true that retrofitting sprawl with TODs is more difficult than building them anew, which is why TODs are especially compelling in the fast-developing new cities, primarily in Asia, Africa and South America.

California has adopted ambitious plans to address CC, plans which also diminish waste heat from tailpipes.

> By 2030, residents will have to travel by foot four times more frequently than they did in 2012, alongside a nine-fold increase in bicycling over the same time, and a substantial boost in bus and rail ridership . . . Getting people out of their cars in favor of walking, cycling or riding mass transit will require the development of new, closely packed housing near jobs and commercial centers at a rate not seen in the United States since at least before World War II.[10]

Walking, biking and transit must not be just available, but delightful and safe. California also wants to cut traffic emissions by replacing gasoline-powered vehicles with electric vehicles (EVs), with Volkswagen's plan to invest $44 million in an electric car sharing program in Sacramento.[11] And they're planning for a significant percentage of Californians to forego or give up automobiles altogether. In that case, more people will want to live near where they work and shop, which means adding more housing in existing neighborhoods, and new residential development of various types in malls and office parks. And the State's recent plans to require rooftop solar collectors on all new single-family houses will cut waste heat from power plants.

Bicycling

Urban biking is booming worldwide.

> NYC expects to have 1800 miles of bike lanes by 2030. In one year, between March 2016 and March 2017, rides increased by 110% there, as well as 70% in Chicago and 66% in Columbus, Ohio; and cities as diverse as Delhi, Moscow and San Francisco are expanding their bike-lane systems.[12]

Bike-share systems are blooming worldwide, with soaring numbers that are quickly out of date. In 2016, there were well over 1,000 cities with systems, up from 68 in 2007 and four at the turn of the century. By the end of 2017 the Chinese dockless bike-share company Ofo claimed to operate 10 million bikes worldwide; its rival Mobike says it had deployed 7.5 million bikes in China and elsewhere. Together they asserted responsibility for 60 million bike rides every day, and Ofo's operations boss thinks China alone could support 300 million rides a day![13] As bike-sharing hits the mainstream, many cities are devoting more of their street space to cycling, as well as to a broader pool of users. Portland, Oregon, has a bike-share program for people with disabilities, including hand-cycles, trikes and tandems, and Detroit plans to institute a similar program.[14]

Bike-sharing is not new. Amsterdam anarchists started a free bike system in the 1960s, but they were either stolen or impounded by the police because a 1928 statute required all bikes have locks. Bike theft plagued other early systems, until Paris's large Velib system succeeded in 2007.[15] Still, some of the Dutch still want to make bikes freer – creating a system in which bikes are not owned by people, or cities, or by companies, but by everybody as part of the public realm. Well-used systems would pay for their own maintenance and purchase new bikes. Blockchains could create and monitor self-managing fleets of bikes. Theft would be technically impossible, although there would be a loss of access to purloined bikes. On a related front in Brooklyn, NY, a network of more than 1,200 new electric vehicle charging stations was built with a blockchain.

Bike-share systems originally depended on a dense network of docking stations, which is relatively capital- and labor-intensive, especially shifting bikes from over-used to under-used locations. This makes planning their locations a critical municipal task, as shared bikes become an important component of public transit. Bikes are particularly good at solving the problem of the "last mile," i.e., the final travel leg between a transit stop and one's ultimate destination. Shared bikes are now typically equipped with a special locking mechanism on the back wheel, meaning users can more or less pick them up and leave them wherever they like. The lock is operated by a cell phone, as is the rental payment.

> There are now more than 16 million shared bicycles on the road in China's traffic-clogged cities, thanks to a fierce battle for market share among 70-plus companies backed by a total of more than $1 billion in financing. These start-ups have reshaped the urban landscape, putting bikes equipped with GPS and digital locks on almost every street corner in a way that Silicon Valley can only dream of . . . In Shanghai, where officials have struggled to maintain order, there is now one shared bike for every 16 people, according to government statistics.[16]

The problem is that the bikes, not infrequently damaged, are strewn like detritus across the urban landscape. This large-scale litter angers local residents and results in mountainous dump piles.

Hangzhou, China reputedly has the world's largest bike-share system. The country's dockless bike-sharing boom came after it

> experimented with various public/hybrids, searching for a balance that would make bike-sharing cheap enough to attract users but profitable enough to cover costs . . . Copenhagen-based AirDonkey, essentially an app-based sharing platform . . . allows bike owners (including, notably, bike shops) to rent out their cycles to others . . . Bike-share systems have proliferated wildly in recent years – Africa just launched its first, in Marrakech.[17]

While reducing waste heat, these proliferating bikes are saving energy and space while moving people and cargo more efficiently and pleasantly than their four-wheel motorized competition.

Bicycling is too rich and promising a subject not to delve into further. It was once considered a morally hazardous temptation for children and women to stray many miles from home,[18] yet Susan B. Anthony said "cycling did more to emancipate women than anything else in the world."[19] We must remember that both Henry Ford and the Wright Brothers started out as bicycle mechanics, before going on to start the two industries that have done so very much to increase our mobility and carbon footprints. Bikes have come a long way technically, but the basic design and componentry of bikes has been strikingly persistent for

Figure 4.1 The many purposes and pleasures of cycles and cycling, from the simple elegance of the classic road bike to the utility of cargo bikes, commuter bikes and the fun of shared cycles. The number, types and uses of human-powered cycles seem to be forever increasing. The bicycle has become the most popular mode of personal transport in the world, and estimates of the number of bikes in use around the globe run upward of 2 billion. (Photos by author)

a century. They are classic objects of technological simplicity and beauty, verging on perfection after so many design refinements. And now there are shared bikes, mountain bikes, cargo bikes, electric bikes, jitney bikes, family bikes, party bikes, camping bikes, vendor bikes, trikes and even drones that are ridden like a bike.

Cycling systems and culture have matured to an exciting level this century. Not only bike-share systems of various sorts have proliferated, but also bike lanes, racks, parking structures, memorial bikes and even bicycle public art. Community bike clubs are not new, but they are burgeoning, along with political advocacy groups. In Bhutan, where they have replaced the GDP metric with GNH – Gross National Happiness – a favorite mantra of cycling boosters goes: "You can't buy happiness – but you can buy a bike, and that's pretty close."[20] As long ago as 1896, Arthur Conan Doyle, the idiosyncratic author of the many Sherlock Holmes novels, voiced the same sentiment: "when the day appears dark, when work becomes monotonous, when hope hardly seems worth having, just mount a bicycle and go out for a spin down the road, without the thought of anything but the ride you are taking."[21]

Bicycle use is everywhere expanding, especially in Europe. The Netherlands and Denmark lead the way, with Germany, Italy, Switzerland and the U.K. not far behind. Amsterdam, a city of 800,000 people has 880,000 bikes, which is four times the number of cars. Some 40 percent of its trips were taken by bike in 2009, when Copenhagen took 37 percent.[22] Copenhagen aims to see half its daily work force commute by bike, and is already over 40 percent. Like Amsterdam there are more bikes than people, and 400 km of dedicated cycle lanes. Remarkably, "99% of the population of Denmark consider themselves experienced cyclists."[23] In the country's 50 most populous cities and towns, the average mileage of on-street bicycle lanes doubled between 2007 and 2016, while the number of physically separated bike lanes across the country more than tripled and is still growing.[24] Commuting by bike in the U.S. is highest in Portland, followed by Washington D.C. The rapid spread of on-street bike lanes is literally paving the way to greater bike usage. The benefit of commuting by bike is a function of the avoided car costs ($0.61/mile as of 2017), the cost of biking ($0.08/mile) and avoided congestion costs ($0.63/mile). The average daily distance for cyclists of all ages is estimated to be 19 miles for 220 working days per year or 180 school days per year for students.[25]

University researchers in the U.S. have dissected data from the American Time Use Survey, which studies what activities people do in a day, how long they do them for, whom they do them with, and where they do them. Travel is one such activity, which is further broken down by mode and trip purpose. Two-thirds of respondents in a study said they enjoy biking and walking, and most people said they wished they traveled more by these modes. The happiest mode of travel appears to be bicycling. Even after excluding those who bike purely for recreational purposes, bicyclists are in a significantly more positive mood than other travelers such as bus riders or walkers. Given that biking is healthy, eco-friendly, inexpensive and enjoyable, it makes sense to consider measures, like more bike lanes, to encourage more riding and safer riding.[26]

Some people maintain a fear of biking on roads and streets, particularly busy urban streets, and the danger of injury or death must be weighed against the positive health outcomes of biking on a regular basis. The numbers indicate this is more an apparent danger than a real one. For instance, even though most bike-share users do not wear a bike helmet, astonishingly over 23 million rides were taken on shared bikes between 2007 and 2014 without a single reported fatality.[27] The first death was not reported until 2017 in New York City. A British study took a comprehensive look at the health benefits of bicycle commuting, and the results were staggering. During the study, the 263,450 subjects who were under review had a 41 percent lower chance of death than those who didn't.

> Cycle commuters had a 52% lower risk of dying from heart disease and a 40% lower risk of dying from cancer. They also had 46% lower risk of developing heart disease and a 45% lower risk of developing cancer at all.[28]

To realize this dramatic improvement, we need to double down on making biking fast, easy and safe, while aggressively promoting the value of active transportation.

A personal anecdote: As I researched and wrote this book, I was on sabbatical leave in Cambridge, England, a university city of some 125,000 residents, about the same size as my university hometown of Ann Arbor, Michigan. Cambridge is a beehive of bikers, which dominate travel in and around its historic center, almost completely displacing motorized vehicles in many areas. Some central streets are limited to cyclists and pedestrians, with few if any vehicles allowed. Almost every street has marked bike lanes, some of which are separate, dedicated bikeways. Crosswalks, sidewalks and bridges have traffic signs and sometimes separate traffic signals for cyclists. The sidewalks are often marked to separate bikes from pedestrians, which is less successful on the crowded thoroughfares and tight medieval streets. Public bike racks abound, plus private ones, which are often covered. And there are nearby national routes for biking and walking that crisscross Britain, many with dedicated, paved bike paths. As a result of all these bike routes and amenities, as well as frequent, bike-friendly transit and intercity rail and bus service, many residents of the city do not own cars. In the meantime, Ann Arbor is getting more and more bike-friendly, but is maybe one-quarter of the way to Cambridge's cycling culture.

The Shared-Use Mobility Center, a not-for-profit organization focused on bringing together the public sector, private industry and local communities around cleaner, leaner transportation in the U.S., has recently set a goal to take 1 million cars off the road in the U.S. over the next five years by scaling up shared mobility and public transit. They claim it would happen if the public just did the following: 7% became transit commuters; 3% bike-share users; 6% became car-share members; and 7% started using carpools, van pools or car-splitting. Together these changes would annually reduce 5 million gallons of fuel use, 6 million tons of GHG emissions and $5 billion dollars in household transportation expenditures.[29]

As you can see, the economic impact of biking is surprisingly strong.

> Europe's cycling industry now employs more people than mining and quarrying, and almost twice as many as the steel industry . . . Some 655,000 people work in the cycling economy – which includes bicycle production, tourism, retail, infrastructure and service. If cycling's 3% share of journeys across Europe were doubled, the numbers employed could grow to over one million by 2020.[30]

In 2012 bicycle sales in the EU outpaced new automobile sales in almost all of the 27 countries (partially because of a slump in car sales). In the poorer eastern EU countries, bike sales were reputed to be five to ten times automobile sales.

> Given the convenience, health benefits, and affordability of bicycles, they could provide a far greater proportion of urban passenger transportation . . . a world with a dramatic increase in cycling could save society $24 trillion cumulatively between 2015 and 2050, and cut CO_2 emissions from urban passenger transport by nearly 11% in 2050.[31]

These last estimates are impossible to substantiate, but they illustrate just how big a role bikes can play in combatting CC and UHIs. And that role will only increase as the number of cold days is diminished, ironically thanks to CC. Yet another study sees "economic gains of $900 million annually for cycling alone and $20.7 billion per year for outdoor recreation more broadly by 2060."[32] Biking has big numbers.

Walking

As good as cycling is, *walking* is the most basic and dependable way to move through space. It's not quite as energy efficient as biking, but both are a tiny fraction of what automobiles and even rail burn per passenger-mile. The bipedal human is extremely well designed to walk, aided by the big toe, which allows it to easily push forward at a pace of 3–4 miles per hour. It is arguably the healthiest, least expensive and most agile and pleasant mode of moving through space. And if the urban network and infrastructure are well designed, it's no doubt the safest mode. The physical health benefits are legion: as aerobic exercise, walking improves circulation, shores up bones, strengthens muscles, helps with weight loss, improves breathing, enhances sleep, helps prevent blood clots, strokes and heart disease. There are also psychological benefits, such as improving mood, slowing mental decline, even lowering the risk of Alzheimer's disease.

For these reasons, walking has been shown to lead to a longer life. From several studies done on the physical benefits of walking:

> Simply walking . . . is, as one former head of the Centers for Disease Control and Prevention put it, "the closest thing we have to a wonder drug." That's not hyperbole: The European Society of Cardiology found a 20-or-so-minute-per-day walk added an average of seven years of life. According to the CDC, more than one out of 10 premature deaths in the U.S. can be pinned squarely on a lack of physical activity, along with more than one-tenth of health care spending. Walking leads to a 14% lower risk of breast cancer for women, an American Cancer Society study reported. A Harvard study found that brisk walking or equivalent exercise cut stroke risk in half. Adding in walking three days a week sharply boosted cognitive performance in older adults, a study in the journal *Nature* reported.[33]

The largest ever study of the link between city walkability and blood pressure looked at around 430,000 people aged between 38 and 73 and living in 22 British cities. It found significant associations between the increased walkability of a neighborhood, lower blood pressure and reduced hypertension risk. The findings remained consistent even after adjusting for socio-demographic lifestyle and physical environment variables, and concluded that public health must consider the intangible benefits of good urban planning and design.[34]

It takes four ingredients to get and keep an average person to walk, all of them essential:

- a compact, dense built environment;
- a rich, convenient mix of uses, with destinations to which people need or want to go;
- a network of small blocks with wide sidewalks lined by trees and buildings, safe from crime and vehicular traffic;
- a transit system to allow pedestrians to move around the whole metropolis and beyond, while entailing the walk that comes at both ends of every transit ride.

If there was a fifth ingredient, it would be the *dog*, as walking this household pet seems to provide universal daily exercise for both master and pet. One sees an endless parade of dogs pulling their masters along. The canine connection is an overlooked boon to walking in cities, which lack the private yards for dogs to move about on their own. Of course, there's an environmental downside: If the world's dogs and cats formed a separate country, their fluffy nation would rank fifth in global meat consumption, and produce as much GHGs per year as 13.6 million cars. And if all their feces were collected, it would be the equivalent of 90 million humans.[35] Pets are no small part of the human carbon footprint.

And good sidewalks are an essential urban ingredient. Although almost every American city surrendered its soul to the automobile in some way, the extent and quality of decent sidewalks varies widely. According to *Streetsblog*, it depends on whether your city was growing at a time when paying for sidewalks was in vogue, rather than an auto-centric time when sidewalks were treated as second-class infrastructure. Boston's handsome historic sidewalks are ubiquitous, while Nashville is trying to fill in the gaps of a sidewalk network that covers less than a third of the sprawling city.[36] Sidewalk maintenance and snow-removal also vary. Dangerous walking conditions tend to disadvantage women, whose trips often are shorter and better suited to walking. However, many streets are not designed to easily get around on foot, especially with children.[37] As part of a "gender-balanced" policy in Sweden, snow-covered walkways are cleared of snow before roads, reflecting the fact that women walk more than men.[38]

Globally, people walk more miles than they drive. The worldwide average exceeds VMT per year – about 1,200 miles driving vs. about 1,500 miles walking.[39] Which nationalities walk the most? The largest ever study of human movement is a 2017 Stanford University report on the number of daily steps taken by 700,000 people worldwide.

The average number of daily steps worldwide, they said, was 4,961. But that number varied widely from country to country. In top-place Hong Kong, which also ranks at the top in transit, survey participants took an average of 6,880 steps a day. In Indonesia, the average was just 3,513, putting it at the bottom of the rankings . . . The United States clocks in at about 4,774 steps a day, a bit below the worldwide average . . . Unsurprisingly, walkability also played a role. In pedestrian-friendly locations where it's easy to get lots of places on foot . . . people walked more.[40]

It is no coincidence that Hong Kong was long the densest city in the world, a title which it now shares with Mumbai and Hanoi. Interestingly, the report showed that places where the amount of walking was unequal, women's inactivity was more prevalent, with a corresponding increase in obesity.

Feeding Americans' increasing demand for walkable neighborhoods is Walk Score, an online service that gives every U.S. address a score of the exact walking distance to destinations that residents typically want or need to be. It's a quick and convenient way to see how far it is to supermarkets, restaurants, drug stores, hardware stores, hospitals, schools, libraries, etc. – a score that figures prominently in real estate sales literature and the portfolios of Wall Street real estate investment trusts. A single point in Walk Score adds an average of $3,000 in value to a home, according to a nationwide study that included more than a million home sales. The added value depends on the local market, with dramatic differences: an increase from 60 to 80 in Phoenix adds $16,000, while the same increase in San Francisco results in an increase of $188,000.[41] That is a powerful premium and more proof that homebuyers value walkable neighborhoods. The score is largely a measure of the density of economic activity, which has a high correlation with walkability, especially in older, pre-automobile cities and towns. It's abundantly clear that people want to walk more and in fact are doing so.

Driverless/Autonomous Vehicles

Before closing the focus on transportation, the ongoing media blitz on driverless AVs and connected, autonomous vehicles (CAVs) warrants more commentary. In a nutshell, it could be a heaven or hell scenario: the emerging technology could radically lessen VMT and space devoted to vehicles, along with the urban carbon footprint and waste heat. Or they could make these factors much worse. Such indirect effects of driverless cars could either slash energy consumption from driving by 60 percent, or increase it by 200 percent, according to a 2016 study by the U.S. National Renewable Energy Laboratory.[42] If the AVs are *personal* vehicles, there will likely be many more cars in motion, including empty ones congesting the streets and consuming more energy while they run errands, pick up children or simply circle the block to avoid parking charges while its passenger pops into a shop. Because some 80 percent of the variable costs of driving – gas, mileage-related wear and tear, maintenance – are in the value of the driver's time, AV travelers on long trips will reclaim part of that value by web surfing, working or sleeping.[43] This reduced cost will likely increase travel. Indeed, most studies predict increased VMT.[44]

The convenience of AVs could result in up to 35 percent more miles for personal AVs and a discouraging 90 percent more for non-shared AV taxis, according to a 2014 study by the International Transit Forum and the Corporate Partnership Board. This increase arises from riders acquiring a greater tolerance for long commutes.[45] There will be driverless vehicles with one young child aboard, as well as "deadhead" trips – vehicles without passengers looking for riders and cheap parking or running errands. *If there's anything worse than a single-occupancy vehicle (S) OV), it's a zero-occupancy vehicle (ZOV).* They are sure to be commonplace in the nightmarish scenario of higher congestion and more VMT. And it's safe to assume that the giant automobile and oil companies, as they quietly give lip service to reducing mileage, will tacitly support and quietly push ZOVs and greater VMT, as they both bring higher car and gasoline sales. The suburban road to hell may once again be paved with good intentions, with deadhead trips replacing dead-end cul-de-sacs as the Achilles heel.

On the other hand, if the vehicles are *shared*, AVs promise to save energy, VMT and urban space. And they could save money: A network of driverless Automated Rapid Transit (ART), with dedicated lanes on many arterials are much less costly, as well as faster than conventional buses. For instance, "the 50,000 minibuses and 150,000 taxis in Mexico City could be better deployed as part of a system that encouraged ridesharing and on-demand re-routing."[46] Fewer vehicles in motion or at rest will free up right-of-way (r.o.w.) for bikes and pedestrians, parking vehicles and even infill development. ART includes driverless bus rapid transit (BRT), smaller buses, jitneys and shared taxis in dedicated travel lanes that connect transit hubs. (The ultimate system would be vehicles that are connected, autonomous, shared, electric – CASE). It's even more promising if smaller, shared, short-haul AVs or other low-energy modes were available at these hubs for "the last mile." This combination of ART on longer, fixed routes with dedicated lanes and shared taxis providing "mobility on demand" for shorter trips could cut street congestion, VMT and the need for more advanced AVs, with their technological problems with mixed traffic, high speeds and thorny legal issues. The combination could also radically reduce space needed for parking.

The city of Los Angeles is building a dozen mobility hubs near light rail stations where people can access a variety of choices from EV car sharing to bike sharing to buses. The project goes well beyond transportation: shady places to sit, games for people to play while they wait, USB ports, real-time travel information, a place to get a cold drink. Mobility hubs bolster the opportunity for neighborhood hubs. The city is considering streets that can flex over the course of a day and month. In the morning, a street can serve mobility needs while it converts to a park in the afternoon and a plaza in the evening. The largest cost of closing a street is the work to manually erect barricades and detour signs. If these tasks are automated and the costs decrease, communities can reclaim under-used streets for other uses. Only a few technological components are necessary: changeable infrastructure that can easily convert a street, the technology to communicate to drivers and vehicles that the street is closed, and algorithms to create appropriate detours.[47]

AVs and CAVS often include cameras, sonar, radar, LiDAR, a GPS navigation system, a computer and support structures. The added weight, electricity demand and aerodynamic drag in autonomous vehicles are not insignificant contributors to energy use and GHGs. However, when savings from the driving efficiencies associated with self-driving vehicles – smoother traffic flows with tight platooning of vehicles on streets and roads – are factored into the equation, the net result is a reduction in lifetime energy use and associated GHG emissions of up to 10 percent. The weight of the onboard computers, which is likely to come down over time, is a key factor. Another finding in the University of Michigan study was that electric AVs have lifetime GHG emissions that are 40 percent lower than vehicles powered by internal combustion engines.[48]

Autonomous trucks and smaller cargo vans are already proving beneficial in goods delivery, which is dramatically up with online retail sales with home delivery. If this exponential growth continues, it will have two physical impacts: First, retail space in cities and suburbs will become vacant, with attendant blighting tendencies, and second, warehouse space will surge. "Citi[bank] estimates that 2.3Bsf of new warehousing – equivalent to about 20,000 football pitches (over 50,000 acres) – will be needed worldwide over the next 20 years."[49] Where might this space be found and what form might it take? Because it's difficult to convert street-oriented urban retail that has been vacated, the warehousing could occupy dying suburban malls. However, the abandoned malls tend to be too remotely located for easy delivery by the Amazons and Alibabas of the world. So, the warehouses will tend to be near central business districts, and will tend to get taller, as many already are in Asia. And some of the vacant urban retail shops will likely become showrooms for the e-commerce giants.

In the preferred AV/ART scenario, vehicle ownership will decline. Some studies estimate that the average U.S. household will drop from 2.1 to 1.2 vehicles.[50] Some experts are predicting autonomous buses on dedicated lanes or roads in the U.S. by 2019. These smaller, more frequent buses eliminate the cost of the driver, which is 50–80 percent of operational costs.[51] Two northern European cities are forging ahead with ART. Oslo has announced it plans to ban private vehicles from the city center by 2019. Helsinki plans to make private car ownership obsolete by 2025, with publicly owned MaaS or TaaS. A homegrown app turns the act of getting around a city – by bus, train, bike, taxi or borrowed car – into a monthly subscription. Trip planning, ride hailing and car sharing, alongside seamless booking, ticketing and payment, can be done for both public and private modes of transit.

A common argument in favor of AVs and CAV is improved safety. As of the date of this writing, there have been only two AV fatalities, with one pedestrian death. Google is working on a safer, fully autonomous car with no steering wheel, which they claim will be available as early as

2018–2020.[52] According to the University of Michigan Transportation Institute, up to 8 million car crashes and 44,000 deaths could be prevented if the federal government mandated connected vehicle technology in 2019.[53]

There are hidden costs, practical and even existential ones. If the advent of AVs results in the need for far fewer cars and trucks, there could be a massive loss of jobs in the vertical, multi-pronged industry that designs, manufactures, sells, repairs, fuels, houses and insures vehicles. Questions abound: Might the ease of mobility-on-demand reduce the use of transit, perhaps dramatically? Will sprawl be exacerbated, with an even greater sense of placelessness brought on by ZOVs? Will we adopt lifestyles that are even less physically active, with the attendant health problems? And there are ethical dilemmas: Should the automated "driver" favor the lives of passengers or pedestrians when it sees a collision ahead? The list of issues goes on. However, as New Urbanist author Ellen Dunham-Jones and others point out, AVs also have the potential to dramatically improve urban livability by making streets narrower, safer and quieter, allowing more space for sidewalks, bike lanes and pedestrian-friendly uses to be built on the expected surplus of surface parking lots.[54]

There are major, direct and indirect impacts of AV/ART and MaaS/TaaS on land use and the design and development of the built environment. If we want more *shared* use of AVs, we need to create livable, walkable communities where car trips are relatively short and can be easily shared among individuals who live and work relatively close to each other and on the same general route. Far more curb space will be needed for ride-hailing and ride-sharing services to drop off and pick up passengers. Think airport arrival and departure areas. As curb access becomes more in demand, it will make sense to charge for it, as the San Francisco Airport already does. Re-purposing obsolete parking areas to compact, mixed-use, walkable redevelopment will become commonplace. Depending on which AV scenario plays out, it could lower the size and the cost of housing by increasing or decreasing the number of required parking spaces, especially carports and garages. And if people work in their cars more, the modality shift could also lessen the use of and need for home office space. These two factors could diminish the size of land parcels, and densify the center of towns and cities.

If greenfield and underdeveloped metro areas continue to be paved with both good intentions and asphalt, at least there will be less asphalt. Extrapolating Professor Dunham-Jones point, the narrower streets that AVs require would allow conversion of some of the existing road to bike lanes, wider sidewalks and shade trees. Cities and urban districts built or rebuilt from scratch can be more compact, with less pavement for the parking as well as the movement of vehicles. With the decreasing need for retail space, as e-commerce and fast home delivery undermines brick-and-mortar stores, there may be mobile retail units visiting neighborhoods to allow customers to see, touch and test products. Suburban big-box stores, which entirely depend on vehicular access, may be the first to implode, whereas walkable retail is less threatened. As some transportation experts state, cities need to understand that *they* own the operating environments for new transportation technologies – the streets. Because this physical network is controlled by cities, the public sector has tremendous leverage to make sure that new technologies serve community goals as well as individual desires and private interests. For this reason, cities should definitely not relinquish control of their public circulatory networks to private companies that seek it. Indeed, coordinated AV and CAV systems require proactive planning, rather than a default to the car-oriented systems inherited from the past.

Fewer and smaller surface parking lots is an urban issue that should not be trivialized. Todd Litman, a transportation economist who studies the effects of subsidies for parking and roads at the vaunted Victoria Transport Policy Institute in British Columbia, estimates that the annualized cost of land, construction, maintenance and operations per parking space in the U.S. comes to $600. Since there are about four parking spaces per vehicle in America, the cost per car is $2,400 each year. But too much parking is "free," as Americans only spend about $85 annually on parking per vehicle. This means the annual parking subsidy per vehicle is more than $2,300, which exceeds what most Americans spend on fuel for a vehicle.[55]

On the negative side, a devastating outcome could be increasing the radius of sprawl. If driverless cars *induce* additional travel, they add to congestion and fuel consumption. They could also increase the area suitable for low-cost, single-family development and the attractiveness of "drive-until-you-qualify" mortgages. If commuters are free to work, socialize or otherwise spend little if any time driving, the mental cost of commuting would be lower. A less-taxing commute would mean that people could live farther away, in homes and neighborhoods perhaps more to their liking or their budget. "This effect could spark a renewed round of exurban development."[56] Imagine tightly-packed platoons of AVs speeding in from distant exurbs with sleeping commuters in the morning, and evening ones with cocktail drinking and board games or Nintendo-playing, à la the bar cars on commuter trains. If the AVs were ARTs, they might spur corridors of compact, walkable energy-efficient towns, like Philadelphia's posh Main Line to London's greenbelt suburbs to Mumbai's overcrowded northern areas.

Another negative, indirect question is the possibility of social control. As cities institute congestion pricing, subsidize ride hailing in poor and under-served areas, or impose taxes on Uber, Lyft and other such mobility services, they can also slip into subtle and questionable forms of social engineering. They could become means of social manipulation in the hands of authoritarian governments. For instance, fleet operators, who know a great deal about the movements of their riders, could provide incriminating information in a police state. There is the risk that some more dangerous and poor areas will not be served by robotaxis, opening the door to more discrimination, segregation and danger. Authoritarian regimes could outright restrict people's movements, a classic right that is political at its core. AVs may represent a seismic shift in transportation equal to the advent of the automobile, which offered so much freedom but held unforeseen social and physical impacts. They must be seen and judged through a socio-environmental as well as technical lens.

Another question outstanding is how AVs are likely to change transit.

> On the one hand, this new technology could be a boon for transit as it helps solve transit's perennial first and last mile hurdle. Lyft, Uber or other personal and group rideshare services can get people to the train, light rail, or bus station, increasing catchment areas and boosting ridership. On the other hand, some riders may simply decide to stay in that vehicle all the way to their destination – especially as the price of the trip drops dramatically as technology replaces the highest cost of the trip – the drivers. Preliminary reports from New York and San Francisco (where ride-sharing is high) point to this trend . . . Some studies have shown a decrease of up to 43% of transit ridership – potentially the death knell of transit as we know it. A survey by researchers at the University of California at Davis suggests ride-share lures people away from mass transit. Because ride-share taxis have cost Chicago $40 million in fares, parking fees and other revenues, the City has been slowly raising its tax on these services.[57]

One expert says ride-hailing services have already cut into public transit in 31 out of 35 large American cities, with a 5 percent drop over two years because of this and other reasons.[58] The fact that more and more American urbanites don't own a car or don't have access to one complicates this equation: almost 55 percent of New York City residents fit this category, as do a third in Boston and Washington D.C.[59]

In addition to the concern about an overall drop in transit ridership, there is the possibility of AVs atomizing transit. What happens when multiple rider/route services such as Via, Chariot, Lyft-line and Uber Pool grow, and there are ten-passenger vans zipping through cities, delivering people directly to where they want to go and not to a bus stop a few blocks or a few miles away. If this happens, the benefits associated with transit proximity and TOD will diminish, and the traditional real estate mantra of "Location, Location, Location" will become close to obsolete.[60] If mobility becomes that much easier and more affordable, the friction of physical movement – one of the factors that creates the value of location – will decrease. This doesn't necessarily mean that current nodes of activity and commerce will decline in value, but the role of proximity may give way to the role of the quality and buzz, as well as to the convenience and comfort of the roundtrip.

Unequal accessibility in large urban areas is becoming more pronounced as congestion increases. Taken to the extreme: With the world's largest fleet of helicopters, a reported 1,300 helicopter flights lift off daily in São Paulo, ferrying the ultra-wealthy around this city of 12 million people for $1,000 per flight. Picture their aircraft gliding above traffic jams that stretch over 100 miles.[61] In 2017

> Uber announced plans to unleash its newest mobility disruption: UberAir, a long-promised "flying taxi" service that would lift-off in the Southern California metro by 2020. By then, the company claims, passengers will be able to book trips on electric vertical takeoff and landing (e-VTOL) aircraft through the Uber app, at roughly the fare of an UberX ride, the company's cheapest private car option . . . A promotional video indicates that they'd depart from "skyports" atop strategically located high-rise buildings.[62]

How it could be so inexpensive is a hanging question in this matter, although autonomous passenger drones without pilots could cut the cost considerably. Several companies are testing multiple-rotor models that carry up to four passengers, but face formidable technical, legal and pricing challenges.

Electric Vehicles

These too are worthy of more detail. How effective will they be in combatting CC and UHIs? There are several advantages of EVs over internal combustion vehicles that are significant: quieter, easier to manufacture and maintain (due to fewer components and moving parts), higher-torque performance and lower emissions. There are disadvantages: shorter driving range, required recharge time (which is seeing breakthroughs), limited size, battery replacement, lack of charging stations and, currently, price. The most consequential factor for CC and UHIs, including waste heat, is their emissions.

> Existing electric cars reduce carbon emissions by 54% compared with petrol-powered ones, according to America's National Resources Defense Council. That figure will rise as electric cars become more efficient and grid-generation becomes greener. Local air pollution will fall, too . . . One study found that car emissions kill 53,000 Americans each year, against 34,000 who die in traffic accidents.[63]

These environmental and health benefits are enormous, when you consider there are now about 1B cars on the road, almost all powered by fossil fuels. Though most of them sit idle, America's car and truck engines can produce ten times as much energy as its power stations. The internal combustion engine is the mightiest motor in history.[64]

While charging car batteries from central power stations is more efficient than burning fuel in separate engines, the net benefit depends on the source of electricity. If the power source for recharging is clean – generated by hydro, solar or wind – electric vehicles are a very big improvement over conventional, fossil-fueled vehicles. It's clear that an electric vehicle in a place like Norway, which produces energy almost entirely from renewable sources of power, is cleaner than one in China, which is still heavily dependent on coal. If the electricity to power EVs is generated by power plants that run on fossil fuel, it's a minimal improvement; if it's a coal-fired power plant, they are barely better and can even be worse in terms of both CC and UHIs. Some 1 million electric vehicles in China produce more CO_2 than some fuel-efficient gasoline-powered cars. However, as power grids all over the world become greener, the benefits of EVs become potentially gigantic. Their competitive advantage is cleverly illustrated by how much more efficient gasoline vehicles would have to be to perform more efficiently than electric cars. In Michigan, a gas vehicle would need to get 38 mpg to beat electric cars, while in upstate New York it would have to do better than 191 mpg. Because power generation is typically dirty in Africa, China and India, internal combustion vehicles would only need to get 29–52 mpg to have equivalent emissions; in 26 countries with clean power like Brazil and Iceland, between 100 and 1,000 mpg would be required; and up to 5,000 mpg in hydropower-rich Albania, Paraguay and Nepal![65] The internal combustion engine has had a notoriously long, good run, but its end is in sight, speeded up by a lengthening list of countries mandating that all new cars must be zero-emission by 2050 or sooner.

France and Britain plan to end the sale of gasoline- and diesel-powered cars by 2040. Norway aims to do it by 2025. It

> offers generous incentives that make electric cars cheaper to buy, and provides additional benefits once the vehicles are on the road . . . About 52% of the new cars sold in the country last year (2017) ran on new forms of fuel . . . while carmakers like Volvo have moved to phase out the internal combustion engine entirely.[66]

The Chinese government is aiming to sell 2 million EVs in 2020, offering incentives as well as restrictions on the purchase of gasoline-powered vehicles.[67] A Morgan Stanley report suggests 30 percent of some 28 million expected new vehicle sales in India could be electric powered by 2030.[68] If electric cars are the future, so are electric buses, which are fast becoming commonplace. In Shenzhen, China – arguably the fastest growing city in history, having gone from less than 100,000 to 12 million in about 40 years – 100 percent of its almost 15,000 buses were electric by the end of 2017, in a country where they are selling "like hot cakes."[69] And mayors from a dozen major cities around the world – including London, Los Angeles and Mexico City – have signed the Fossil-Fuel-Free Streets Declaration, which pledges they'll purchase only electric buses by 2025. The agreement, with more cities expected to sign on, calls for

> a future where walking, cycling and shared transport is how the majority of citizens move around our cities. The long-term goal, agreed to by the C40 Cities, is to ensure that substantial areas of each city are emission-free by 2030 and to collectively combat CC.[70]

Reducing waste heat in the transportation sector is clearly a very effective strategy to reduce UHIs, as well as CC. Reducing tailpipe and chimney heat can be achieved by both low- and high-tech techniques, with the most effective antidote being the "negatrip" – simply staying where you are, followed by walking and biking rather than driving, or working at home more, as contemporary jobs and live–work dwellings make easy. Indeed, the idea of leaving home to go to work is a modern idea; people generally labored at or around the home and its gardens or workshop before the Industrial Revolution gave birth to commuting to large factories and later to office buildings. A new study in the journal *Joule* suggests that the spread of technologies enabling Americans to spend more time working remotely, shopping online – and watching Netflix and chilling – has a side benefit of reducing energy use.[71]

It would be remiss not to mention a final transport mode: *drones*. These self-propelled, unmanned aerial vehicles (UAVs) are agile, little aircraft that have captured many an imagination, not to mention the attention of many entrepreneurs. U.S. futurist Thomas Frey argues that there will be 1 billion in the world by 2030. "They can also roll on the ground, they can stick to the side of a building, float in the river, dive under water . . . they can climb a tree and attach themselves like a parasite to the side of a plane."[72] Uses vary; one is providing medical services to remote, poor communities in developing countries. For example, Vayu, a start-up based near my hometown in Michigan, sells drones that carry up to five pounds of medicine deep into the jungle or mountains, and return with test samples – all automatically, with nothing more than local natives pushing a button. Amazon and other retail companies are on the verge of delivering packages by drone. The potential list of applications is very long.

Drones have potentially momentous implications for our cities and towns, even our countryside, as land delivery vehicles can be reduced in number and frequency of use. Their potential impact on urban congestion and VMT could be substantial. Here are numbers presented by McKinsey & Company: One-third more commercial vehicles were in use in 2014, compared to 2006; Related urban congestion costs in the U.S. are expected to be up 20 percent between 2015 and 2020; E-commerce is estimated to increase by 85 percent during the same time period. Their report goes on to promise signal improvement in these numbers through several changes in the standard delivery mode: night deliveries from urban consolidation centers, load-pooling and EV delivery vans. The expected drop in tailpipe emissions is 30 percent (up to 100 percent with EVs) and 25–55 percent in costs per parcel.[73] "Stay tuned" is the operative message.

How do strategies to cut energy usage, emissions and waste heat in the *transportation* sector compare those proposed in the *building* sector? Which sector is more cost-effective?

> The energy content of the gasoline used by a typical office commuter each year is comparable to the energy used by his or her share of the building where he or she works . . . So in fact, getting someone out of a car and onto a bike is equivalent to going net-zero (in the building), which costs a hell of a lot more than a bike rack and a shower. In fact, it appears to be the single most important energy and fossil fuel saving measure we can do.[74]

As we will see next, some engineers would disagree, arguing that building insulation is the lowest-hanging fruit in the world of energy conservation.

Architectural Strategies

Cities are chock-full of buildings, all kinds and all sizes, created in almost infinite combinations that result in the rich panoply of architecture and urbanism. Their design is about *form*, which is a subjective quality difficult to quantify in numbers or even describe in words. Their design is also about performance, which is much easier to quantify. In terms of energy performance, the built environment consumes more energy than transportation does. If industrial buildings are included, the U.S. building sector approaches half of the national energy pie, and contributes almost half of the GHG emissions, while accounting for about three-quarters of electricity consumption.[75] While intensifying global CC, all the combustion associated with this energy use churns out a great deal of local waste heat. Some combinations of form and performance work well together to slash energy use and environmental deficits, while other architectural combinations are environmental train wrecks, with two or three times the ecological footprint per square foot. There is no substitute for good, responsible architects and urban designers.

The ubiquitous glass skyscraper can be a deep energy sink, taking a great deal of energy to heat and cool. These sealed glass towers

> around the world will become a liability over the next twenty or thirty years' time if climate modelling predictions and energy price rises come to pass as expected . . . [there's] the perfect storm of the skyscraper boom in China, where huge high-rise, all-glass metropolises expand at an exponential rate . . . [with] increasing reliance on air conditioners."[76]

Oddly, glass buildings are proliferating even as cities set ambitious goals to deal with climate change. One Bostonian architect says that "glass, like sugar, has negative consequences when used in excess. My perspective is that we're overdosing on glass."[77] And skyscrapers are getting taller and more numerous. The number of them that are over 650 feet (200 meters) tall has tripled since the year 2000, according to a study by the New Jersey Institute of Technology.[78] There are other examples of why contemporary architecture is on a collision course with CC and UHIs, too many for this book to present.

AC is one of the world's most overlooked technologies and industries. It is commonplace in the United States.

> By 2014, 87% of U.S. homes had some form of air conditioning . . . We consume more energy for residential air conditioning than all other countries combined, although, with other countries such as China and India in pursuit of glass-walled visions of modernity, that is going to change, and not in a good way.[79]

The technology of air conditioning, which is such a growing slice of the global energy pie, is worth a historical note. Willis Carrier's first device in 1902 was meant to dehumidify to keep tobacco, wallpaper and textiles from getting moldy. Most systems still work off his original designs, which require a combo of compressor-driven chilling, ventilation, filtration and dehumidification. Residential AC is only 70 years old.[80] Thus AC started at roughly the same time as automobiles, and both have had a huge impact on where and how people live and work.

Unlike cars, though, air conditioners have drawn little criticism for their emissions, waste heat, energy inefficiency and social impact. Improving AC is arguably the single most effective way to reduce GHG emissions. For instance, replacing refrigerants that damage the atmosphere would reduce total greenhouse gases by 90B tonnes of CO_2E by 2050. Making the units more energy-efficient could double that. By contrast, if half the world's population were to give up meat, it would save 66B tonnes of CO_2E. Replanting 2/3rds of degraded tropical forests would save 61B tonnes. A one-third increase in global bicycle journeys would save just 2.3B tonnes.[81]

Hot Saudi Arabia will be using more energy on AC than it exported as oil in 2018. On hot days in its capital Riyadh, AC already utilizes 70 percent of the city's peak electricity demand.[82] At the rate AC is spreading in developing countries, it's crystal clear that more effective ways to stay cool without consuming so much electricity are needed.

It's clear that global demand for space cooling and the energy needed to provide it will continue to grow for several decades. Of the 2.8 billion people living in the hottest parts of the planet, only 8 percent currently possess ACs, compared to 90 percent ownership in the U.S. and Japan. In all major markets, people are typically buying air conditioners whose average efficiencies are less than half of what is available. The IEA developed several scenarios to assess the implications of current trends for air conditioning in buildings and the potential benefits of improvements in energy efficiency. In a reference scenario for 2050 based on current policies and market trends, CO_2 emissions almost double from 2016 and the share of air conditioning in power sector emissions worldwide rises from 8 percent to 15 percent. Avoiding this troubling outcome is possible if AC and chillers are much more energy efficient and power production shifts away from fossil fuels.[83]

AC use is rapidly growing in warm or tropical countries with large populations. In India, there are

> more than three times as many cooling degree days per person than in the United States. (A cooling degree day is [when] the average temperature is over 65[°F for 24 hours].) . . . It is important to note that this future trend is not forecast to occur because the world will be warmer – though it will be – but rather, because it will be richer.[84]

Whatever the reason, the numbers are mind-numbing: "[I]f the second, fourth, and fifth most populous nations – India, Indonesia and Brazil, all hot and humid – were to use as much energy per capita for air-conditioning as does the U.S., it would require 100 percent of those countries' electricity supplies, plus all of the electricity generated by Mexico, the U.K., Italy, and the entire continent of Africa."[85] The cost of such an exorbitant investment would be disastrous to their economies, not to mention CC. Even in the wealthy U.S., where peak demand is increasing, to avoid brownouts, "utilities will need to spend between $70 billion and $180 billion in grid upgrades."[86]

Figure 4.2 Air conditioners are ever-increasing in number as developing
countries become hotter and more able to afford them. A
University of California, Berkeley study claims: "The growth in
air conditioning has been staggering. China is the sweet spot. The
number of households that have it has doubled in five years. Every
year, 60 million more units are being sold there, eight times as
many as are sold annually in the United States."[1] (Matthew Klein)

1 Catherine Hausman, "Climate change is projected to have severe impacts on the
frequency and intensity of peak electricity demand in the United States," Michigan
News in *The University Record*, 2/7/17

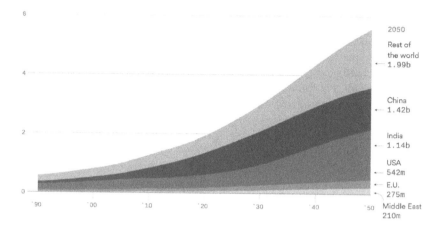

Air conditioners, 1990-2050

Billions of units

2050

Rest of
the world
← 1.99b

China
← 1.42b

India
← 1.14b

USA
←- 542m

E.U.
←- 275m

Middle East
210m

Figure 4.3 The global number of air conditioners may triple between 2018 and
2050, with the bulk being outside the U.S. and the EU, especially
in China and India. There are only a handful of cities in Africa,
the Arabian Peninsula, India, Southeast Asia and Central America
that don't need air conditioning.[1] (Reproduced from IEA, Future of
Cooling report; Chart: Axios Visuals)

1 Antonio Voce, "Which cities are liveable without air conditioning – and for how much
longer?" *The Guardian*, 8/14/18

Figure 4.4 Cities that are considered to need AC to be comfortably livable.
(Image redrawn by author, data from Nolan Gray, Antonio Voce
based on *The Guardian Cities*)

It's easy to overlook just how big the differential is between the richest and the poorest countries. In Southeast Asian countries like Cambodia, statistics show that households in Myanmar and Bangladesh recently consumed less electricity in a year than a typical U.S. refrigerator! Seen through the broadest socio-political lens, this differential seems almost criminal. Americans have become more habituated to high energy usage than they realize. A typical home has slowly become overrun with electric and electronic equipment. My research suggests that the typical home would need an average of 14 cyclists pedaling 24/7 to generate enough electrical power. And because of generation and transmission losses, 44 full-time cyclists would be needed at the regional power plant![87] This is precisely why we're addicted to fossil fuels. One cup of oil produces as much energy as 16 cyclists. "[I]f oil didn't exist, we would have to invent it. No other substance comes close to oil when it comes to energy density, ease of handling and flexibility."[88] It will be difficult to wean ourselves of this power-packed gift from the literal bowels of the earth.

Air conditioning may not be as exciting or trendy a technology as wind and solar, but as already flagged, it's a major CC and UHI issue worldwide. It really matters, because cooling has a direct relationship with the building of coal-fired power plants to meet cities' mushrooming peak demand.

If more air-conditioners are humming in more homes and offices, then more capacity will be required to meet the demand. So, 1.6 billion new air-conditioners by 2050 means thousands of new power plants will have to come on line to support them. A Lawrence Berkeley National Laboratory study argues that even a 30% improvement in efficiency could avoid the peak load equivalent of about 1,500 power plants by 2030 . . . The countries driving the bulk of demand for air-conditioning – China, Brazil, India, and Indonesia – have energy efficiency improvement policies like labels and incentive programs. Improvements to China's policies could have sweeping gains, because it is the primary exporter of air conditioners (and other electric appliances) to countries primarily in Southeast Asia, where demand is growing. India's Ministry of Power is working to develop a program for bulk purchases of superefficient air-conditioners, which may include refrigerant alternatives to HFCs . . . Many believe India will outpace China, which grew from 5 percent market penetration in the mid-1990s to more than 140% today, meaning millions of families have more than one air conditioner.[89]

The efficiency of air conditioners, heat pumps and refrigerators has improved over the years, but a major hurdle remains. Even after the Montreal Protocol reformed their ozone threat, AC units continue to exhaust HFCs, a potent if short-lived GHG. The refrigerant chemicals still used in air conditioners and refrigerators can have a global warming potential thousands of times greater than CO_2. In a deal struck in 2016, the world agreed to phase out those chemicals over the next 30 years, avoiding about 90 gigatons of CO_2E. This solution has the greatest total potential for carbon reduction. New research

indicates that adding improved efficiency in refrigeration and phasing out fluorinated gases used for cooling, as mandated by international agreement, could eliminate a full degree C of warming by 2100. Given that the "business as usual" trajectory leads to 4 to 5°C of warming, that is shaving off a pretty big slice.[90]

In fact, "refrigerant management" is the biggest and lowest-hanging fruit that can be picked, according to Paul Hawken's 2017 book, *Drawdown: The Most Comprehensive Plan Ever Proposed to Reverse Global Warming.*[91] *The book describes 80 strategies to reverse CC in terms of their potential to reduce and absorb carbon emissions. Its metric is gigatons, and the total global potential for carbon reduction and removal is the equivalent to the weight of the water in 400,000 Olympic-sized swimming pools.*

A building's *physical size* is very consequential, not only in terms of energy to heat, light and cool it, but also the energy that goes into its materials and erection – all of which produce waste heat. As mentioned, 5 percent of world energy goes into producing cement for concrete, half of it poured in China.[92] Reducing the size of buildings, especially bloated American homes, will reduce waste heat from furnaces and air conditioners.

According to the US Census' most recent study of new housing, which concluded with the year 2015, homes on average continue to grow in square footage, though families simultaneously continue to get smaller. Nationally, the average square footage for a single-family home was about 2500sf in 2015, compared with about 1600sf in 1980.[93]

European homes are typically about half that size. Accordingly, the migration to smaller dwelling units in cities by younger and older Americans is on the promising side of this ledger. U.S. offices and labs also have more floor area per occupant, sometimes extravagantly so. A science lab that achieves a high energy rating – LEED Gold, for instance – but has two or three times as much space per worker compared to, say, India is an embarrassing irony.

There is good architectural news as well. As CC and UHIs have made energy efficiency more and more important, there has been a steady reduction in waste heat, due to the popularity and spread of higher performance buildings.

Without energy productivity improvements, America's energy needs would have tripled since 1970, according to a report by the Bipartisan Policy Center. Actual growth was only one-fifth of that. Energy efficiency has emerged as the largest and cheapest antidote to burning fossil fuels to generate electricity.[94]

There are many reasons for this improving trend, chief among them being the Architecture 2030 initiative, founded by Ed Mazria, a fellow passive solar pioneer from the 1970s. It has a host of voluntary and mandatory codes and regulations, and importantly, it promotes the rise in public consciousness of CC and other environmental challenges. According to Mazria, energy usage and GHG emissions from the building sector have dropped appreciably – by about 20 percent between 2005 and 2015. The real estate and financial markets are also helping. A study of loans in the Commercial Mortgage-Backed Securities market shows green buildings carry 34 percent less default risk, all else being equal. The benefit comes at least partly from the level of performance, not only the label itself. Loans on buildings that were green at loan origination also have slightly better terms than loans on non-green buildings – a difference that is growing but whose economic effect is small compared to the lower default risk.[95]

There are numerous active and passive design strategies for buildings to reduce energy consumption and reduce waste heat as a co-benefit. "Passive" means that it is fundamentally an architectural rather than an engineering strategy or system. The only moving part is the sun itself, whereas active systems have motorized pumps, fans, dampers, etc., as well as thermostatic controls. New and better-engineered mechanical systems that heat, ventilate and air condition buildings have the potential to not only burn less fossil fuel, but also exhaust cooler fumes into the urban air shed. On the architectural side, there are low-tech, passive solar space heating systems, such as Trombe Walls, Attached Sunspaces and Direct Gain. And there are photovoltaic solar systems, which can also be considered passive, as their energy flows are not mechanically driven.

Passive cooling and dehumidification devices can significantly reduce the voluminous stream of hot air pumped into the urban air shed by AC systems, which have allowed populations to swell in previously uninhabitable places. Large, new cities like Dubai would be essentially unlivable without air conditioning most of the year. Passive systems like their traditional wind towers help but can't adequately deal with the rising temperatures. "In Dubai at the height of summer, people already go outside as little as possible. By 2100, according to one recent study, there may be days so hot and humid that going outside could kill you."[96] The cities of the American South and Southwest would not have boomed without AC. Yet, this makes these places more vulnerable, should electricity become more expensive, scarcer or more intermittent. Some experts say "there may be a time in the future when the climate in some places will be so hot that air-conditioning won't be able to maintain comfortable temperatures."[97] Such a development will require radical changes in both building design and lifestyles.

It is well-known how buildings can reduce energy flows by tapping basic natural heating and cooling techniques and renewable energy sources in ways that are region-specific and climate-sensitive. Defensive and offensive strategies – from use of local and recycled materials to heavy insulation to building orientation and passive solar systems to dense urban configurations – can cost-effectively address the reduction of material and energy consumption in the U.S and other climates and terrains. Many shelves of books and articles have been written about these strategies since the Oil Embargo of 1973. Energy-efficient buildings engage both energy and ecology. They deal with *material* resources – both organic and inorganic – and with *energy* consumed by buildings for their heating, lighting, cooling and running equipment, as well as for maintenance. As for material resources, there are some radical new building products being experimented with: super-glazing, interactive surfaces, self-healing materials, bio-composites, 3D fabrics, Engineered Living Materials, bone-like and eggshell-like structural material, with surely more to come. New soy-based phase-change materials, which can be used as a heat sink to absorb solar heat, are estimated to save up to 30 percent heating and cooling costs.[98] The availability of new materials – underwriters' slow approvals notwithstanding – is sure to improve building performance or bring costs down, or both.

There are two basic ways to measure energy – by *quantity* and by *quality*. These two ways are described by the First and Second Laws of Thermodynamics. The metrics of the First Law are units of energy, like BTUs and watts, while the Second Law measures the intensity or temperature of energy, sometimes called exergy, both of which denote its ability to do work. The seven principles listed below are primarily about reducing the *quantity* of energy used. The passive solar systems mentioned above use relatively low temperatures for space and water heating and are therefore also *qualitatively* more elegant than fossil-fuel-fired systems, which run at much higher temperatures. The principles tend to focus on thermal energy, as opposed to luminous and electrical energy, but they do include the energy consumed by electrical lighting and equipment, as well as heating, cooling and the energy embodied in a building's materials. As powering and heating buildings become more efficient, a structure's materials can account for a half or more of its total environmental and carbon footprint over its lifespan.[99] Fortunately, recycling and reusing existing materials can drastically reduce the wasting of embodied energy.

As noted, there has been significant progress over recent decades in cutting energy use in buildings, but there is a long way to go to fully and wisely steward our energy resources. We want simple and understandable ways to do more with less energy, as well as to cut overall energy use. Lean, passive design is all the more essential as we run out of low-hanging fruit, and have to reach higher to conserve and generate energy. The lowest fruit is reducing the energy *demand* of buildings. A BTU or a watt saved – the "negawatt" – is far cheaper than one produced even from "free" energy sources like wind and solar, which have capital costs. *Defensive* strategies – primarily insulation and weather-stripping – usually have the quickest economic payback. Reused and recycled building materials and components are preferable to new ones, especially synthetic and high-tech materials whose manufacture requires high energy and chemical inputs. Buildings that share walls, floors and roofs require less heating and air conditioning per person, as well as less building material and maintenance. Downsizing buildings as much as possible is always good defense. Even better is renovating or retrofitting existing buildings. Like the negawatt, the best option of all can be the "negabuilding" – not building at all – and getting by with existing facilities, assuming their energy performance can be upgraded. If so, "the greenest building is the one already built."[100]

Offensive strategies include renewable energy, typically solar, wind and geothermal. If done at the community scale, hydro, biogas and biomass is cost-effective in many situations. The sun is an intense light source, and its most common and effective architectural use is *illuminating* building interiors with daylight. Passive solar heating – in which the building itself collects, stores and distributes heat – is another proven use of the sun's generous supply of energy. Passive systems are more architecturally integrated than active solar systems, whose panels are discrete, often awkward add-ons to a building, and require fluids, pumps, thermostats and racks. Other than movable vents, flaps and curtains that some passive systems have, they typically have only one moving part – the sun. Although usually less architecturally integrated, photovoltaic panels or cells and solar hot water collectors can be added to the building, typically on the roof, where they can be arrayed and tilted to face and even track the sun. Some PV systems look like conventional roof shingles. Importantly, passive solar and PV systems emit no sensible heat, GHGs or other pollutants, other than in their manufacture and construction.

Solar radiation is intermittent, diffuse and relatively weak compared to fossil fuels, which are too power-packed and underpriced to be utilized so cavalierly. (Oil should be treated with more respect and priced more like olive oil.) Nonetheless, the sun's rays are intensive and frequent enough to provide ample light, heat and electricity for buildings. As mentioned, PV panels have dropped dramatically in price and are competitive with utility-provided electricity in many places. They are already part of the standard repertoire in sunny regions, and have been deployed in remote, off-grid locations for decades. "Following an amazing 30-fold increase in PV sales over the past nine years, the solar industry in the U.S. now employs more than 260,000 workers nationwide. That's more employees than work for Apple, Facebook, and Google combined."[101] The International Renewable

Energy Association reports that as of 2017, there were over 10 million jobs globally in renewable energy, from hydropower to wind to solar, with PVs employing over 3 million. Speaking of corporations, by 2017 there were "nearly 100 large companies that have committed to transitioning to 100 percent renewable generation . . . (including) Johnson & Johnson, Procter & Gamble and Nike."[102] Energy codes, regulations and red tape have steadily increased over the decades. Both mandatory and voluntary, they have significantly reduced energy consumption, but have added to the bureaucratic delay and hassle of design and construction. They include LEED ratings, which are voluntary but complicated and expensive. Moreover, most systems consist of a laundry list of criteria, which is more reductionist than integrative or synergistic. Architecture 2030 is a simpler, less expensive and more workable voluntary rating system, as it focuses almost solely on reducing GHGs and ultimately making buildings carbon- and energy-free. BREEAM, a code developed in the U.K., is used in other countries. A simpler and more locally tailored regulatory system would be welcome, even if it were initially limited to certain building types or zones within a region.

The metrics used should also be appropriate. Small buildings are typically skin-load-dominated, which means their thermal performance is driven by energy flows through their walls, windows and roofs. Their performance is usually intuitive and can often be predicted by simple rules of thumb and charts. But large, multi-story buildings are dominated by internal loads – lights, equipment, people, etc. – and typically need engineers to do computer calculations during the design process. When energy consumption is calculated, the best overall metric is Watts or BTUs/sf/yr/occupant, which is roughly equivalent to carbon footprint per capita. It is essential to include people in the denominator, as it gives due credit for buildings with higher occupancy levels, which vary widely by use and culture. It thereby penalizes overly spacious or luxuriously wasteful buildings, which is essential if there is to be a sense of equity and fair share in energy consumption across the wide spectrum of countries.

There are many design techniques and building technologies that can significantly reduce the use of energy and the production of waste heat and GHGs. Here is a list of seven basic, passive architectural design principles that I first published 40 years ago, and have recently updated. They address buildings – especially smaller buildings and new buildings – across all climate zones in the U.S., although locales that are extremely cold, hot or humid need further elaboration. They also apply to similar climate zones throughout the world, with some of the principles reversed in the southern hemisphere:

The Seven Principles of Passive, Energy-efficient Buildings

These principles are offered as a short, irreducible but complete list for designers and builders, as well as for the public. When further detail for actual, site-specific applications is needed, expert advice is recommended.

To consume less energy and produce less GHGs, buildings should:

1   *be built with local, low-energy materials and methods, and designed no bigger or more extravagant than needed, as well as sensitively taking their place in the natural landscape or urban setting.*

  – Building materials that are in their natural or near-natural state are preferable to processed ones that have additional energy and chemical inputs. Locally sourced wood, stone, brick and glass are less energy-intensive than aluminum, plastic, concrete and steel (unless they are reused or recycled).
  – Materials that are salvaged, non-toxic, renewable and biodegradable are also superior, in both environmental and energy terms. Buildings should comfortably take advantage of their site in the built or natural context.

2   *have an envelope capable of isolating or buffering it from heat, cold and humidity, consistent with the climate zone.*

  – In temperate and cold climates, walls, roofs and floors should be heavily insulated, with double-glazed or triple-glazed windows, as well as minimal air infiltration and cold bridges through the building envelope. Insulation has one of the highest paybacks of any investment, especially in smaller buildings with a high skin-to-volume ratio. Careful attention should be given to vapor barriers, which belong on the warm side of insulation. Glazing on all faces should be covered at night with interior or exterior air-tight movable insulation, such as insulating curtains, shutters and panels.
  – Light colored roofs and walls reflect unwanted solar heat gain, but their primary benefit is reducing local heat islands. Shade from trees and other vegetation is often essential.
  – Larger, multi-floor buildings have a more favorable ratio of volume to skin than smaller buildings and are thermally more energy-effective per occupant. Engineering studies have shown that defensive strategies are usually the most cost-effective. It is worth noting that, according to McKinsey & Company, wall and roof insulation have the fastest payback of *any* energy-saving technology on the planet![103]

3   *be oriented to take advantage of local climate and terrain, facing south (in the northern hemisphere) if possible, with sufficient glazing to passively collect solar gain if there is a heating season; have appropriate shading of south and west glass when solar gain is unwanted; and welcome natural light.*

  – In temperate and cold climates, if at all possible buildings should have the largest face oriented to the south, preferably within less than 20 degrees. Buildings and rows of buildings should be stretched east to west to maximize solar exposure. The south face(s) should be generously glazed, as each square foot of vertical double-glazing gains more heat than it loses over the course of most heating seasons. East, west and north faces perform better with minimal window area, preferably no more than needed for daylight, views and natural ventilation, any of which can sometimes trump thermal efficiency in architectural importance.

– At appropriate times of the day and year, glazing should be protected from sunlight with exterior fixed or movable shading devices, without compromising appropriate levels of daylight. In most climates, west-facing glass is particularly susceptible to visual glare and overheating, and exterior fixed or movable vertical louvers, shutters, trellises and living walls can shade glass from the hot sun. There are similar benefits from *interior* window blinds and shades, which are lower in cost, but devices installed inside of the glass are thermally less effective. (This loss occurs because when the incoming solar radiation hits the interior shading device it is converted from long wave to short wave, or infra-red, radiation, which in turn, is absorbed by the glass on the outgoing bounce.) It is always better to intercept the sun's radiation, especially direct sunlight, before its heat is trapped by glass.

– South sloping roofs, steeper in latitudes further from the equator, can be devoted to PV solar panels and to thermo-siphoning solar DHW systems with flat-plate or evacuated tube collectors. Climates with freezing temperatures must be drained down at night, or use freeze-resistant fluids and heat exchangers with the potable water. These systems can also be deployed in tilted arrays on flat roofs.

4 *have sufficient mass to store solar gain and to act as a thermal flywheel, radiating warmth in the heating season and absorbing it in the cooling season.*

– Where heating is needed, there should be enough thermal mass inside the thermal envelope to carry any excess heat gain from the day into the night or next day. Heavy, dark-colored masonry with *direct* exposure to the sun is among the best thermal storage/flywheel devices, especially if it is also part of the building's structural system (e.g., Trombe Wall, where the mass, which is between the occupants and glazing, holds up part of the roof.) Dark-colored water barrels can be useful for thermal storage, especially in attached greenhouses and sunspaces. Multi-zone buildings should redistribute excess solar gain or internally generated heat to other zones that need heat.

– Where cooling is needed during the day, there should be enough thermal mass inside or outside the thermal envelope – often in the form of masonry – to delay the arrival of the afternoon heat wave until cooler night air can cool and ventilate the building. Interior thermal mass can also help smooth exterior temperature swings, and can work effectively together with natural ventilation.

– Geothermal takes advantage of a much longer thermal fly-wheel – the slow annual swing of soil temperature under or near the building. By tapping into it with circulating water, it can lessen both heating and cooling loads, and is cost-effective in many climes.

5   *when cooling is needed, be open to and induce natural ventilation, have low albedo roofs, and shade with vegetation, fixed and movable devices.*

– Cross-ventilation and chimney-effect, vertical ventilation should be used in hot, humid climates as needed to cool building spaces and building mass, especially at night when outdoor air is cooler. Night sky radiation and evaporative cooling are effective in hot, dry climates with clear skies. Tall buildings can help induce natural ventilation in the cooling season by taking advantage of the chimney effect in double-skin walls. Cross ventilation in large-floorplate office buildings and in multi-family housing with double-loaded corridors is a challenge.

6   *be readily adapted, renovated and repaired over time, with materials and components reused at the end of their useful lives.*

– The building foundation, structure and shell should be usually built to last a century or more in order to shelter different users and needs over time. Buildings should be constructed of materials that are reusable or recyclable. Movable, short-lived and personalized building components should be flexible on a daily and seasonal basis, as well as adaptable over the years.

– Buildings should recycle gray water for flushing of toilets and irrigation of plants. Occupants should recycle inorganic and compost organic waste, as well as minimize water consumption.

7   *employ the first six principles in connected, multi-story urban buildings within cities, and always in ways that are site-specific, context-sensitive and that do not prevent other buildings from employing them.*

– Urban buildings have smaller exterior surface area per occupant, because their party walls and shared floors reduce the need for heat in the heating season and for air conditioning in the cooling season. Urban buildings also contain less embodied energy and require less energy to construct and maintain per occupant. Buildings that are 100 percent solar or zero-energy are often less cost-effective than an equivalent investment in multiple buildings that are 80 percent solar, as 100 percent is higher on the curve of diminishing returns and reaches for higher, more expansive fruit. Hitting this sweet spot – sometimes called the 80 percent rule – is especially important when affordability is paramount.

- Daylight and solar access for neighboring buildings should be blocked as little as possible. Buildings can slope or step down to the north to cast shorter shadows.
- Wherever possible, buildings should connect to district heating, cooling and electricity generation systems, taking advantage of scalar efficiencies: district infrastructure such as integrated building energy management, renewable energy, energy storage, water recycling and on-site wastewater treatment that actively reduce energy and climate impacts.
- Other economies are possible with code "workarounds," such as multi-family housing of three stories, which can meet accessibility codes with a single fire stair and no elevator.
- Finally, if the building is not located in an area that has ample amenities and services in easy walking/biking distance, or if it is not well served by transit, dependence on automobiles can offset the energy and climate benefits promoted by these principles.

These seven principles of energy-efficient buildings will increasingly prevail as energy prices rise, as more and more good exemplars are built in different climates, and as new economic, political and climatic realities make sustainable, resilient architecture more essential.

Electrical Power Production

There is a sea change occurring in the way we *produce* energy. The first Industrial Revolution (IR) which peaked in the nineteenth century, was a coal-powered, steam-driven economy. The second IR flourished in the twentieth century, with the gasoline-fueled, internal combustion engine and the electrical power grid. In *The Third Industrial Revolution*, Jeremy Rifkin offers five pillars for a more energy-sustainable future:[104]

1 shifting from fossil fuels to renewable energy;
2 distributing micro-power plants within and on buildings (PV, wind, biomass, hydropower);
3 deploying hydrogen for energy storage in buildings and infrastructure (as a zero-carbon backup to renewables);

4   building a smart grid to save, store and buy back energy;
5   powering vehicles with batteries and fuel cells.

He also describes an equally profound shift in communications, with the telephone giving way to television in the second IR, and the cell phone and World Wide Web gaining dominance in the third IR.

Oil and electricity are a study in opposites. Oil is a

> wonder fuel, packed with more energy by weight than coal and by volume than natural gas (both of which remain the main sources of electricity). It is easy to ship, store and turn into myriad products from petrol to plastics to pharmaceuticals. But it is only found in specific places favored by geology. Its production is concentrated in a few hands . . . Concentration and cartelization make oil-rich states prone to corruption and abuse.[105]

On the other hand, electricity is harder to store and to transmit over long distances, and its distribution requires regulation as a public utility. It is harder to monopolize because it can be generated by different sources, from natural gas and nuclear to wind, solar, hydro and biomass, many of which are widely abundant. Almost anyone can produce electricity, from the most developed to the least developed countries. Because its renewable sources are intermittent, its storage and distribution need and reward cooperation. Switching from oil to electricity could potentially lead to a less competitive and more peaceful world. However, the transition will surely be non-linear and messy, particularly in autocratic countries where falling oil revenues lead to economic turmoil, regional tension and social unrest.

There are bridging measures while we make this inevitable shift. For example, substituting a lower carbon-intensive fuel, such as natural gas, for a higher carbon-intensive fuel, such as coal, is an effective means of lowering CO_2 emissions in the short run. But it provides no relief from UHIs and few benefits related to CC adaptation. More efficient and more distributed fossil-fuel-fired power plants are also beneficial in the battle against both CC and UHIs, but only as a very short bridge to distributed renewable energy systems. Although large power plants are usually situated outside city centers, some are in urban locations, especially since smaller, decentralized power and co-generation plants have begun to proliferate. Denmark now is powered and heated by a connected network across cities and countryside that consists of hundreds of renewable energy systems and combined heating and power plants (called co-generation in the U.S.). Brooklyn, NY has a "micro-grid" of 60 local energy producers, mostly solar photovoltaic systems. Parenthetically, it uses a blockchain to automate peer-to-peer transactions between 800 local consumers. In the developing world, from

Myanmar to Mozambique, 100 "mini-grids" are being set up a year. Smaller than micro-grids, the IEA forecasts hundreds of thousands of them could connect 440 million people by 2030.[106]

Renewable energy systems, which don't combust fossil fuels to produce electricity, are a key component of reducing waste heat. Currently and for the foreseeable future, these systems primarily consist of PVs and wind turbines. PVs are particularly suitable in urban settings, as they can be installed on rooftops, on racks hovering over surface lots and rooftop parking areas. "Thanks in part to a new offshore wind turbine installation, Denmark was recently able to power the entire country for a day with wind energy alone."[107] Although wind machines are currently very cost-effective, they don't tend to be installed in cities, as winds are flukier in direction and speed, with rooftop wind machines hampered by air turbulence. Geo-thermal is also becoming widespread, but other renewable energy systems like tidal and wave systems are not widely deployed.

In 2016, the world invested for the first time more in photovoltaic systems than in coal- and gas-fired power plants combined, as vivid testimony of their uptake.

By 2050 non-hydro renewables will account for a third of global power generation – a huge increase from the 2014 level of 6%. To put it another way, between now and 2050, wind and solar are expected to grow four to five times faster than every other source of power.[108]

Nonetheless, PVs actually rose from a paltry 1% of U.S. generation to only 1.4% in 2016, with a whopping 65% of electricity generation still done with fossil fuels, plus 20% nuclear, 6.5% hydroelectric, 2.0% biomass and geothermal, and 5.6% wind.[109] China, which has more solar capacity than any other country, plans to triple it by the end of the decade.[110] Europe had over 4,000 wind turbines across 11 countries by 2018, and the U.S. lags behind with a small fraction of that capacity. The cost of offshore wind fell by a third between 2012 and 2016.[111] As of 2018, the world's largest wind turbines, which stand 650 feet high offshore of Liverpool, can each generate enough electricity to power 135,000 British homes.

There is more good news on energy and its efficient utilization. By 2050, global "energy intensity" – that is, how much energy is used to produce each unit of GDP – will be half what it was in 2013.[112] For instance China, which was previously criticized for too little co-generation/CHP, improved its overall energy efficiency by 25 percent between 2000 and 2013, which was faster than its population grew. In other words, it would have used a quarter more energy without these improvements. The American Council for an Energy Efficient

Economy, which publishes an annual energy efficiency scorecard for comparing the energy intensity of national economies and for scoring each country on efforts to become more efficient, ranked China sixth, two levels above the U.S. It cited its commitments to and investments in efficient buildings, equipment and transportation.[113] Aside from addressing CC at the macro scale, these dramatic increases in efficiency decrease the waste heat issuing out of tailpipes and power plant stacks in urban areas.

A Related if Inconvenient Paradox – Jevons

Alas, despite all the efficiency gains, there is the notorious "rebound effect," whereby increased efficiency undermines energy savings and complicates the economics of energy efficiency. Jevons Paradox states technological progress that increases the efficiency with which a resource is used tends to increase – rather than decrease – the rate of consumption of that resource. It's counter-intuitive, but has been demonstrated many times and in many ways since Jevons first applied it to nineteenth-century efficiency gains in the use of coal that led to a more coal-intensive economy. It's an economic principle, not a natural law, meaning there has to be a reduction in price for it to apply. As price goes down, demand goes up. Hence the rebound effect describes the way efficiency can backfire in unwanted ways, in this case more burning of dirty fossil fuel. But if the price goes back up, consumption will almost always decline. Energy conservation policies and regulations, such as a carbon tax or cap and trade system, can reduce or eliminate the rebound.

The paradox helps explain why automobile VMT tends to go up when the average mpg improves.

> Since 1980, the number of miles Americans drive has grown three times faster than the U.S. population, and almost twice as fast as vehicle registrations. Average automobile commute times in metropolitan areas have risen steadily over the decades, and many Americans now spend more time commuting than they do vacationing.[114]

As fuel and some cars have gotten less expensive, people drive more and tend to buy bigger, gas-guzzling vehicles, including more vehicles. It's another form of induced demand, akin to the way adding lanes to freeways tends to increase VMT.

Another example of the paradox is more efficient electrical lighting, such as LEDs.

> Despite a global move to more efficient lighting and various efforts to lessen the impact of lighting on humans and the environment, scientists say both the brightness and the area of Earth lit at night continue to increase by 2.2% each year on average, per a 2017 study.

That's likely because people are using more lighting now that it is cheaper and more efficient.[115]

Arguably, cheaper LEDs lead people to be less conscientious about turning lights off. Not only does any increase add to society's collective carbon footprint but also to light pollution, which has been shown to negatively impact human health, environment and ecosystems, not to mention astronomical research. The rebound effect from induced demand has been and will continue to be counter-productive in the fight against CC and UHIs.

Happily, wind machines and solar photovoltaic cells are on the right side of Jevons Paradox: as they get cheaper, more are utilized and GHG emissions fall. In what might be called the "gateway effect," both are booming, leading to more and more replacement of fossil fuels. "On a global scale, more than half the investment in new electricity generation is going into renewable energy. That is more than $300 billion a year, a sign of how powerful the momentum has become."[116] A particularly stunning statistic shows that "every day, 500,000 solar panels are being installed across the globe."[117] As previously mentioned, a big reason is much lower cost as in recent years there has been a substantial drop in the price of photovoltaic panels. The annual mega-wattage of installations in the U.S. went up 24-fold between 2000 and 2015.[118] It is timely: the U.S. Department of Energy estimates that by 2035 residential and commercial buildings will use 77 percent of the total electricity in the United States, up from 73 percent in 2012.[119] This burgeoning, clean energy generation is also highly beneficial because traditional generations that produce and transmit it vent two-thirds of the energy as waste heat.

There is an interesting reverse spin that has been noted about Jevons Paradox: improvements and lower prices in information technology have increased, rather than reduced, the desire for face-to-face interaction. Edward Glaeser calls it Jevons Complimentary Corollary, pointing out that electronic communications, like email and Skype, have made for a more relation-intensive world. As people spend more time transmitting information, they make life more information intensive and knowledge more valuable.[120] That has increased the value of learning from other people in real time and real place. And there is no richer and more effective way to share and enrich knowledge than face-to-face exchange in cities. Indeed, that's why young Silicon Valley multi-millionaires, as well as successful urban entrepreneurs, live in walkable, café neighborhoods, not in suburban McMansions.

Notes

1 Brian Stone, *Louisville Urban Heat Management Study*, for Public Comment, April, 2016, p. 9
2 Lisa Gartland, *Heat Islands*, Earthscan, 2008, p. 23

3 J. Raven et al., "Urban planning and urban design," in C. Rosenzweig et al. (eds), *Climate Change and Cities: Second Assessment Report of the Urban Climate Change Research Network*, Cambridge University Press, 2018, p. 148

4 Gregory Newmark and Peter Haas, "Income, location efficiency, and VMT: affordable housing as a climate strategy," *CNT Working Paper*, 12/16/15

5 Tod Litman, "Understanding location-efficient affordability impacts," *Planetizen*, 4/29/18

6 Rob Steuteville, "The amazing route diversity of street grids," *Public Square*, 8/9/18

7 Newmark and Haas, "Income, location efficiency, and VMT: affordable housing as a climate strategy," p. 147

8 Kevin Klinkenberg, "Responding to the 'Klinkenberg Retreat,'" *The Messy City*, 5/8/18

9 Email from Robinson Brown, a housing developer, 8/30/17

10 "California won't meet its climate change goals without a lot more housing density in its cities," *LA Times*, 3/7/17

11 Randall White, "California accepts Sacramento-area electric car share program," *Capital Public Radio*, 7/27/17

12 Quote and paragraph are based on articles in *Sustainability and Resource Productivity*, 4, McKinsey & Company, 2016

13 "How bike-sharing conquered the world," *The Economist*, 12/19/17

14 Stefani Cox, "Two cities explore adaptive bike rentals for people with disabilities," *betterbikeshare*, 5/10/17

15 "How bike-sharing conquered the world," *The Economist*, 12/19/17

16 Javier C. Hernandez, "As bike-sharing brings out bad manners, China asks, what's wrong with us?" *The New York Times*, 8/2/17

17 Rob Walker, "China's app-based bike share market," *Land Lines*, Winter, 2017

18 David McCullough, *The Wright Brothers*, Simon and Schuster, 2015, pp. 21–22

19 National Museum of History, as reported in *The New York Times*, 7/13/15

20 Travel Section, *The New York Times*, 11/2/14

21 Ibid.

22 www.copenhageniZe.com

23 Lewis Macdonald, "New report on encouraging cycling (Denmark)," *Eltis*, 1/5/16

24 *Zocalo*, 9/6/16

25 Valerie Vandermeulen et al., "The economic evaluation to create public support for green infrastructure investments," *Landscape and Planning*, 11/30/11, pp. 198–206

26 Eric Morris, "Is travel really that bad?" *Access*, Spring, 2017

27 Update section of *Better Cities & Towns*, September–October, 2014

28 Tom Babin, "Forget all the other reasons you should be riding a bike: this is the one that matters," *Shifter*, 8/9/17

29 Tom Frisbie, "Why SUMC wants to take 1 million cars off the road in the next 5 years," http://sharedusemobilitycenter.org, 8/8/17

30 "Europe's cycling economy has created 650,000 jobs," *The Guardian*, 11/12/14

31 Jacob Mason, Lew Fulton, Zane McDonald, *A Global High Shift Cycling Scenario*, Institute for Transportation and Development Policy and the University of California, Davis, 11/12/15, p. 4

32 Nathan W. Chan and Casey J. Wichman, "The effects of climate on leisure demand: evidence from North America," *Resources for the Future*, 12/5/17

33 David Chayka, "How your suburb can make you thinner," *Politico*, 5/10/17

34 Elle Hunt, "Walkable cities reduce blood pressure and hypertension risk, study," *The Guardian*, 2/5/18

35 Alison Hewitt, "UCLA researcher finds that feeding pets creates the equivalent of 64 million tons of carbon dioxide a year," *UCLA News*, 8/2/17

36 "The case against sidewalks," *Alissa Walker@awalkerinLA*, 2/7/18

37 Angie Schmitt, "How dangerous walking conditions disadvantage women," *Streetsblog*, 1/19/18

38 Angie Schmitt, "Why Sweden clears snow-covered walkways before roads," *Streetsblog*, 2/24/18

39 Nigel Griffiths, Future Mobility Workshop, Ann Arbor, MI, 4/30/18

40 Amanda Erickson, "The world's laziest countries," *Washington Post*, 7/14/17

41 Robert Steuteville, citing Redfin in "The value of walkability and walk score inaccuracies," *Public Square*, 3/16/18

42 Peter Fairley, "Exposing the power vampires in self-driving cars," *IEEE Spectrum*, 2/15/18

43 Jonathan Levine, "The energy risk of self-driving cars," *Axios*, 5/17/18

44 Future Mobility Workshop, University of Michigan, Ann Arbor, MI, 4/30/18

45 Peter Calthorpe and Jerry Walters, "Autonomous vehicles: hype and potential," *Urban Land*, 3/1/17

46 "It starts with a single app," *The Economist*, 10/1/16

47 Seleta Reynolds, "How Los Angeles is adopting mobility for our digital age," *Eno Transportation Weekly*, 3/26/18

48 Jim Erickson, "Maximizing the environmental benefits of autonomous vehicles," *Michigan News*, 2/15/18

49 "Special report, e-commerce," *The Economist*, 10/28/17, p. 12

50 Frank Shafroth, "Breaking down the financial impact of self-driving cars," *Governing*, January, 2017

51 Angela Ruggierio, "San Ramon: driverless shuttles make their debut," *East Bay Times*, 3/6/17

52 This paragraph is based on a talk by Ellen Dunham-Jones at the ROWE/ ROME conference, Rome, June 21–23, 2013

53 "Connected vehicle tech: mandate now to save lives," *Michigan News*, 3/7/18

54 Ellen Dunham-Jones, "Downtown Atlanta 2041: autonomous vehicles and A-street grids," Georgia Tech Library, August, 2016

55 Angie Schmitt, "If Americans paid for the parking we consume, we'd drive 500 billion fewer miles each year," *Streetsblog USA*, 7/26/18

56 Robert Dietz, "How will driverless cars impact housing?" *Homebuilder Magazine*, 5/25/17

57 Editorial Board, "Making room for Uber, taxis and transit," *Chicago Tribune*, 10/27/17

58 Nigel Griffiths, Future Mobility Workshop, Ann Arbor, MI, 4/30/18

59 Mike Macaig, "America still loves cars, but some cities are starting to ditch them," *Governing*, 12/5/17

60 Nico Larco, "AVs and real estate: a guide to potential impacts," *Urbanism Next*, 8/21/17

61 Mary Beth Griggs, "Sao Paulo traffic jams extend 112 miles, on average," SmartNews, *Smithsonian.com*, 9/25/12

62 Laura Bliss, "The anti-urbanism of Uber Air," *citiscope*, 11/9/17

63 "Road kill: the death of the internal combustion engine," *The Economist*, 8/12/17, p. 7

64 Ibid., p. 7

65 Bernie DeGroat, "Comparing emissions worldwide from gas, battery-powered vehicle," Michigan News in *The University Record*, 11/13/17

66 Amie Tsang and Henrik Pryser Libell, "In Norway, electric and hybrid cars outsell conventional models," *The New York Times*, 1/4/18

67 Trefor Moss, "Electric-vehicle sales amp up in China," *Wall Street Journal*, 5/11/18

68 "Why India dreams of electric cars," Morgan Stanley, *Research*, 6/28/18

69 Nicholas Zart, "100% electric fleet for Shenzen (population 11.9 million) by end of 2017," *Clean Technica*, 11/12/17

70 Sean Szymkowski, "These 12 cities buy only electric buses from 2025 on; more expected to join," *Green Car Reports*, 11/14/17

71 Kendra Pierre-Lewis, "Americans are staying home more: that's saving energy," *The New York Times*, 1/29/18

72 Marco Margaritoff, "Futurist Thomas Frey predicts 1 billion drones by 2030," The Drive, *Aerial*, 8/31/17

73 Shannon Bouton et al., "Urban commercial transport and the future of urban mobility," *Sustainability & Resource Productivity*, McKinsey & Company, September, 2017

74 Lloyd Alter, *Treehugger*, 8/3/15

75 Edward Mazria, Fact Sheet, *Architecture 2030*, based on U.S. Energy Information Administration, *Annual Energy Outlook 2009*

76 Alan Short, *The Recovery of Natural Environments in Architecture*, Routledge, 2016

77 Courtney Humphries, "Boston wants to fight climate change: so why is every new building made of glass?" *Globe Contributor*, 7/14/17

78 Roopinda Tara, "Fun facts about skyscrapers," *engineering.com*, 8/29/17

79 Patrick Sisson, "How air conditioning shaped modern architecture – and changed our climate," *curbed*, 5/9/17

80 Scott Bernstein, personal email, 11/7/17

81 "How to make air conditioning more sustainable," *The Economist*, 8/25/18

82 Ibid.

83 "Chilling prospects: providing sustainable cooling for all," www.SEforALL.org, 2018

84 Chris Mooney, "Cool homes, hot planet: how air conditioning explains the world," *Washington Post*, 4/27/15

85 Stan Cox, quoted in Rick Noack, "Europe to America: Your love of air-conditioning is stupid," *Washington Post*, 7/22/15

86 Catherine Hausman, "Climate change is projected to have severe impacts on the frequency and intensity of peak electricity demand in the United States," Michigan News in *The University Record*, 2/7/17

87 Based on personal research and calculations, ca. 2014

88 Robert Bryce, *Smaller Faster Lighter Denser Cheaper*, Public Affairs, 2014

89 Lisa Friedman, "If you fix this, you fix a big piece of the climate puzzle," *The New York Times*, 8/3/17

90 Ibid.

91 Paul Hawken, *Drawdown: The Most Comprehensive Plan Ever Proposed to Reverse Global Warming*, Penguin, 2017

92 Clair Brown, *Buddhist Economics*, Bloomsbury, 2017, p. 53

93 "America could be killing the McMansion for good," *Business Insider*, 3/6/17

94 Ralph Cavanugh, "Good news on energy," *The New York Times*, 11/24/14

95 Xudong An and Gary Pivo, "Green buildings in commercial mortgage-backed securities: the effects of LEED and Energy Star certification on default risk and loan," *Real Estate Economics*, 1/3/18

96 Robert Kunzig, "The world's most improbable green city," *National Geographic*, August, 2017

97 Tatiana Schlossberg, "How bad is your air conditioner for the planet?" *The New York Times*, 8/9/16

98 J. Raven, J. et al., "Urban planning and urban design," pp. 154–155

99 Stephen Miller, "How Seattle's appetite for construction is creating a growing waste problem," *Seattle Magazine*, June, 2018

100 Carl Elephante FAIA, *AIA Record*, 10/30/15

101 Karla Lant, "More Americans work in solar power than for Apple, Facebook, and Google combined," *Futurism*, 4/17/17

102 "Large corporations becoming biggest buyers of renewable energy," *Power Engineering*, 6/21/17

103 Per-Ander Enkvist, Tomas Naucler and Jerker Rosander, "A cost curve for greenhouse gas reduction," *The McKinsey Quarterly*, 1, 2007

104 Jeremy Rifkin, *The Third Industrial Revolution*, Palgrave Macmillan, 2011

105 "Welcome an electric world. Worry about the transition," *The Economist*, 3/15/18

106 "Empowering villages," *The Economist*, 7/14/28

107 Wrap Up, *Futurism*, 3/5/17

108 Scott Nyquist, "Energy 2050," *Sustainability and Resource Productivity*, 4, McKinsey and Company, 2016

109 Paul Driessen, "Yet another renewable energy boondoggle," *WUWT* (blog), 9/1/17

110 "Blinded by the light," *The Economist*, April 2–8, 2016

111 "Biggest wind turbines hailed as a star turn," *The Guardian*, 5/17/17

112 Scott Nyquist, "Energy 2050"

113 Email exchanges with Scott Bernstein, head of CNT, May, 2016

114 Reid Ewing et al., *Growing Cooler: The Evidence on Urban Development and Climate Change*, Urban Land Institute, 2008

115 Eileen Drage O'Reilly, "The 'lighting revolution' may be increasing light pollution," *Axios*, 11/25/17

116 "Trump can't stop energy transition," *The New York Times*, 1/3/17

117 "Renewable have taken over as the dominant source of new electricity generation," Earth & Energy, *Futurism*, 10/27/16

118 Solar Energy Industries Association, graph by gtmresearch, 2016

119 J. Raven et al., "Urban planning and urban design," p. 145

120 Jevons Paradox, Wikipedia, 4/16/17

5   Cool Micro-climates and Urban Trees

To continue with ways to mitigate and adapt to extreme heat, we come to the last of the four strategies to mitigate and adapt to UHIs.

Creating Cool Micro-climates within the City

Cool micro-climates are places where the air temperatures, humidity, radiant temperatures and wind speeds are more comfortable than surrounding areas. They are created primarily with plants, especially shade trees. A city's vegetative cover can simultaneously lower the cooling loads of buildings, air pollution and the temperatures of outdoor air, pavements and storm water runoff, while sequestering carbon and performing other tasks and services. An extreme example is an oasis in a hot desert. Comfortable micro-climates are also created by evaporative cooling from fountains and pools in arid climates. But it's urban trees that do the yeoman work cooling hot cities.

In *The Man Who Planted Trees*, Jim Robbins opines on the value of trees.

> What an irony it is that these living beings whose shade we sit in, whose fruit we eat, whose limbs we climb, whose roots we water, to whom most of us rarely give a second thought, are so poorly understood. We need to come, as soon as possible, to a profound understanding and appreciation for trees and forests and the vital role they play, for they are among our best allies in the uncertain future that is unfolding . . . Trees are responsible for half the photosynthesis on land . . . Trees feed oxygen and minerals into the ocean; create rain; render mercury, nitrates, and other toxic wastes in the soil harmless; gather and neutralize sulfur dioxide, ozone, carbon dioxide, and other harmful pollutants in their tissue; create homes and building materials; offer shade; provide medicine; and produce a wide variety of nuts and fruits. They sustain all manner of wildlife, birds, and insects with an array of food and shelter. They are the planet's heat

shield, slowing the evaporation of water and cooling the earth. They generate vast clouds of chemicals that are vital to myriad aspects of the earth's ecosystems.[1]

Indeed, trees are miraculous assets in many ways.

The distinguished English author John Fowles' *The Tree* exfoliates on the complexity of tree culture: evolution did not intend trees to grow singly. Far more than ourselves they are social creatures."[2] They also connect to humans:

> Trees are an intricate part of our sapien wiring. Once, we were sheltered merely by dense upper story canopy; then slowly, we began to reshape the forest into increasingly complex variations of artificial canopy until utility became tradition, and tradition became architecture.[3]

Trees are the great natural multi-taskers of the urban environment, remarkable in so many ways. The list of the environmental contributions of trees and other vegetation is extraordinarily long: they offer cool shade, evapotranspiration from leaves that cools and moistens the air; they provide animal habitat, nuts, fruits, flowers and fragrance, while changing color with the seasons, absorbing sound, providing mulch, dampening heavy winds, shaping public space, screening parking lots, softening infrastructures, soothing the psyche and bestowing beauty and biophilic presence – not to mention sequestering carbon while exhaling oxygen, filtering particulate pollution, retaining soil and water. Trees also raise real estate values, and slow down cars on the street to make both pedestrians and motorists safer. As good as carbon-sequestering forests are at combatting global CC, urban trees reduce GHG emissions more by shading buildings than by sequestering carbon. Along streets and in parks and parking lots, trees are a particularly effective way to cool the city. They are also the source of wood for fuel and construction. It is a remarkably long list, and happily, it can be applied not just to trees but to green space in general.

The dappled patterns of tree shadows on pavements and buildings is an added delight, as is the spatial depth given by shadows and shade. Every culture seems to relish trees and the dappled light their canopies filter. One theory posits that humans like this ambience because they originally evolved at the forest edge, overlooking the savanna in East Africa. Urban trees often grow larger, with a bigger canopy, than trees in a forest, because of less competition from other trees. In 1994, municipal foresters in Chicago found that of over four million trees in their city, "only a tenth of the overall urban forest was street trees, (but) they provided a *quarter* of the canopy."[4] Accordingly, a street tree can have many times the cooling capacity of a forest tree.

Figure 5.1 This tree at the center of an English village is an urban amenity in multiple ways – a vehicular roundabout, a shelter with public benches, bulletin board and clock, all of which are pleasantly shaded. Urban trees can be friendly, even beloved local icons. (Photo by author)

The thermal impact at ground level of greenery varies from city to city, depending on urban morphology. In a high-rise city like Hong Kong, which has very high building-height-to-street-width ratios, a 2011 empirical study revealed that greening rooftops is ineffective for thermal comfort near the ground. Trees were also shown to be more effective than grass surfaces in cooling pedestrian zones. In this extremely dense, that is hot, humid city in the summer,

the amount of tree planting needed to lower pedestrian level air temperature by around 1.8°F (1°C) is approximately 33% of the urban area, which pushes the landscaping limit in most parts of the city ... According to the field measurements in Kumamoto, Japan ... a small green area (60m × 40m) ... can be beneficial. The maximum difference between inside and outside the small green area was found to be 5.4°F (3°C) . . . in Tokyo, vegetated zones during summer are on average about 3°F (1.6°C) cooler than non-vegetated zones; and in Montreal, urban parks can be 4.5°F (2.5°C) cooler than surrounding built areas.[5]

New trees could help shave up to 15°F from unshaded hot zones in Phoenix and drop unshaded parts of Dallas from 101°F to 90°F on their hottest summer days, according to UHI expert Brian Stone.[6] Shade cools people, but it also cools the neighborhood indirectly as the cooler air moves through it. While not always enough to deal with extreme heat, these considerably lower temperatures make everyday life healthier and more pleasant.

Green "living walls" and planted "green roofs" also have cooling benefits, but are less cost-effective and require more maintenance and irrigation than trees planted in terra firma. And green roofs on mid- and high-rise buildings are too removed from street level to have much impact on pedestrian comfort.[7] However, as in the case of Chicago City Hall's green roof, these high gardens can help cool buildings of similar height down wind. In hot, arid climates, water fountains and pools can also cool the air by evaporation. Mechanical "swamp coolers," popular before the advent of AC, can cool buildings in such climates while discharging less hot air and using less electricity than air conditioning.

Many cities have lost their forest cover. Atlanta has lost half its tree cover in the last quarter century, while Seattle has lost a third. Studies have shown that recouping Atlanta's original tree cover could lower air temperatures by more than 12°F on the hottest days and diminish heat waves even more.[8]

Measurements of ambient temperatures taken on exposed versus canopied streets around the U.S. document temperature differentials ranging from 5–15°F between the two, which can make a big difference when temperatures hit triple digits . . . According to the U.S. Department of Agriculture, the cooling impact of a single healthy tree "is equivalent to ten room-size air conditioners operating 24 hours a day."[9]

Even if this impact is overestimated, it's incredibly positive.

Trees also have impact on local wind conditions, which in turn affect temperature and humidity – two essential determinants of how much time people spend outdoors. Wind also affects the pressure gradient between the interior and exterior of buildings. The stronger gradient forces more air from outside into buildings through small gaps and openings, requiring greater consumption of energy to heat or cool the building.

Figure 5.2 Rooftop gardens, a.k.a. green roofs, can be wonderful amenities, as well as detain storm water and provide thermal and acoustic insulation. And growing food is popular, as shown here on a Brooklyn rooftop. The other example, atop Chicago's City Hall, is for public pleasure. It cools downwind buildings of similar height more than its occupants or pedestrians below. (The Eagle Street Rooftop Farm photographed by Annie Novak; "TonyTheTiger" Antonio Vernon)

Researchers from the University of British Columbia created a computer model showing that when there are no trees in a neighborhood, that pressure gradient goes up by a factor of four. Because wind pressure can be the root cause for about a third of a building's energy consumption, the finding means that if there are no trees around, the cost to maintain a building's temperature can rise. The researchers estimate that trees in the Vancouver neighborhood they modeled save 15% on energy bills in the summer and 10% in the winter.[10]

At least 135 American cities maintain tree inventories and have planting and maintenance programs, and almost half of them have adopted canopy goals.[11] New York City planted its millionth tree in 2015, in a program started eight years earlier, and Phoenix plans to double its tree canopy by 2030.[12] It is looking to create long corridors of shade-providing trees to allow people to venture out of their homes and cars during the day. Seattle plans to increase its tree canopy from 18 percent to 30 percent over the next 30 years. Washington D.C. has incorporated a city-wide tree canopy goal of 40 percent of the city's land area. To achieve this goal by 2032, the city must increase its canopy cover from the existing 35 percent by planting 8,600 trees per year.[13] Many of the trees are being wisely planted along streets, roads, sidewalks and bike/pedestrian paths. In San Francisco, the city government did a complete "street tree census," counting about 125,000 trees of more than 500 different species throughout the city's 33 neighborhoods – while also identifying 40,000 potential planting locations. "All those trees suck up 19 million pounds of CO_2 and filter 100 million gallons of storm water annually – and the city's Urban Forest Plan plans to add 50,000 street trees over the next 20 years."[14] Melbourne, Australia plans to double the forest canopy from around 22 percent to around 40 percent over the next 20 years to deal with increasing temperatures. In a city that is 4–7°C hotter than its suburbs, they expect a drop of four of those degrees.[15] Again, addressing CC and UHIs is too urgent to plant trees that need 25–50 years to grow mature canopies. Faster-growing ground cover, later to be overshadowed by maturing trees, can also help.

There is also a growing, proactive interest in urban tree cover in the developing world, including Africa and the BRIC countries, especially China. In Africa,

> Kumasi, a Ghanaian city of more than one million people, embarked on a successful urban forestry project with support from international donors. Its goal was to energize schoolchildren and households to plant over a million trees . . . China's National Forest City programme . . . combines national targets with local community involvement with the aim of inculcating a sense of environmental stewardship among residents . . . more than 170 cities and 12

provinces were actively involved in the initiative . . . Tree cover in these urban communities . . . increased to 40% or more, up from less than 10% in 1981.[16]

And Hong Kong planted over 10 million trees during the first decade of this century, along with almost 68 million shrubs and 9 million annuals.[17] Pakistan is also investing in forestry, with "a massive budget of $20B in 2017–18 to maintain and maximize forest resources in a scientifically, socially, ecologically and environmentally sustainable manner."[18] India is also being very aggressive:

> More than 67 million trees were planted by millions of people in a span of 12 hours in India, setting a new Guinness reforestation record . . . India pledged to increase forest cover to 95 million hectares (235 million acres) by the year 2030. India's government is putting forward $6.2 billion for this effort.[19]

The sooner and the bigger the trees planted, the better, especially in hot developing countries that have millions of people moving to cities.

> China is constructing one of the world's first "forest cities" to fight air pollution and curb the production of toxic gases. The city is expected to house up to 30,000 people and absorb approximately 10,000 tons of carbon dioxide, 57 tons of pollutants and produce about 900 tons of oxygen per year as a result of the abundance of trees and plants . . . The city . . . will have roughly a million plants of over a 100 species along with 40,000 trees planted . . . in almost every possible surface. The architect's website states, "The diffusion of plants, not only in the parks and gardens or along the streets, but also over building facades, will allow the energy self-sufficient city to decrease the average air temperature, to create noise barriers and to improve the biodiversity of living species."[20]

The Economics of Urban Trees

Loss of ecosystem services from trees can pose enormous costs. There are incalculable, irreplaceable losses, such as the loss of bees to pollinate flowering trees to absorb GHGs and rainwater to desalinate saltwater. Conversely, a better integration of green infrastructure in cities can lead to cost savings. For example,

> an evaluation of the economic benefits of rainwater runoff reduction by urban green spaces in Beijing showed that 2494 cubic meters of potential runoff was reduced per hectare of green area and a total volume of 154 million cubic meters of rainwater was stored in these

urban green spaces, which almost corresponds to the annual water needs of the ecological landscape in Beijing. The total economic benefit of $19B is equivalent to three-quarters of the maintenance cost of Beijing's green spaces.[21]

Trees are also generally credited with increasing individual real estate values, especially along tree-lined streets. "In a 2008 study, economists at the University of Pennsylvania . . . valued a single tree planted within 1,000 feet of a house as raising the building's value by 7 to 11%."[22] While this value accrues to the property owners, there are also immense public and social benefits. Trees in urban areas save megacities more than $500 million a year in public health costs, energy expenses and environmental protection, according to a scientific study of trees in ten megacities across the globe, including Beijing, Los Angeles, Mexico City and Mumbai. They found that trees cover about a fifth of the cityscapes and save these communities almost half a billion dollars a year by reducing air pollutants like fine particulate matter and sulfur dioxide; $11 million in handling storm water runoff; $8 million in CO_2 sequestration; and another half million in building heating and cooling costs. That ends up equaling roughly $1.2 million per square mile, or $35 per resident each year. The study also found that cities had on average 19 percent more land available to plant more trees. If planted, the economic benefits could be nearly doubled.[23]

London and New York City have pioneered the economic measurement of an urban forest's value. Last year, its "i-Tree Eco Report (a public web service open to all) determined that the city derives . . . $161.5 million annually in quantifiable ecosystem services such as pollution removal, carbon sequestration and storm water alleviation from its tree cover."[24] The report further estimated that it would cost about $8 billion to replace the U.K. capital's nearly 8.5 million trees. London has conducted and audit of its central business districts, and found over 10 million square feet of space that could be converted to rain gardens, green roofs and green walls.[25] When a U.S. Forest Service scientist produced the 2007 i-Tree report for New York City, "it showed that its 600,000 street trees saved $35.6 million just in storm water mitigation, not to mention $28 million in energy costs."[26] As mentioned above, the city then embarked on a massive planting program. In 2015 the program TreesCount![27] enlisted over 2,000 volunteers to learn about the state of the city's trees, their dimensions and community benefits. After months of walking the streets of the five boroughs, their massive effort resulted in an urban forest registry, with statistics on each of almost 700,000 registered trees, including the amount of rainwater retained and the money each individual tree saves per year. The amount of electricity conserved is also estimated, as well as the reduction of air pollution. More recently the City worked out that for every dollar they invested in their urban trees they got a return of $5.60.[28]

The economic value of urban trees over their lifetime is perhaps even more impressive.

> Over a 50-year lifespan, a tree generates sufficient oxygen, controls air pollution, recycles water, and controls soil erosion worth an approximate $161,000 in total value per tree . . . a single mature tree can absorb 48 pounds of carbon dioxide a year and release enough oxygen to support two humans.[29]

That breaks down into $31,000 of soil erosion, over $30,000 worth of oxygen, $37,500 worth of water recycled and more than $60,000 worth of air pollution control. Another study, which was conducted by the U.S. Department of Agriculture Forest Service and the University of California, Davis, found that by increasing the canopy over Los Angeles by 1.3 million trees, the city would garner up to a billion dollars in benefits over the next 35 years.[30] From these many surveys and statistics, it's abundantly clear that trees are not only essential eco-psycho-social assets, but also of very significant economic value to cities. (In the first example, in the wet Pacific Northwest, a tree saves over $3,000 per year, and in the Los Angeles example only $25 per year – far too large a discrepancy for even approximate estimates over a long period of time, with different climates and categories – suggesting there's still progress to be made in standardizing these metrics.)

Other cities inspired by i-Tree data are Philadelphia, Milwaukee, Sacramento, Baltimore, Atlanta, Denver and others.

> But the solution is not to just plant new vegetation everywhere. For one thing, not all trees are equal, including some detrimental aspects. The pungency of a cedar, eucalyptus, or pine woodland, to name a few examples, comes from a blend of volatile organic compounds (VOCs) in these species. When these VOCs interact with the nitrogen oxide that is in car emissions, in the presence of sunlight and hot air temperatures, they produce ozone at ground level.[31]

As we've learned in recent years, this gas can be harmful to health, causing ailments like asthma and heart disease. So, ozone in the lower atmosphere is unhealthy, while being beneficial in the upper atmosphere because it reduces climate change by bouncing back solar radiation.

> In the world's already smoggy metropolises, pollution is likely to grow worse, a phenomenon that scientists have taken to calling "the climate penalty." Ozone is a key ingredient. This lung-damaging compound, often formed from chemical reactions involving sunlight and automobile exhaust and other pollutants, plagues major cities around the globe. As the climate grows warmer, it is projected that more of it will form in polluted areas on sweltering days.[32]

A Little Arboricultural Science

Here is a quick detour into the equally impressive science of trees and photosynthesis. Each leaf has little Cheerio-like openings, which are breathing tubes called stomata:

> There are so, so many of them! On . . . one thousandth of a square inch – you might find a hundred to a thousand little lungs . . . If we multiply all those leafy lungs times all those leaves times all those trees and add grasses into the bargain, we're talking about an unimaginably vast planetary breathing system – a giant green machine that pulls enormous quantities of carbon dioxide out of the air, especially in the warmer months . . . Come winter, the leaves fall off, trees go bare. Without leaves, trees go quiet. Any extra CO_2 is more likely to hang in the atmosphere – until June. That's the month when trillions upon trillions of leaves are opening, growing, and starting to breathe . . . their collective breath literally cleaning the sky . . . It's like the world's northern forests become a giant vacuum cleaner, scouring the air, sucking down the CO_2 till around November. Consider the fantastic scale of this global dance. It starts . . . with 3.1 trillion trees. That's the latest census, published . . . in the science journal *Nature* by Yale's Thomas Crowther . . . If he's right, there are more trees on Earth than there are stars in the Milky Way. Now imagine how many leaves might be on all those trees. It's a very big number. The University of Washington tried to come up with a leaf count for a "mature oak," but oaks are so variable that they could only give us a range: 200,000 to half a million leaves per tree.[33]

During photosynthesis, vegetation converts sunlight and CO_2 into glucose and O_2, thereby making life possible. Without this gift from leaves, there would be neither the food nor the oxygen that all animals need to live!

> The pace of change in photosynthesis is unprecedented in the 54,000-year record . . . While photosynthesis increased at the end of the ice age, the current rate is 136 times as fast. With all that extra carbon dioxide going into plants, there has been less in the air to contribute to global warming. The planet has warmed 1.4°F since 1880, but it might be even hotter if not for the greening of the Earth.[34]

During photosynthesis plants also release water vapor from their leaves. Called transpiration or evapotranspiration, it serves as natural air conditioning that directly helps mitigate UHIs. The transpiration from a mature, well-watered tree with a 30-foot crown can be equivalent to 40 gallons of water per day. The cooling effect of this transpiration can reduce the annual cooling load within a nearby building by 2–8 percent, and reduce peak cooling by 1–10 percent per tree.[35] A plant also stores that carbon as biomass until it eventually dies and decomposes into fertilizing mulch, releasing most but not all the carbon back into the environment. Carbon sequestration and storage in biomass is not the only way that vegetation reduces CO_2 in the atmosphere. The other way is *avoided* CO_2 from reduced building cooling loads due to shade from trees and other vegetation.

According to Brian Stone, the combination of albedo enhancement and reforestation "are the single most effective option available to cities to counteract the very real threats of CC during the next half century . . . none is more effective and less energy-intensive than planting trees."[36] And, unlike infrastructure, which begins to degrade and lose value the moment it is installed, a tree increases in value and size for decades. Combining tree planting with avoided deforestation and agroforestry (where shade trees are interspersed with crops) is a very promising combination. There are good forms of carbon, and bad ones. Urban trees are very much on the right side of the carbon ledger. They are part of a larger global reforestation effort, ironically one that is *recarbonizing* the environment, while we humans try to *decarbonize* our lives.

While trees can combat both UHIs and CC, it's also worth noting that CC combats trees. With the increase in extreme weather, forests could be disturbed permanently by heavy wind storms. As the cycle of damage and regrowth – what ecologists call a disturbance regime – occurs more often as extreme storms become more frequent, some forests may fail to recover completely. Over decades, the reduction in carbon stored in trees would likely become permanent, meaning more carbon would have to be removed in other ways. Jeffrey Chambers, a geographer at the University of California, Berkeley states "If the climate warms . . . That could work on the ability of those systems to remove CO_2 from the atmosphere."[37]

Urbanization is also combatting trees, with urban footprints expected to almost double in the U.S. by 2060. That would be the equivalent of an expanse of concrete the size of Montana. Cities in small states like Rhode Island, Delaware and Connecticut are likely to expand the most in proportion to their state's area, but fast-growing states like California, Texas and Florida will likely convert the most acreage to urban development.[38] The National Forest Service figures there are currently between 5 and 6 billion trees in our urban forests, providing $18 billion in pollution removal, $5 billion in energy savings, and almost $3 billion in avoided emissions.[39] Urban forests are likely to be among the most important and beneficial forests in the future. One last, surprising bit of tree science: On a completely different front, an MIT laboratory is exploring fauna that glows. It may be possible to transform trees into self-powered streetlights, using enzymes and nanoparticles similar to those found in fireflies. Plant nanobionics, a new research area, aims to engineer plants to take over many of the functions now performed by electrical devices.[40]

Trees as Environmental Foot Soldiers: Advancing and Retreating

Trees are environmental foot soldiers when distributed throughout the city. A single street tree does not sequester that much CO_2 or other pollutants, but in aggregate they can absorb a great deal of both. They also soak up rainfall.

> Trees absorb the first 30% of most precipitation through their leaf system, allowing evaporation back into the atmosphere. The moisture never hits the ground. Another percentage (up to 30%) of precipitation is absorbed back into the ground and taken in and held onto by the root structure, then absorbed and then transpired back to the air.[41]

Trees are foot soldiers in another, more literal war, where they offer another kind of absorption. Trees in heavy planters can prevent terrorist-driven vehicles from targeting pedestrians. "A big pot full of soil has the same resistance as a 'Jersey Barrier,' but it can host a tree – a living being that offers shadow; absorbs the dust, subtle pollutants and the CO_2; produces oxygen; homes birds."[42]

When trees grow together in urban parks, canopies and forests, they are very different than street trees lined up straight like a disciplined parade of foot soldiers. The tree canopy in cities like Savannah, Georgia, integrates the physical and social fabric. Parks generate social cohesion in informal ways that streets are not able to. They allow people to sunbathe, picnic, play games, throw frisbees, fly kites, play with their pets, snooze, etc. In short, they help people alone or in groups to relax and enjoy the city, a *sine qua non* for the continued flourishing of cities and ultimately our species. Other forms of park vegetation, such as shrubs, vines and grasses perform the same beneficial environmental and social tasks. And community gardens encourage people to grow food and flowers together. The immediate presence of attractive greenery or high-quality parks can add significant real estate value.

> However, at the city-wide level, the presence of more greenery can be associated with *lower* as well as higher value. What it is and how it is managed really matters. For example, in London, the cost of a home closer than average to a high-quality park is on average 11% (or £51,000) higher than one that is not, holding everything else equal. However, in Liverpool, a home located closer than average to a high-quality park is worth, on average, 7 per cent (or £7,760) less.[43]

One can only conclude that the park in Liverpool is not as safe, well managed or maintained.

Some observers have found that trees lower the crime rate. A study in Baltimore showed there is a strong inverse relationship between tree canopy and our index of robbery, burglary, theft and shooting. The more conservative spatially adjusted model indicated that a 10% increase in tree canopy was associated with a roughly 12% decrease in crime.[44]

When the study went on to break down tree cover in public rather than private space, it found that there was a 40 percent decrease in these crimes. The researchers were careful to point out that in a few isolated areas, the findings were reversed, presumably because the vegetation's concealment value outweighed its deterrent effect. Appropriate spacing and frequent pruning of vegetation is needed in these cases. The Chicago Regional Tree Initiative compiled all the benefits that trees provide, with citations backing up the claims. One of the studies suggests that trees "may deter crime both by increasing informal surveillance and by mitigating some of the psychological precursors to violence."[45] In general, more trees and green spaces mean more eyes on the street, and more eyes on the street reduce crime, as the legendary urbanist Jane Jacobs so famously proclaimed over a half century ago.[46] It's safe to generalize that cooler tree-lined streets and parks are freer from violent conflict.

The Japanese have been promoting the physical and psychological benefits of what they call "forest bathing," a fetching term for spending more time in wooded settings. Their studies show that stands of trees lower blood pressure and pulse, while reducing the risk of heart disease and the level of stress hormones. They also feel forest settings are "balm for urban children and those wanting to escape technology . . . Some city-dwellers are even joining 'forest bathing clubs.'"[47] From 2004 to 2012, officials spent about $4 million studying the benefits of just being with trees – not hiking in rural woodlands but simply sitting or meandering under trees, relaxing rather than accomplishing anything. A subsequent survey on forest bathing's psychological effects on 500 healthy volunteers showed significantly reduced hostility and depression scores, coupled with increased liveliness, after exposure to trees.

> Brief exposure to greenery in urban environments can relieve stress levels, and experts have recommended "doses of nature" as part of treatment of attention disorders in children. What all of this evidence suggests is we don't seem to need a lot of exposure to gain from nature – but regular contact appears to improve our immune system function and our wellbeing.[48]

Similarly in China, elderly citizens are increasingly leaving polluted cities and taking their ailments to "longevity villages," where the more natural setting, cleaner air and purer water are seen as miracle cures.[49]

Urban forestry is particularly good at sequestering CO_2 and producing oxygen, as well as providing wood for construction, often replacing carbon-intensive steel and concrete. The rising economic value of timber building materials and other forest products encourages more afforestation. And, if legally permitted, fallen and harvested trees can be used as a wood-chip fuel in power plants or to provide the cozy warmth in a home fireplace or wood stove. Urban agriculture, now popular in North American cities, can provide similar benefits to individuals and communities. Small allotment gardens can be planted almost anywhere in the city, and are especially sensible in abandoned areas. "A display of growing plants, made accessible to all and cared for by conscientious gardeners, provides an alternative to sterile development and derelict spaces and offers a vision of hope for the city."[50] Together street trees, parks, gardens and urban forests are large enough in scale to provide cool urban micro-climates and to play a significant positive role in both urban metabolism and urban pleasure.

Some urban foresters and arboriculturalists insist on planting native species.

> Perhaps the most substantial point lost on many of those who advocate a "natives only" policy is that most if not all urban forests (and woodlands and other treescapes) are situated in probably the most artificial and man-made landscape that humans have devised and constructed. Arguments for the insertion or reconstruction of wildlife habitat in urban areas miss the point that such areas are, by definition, devoted to people. That is not to preclude the establishment of native vegetation in and around towns and cities, but it should be in keeping with what people want. This aspect is rarely considered by those who argue most vociferously for the ecological value of urban forests.[51]

A lack of community participation in tree selection leads to less advocacy for trees in general.

The costs of trees are not trivial: increased water demand, pruning their branches, raking and removing their fallen leaves, and repairing rumpled sidewalks and root-invaded underground pipes. The roots of trees not only heave sidewalks, they can make land and buildings subside by absorbing moisture. For instance, shrinking clay subsoils in London require the costly underpinning of inadequate foundations, with some insurance companies demanding removal of whole blocks of shade trees. Trees can start or spread fires and, as already stated, they emit VOCs that form ozone. And trees in dense, tight urban spaces also can limit cooling breezes in hot weather, and their leaves can trap particulate pollutants from vehicles. "Leaves and branches slow air flow, causing pollutants to settle out."[52] On the other hand, research has also shown a 60% reduction in particulates from exhaust fumes in tree-lined streets . . . sulphur dioxide, nitrogen oxides and particulates, carbon monoxide, cadmium, nickel, and lead are all substances that a tree works 24 hours a day, 7 days a week to remove and store.[53]

Some American residents don't want trees on their street, often because perched birds spatter parked cars with their droppings. Town and city dwellers in England can be ambivalent about trees: "arboriculturists know well that many people seek to remove or reduce them because of negative effects such as light obstruction or . . . nectar dripping on cars in the immediate environment."[54] "Treephobia" sometimes sets in among people who have had trees fall on their homes or cars. For others, the raking and removal of fallen leaves and branches is a proverbial problem that is seen as not worth the benefits. Another study of attitudes about street trees in the U.K. and the U.S. concluded that while

> there often exists a significant negative attitude to street trees in some people, generally those communities sampled had a benevolent attitude to them. However, it is doubtful whether positive ecosystem services . . . such as carbon sequestration or biofuel production register as important with many people, if at all.[55]

Another urban challenge is that dense urbanism restricts the availability of large greenspaces, especially in cities constrained by extensive areas of water and mountains. There is limited available land in dense cities to retroactively provide parks, greenways and tree canopies. Physical infrastructure above- and below-grade also constrains the planting of trees. Insinuating smaller bits of greenspace – "interstitial greenery" – into existing built public space and infrastructure is needed to supplement the planting of large trees. Instead of only providing expansive green spaces for passive and active recreation, smaller green spaces can be planted throughout the city to increase walkability, shade, scale and aesthetic appeal. These plantings include shrubbery, trellises, arbors, bio-swales and vertical green walls. In the aggregate, they can add significant beauty, shading and lung capacity to the city. In 2015, University of Georgia researchers showed that "networks of small urban green spaces, such as parks, gardens and green roofs, were *more effective* at reducing a city's temperature than a singular park of the equivalent size."[56] Both Chicago and Los Angeles, cities with little available open land within their boundaries, have committed to greening their alleys and interstitial spaces. Berlin's "Sponge City" initiative also tackles the two issues with which most cement- and asphalt-covered urban centers struggle: heat and flooding. It addresses them with heat-repelling and water-absorbing green space.[57]

Some tree and shrubbery loss is inevitable with urbanization, especially with the unfortunate clear-cutting associated with developments on the urban edge. But deforestation and loss of groundcover result from more than development and clear-cutting. There is not enough institutional and government support for maintaining urban vegetation and planting new vegetation. For instance, not all cities have adequate tree replacement policies and programs. Energy and other utility companies are allowed to prune and remove vegetation on private land without getting permission each time. Overcutting has to be curtailed in any successful effort to maintain and increase the urban greenery that is so critical to addressing UHIs. The obstacles to planting and maintaining trees must be overcome, for their benefits are more legion than even tree-huggers realize. Figure 5.3 lists 18 benefits, to which more can no doubt be added.

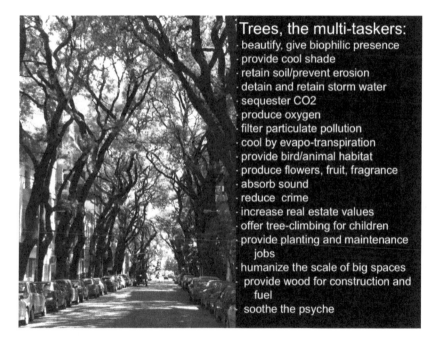

Trees, the multi-taskers:
- beautify, give biophilic presence
- provide cool shade
- retain soil/prevent erosion
- detain and retain storm water
- sequester CO2
- produce oxygen
- filter particulate pollution
- cool by evapo-transpiration
- provide bird/animal habitat
- produce flowers, fruit, fragrance
- absorb sound
- reduce crime
- increase real estate values
- offer tree-climbing for children
- provide planting and maintenance jobs
- humanize the scale of big spaces
- provide wood for construction and fuel
- soothe the psyche

Figure 5.3 Street trees are stalwart foot soldiers in cooling and beautifying the city, which in turn attract and retain urban residents. Coupled with cool roofs and pavements, they can reduce a city's ambient air temperatures by 4°–9°F (2.2°–5°C) during summer months.[1] Taken together trees are an immense breathing system for the earth that is essential for both plants and animals, including humans. Trees breathe out what we breathe in; we breathe out what trees breathe in; we inter-breathe with trees. (Photo by author)

1 Benjamin Barber, *Cool Cities: Urban Sovereignty and the Fix for Climate Change*, Yale University Press, 2017

Also, there is the awkward relationship of trees and parks to the perennial problem of urban gentrification. This hidden cost of greening is sometimes labeled "eco-gentrification," referring to the inequitable distribution of greenery throughout the city. Districts with greater access to green space, including yards, street trees and public parks, are often more desirable and therefore more expensive. "Numerous studies have shown that lower-income neighborhoods and ethnic or racially diverse communities are more likely to have decreased access to urban green space."[58] This inequity has given rise to the "just-green-enough" tactic, which strives to "increase the environmental quality and public health of a neighborhood, but without changing its socio-economic character."[59] There needs to be more sensitive attention to under-greened areas by urban planners, developers, city officials and policymakers.

Finally, there is the long length of time required to grow large shade trees. "The only better time to plant a tree than today, is 10 years ago."[60] If all cities facing overheating from CC and UHIs need extensive tree canopies, getting street trees large enough, quick enough is expensive. There is not sufficient time to grow them from small caliber trees, much less saplings. Reasonably large trees need to be planted, preferably with 6-inch or bigger trunk diameters and 20-foot or wider canopies. Extreme weather events may require a rejuvenation of existing canopies. Tree planting, as already elaborated, is ambitious in many cities. Large urban trees are cherished civic assets that need the support of foundations, citizen groups and land owners.

Old-growth forests are not found in cities, but they are nonetheless worthy of mention, because they are such powerful carbon workhorses, as well as awesome places to visit. The World Resources Institute estimates that nearly 80 percent of the old-growth forest on the planet is now gone, with the figure jumping to more than 90 percent in the contiguous U.S.

> Much of the loss is due to the march of civilization; we have clear-cut ancient trees to make way for our settlements. But chainsaws and bulldozers and harvesters are not the only threats, or even the most powerful: forests are now weakening or dying at alarming rates due to natural processes that are intensifying as a result of our warming planet. The major threat . . . can be traced to relatively recent, climate change-driven events, including prolonged infestations by pests whose destructive actions are no longer curtailed by long cold winters.[61]

Trees are under attack from a wide variety of other threats. New aerial monitoring techniques indicate that the increasing frequency and size of forest fires are having a marked impact on global carbon emissions. In the third of a century between 1984 and 2017, the total area of land that burns in any given year was up 300 percent; the area of forests per se that burns annually was up 1,000 percent.[62] Intentional and accidental deforestation has been a growing problem globally, especially to create pasture for beef-producing cattle, whose belching and flatulence produce enough methane to be another major contributor to CC. The Amazon River Basin has been visited by drought that is slowing forest growth, and the added heat is forcing animals to migrate to higher land on the eastern slope of the Andes mountains. And too many elephants in some African reserves are destroying forest habitat at alarming rates.[63] Forest loss has become a large enough ecological and CC issue to receive growing media attention and action by NGOs.

Deforestation by humans is currently the major threat to the global loss of both trees and tree species. Fragmentation of the landscape by human intervention has also diminished the global number of trees and species. The spread of insect pests, such as the emerald ash borer that has wiped out so many ash trees in northwest Europe and in eastern and central U.S., is often accidental. In this case it was carried by cargo ships from Asia to Michigan in 2002, and then migrated to other states, killing hundreds of millions of ash trees, with many more still at risk. Increasingly CC is contributing to global deforestation and species loss, due to increased evapotranspiration from warmer temperatures and more intense, erratic precipitation. According to the World Conservation Monitoring Center, the mounting combination of causes this century is forcing the extinction of 10 percent of the planet's 100,000 tree species.[64] While the ongoing extinction and invasion of species is an ongoing process of regenerating and advancing the evolution of trees, humans need to guard against the loss of key species on which they depend. Trees are essential for our species' continued success for the habitat they provide to so much life and for the carbon they absorb and oxygen they produce.

Homo sapiens cut down more trees than they replant. The global tree count is down to about three trillion from between an estimated five to six trillion in prehistoric times. That's 422 trees per human,[65] most of which are not in cities. We need their help absorbing carbon all over the planet, but especially in cities, where humans exhale about 1 kg (2.2 lbs.) of CO_2 every day, while our cars typically emit as much in 3 miles. While urban trees are helpful carbon sinks, they reduce GHG emissions more by shading buildings, thereby reducing the need for fans and air conditioners. There have also been some promising new findings that suggest that trees may be able to absorb more carbon dioxide than previously thought. According to a 2017 study at Wyoming University, global climate models have failed to adequately account for a positive feedback loop: as carbon dioxide increases in the atmosphere, plants thrive, grow larger and are able to absorb more CO_2. This may help explain why the atmospheric GHG levels have not been rising as fast as some models have predicted. "The team estimates that climate scientists have underestimated the ability of plants to grow and absorb carbon dioxide by as much as 16%."[66]

Less known is the fact that forests – despite an overall planetary decline – are actually on the increase in parts of Europe and America. Trees are spreading in almost every European country, especially Spain, Greece, Ireland and Italy, where the increase was 5–10 percent between 1990 and 2015.

> Forests now occupy a third of America's land, having grown by 2% in the past decade. They are even expanding in Australia, following a long decline . . . Deforestation in South America and Africa rightly gets most of conservationists' attention. That loss is huge – equivalent to about 4.8M hectares a year, which far outweighs gains elsewhere. Yet the foresting of rich countries is still one of the world's great land-use changes. It seems just as unstoppable as the deforestation of poorer places.[67]

Trees may be the most remarkable species of the plant kingdom. Pando, a clonal colony of quaking aspen trees in Utah that is a single genetic organism with a common root system, is 80,000 years old![68] Some individual trees are 4,000–12,000 years old, living longer than any organism on the planet. And

> the older they get, the better they get at being trees. The rate at which they sequester carbon increases each year, and the amount of life they can sustain increases proportionally. Scientists know of no fundamental reason why trees must inevitably die, and many times one or more genetically identical "scion" grows where a mature tree once stood. There is no equivalent reincarnation in the animal world, other than in Buddhism.
>
> In forests, trees clump together "like human families: tree parents live together with their children, communicate with them, support them as they grow, share nutrients with those who are sick or struggling, and even warn each other of impending dangers."[69]

Taller, older trees tend to receive more sunlight and produce more sugar than they need.[70] These hub or mother trees can help over 100 offspring trees, by sending nutrients and rhizomes to their "family of children," as well as making root space for them![71] Some species, like birches, are unfriendly and behave like bullies, while beech trees are collaborators, according to years of work by former German State Forester Peter Wohlleben. He sees a study of African acacias, which shows how they release a chemical when giraffes start eating them, as evidence of how trees communicate. The chemical released drifts through the air warning other trees of the danger and they in turn begin producing toxic chemicals before the giraffe has reached them.

Trees magically interact with and support their fellow trees, but they also compete with other trees for light and water. They behave uncannily like human species, with its selfish and altruistic gene . . . When he talks about oak trees using 600 words, he is referring to a chemical language. "Above all most trees want to live socially," says Wohlleben. "Trees don't want to grow fast. They want to have companions. They want to live in social groups . . . they support each other."[72]

The fact that trees can communicate and cooperate with each other boggles the mind. Some Buddhists see them as sentient, conscious organisms.

A seventeenth-century gardener wrote of how trees "speak to the mind, and tell us many things, and teach us many good lessons." Hermann Hesse called them "the most penetrating of preachers" . . . Since long before researchers began to illuminate the astonishing science of what trees feel and how they communicate, the human imagination has communed with the arboreal world and found in it a boundless universe of kinship . . . We extol our intelligence as the uniquely human faculty that sets us apart from other animals, but even our definitions of intelligence are narrowly anthropocentric and based on things we humans happen to be good at. Surely there's a special kind of biological and existential intelligence in an organism capable of such remarkable resilience – an organism that can outlive us by millennia and witness all of our fleeting struggles while it remains unflinchingly rooted in its particular corner of the ecosystem.[73]

The arboreal gifts continue: "Even when a tree dies, it continues to give life. First it nourishes insects that bore into its wood and birds that eat them. Eventually it falls, rots, and becomes a seed bed for new trees and plants."[74] Urban trees are like little hospitals, doing so much to enhance micro-climates and to make us feel better psychologically and physically. They've long been appreciated as urban amenities and oases. Indeed, seventeenth-century Amsterdam's City Council mandated the planting of trees for "sweet air, adornment and pleasantness."[75] Rarely do so many virtues line up on one side of an equation. The earth needs trees. Humans need trees. Cities need trees.

Notes

1 Jim Robbins, *The Man Who Planted Trees*, Spiegel & Grau, 2012
2 John Fowles, *The Tree*, Vintage, 2000
3 Clay Chapman, mason/master builder, personal email, 7/22/18
4 David Maxwell Braun, interview with Jill Jonnes, author of *Urban Forests*, *National Geographic*, posted 11/2/16

5 Edward Ng et al., "A study on the cooling effects of greening in a high-density city: an experience from Hong Kong," *Building and Environment*, 2012, pp. 256, 261

6 Brandon Loomis, "In Dallas as in Phoenix, people look to trees for relief from urban heat islands," *The Republic*, azcentral.com, 12/29/17

7 Ng et al., "A study on the cooling effects of greening in a high-density city: an experience from Hong Kong," p. 261

8 Brian Stone, *The City and the Coming Climate*, Cambridge University Press, 2012, pp. 99–104

9 Jeff Speck, *Walkable City*, North Point Press, 2012, p. 226

10 Katherine Schwab, "Scientists discover yet another reason cities need more trees," *Co.Design*, 8/2/17

11 "Protecting and developing the urban tree canopy," *U.S. Conference of Mayors*, 2008, p. 8

12 Madeline Ostrander, "As cities grow hotter, how will we adapt?" *The New Yorker*, 9/18/16

13 Emily Oaksford, APA Sustaining Places, website/blog, 3/18/15, citing source in footnote 9

14 "EveryTreeSF – street tree census," http://sf-planning.org, S.F. Planning Department, 2017

15 Hayley Birch, "Where is the world's hottest city," *The Guardian*, 7/22/15

16 Gregory Scruggs, "Urban forests increasingly central to planning in poor and rich countries alike," *citiscope*, 1/30/17

17 "Planting records," Greening, Landscape & Tree Management Section, Development Bureau, Hong Kong, www.greening.gov.hk/en/people_trees_harmony/planting_record.html

18 Marian Shafqat, "Forests get a whopping Rs2B in budget," *The Express Tribune*, 6/7/17

19 K. Unnikrishnan, "India has planted nearly 66 million trees in 12 hours," *Environment*, 7/2/17

20 "China is building the first forest city of 40,000 trees to fight air pollution," *The Express Tribune*, 6/28/17

21 J. van Zoest and M. Hopman, "Taking the economic benefits of green space into account: the story of the Dutch TEEB for Cities Project," *Urban Climate*, May, 2004, pp. 107–114

22 Gregory Scruggs, "Urban forests increasingly central to planning in poor and rich countries alike"

23 "Urban trees save megacities $500 million a year," *Yale Environment 360*, 9/5/17

24 Gregory Scruggs, "Urban forests increasingly central to planning in poor and rich countries alike"

25 Brad Plumer, "Really big ideas to beat the heat," *The New York Times*, 8/9/18

26 David Maxwell Braun, interview with Jill Jonnes, author of *Urban Forests*, National Geographic, posted 11/2/16

27 Constanza Martinez Gaete, "New York City mapped all of its trees and calculated the economic benefits of every single one," *ArchDaily*, 11/28/16

28 Kirsten Bauer, "From grey to green infrastructure: how local governments are re-making Melbourne," *foreground*, 4/6/18

29 Olaf Ribiero, insidebainbridge.com/tag/probuild, 1/27/14

30 GreenStreets LA, "Planting trees where people live," http://greenstreetsla.org/

31 Ananya Battacharya, "Trees could make urban pollution even worse," *Quartz*, 12/6/16

32 "Cities' air problems only get worse with climate change," *The New York Times*, 8/20/14

33 Robert Krulwich, "The earth has lungs," Phenomena, *nationalgeographic. com*, 3/9/16
34 J. Elliott Campbell, University of California, Merced, quoted in Carl Zimmer, "Antarctic ice reveals earth's accelerating plant growth," *The New York Times*, 4/5/17
35 A. Rosenfeld, H. Akbari, J. Romm and M. Pomerantz, "Cool communities: strategies for heat islands mitigation and smog reduction," *Energy and Buildings*, 28, 1998, pp. 51–62
36 Brian Stone, *The City and the Coming Climate*, p. 99
37 Henry Fountain, "Forests protect the climate: a future with more storms would mean trouble," *The New York Times*, 3/13/18
38 Mark Wilson, "The national forests of the future need to be in cities," *Co. Design*, 3/15/18
39 Ibid.
40 "Could cities replace street lights with glowing trees?" Concepts, *The Urban Developer*, 2/28/18
41 Dan Burden, "Urban street trees, 22 benefits," Glatting Jackson and Walkable Communities, Inc., August, 2006
42 Gunseli Yalcinkaya, "Stefano Boeri proposes trees instead of barriers to protect against terror attacks," *dezeen*, 8/24/17
43 Alessandro Venerandi, "What are the factors that give a place value," *CityMetric*, 10/16/17
44 Austin Troy, J. Morgan Grove and Jarlath O'Neill-Dunne, "The relationship between tree canopy and crime rates across an urban–rural gradient in the greater Baltimore region," *Landscape and Urban Planning*, 106, 6/15/12, pp. 262–270
45 Delaney Nolan, "A very detailed, interactive map of Chicago's tree canopy," *Atlas Obscura*, 8/14/17
46 Jane Jacobs, *Life and Death of Great American Cities*, Random House, 1961
47 Ephrat Livini, "The Japanese practice of forest bathing is scientifically proven to be good for you," *World Economic Forum*, Agenda, 3/27/17
48 Ibid.
49 Nina Strochlic, "In search of a longer life," *National Geographic*, March, 2018
50 Richard Ingersoll, "Eat the city," *Places*, June, 2013
51 Andy J. Moffat, "Communicating the benefits of urban trees: a critical review," *Arboricultural Journal*, 38, 2016, published online 5/26/16
52 Ibid.
53 "9 reasons our cities need mature urban trees," *GoBlueUrban* (blog), 8/28/15
54 G.F.M. Dawe, "Street trees and the urban environment," in Ian Douglas, David Goode, Michael C. Houck and Rusong Wang (eds), *The Routledge Handbook of Urban Ecology*, Routledge, 2011, pp. 424–449
55 H. Schroeder, J. Flannigan and R. Coles, "Residents' attitudes toward street trees in the UK and U.S. communities," *Arboriculture and Urban Forestry*, 32, 2008, pp. 236–246
56 Laurie Winkless, "The rise of the urban rooftop," *Forbes*, 8/10/18
57 Gloria Kurnik, "Berlin is becoming a sponge city," *Bloomberg Businessweek*, 8/18/17
58 Calli Vander Wilde, "Striving for just green enough," *Agora*, 11, 2017, p. 63
59 Jeanne Haffner, "The dangers of eco-gentrification: what's the best way to make a city greener?" *The Guardian*, 5/6/15
60 Wayne Appleyard, Ann Arbor Energy Commission, personal memory
61 Mark Hough, "Champion trees and urban forests," *Places*, September, 2013
62 Miles O'Brien, "Leading edge of science," *PBS NewsHour*, 12/13/17

63 Ibid.
64 Johannes Foufopoulos, Professor of Natural Resources, speaker at Science Cafe, Ann Arbor, MI, 2/21/18
65 Robert Krulwich, "The earth has lungs"
66 Sarah Knapton, "Global warming: plants may absorb more carbon dioxide than previously thought," *The Telegraph*, 5/23/17
67 "The foresting of the West," *The Economist*, 12/2/17
68 "Pando (tree)," Wikipedia, June, 2017
69 Peter Wohlleben, *The Hidden Life of Trees*, Greystone Books, 2015 (inside book flap)
70 "Talking trees," Explore, *National Geographic*, June, 2018, p. 26
71 Suzanne Simard, "How trees talk to each other," *TED talk*, July 2016
72 Mark Brown, "Trees talk to each other, have sex, and look after their young says author," *The Guardian*, 5/31/17
73 Mary Popova, "The world's oldest living things," *BrainPickings*, 5/14/17
74 Gabriel Popkin, "What the death of an oak tree teaches us about mortality," *Aeon*, 12/6/16
75 Jonathan Rose, *The Well-Tempered City*, Harper Wave, 2016, p. 87

6 Policies and Case Studies

The prolific CC blogger Joyce Coffee waxes optimistic on CC:

> Walking through my Midwestern neighborhood, I spy innovations
> that suggest we are up to the challenges that a changing climate trig-
> ger. I see storm sewers with "rain blockers" that delay rainwaters'
> approach to them during and after big rains; "permeable alleys" that
> absorb water through pores in their concrete; and bioswales of plants
> and spongy soil that absorb water runoff from roofs and roads. And
> underground a mile or so away, deep tunnels take precipitation from
> heavy rains and snow melts to large distant reservoirs to prevent
> overflows of sewage and storm water.

Let's look at other examples, primarily in the public sector, of demonstration and policy initiatives,[1] followed by longer case studies of
particular cities.

A Panoply of American Examples

Across the U.S., stakeholders from citizens to government agencies to
corporations have adopted strategies and demonstrations to reduce
UHIs and CC as voluntary efforts and official policies and practices.
Demonstrations and practices include green and cool roofs, reforestation and cool pavements; the policies involve mandatory cool roofs
and other antidotes, including incentive grants and rebates. Other
entities, like university and other campuses, also implement voluntary
initiatives and required practices, often as a result of public policy.
Different types of efforts can complement each other: sometimes an
initiative that begins as voluntary becomes required over time. In addition to examples already cited in earlier chapters, the following ones
ostensibly address CC, but simultaneously deal with UHIs.

Voluntary/Demonstration Efforts

Demonstration Projects

As noted earlier, the City of Chicago installed a green roof on its City Hall that includes some 20,000 plants, shrubs, grasses, vines and trees. In addition to assessing energy impacts, the green roof has been designed to test different types of rooftop garden systems, the success rates of native and non-native vegetation, and the detention of storm water. The project has drawn media attention, and helped to raise the visibility and public understanding of green roofs in the city. The City of Tucson, Arizona demonstrated and documented how a cool roof reduced the temperature inside and on the roof of a city administration building, and saved 400 million BTUs in cooling energy annually. The city installed 28,000 square feet of white elastomeric coating on the unshaded metal roof, resulting in a 50–65 percent saving on cooling costs.

Incentive Grants and Rebates

Starting in 2006, Baltimore County has provided $10 coupons to home-owners toward trees purchased at local nurseries. In spite of the modest inducement, 1,770 trees were planted in the first two months, with many more to follow. Sacramento has partnered with a foundation to provide $350,000 worth of free 4–7 feet tall shade trees to residents who agree to plant and maintain them. They also give utility bill rebates on cool roofs of $0.20/square foot to customers with flat roofs, as does Austin, Texas. After succeeding with its green roof demonstration, Austin has since given out grants of $6,000 for about 100 rooftops. Philadelphia has provided over 550 buildings with cool roof coatings, which has reduced air conditioning by about one-third in a typical row house. Pennsylvania's EPA has given out more than $500,000 in green roof grants, while Houston has given individual grants of up to $10,000 for adding plantings along and attached to blank walls for improving aesthetics and fighting UHIs. Pennsylvania also has an $8 million tree-planting program that targets older cities and towns with less than 25 percent tree cover. New Jersey's Cool Cities Initiative plants trees in its large cities with low tree coverage.

Voluntary Private Sector Initiatives

Roughly half of the biggest corporations and companies in the U.S. have set targets to shrink their carbon footprints. "Almost two dozen companies, including Google, Walmart and Bank of America, have pledged to power their operations with 100% renewable energy, with varying deadlines. Google's data centers worldwide now run on renewable energy."[2]

These examples are the tip of a growing iceberg of private initiatives. However, while large corporations have the financial structure and wherewithal to pay for energy upgrades, production homebuilders in the U.S. are less able to afford them, particularly for middle-income housing.

Public Education and Awards

Almost all cities engage in some type of public outreach and education. Cities in Utah, for example, take advantage of a program that uses advertising, outreach and educational workshops to plant trees to reduce energy consumption and diminish urban heat. Utah Kool Kids program teaches elementary and secondary school students about UHI impacts and reduction techniques. The Cool Schools program in Los Angeles teaches environmental stewardship with hands-on and classroom experience, including the planting of hundreds of trees. The national EPA has long hosted the ENERGY STAR awards. The San Diego school district, for instance, won one of these awards because 140 of its 200 schools met the program's criteria, including cool roofs. The Home Depot Foundation gives out over $100,000 in awards per year for tree planting. The Green Roofs for Healthy Cities gives awards for green roof initiatives, as well as funding research teams and citizens who have advanced the implementation of green roofs through policy, which brings us to the next category.

Policy Initiatives

Procurement

Many local governments committed to addressing UHIs started with procurement policies for municipal facilities by revising their construction and bid specifications. Tucson requires that air-conditioned city buildings use cool roofing materials for most new buildings and replacement roofs, a policy that has also encouraged use of these products on private projects. Chicago, after demonstrating its Green Alley initiative, encourages repaving of alleyways with porous materials. Some 2,000 miles of alleys are or will be permeable.

Resolutions

Austin City Council has adopted a heat island mitigation resolution, and awarded $1 million toward enforcing its tree-saving ordinance and is developing a cool roofs strategy. Annapolis, Maryland has adopted a comprehensive energy-efficiency resolution, including increasing street trees to lower its ambient temperatures and levels of CO_2 and ozone.

Tree and Landscape Ordinances

Tree protection ordinances prohibit the removal or pruning of trees, often native or historic ones, without a permit. One type requires tree protection during building construction. San Antonio specially protects significant and heritage trees, as well as ones in 100-year floodplains. Street tree ordinances typically govern the planting and removal of trees along public rights of way that are owned privately but accessible to the public. Orlando, Florida requires planting trees every 50 to 100 feet on both sides of the street. Some cities require shade trees in parking lots to lower heat emitted by pavement and parked cars. Chicago requires landscaped trees and shrubs on parkways, parking lots and around loading docks on both new and renovation projects. Baton Rouge, Louisiana requires two shade trees for each 5,000 square feet of property and one street tree for every 600 square feet of street frontage. It also requires a shade tree for every 10–15 parking spaces, depending on the size of the lot.

Since 1993, an Atlanta city ordinance has set rules and imposed fees for cutting down the trees that make the city distinctive. Cutting down a healthy tree of 6 inch caliber or greater requires city approval and a size-based fee, which can be reduced. Signs let neighbors know when trees are slated for removal, giving them a chance to appeal. Violations come with fines of $500 for a first offense, $1,000 for each one after that – and

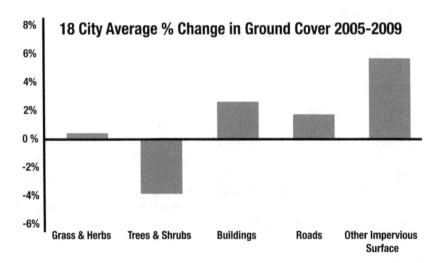

Figure 6.1 During a 5-year period, the area covered by trees and shrubs in 18 American cities fell significantly, while buildings, roads and other impervious surfaces increased as a percentage of total land area. The rate of change sets the stage for flooding and heat emergencies among other climatic impacts.[1] (Center for Neighborhood Technology)

1 David Nowak and Eric Greenfield, "Tree and impervious cover change in U.S. cities," *Urban Forestry and Urban Greening*, USDA Forest Service, 2012

up to $60,000 an acre depending how many were cut down illegally.[3] In Georgia, Savannah's downtown has a dense, mature tree canopy of Southern Live Oaks, Magnolias and Crepe Myrtles, all carefully protected by a local conservation society. It's a superb asset that helps bring millions of tourists per year, as well as offering delight to residents. As cities get hotter, it's all the more essential to have ordinances with penalties and/or incentives to protect urban trees.

Comprehensive Plans and Design Guidelines

Comprehensive or General Plans set forth policies, goals and objectives to direct development and preservation, while design guidelines are more descriptive and suggestive about the preferred quality or character of a place. Gilbert, Arizona lists reducing heat as a core goal of their General Plan, with a host of criteria for evaluation techniques, co-sponsorships and mitigation techniques. The Official Plan of Toronto, Canada includes policies to specifically address UHIs through shade trees, permeable and reflective pavements and other strategies to reduce flooding and air temperatures.

Zoning Codes and Green Building Standards

The zoning codes of Portland, Oregon and Chicago allow larger buildings if roof gardens or green roofs are installed. Cities like Arlington, Virginia, Ann Arbor, Michigan and San Jose, California base some of their building requirements on the LEED rating system. Green Globes, operated by the Green Building Initiative, is another rating system that other American and Canadian cities use. Both systems give credits for shade vegetation, cool or green roofs, highly reflective, emissive or permeable pavements. Seattle, Washington requires vegetative cover on the equivalent of 30–60 percent of the applicable property, depending on its use, and it has cost-shared over 17,000 trees to 600 neighborhood groups. It's worth noting that even though Seattle historically has had cool summers, the language of this regulation specifically – and surprisingly – targets heat waves. As of 2018 in Orlando, any commercial or multi-family residential building larger than 50,000 gross square feet, and any city-owned building of over 10,000 gross square feet, is required to obtain an energy benchmarking score, which is *publically posted*. To be held publically accountable in this manner seems like an effective way to improve energy performance through peer pressure, without mandating it.

Building Codes

Energy codes, which are often part of local and state building codes, have begun to require cool roofs. In 1995 Georgia was the first state to add them to its energy code. Chicago mandates a minimum reflectance of 25 percent for low-sloped roofs, and such roofing products qualify for an ENERGY STAR label. Florida and California have added cool roof provisions, as their popularity increases across the country. As previously noted several times, Los Angeles has been very aggressive.

Air Quality Requirements

As mentioned in Chapter 4, lowering urban temperatures can help reduce ground-level ozone, as many cities struggle to meet national standards. Cities are using urban forestry and cool roofs, in particular, to help them reach attainment. EPA has developed three strategies that include UHI reduction to help with State Implementation Plans (SIPs). The U.S. Forest Service's Center for Urban Forest Research estimates that one million additional trees could lower NO_x by almost a quarter ton per day, and if trees emitted low levels of VOCs, ozone could be reduced by 1.5 tons daily. As part of the Washington D.C. region's SIP, Fairfax County set a precedent in 2007 with a tree canopy goal of 45 percent, and proposed increasing the number of trees planted from 21,000 to 84,000, justifying the added expense by citing trees' multiple benefits.

Government Insurance

As society keeps building in flood-prone coastal areas, we are

> pretty much daring Mother Nature to whack us. We even subsidize such dares through the dysfunctional National Flood Insurance Program. This offers underpriced insurance, encouraging people to live in low-lying areas, compounded by flood maps that are old and unreliable. One Mississippi home flooded 34 times in 32 years, resulting in pay-outs worth almost ten times what the home was worth.[4]

One hopes that flabby, out-of-date insurance programs at all levels of government will be revisited in light of the growing impacts of CC and UHIs.

Government Subsidies

The available set of smart surface solutions include cool roofs, green roofs, solar PV and permeable and reflective pavements and road surfaces. They can be expensive, especially for low-income areas, where the problems are greatest. These neighborhoods are characterized by little greenery and dark impervious surfaces that result in excessive summer heat, air pollution, respiratory illness, heat stress and high health costs. "One of the findings that is most robust in the disaster literature is that low-income families and families of color will receive a greater degree of damage to begin with."[5] Recovery can take two to four times longer for low-income families or families of color than for other households. Municipal, metro, state and federal subsidies are more and more needed.

American Case Studies

These case studies highlight what some American cities have done, including some of the cities already mentioned. The selected cities represent different climates, from cold winter, hot summer to dry mountain to hot, humid prairie.[6]

Chicago

The City of Chicago, located on Lake Michigan in the North Central region of the U.S., has a population of over 2.7 million and covers over 225 square miles. The metropolitan region is the third largest in the U.S., with roughly 10 million people in a six-county area that covers approximately 3,750 square miles. Chicago's climate is predominantly continental, ranging from warm in the summer to cold in the winter. Its climate is partially modified by Lake Michigan, and to a lesser extent by other Great Lakes. The flat terrain of the Midwest and the lake make Chicago's weather unpredictable and frequently extreme. Summer is very warm and often humid, with temperatures reaching 95–100°F (35–38°C). The coldest days in the "windy city" are usually in January when the temperature can drop well below 0°F (-18°C). The city averages about 750 cooling degree days and 6,500 heating degree days (based on a trigger temperature of 65°F or 18°C), with a cooling season that lasts from mid-June through early-September. Air conditioning saturation in the metro area is fairly high, particularly in residences built after 1980, and in commercial buildings.

With an estimated 3.5 million trees, the city's tree canopy and ground cover is about 40%, followed by mostly asphalt paved surfaces of 31% and roof surfaces of 27%, plus about 2% bodies of water. The vegetative coverage varies from 16% in urban commercial areas to 45% in medium/high density residential areas to 71% in the outer suburban residential areas. Street trees within the City, including those growing in the several hundred miles of median strips, comprise about a third of the tree cover. The highest percentages of paved surfaces are transportation rights of way, commercial suburban areas, commercial urban areas and industrial areas.

Chicago has been a leading city in launching measures to reduce UHIs. Highlights of the City's activities make an impressively long list:

landscape ordinance, energy code, rooftop garden on City Hall, energy savings, open space impact fee, asphalt alley reconstruction, parking lot resurfacing and greening. The Tree Ordinance, established in 1991 and updated in 1999, covers three categories of landscaping: planting trees or shrubs on parkways; landscaping to screen parking lots, loading docks and other vehicular use areas; and landscaping within the parking lots, loading docks and other vehicular use areas. Tellingly, the City no longer plants the state's official tree, the White Oak, because it anticipates the local climate slowly becoming equivalent to the current climate in northern Texas and Mississippi within the lifetime of newly planted trees.

In January 2003, Chicago amended its energy code requirements for reflective roofs, which applies to all buildings with some exceptions. Already referenced is the acclaimed rooftop garden on City Hall. The total available cooling effect from evapotranspiration by the garden is

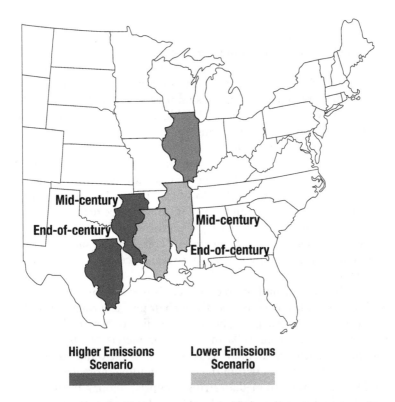

Figure 6.2 This graphic illustrates that the City of Chicago estimates Illinois' climate will become equivalent to today's climate in Louisiana or Texas. The City is planting trees on their streets and in parks accordingly, as well as taking other initiatives to deal with a warmer, wetter climate. (Redrawn by author, data from USGRCP 2009)

claimed to be 730 percent of what is needed to eliminate the cooling load of the roof per se. Because the roof is well insulated, the surplus cooling effect is mostly available to the surrounding microclimate and tends to reduce cooling costs in buildings downwind. The city estimates that if green roofs were installed on all Chicago roofs the avoided peak energy demand would be 720 megawatts, and load on the storm sewer system would be reduced 70 percent. Air quality would improve due to removal of particulates, nitrogen dioxide and ozone by the vegetation, and power plant emissions would decrease. The green roofs would also increase the amount of wildlife habitat for squirrels, birds and butterflies.

The repaving of alleys is part of the Green Alley initiative. Chicago also has a series of greening projects involving replacing concrete and asphalt with green space and reflective surfaces throughout the city. In addition to the above activities, Chicago has launched a series of neighborhood projects intended to demonstrate UHI reduction techniques at the community level. Much as lighter-colored pavements cool the city and the planet, permeable pavements reduce flooding. Introducing grass and other ground cover in the interstices of pavers is positive: despite the relatively dark green leaves, evapotranspiration tends to offset its greater absorption of solar heat, on top of its carbon sequestration.

The municipal government launched one of the country's most ambitious climate action planning processes, engaging experts and residents alike. Leading scientists and a nationally recognized research advisory committee helped develop various future climate scenarios and strategies for reducing emissions and adapting to changes already affecting the city and region. This effort resulted in the Chicago Climate Change Action plan, with supporting reports that cover climate, water, health, ecosystems and infrastructure. It constitutes a roadmap of 35 actions and five strategies: energy-efficient buildings, clean and renewable energy sources, improved transportation options, reduced waste and industrial pollution, and adaptation.

While Chicagoans may grouse about the occasional late train or bus, the Chicago Transit Authority (CTA) is one of the U.S.'s largest urban rail transit systems, and it generally works well. There are projects afoot to make it better, like a $2.1 billion modernization of several lines and stations. And the CTA is carrying out preliminary engineering studies for the extension of another line to serve transit-starved neighborhoods on the Far South Side. Transit-oriented development (TOD), which situates high-density housing and retail near train stations, has become a priority.

The plan includes dealing with heat waves, as the number of days over 90°F is projected under their higher emissions scenario to increase from the current level of 15 days to 8 weeks per year, with more than 30 of these days over 100°F and several severe heat waves each summer. The city plans to:

1   Prepare for heat waves through implementing a heat-watch warning system already proven to save lives; evaluating power vulnerability and the potential risks of heat stress among key populations most at risk in Chicago; developing collaborative action plans to manage these risks; and updating current heat-stress regulations for future amendments.

2   Reduce summer energy use through a home weatherization program, a green infrastructure program (including landscaping, reflective roofing, reflective and permeable pavement and rooftop garden requirements) and a cooling initiative to spur innovation.

3   Improve air quality through reducing ground-level ozone "precursor emissions" of pollutants from vehicles and other sources; prepare for increases in the frequency of heavy rainfall events and flood risk.

4   Adapt Chicago's trees and plants to a changing climate through a new planting plan recommending plants that remove pollutants, help manage heat, absorb storm water and can tolerate expected climate changes.[7]

As ambitious and positive as these plans are, the critical question is how fast the city can realize them. To end on a higher, contrapuntal note, residents of cold cities like Chicago can look forward to fewer and less severe cold spells. According to some scientists:

> The Arctic has warmed so much – twice as fast in recent decades than other parts of the world – that when polar air descends to lower latitudes, the cold snaps are warmer on average . . . a spell of extremely cold weather (is) about 15 times rarer than a century ago.[8]

Some good news for the windy city.

Salt Lake City

The metro area includes over 1.7 million people spread over about 1,600 square miles, which makes it less dense than metro Chicago. Salt Lake City's climate is characterized by hot, dry summers and cold, mild winters. The Great Salt Lake, which lies to the northwest of the city, heavily influences the climate. The average summer temperature in Salt Lake City is 92°F (32°C), and the average winter temperature is 36°F (2.2°C). The U.S. Department of Energy's Lawrence Berkeley National Laboratory (LBNL) modeled Salt Lake City's urban heat island, which represents near-ground air temperatures, as opposed to the surface temperatures that were measured by thermal imaging. They found that topography greatly influences Salt Lake City's heat island, with higher elevations being consistently cooler than the lower elevations. LBNL simulations indicate that Salt Lake City's heat island can reach 7.2°F (4°C) at night and about 3.6°F (2°C) during the afternoon. The lab concluded that although Salt Lake City is fairly well vegetated, the potential benefits from additional vegetation are large. Considering that trees potentially can shade 20% of the roof area, 20% of roads, 50% of sidewalks, and 30% of parking areas, Salt Lake City could increase additional tree cover by approximately a sixth. LBNL also found that with almost half of Salt Lake City's roofs and pavement being impermeable, the metropolitan area has a large potential to lighten its albedo.

In addition to offering the Kool Kids program, the Utah Cool Communities group has worked with Envision Utah, a nongovernmental organization that focused on growth issues including preserving critical lands, conserving water and improving housing and transportation options. The effort, led to a large extent by New Urbanist Peter Calthorpe, developed a toolbox to offer state and local decision-makers information on community-development options, including urban-heat-island reduction. This toolbox and cooperative effort provided a successful way to educate communities about Smart Growth, heat islands, heat waves and energy savings. Calthorpe Analytics has since gone on to develop Urban Footprint, the most comprehensive computer program for detailed analysis of different development scenarios

TreeUtah and other organizations in Utah and Salt Lake City are also taking actions that reduce heat island impacts. It is a statewide nonprofit organization that aims to improve the state's quality of life by enhancing the environment through planting, stewardship and education. It partners with a variety of local and national groups, and since 1995 it has been focusing on educating communities about urban forestry. Some examples of TreeUtah projects include planting 6,000 tree seedlings along the Jordan River to augment the 8,000 previously planted in honor of Utah's one hundredth birthday. As solid as Salt Lake City's tree-planting initiative is, it falls short of what some American cities are planning. For instance, Phoenix, AZ is promoting an ambitious plan to cover a quarter of the city with tree canopy, a huge undertaking in a metro area considered a poster child for sprawl, and one that, according to at least one national report, is one of the fastest-warming in the country.[9]

In 2016, Salt Lake City adopted Climate Positive 2040, which very ambitiously commits it to utilize 100 percent renewable energy sources to generate electricity by 2032 and create an 80 percent reduction in energy and transportation-related GHG emissions by 2040. The City also aims to reduce its footprint by at least half before 2030. The plan is broken into nine different sections: renewable energy, clean transportation, highly efficient buildings, air quality, sustainable food, zero waste community, collaborative solutions, city operations and resilient city. While it addresses CC, there are no specific plans for directly addressing UHI or heat waves.

Houston

This largest city in the southern U.S. has a city population of 2.4 million
and a sprawling metro count approaching 7 million. Houston's climate
is subtropical and humid. Built on Texas wet prairie, it is the country's
energy capital, home of oil and gas giants, the space industry, medical research, waterways hardened by the Army Corps of Engineers and
sprawl of highways and single-family homes that are a quintessential,
post-World War II version of the American dream. No city makes a bigger
effort to put distance between its residents, and spends more time in cars
overcoming that distance. Houston has the highest per-capita GHGs of
all U.S. cities, with transportation responsible for a whopping 48 percent
of the city's total emissions.[10] It also is home to proud, pro-business, anti-
government sentiment. It's set in a state that is deeply divided between
urban and rural, Democrat and Republican. It's a relatively blue city,
currently with an African American mayor, set in a red state. Hurricane
Harvey brought all these tensions into sharp relief in its aftermath. The
occurrence of three 500-year storms in three years, resulting in some
$80 billion in recovery costs,[11] is a very loud and undeniable wake-up call.

The sun shines for most of the year, and Houston has an annual growing season of nearly 300 days, with an annual average rainfall of about
50 inches. The average low temperature is 72°F (22°C) in the summer
and 40°F (4°C) in the winter. The average high is 93°F (32.5°C) in the
summer and 61°F (16°C) in the winter. Humidity in June is typically
around 93 percent at 6 a.m. and 63 percent at 6 p.m. With about 2,700
cooling degree days and 1,600 heating degree days, air-conditioning
loads are higher than heating loads. LBNL staff have determined that the
city's UHIs are often about 3°F (1.7°C) hotter than the suburbs, and it
can peak at up to 6°F (3.3°C). A personal anecdote: Over a half-century
ago when I went to high school in Houston, cutting lawns provided summer work; it was so miserably hot and humid, that a break in the shade
was necessary about every hour. Now it would be more unbearably hot.

The west side of the metro region contains many acres of native prairie,
a large portion of which has been converted to developments on which
trees have been planted. On the north and northeast sides of the region,
approximately 50 percent of the natural land cover consists of densely
vegetated canopies – what Rice University Professor Lars Lerup calls the
"Zoohemic Canopy" in his provocative books *One Million Acres and
No Zoning* and *The Continuous City*. The south side of the region is covered with a mixture of prairie, marsh, forest and abandoned agricultural
land. Among the numerous native trees, there are many that are suitable
for planting in the effort to reduce UHIs. The use of reflective roofing on
commercial buildings has increased rapidly, because of the large energy
savings it provides in this hot, sunny climate. Interestingly, over half the
city's paved area has concrete as its surface material, which has a higher

albedo than the asphalt that covers the remaining 2,000 or so miles of roads, streets and parking lots, the last of which are notoriously pervasive in Houston.

The city is home to several organizations whose focus includes the local air quality. The Houston Advanced Research Center (HARC) works on "sustainability solutions to problems that demand balancing environmental quality, economic health and social equity . . . (including) policies and technologies that promote sustainability and are based on scientific principles."[12] Trees for Houston is a nonprofit organization dedicated to urban reforestation in the metro area. It promotes tree planting throughout neighborhoods, along major thoroughfares and freeways, and in large open spaces. Since its founding in 1983, the group has planted over 500,000 trees and seedlings, including many of each along the city's major streets and freeways. In addition to tree planting, the organization educates adults and school children about the value and environmental benefits of urban trees, with a focus on preservation.

The Gulf Coast Institute focuses in the Houston area on the protection of green space and natural resources and building a sense of place and community. As a part of its effort, it promotes urban cooling and is currently working with the City to coordinate local efforts. The municipal government has a Green Houston initiative, within the Office of Sustainability. It includes a Green Building Resource Center, the 345 miles of interconnected bikeways trails, another 500 miles of bike lanes across the city, and a voluntary financing program of low-cost, long-term loans to finance energy efficiency, renewable energy and water conservation projects.[13]

The Quality of Life Coalition is a volunteer group that aims to capitalize on the city's natural advantages. Its goals include increasing urban vegetation and creating, improving and preserving existing parks and bayous. The coalition has the endorsement of over 60 different groups, including HARC, Trees for Houston and the Gulf Coast Institute. In 2010, it teamed up with the Greater Houston Partnership to promote a master plan along ten of the metro area's bayous to create a 150-mile greenway system and new parks, which can double as flood-retention basins or wetlands. In the 2012 election, voters overwhelmingly approved a major bond referendum that provides $100 million dedicated to bayou greenways, with over $100 million in additional private funding. It is not clear how impactful the ambitious plan will be on UHIs, but the additional greenery will provide some cool shade for the improved water-detention facilities, which proved inadequate in Hurricane Harvey.

Flooding is a very big deal in Houston. It often extends well beyond designated floodplains, in this case outside both the 100-year and 500-year limits. To make matters worse, the city is also sinking, as the result of water, oil and gas being pumped out of the ground. Some parts of the area "have sunk 10 to 12 feet since the 1920s, according to data from the U.S. Geological Survey."[14] The backstory on flooding is indicative of how CC is still denied, or at least defiantly downplayed, in parts of America:

> "More people die here than anywhere else from floods . . . More property per capita is lost here. And the problem's getting worse." . . . Houston has seen the most urban flooding of any other area in the country in the past four decades . . . because it sits so close to the Gulf of Mexico, where waters have been warming as the planet gets hotter. Warm water means more evaporation and more water vapor in the air. So, when a storm comes along, there's more water to pick up and dump on nearby land. "The exact same storm that comes along today has more rain associated with it than it would have 50 or 100 years ago" . . . almost 30 percent of freshwater wetlands were lost between 1992 and 2010 . . . As wetlands have been lost, the amount of impervious surface . . . increased by 25% from 1996 to 2011 . . . But county and city officials responsible for addressing flooding largely reject these arguments . . . The longtime head of the flood control district flat-out disagrees with scientific evidence that shows development is making flooding worse . . . the flood control district has no plans to study CC or its impacts on Harris County, the third-most-populous county in the United States.[15]

The memory of the horrendous flooding during Hurricane Harvey in 2018 is still vivid. It was, after all, the heaviest rainstorm in recorded U.S. meteorological history, dumping 33 trillion gallons in the Houston area – equivalent to a million gallons for every Texan![16] It tied Hurricane Katrina as the costliest tropical cyclone on record, inflicting $125 billion in damage.[17] As lamentable as the extensive damage was, increasingly warmer and more water-logged air is likely to soon whip up even bigger storms. Perhaps the deluge – nearly 19 times the daily discharge of the Mississippi River,[18] which drains the central half of the country. Perhaps it will convince the CC skeptics and denialists in local and state government that something more than random climatic events is happening, and that it is more climatically serious than previous extreme weather events. It may also serve as an urban planning wake-up call in a city that has proudly exulted in sprawling, free-form growth unfettered by zoning.

> No city could have withstood Harvey without serious harm, but Houston made itself more vulnerable than necessary. Paving over the saw-grass prairie reduced the ground's capacity to absorb rainfall. Flood-control reservoirs were too small. Building codes were inadequate. Roads became rivers, so while hospitals were open, it was almost impossible to reach them by car.[19]

Since 2010 Harris County has allowed more than 8,600 buildings to be built inside 100-year floodplains (where there's a 1 percent chance of major flooding in any year). Most neighborhoods here were built on low-lying prairies, and now nearly 40 percent of local flood plains house commercial or residential buildings, according to research done at Texas A&M University.[20] There has also been lax enforcement of requirements for detention ponds to hold runoff, as well as out-of-date floodplain maps.[21] Overall, as a *New York Times* special report described Houston: "much of the devastation was a direct result of a quintessentially American defiance of nature's boundaries."[22] In 2018, the City's Department of Public Works proposed that all new structures in 100-year and 500-year floodplains be built 2 feet above 500-year levels in order to avoid a repeat of the massive flooding that occurred during Hurricane Harvey.

Harvey damaged close to 16,000 housing units, and homeowners saw increases as high as 30 percent on flood insurance renewals in 2018. A local multi-family housing analyst estimates that some 19,000 units were leased by residents displaced by the devastating hurricane, predicting: "The numbers of people moving back to homes is going to be much less than anticipated."[23] Coupled with changes in the federal mortgage interest tax deduction which has now made owning homes less financially attractive, the incentive to rent has increased, with apartment rents climbing. On top of younger Americans' desire to rent rather than own, the impacts of CC could accelerate this trend within the built environment.

A promising anecdote about the Harvey disaster. It was estimated that about one million cars were flooded out of use, stranding many people in this auto-dependent city. Not only did its bikeshare system get plenty of use by those in need and those who wanted to take a look at the flooded bayous, but some residents were hoping to start a "Keep Houston Rolling" campaign.[24] And the city soon had six dockless bike-sharing companies. Necessity once again proved to be the mother of invention, with the systems' ability to open up previously unserved areas beyond the city's core.

Houston not only lags behind other cities of its size in developing and implementing flood control plans, it also is slow to directly address CC and UHIs. Ironically, a 2002 case study[25] done by LBNL's Heat Island Group found that the potential savings from Heat Island Reduction strategies are very large. Their analysis estimated annual energy savings of $82 million, with an avoidance of 730 megawatts in peak power and a reduction of almost 400,000 metric tons of CO_2 in annual carbon emissions. This compares very favorably to their estimates for Chicago of $30 million of annual savings, 400 megawatts of power avoidance and an annual carbon reduction of over 200,000 metric tons.

In 2016, Houston's reputation as a whipping boy of the urban-planning world was improved when it was lauded for its "green transformation" by the national Cultural Landscape Foundation. It brought visitors from around the country to study new investments in the city's parks, as well as the 150-mile network of trails along its bayous.

> [T]he fourth-largest U.S. city will soon have half a dozen signature parks designed by internationally known firms . . . Yet Houston's attempts to appear greener have thrown longstanding inequities into sharper contrast . . . Beyond financial disparities, the region's signature industry inflicts a staggeringly disproportionate burden on east-side residents. According to the Union of Concerned Scientists' report, the airborne concentration of 1,3-butadiene, which causes cancer and a host of neurological issues, is more than 150 times greater . . . than . . . relatively affluent neighborhoods on Houston's west side . . . Policy that would help Houston control its pollution problem is tough to enact in a town dominated by the petrochemical industry.[26]

Indeed, the powerful corporations and the entrenched, wealthy elites in the capital of the oil and gas industry do not seem as inclined to deal with UHIs and CC as much as in other cities with similar climates. Time will soon tell the thermal results, but the area's uncomfortable heat and humidity, as well as its flat, flood-prone terrain in hurricane country, may signal a reversal of fortune and a decline after many decades of economic and population growth.

International Case Studies

Stuttgart, Germany

The city of Stuttgart, home to 600,000 people in the center of an industrial metro area of 2.7 million people in southwestern Germany, is a leader in integrating urban climate into its land use planning practices. Located in a valley, the lowest point of the city is 800 feet above sea level while the surrounding hillsides rise twice as high, an elevation change important to its local climate. The urban region has a mild, temperate climate with warm summers. Wind-speed profiles throughout the city are typically low, which, along with UHIs, contribute to poor air quality. The future climate projections for 2071–2100 suggest a 3.6°F (2°C) increase in annual mean temperature. The estimates for heat waves (above 86°F or 30°C) suggest that the number of days with heat stress (which has a lower threshold than in hotter regions of the world) will increase to more than 30 days in over half of the metro area, and to over 60 days in the low-lying areas.[27]

To its great credit, Stuttgart has had an urban climatology department since 1938. Four decades later the City issued its first of two climate atlases, both of which acknowledge the importance of topography and identify sources of fresh air from agricultural lands, forested areas and surrounding slopes. Seven decades after 1938, the second Climate Atlas was updated and extended to the metro area (179 towns and municipalities), adding air pollution as a challenge.

> Open spaces are subdivided into one of three categories dependent upon their relative climatic importance. In climate-important open space, large-scale development or soil sealing are not permitted. Restrictions are lightened in open space areas of less climatic importance. Developed areas are subdivided into four categories, sorted by climate importance, with increasing requirements for the integration of green space, reduced emissions, creation of green ventilation corridors, and removal/relocation of obstructive existing buildings.[28]

In addition to responding to local climate characteristics, the planning is based on broader recommendations:

1   Vegetation should be placed to surround developments and larger, connected green spaces should be created or maintained throughout developed areas to facilitate air exchange.
2   Valleys serve as air delivery corridors and should not be developed.
3   Hillsides should remain undeveloped, especially when development exists in valleys, since cold and fresh air comes from here.
4   Saddle-like topographies serve as air induction corridors and should not be developed.
5   Urban sprawl is to be avoided.
6   All trees growing in the urban core with a trunk circumference of more than 80 cm at a height of 1 meter are protected with a tree preservation order.

"On both a citywide and human scale, the parks and working landscapes within and surrounding Stuttgart are among the most climatically functional, socially useful and aesthetically pleasing of any modern city in the Western World."[29] About 40 percent of Stuttgart's surface area has been put under the protection of nature conservation orders, a record high in Germany. Greenery covers more than 60 percent of the city proper, which contains over 12,000 acres (5,000 hectares) of forests and woodland, 65,000 trees in parks and open spaces and 35,000 street trees. As early as 2007, 3 million square feet of rooftops had been greened and 25 of over 150 miles of tram tracks had been grassed. In line with the city development vision, 150 acres (60 hectares) of open greenfield land previously earmarked for development have been removed from the 2010 land development plan. Specific interventions include banning buildings in the hills around the town, as well as projects that might obstruct the natural ventilation of nocturnal air flows. Throughout the city there are ventilation corridors: "wide, tree-flanked arterial roads that help clean air flow down from the hills at night to cool the city."[30] Over several decades, Stuttgart has used its planning and landscaping powers to design and implement an entire system of urban air circulation.

The case demonstrates several salient points. First, cities in relatively cool climates – including the American cases of Salt Lake City and Chicago – are already getting uncomfortably hot in summer because of the double hit of CC and UHIs. Second, there are advantages to a municipality with in-house climatic research capacity, which can provide actionable knowledge of local conditions, as opposed to relying on general principles. This sensitivity to local climates is critical, because extreme heat is very much dependent on local, site-specific conditions, such as terrain as this case study so vividly demonstrates. Last, Stuttgart illustrates the importance of a *regional* approach to dealing with UHIs.

Muscat, Oman

This case study relies almost entirely on an in-depth study done in 2010 by TRANSOLAR, an engineering firm located, ironically, in Stuttgart. Jan Gehl, the famous Danish expert on public space, was also involved in the project, enriching the human dimensions of the study. As Middle Eastern societies have increasingly grown accustomed to air conditioning, the old traditions of passive cooling have been weakened or lost. The report states how new technologies, when combined with traditional approaches, could create even better ways to mitigate heat stress and create lively, vibrant and pleasant outdoor spaces.

Muscat, a metro area of over one million people on the Arabian peninsula's coast facing the Indian Ocean, is in a very sunny and arid climate, with mild winters but hot and humid summers. Winter months have low temperatures of around 60°F (16°C) and daytime maximums of around 75°F (24°C). The summer months are quite hot, with maximum air temperatures of almost 115°F (44°C), often making it prohibitively hot to spend much if any time outdoors. There is little relief from the uncomfortable conditions at night because of the thermal mass of the buildings. In fact, the highest *low* temperature ever recorded on earth was June 28, 2018, when it hit 109°F (43°C) in a nearby town. Whereas during winter, the water content and temperature of the air is significantly lower, providing pleasant outdoor conditions. Due to steep mountains surrounding the metro area, the direction and speed of the wind is fluky, with much of it coming from offshore and being redirected back to the sea. Due to the lower temperatures, especially in winter, and a daily swing of 18–25°F (10–15°C), there is the potential for passive cooling of both interior and exterior spaces. And due to the location almost on the Equator, there is a high potential for solar energy systems. Muscat receives about twice as much sun as Stuttgart.

The vision for the metro area is to make public outdoor space more inviting and comfortable for longer periods of the day and of the year. There is an additional challenge of simultaneously reducing energy generation and water consumption in an environmentally sound manner. The city ambitiously aspires to carbon-neutral energy generation in the long term, with a stepwise reduction in the natural gas used in energy generation in the meantime. The energy future of sunny Oman is clearly solar, which can be supported with other renewable energy sources like wind. Not only does the energy for heating, cooling and power need to be greened, but also the energy for water desalination, which has more than doubled as the economy and tourism have grown in the last decade.

Muscat has adopted three main principles for enhancing outdoor thermal comfort, which are shading strategies, air movement and local cooling systems:

1 Shading strategies – The highest potential to increase outdoor thermal comfort was found to be the cluster of trees, followed by fixed or operable shading devices, such as canopies, awnings and louvers. The study found that fixed devices must be relatively opaque, with very low solar transmission. Surprisingly, a horizontal shading device with a high transparency to the sun's rays is worse than no device, because the heat absorbed during the day is trapped at night, a common problem in places where there are no night breezes from the sea. If the solar transmittance of the fabric or solid material is reduced from 30 percent to 2 percent, the share of uncomfortably hot evening temperatures is cut in half. There is a proposed design in Phoenix, Arizona – a city with a similar hot, arid climate that is purportedly warming at three times the rate of the planet[31] – for a diaphanous rope canopy to cover seven miles of its downtown that would purportedly reduce the intensity of the sunlight by more than half. These shading strategies have the potential to be deployed in various locations, primarily in horizontal configurations over streets and plazas. These passive options require no additional power or chilled water to work, and the movable components, which can be opened up to the sky as needed after sunset, can be manually operated.

2 Air movement – The wind has on the one hand the potential to improve comfort during appropriate periods of the year and the day, and conversely to lower outdoor comfort when ambient conditions are too chilly. Therefore, an adaptable system with user control is needed. The physical principle behind all the approaches is to create air turbulence and velocity, which results in a higher heat transfer rate from the body and more evaporative cooling

from the skin. Hot and humid winds can create the opposite effect, making wind shielding a desirable option. The wind shielding analysis assumed a very sizable reduction in velocity to 10 percent of the actual wind speed. Although there will be periods of the year when wind shielding is beneficial, the strategy actually turns out to have a negative effect if the shields are fixed in place and configuration, because of shifting wind direction and speed. Wind shields and large movable vanes are only partially recommended, because their efficiency depends on site-specific conditions and they only make sense where the winds are too hot and humid.

3　Other strategies include radiant cooling, utilizing water wells, geothermal systems, sea water, district systems, air conditioning powered by solar electricity and even nighttime evaporative cooling of water (preferably gray water) if the humidity is low enough. Generally, the humidity levels are too high, which also makes natural ventilation unsuccessful. If mechanically chilled water is resorted to, district systems are preferable to individual units. Because the annual sea surface temperature in winter is cool, there is a high potential for seawater cooling. In districts next to the coast, it is possible to cover a hefty part of the cooling load, especially where steep topography of the seabed allows taking water from deeper, cooler depths that are relatively close to the shore.

Muscat has very abundant solar insolation and therefore a high potential for using solar energy. During hot sunny hours, when the cooling demand is highest, photovoltaic panels can deliver maximum power. At the same time, solar panels can act as shading devices atop buildings, public spaces, parking lots, etc. Their application is architecturally versatile, with colored and/or patterned photovoltaic cells integrated into façades. Thermal solar collectors to heat domestic hot water can be the passive, self-siphoning type with an integral storage tank – relatively inexpensive products with very swift pay-backs. Sitting on the roof, they shade it while heating the water to temperatures suitable for washing clothes and dishes. And during cloudy spells, they pre-heat water to a lower temperature, which is then more easily raised by a conventional hot water heater. Large-scale solar thermal systems can also be cost-effective, typically located outside of urban areas where large mirror arrays can concentrate the sun's rays in a system of concentrated solar power. Tanks store the heat produced during the day and can drive steam turbines during the night. It is possible to combine these solar thermal systems with desalination plants or district cooling systems.

Other renewable energy systems include wind machines, bio-gasification, wave and tidal machines. The Oman coast has many stretches with sufficiently high wind speeds to make wind turbines cost-effective, both horizontal and vertical axis machines. Offshore wind turbines can be even more efficient. And unlike solar energy, sufficiently high wind speeds are often available day and night. Biogas plants, which combust gas produced from the biological break-down of organic matter, can be used to generate electricity or distributed to dwelling units for cooking or space heating. They can be installed in a CHP. Wave and tidal energy systems are more exotic ways to harvest energy. A "wave farm" might typically have 40 machines over an area of a half square mile (about 1 square km), which can bob up and down enough to power 20,000 homes. Tidal energy can also be produced by tidal currents flowing through a dam constructed across an estuary, generating electrical or mechanical power with each rising and ebbing tide.

The study applies these various techniques and strategies to six different districts in metro Muscat. They vary widely, even in this relatively small area, because of numerous differences in micro-climates and terrain. It can't be over-emphasized that the design and implementation of these systems are very site-sensitive, and that very hot cities like Muscat will be heavily, if not disastrously challenged by CC and UHIs.

Ahmedabad, India

Ahmedabad is a rapidly growing city of 7.2 million inhabitants, the largest city in Gujarat state, located in western India. For architecture aficionados, it is home to famous buildings by the international Modernist masters Le Corbusier and Louis Kahn, as well as the highly accomplished Indian architect B.V. Doshi. Situated on a sandy, dry area along a river that shrivels to a stream during the driest part of the year, the climate is arid year round, with very high summer temperatures. The City has zoomed in on raising public awareness of extreme heat and on building community capacity to respond to it, rather than the physical adaptation to or mitigation of UHIs. This case study is about *heat vulnerability*, especially among slum dwellers. As such, it focuses on public health preparedness, such as warnings, surveillance and education.

"While it has always been hot, the temperatures we are seeing in India are beyond what the human body can adapt to."[32] Thousands of people have died from the heat waves in recent years, with one in 2010 and another in 2012 and 2015. The 2010 high of 121°F (46°C) set a 40-year record.[33] A new study found that the number of heat waves killing more than 100 people increased 2.5 times between 1960 and 2009 – a large increase likely due to CC. The devastating May 2015 heat wave ranked the fifth deadliest in the history of cities. Yet the subcontinent's mean temperature has only increased 0.9°F (0.5°C) in the past 50 years, a mild increase in comparison to other parts of the world.[34] Only 3 percent of urban households in India currently have air conditioning – and even many hospitals lack it – making extreme temperatures a major health threat. Exacerbating this, India is home to 20 percent of the world's population, yet the country has only 4 percent of global freshwater resources.

> And the projected migration of 250 million people from rural areas to urban centers between 2008 and 2030 is straining cities' limited resources and infrastructure. That migration is the equivalent of the population of Indonesia, the fourth most populous country in the world, moving to Indian cities over the course of two decades.[35]

The Ahmedabad Municipal Corporation partnered with a coalition of local and international scientists and policy experts to develop the Heat Action Plan in 2017, two years after the city experienced the devastating heat wave that killed 1,700 people. Its four prongs are tailored to protect the most vulnerable populations – elderly, young children, slum inhabitants and outdoor workers:[36]

1   Building public awareness and community outreach to communicate the risks of heat waves and implement practices to prevent heat-related deaths and illnesses. This includes disseminating public messages on how to protect people against extreme heat through inter-personal contact, traditional media outlets and modern media such as WhatsApp, and informational materials such as pamphlets and advertisements on heat stress prevention.
2   Initiating an early warning system and inter-agency coordination to alert residents of predicted high and extreme temperatures. The City has created formal communication channels to alert governmental agencies, the meteorological department, health officials and hospitals, emergency responders, local community groups and media outlets that forecast extreme temperatures.
3   Capacity building among health care professionals to recognize and respond to heat-related illnesses, particularly during extreme heat events. These strategies are paired with straightforward measures like stocking emergency rooms and ambulances with ice packs, as well as opening specialist heat wards in hospitals.
4   Reducing heat exposure and promoting adaptive measures by launching new efforts including mapping of high-risk areas of the city, increasing outreach and communication on prevention methods, access to increased potable drinking water stations and cooling spaces during increasingly frequent episodes of extreme heat.

Part of the Heat Action Plan is the Cool Roofs program, which involves volunteers painting rooftops with a reflective coating that typically helps lower indoor temperatures by about 5.5°F (3°C). It includes painting or otherwise converting at least 500 slum rooftops and improving the reflectivity of government buildings and schools.

This doesn't just make being indoors more comfortable for poor people who can't afford air conditioners. It also protects them from heat stroke and other health impacts that can easily turn fatal in a city where May temperatures regularly reach degrees 110°F (43°C) . . . One of the most important aspects of the Heat Action Plan . . . is training medical personnel how to spot and treat heat-related ailments . . . Nearly 350 medical staff have been trained how to identify such illnesses, and about precautions and treatment.[37]

Figure 6.3 In a public ceremony in Ahmedabad, local officials start painting a rooftop in an informal settlement as part of the City's widely copied "Cool Roofs" campaign. Volunteers paint the roofs white to keep indoor temperatures cooler under these uninsulated corrugated metal roofs, which are so ubiquitous in squatter communities around the world. One study suggests that by increasing the amount of white roof area by just 1 percent across the globe, the added reflectivity would have enough cooling effect to keep more than 100 billion tons of carbon dioxide out of the atmosphere over the next century because of reduced air conditioning.[1] (Sayantan Sarkar, NRDC)

1 Hashem Akbari et al., "The long-term effect of increasing albedo of surface areas," *Environmental Research Letters*, 4/12/15

The initiatives have saved lives and protected residents' health and comfort from dangerously high temperatures. Other cities and states across India are now using Ahmedabad's pioneering Heat Action Plan as a model for shaping preparedness plans and early warning systems for their own citizens, a high priority after the historic 2015 heat wave. In summary, convincing local government leaders to plan and support climate preparedness is critical in the face of UHIs and CC. Ahmedabad vividly illustrates low-cost policies and practices that are sometimes about physical antidotes, but more often about building public awareness and community capacity. Evaluations between 2013 and 2015 offer proof the program is working; heat-related casualties in Ahmedabad were low during the major 2015 heat wave, while thousands died elsewhere across India. The program has evolved and expanded over time and is becoming a model for other cities. As of 2017, 17 cities and 11 states across India had released or were developing heat action plans.[38]

In closing this chapter on case studies, C40 should be mentioned. This network of the world's megacities committed to addressing climate change has published 100 case studies of cities of every size, geography and stage of development around the earth. Their *Good Practice Guides* provide tangible examples of climate solutions and nearly 70 categories of good practice and actions in energy, transport, solid waste management, urban planning, adaptation and finance. Their pamphlet *Cool Cities* is cited later in this book, and companion booklets are a good resource for professionals and officials involved with cities in the war against CC.

Notes

1 This entire section is based on and paraphrases or copies "Heat Island Reduction Activities," U.S. EPA website archive
2 Hiroko Tabuchi, "With government in retreat, companies step up on emissions," *The New York Times*, 4/25/17
3 Matt K. Smith, "Atlanta's building boom is destroying its famous forests," *Daily Beast*, 5/16/18
4 Nicholas Kristof, "It's not too late to learn from our mistakes," *The New York Times*, 9/3/17
5 Adele Peters, "How Houston can become more resilient to future floods," *Fast Company*, 8/29/17
6 This entire section is based on and paraphrases or copies "Heat Island Pilot Project," U.S. EPA website archive
7 Executive Summary, *Chicago Climate Action Plan*, 2008, chicagoclimateaction.org
8 Henry Fountain, "That recent brutally cold weather? It's getting rarer," *The New York Times*, 1/11/18
9 Patrick Sisson, "How air conditioning shaped modern architecture – and changed our climate," *curbed*, 5/9/17
10 Alissa Walker, "Mayors are fighting the EPA's fuel-efficiency rollback: what cities need are fewer cars," Opinion, *Curbed*, 8/2/18

11 Adam Kamins, "Hurricane Harvey's U.S. cost: an update," *Moody's Analytics*, 10/2/17
12 HARC website, "Our focus," HARCresearch.org
13 Office of Sustainability website, greenhouston@houstontx.gov
14 John D. Harden, "For years, the Houston area has been losing ground," *Houston Chronicle*, 5/28/16
15 Neena Satija and Kiah Collier, "Boomtown, flood town," *Pro Publica*, 9/17/16
16 Jeff Goodall, "Welcome to the age of climate migration," *Rolling Stone*, 2/25/18
17 "Hurricane Harvey," Wikipedia, 8/7/18
18 Jason Samenow, "60 inches of rain fell from Hurricane Harvey in Texas, shattering U.S. storm record," *Washington Post*, 9/22/17
19 Peter Coy and Christopher Flagella, "Harvey wasn't just bad weather: it was bad city planning," *Bloomberg Businessweek*, 8/31/17
20 Noble Inram, "As flooding frequency increases, more US cities opt for green infrastructure," *The Christian Science Monitor*, 3/30/18
21 "How to cope with floods," *The Economist*, September 2–10, 2017
22 Michael Kimmelman, "Lessons from Hurricane Harvey: Houston's struggle is America's tale," *The New York Times*, 11/11/17
23 Nancy Sarnoff, "Harvey, tax code changes may spur apartment demand," *Houston Chronicle*, 1/24/18
24 Leah Binkowitz, "How bikes are helping Houstonians after Harvey," *Houston Chronicle*, 9/14/17
25 S. Konopacki and H. Akbari, "Energy savings of heat-island reduction strategies in Chicago and Houston," Lawrence Berkeley National Laboratory, February, 2002
26 "Hurricane Harvey," Wikipedia, 8/7/18
27 European Climate Adaptation Platform, http://climate-adapt.eea.europa.eu/metadata/case-studies/stuttgart-combating-the-heat-island-effect-and-poor-air-quality-with-green-ventilation-corridors
28 Larissa Larsen, "Urban climate and adaptation strategies," *Frontiers in Ecology and the Environment*, 11/1/2015
29 Michael Hough, *Cities and Natural Process*, Routledge, 1995
30 Brad Plumer, "5 Ways to Keep Cities Cooler During Heat Waves," *The New York Times*, 7/24/18
31 Brian Stone quoted in Brandon Loomis, "In Dallas as in Phoenix, people look to trees for relief from urban heat islands," *The Republic*, azcentral.com, 12/29/17
32 Andrew Kornblatt, Berkeley, California, 10/7/15
33 Kathy V. Tran et al., "A cross-sectional, randomized cluster sample survey of household vulnerability to extreme heat among slum dwellers in Ahmedabad, India," *International Journal of Environmental Research and Public Health*, 2013, pp. 2515–2543
34 Steven Leahy, "By 2100, deadly heat may threaten majority of humankind," *National Geographic*, 6/19/17
35 Anjali Jaiswal, "From Austin to Ahmedabad: building heat-resilient cities on the frontlines of climate change," *NRDC Expert Blog*, 10/15/15
36 Ibid.
37 Patralekha Chatterjee, "Lessons and challenges as Indian cities step up planning for heat waves," *cityscope*, 7/13/17
38 "Chilling prospects: providing sustainable cooling for all," www.SEforALL.org, 2018

7 The Sharing Cosmopolis
Prosperity without Growth

Cosmopolis

A cosmopolitan world is about neither romanticizing or preserving authentic local traditions, nor giving in mindlessly to the forces of globalism, to paraphrase political philosopher Kwame Anthony Appiah.[1] As cities continue to become bigger and denser, it is critical that cities are all-embracing and tolerant. To quote Bart Giamatti, President Emeritus of Yale University and of Major League Baseball's National League:

> Over millennia, this refinement of negotiation – of balancing private need and public obligation, personal desire and public duty, and keen interests of the one and the many into a common, shared set of agreements – becomes a civilization. This is the public version of what binds us. That state is achieved because city dwellers . . . have smoothed the edges of private desire so as to fit, or at least work in, with all the other city dwellers, without undue abrasion, without sharp edges forever nicking and wounding, each refining an individual capacity for those thousands of daily, instantaneous negotiations that keep crowded city life from becoming a constant brawl or ceaseless shoving match.[2]

This unspoken covenant is the difference between urbanization and urbanism. Moreover, it's the difference between the democratic polis and urban chaos.

Cities cultivate social tolerance among diverse groups, but periodically they can be the locus of severe conflict and violence. Much has been written on this topic, including by Conflict in Cities (CinC), a group of researchers at the University of Cambridge and their partners in Ireland and Israel, two countries that have experienced more than their share of civil violence. Their studies have underscored how indispensable it is to focus on the urban condition to understand ethno-national and religious conflicts. CinC's research on urban conflict shows that people tend to interact more than they think. Sharing space may simply mean that people from either side of ethno-national or religious divides get to see each other, observe their customs, and hear their languages as they go about their daily lives. Slight as such contact may seem, it begins to open cracks in preconceived perceptions, whilst its absence can mean a reduced potential for improving relations in the future. Moreover, experience and memory of the spaces themselves create some form of common ground, even if little or no direct social interaction takes place.[3]

This analysis confirms once again Jane Jacobs' observations a half century earlier about the daily urban "ballet" of urban sidewalks, of people interacting, going about their plans and shaping the life of the city, from the smallest scale to the largest.

Public space is a *sine qua non* if the city is to tolerate difference and resolve conflict. "Public spaces enable synergistic interaction and exchange, creativity and delight, and the transfer of knowledge and skills. Public spaces can help residents to improve their prosperity, health, happiness and well-being, and to enrich their social relations and cultural life."[4] No one captures the spirit of the public realm more poignantly than Pope Francis, who in his 2018 New Year's Homily praises "the artisans of the common good . . . Small deeds express concretely love for the city . . . without giving speeches, without publicity, but with a style of practical civic education for daily life."[5] The alternative is a privatized urbanism, socio-economically segregated and often physical separated by walls and gates. Physical boundaries breed social isolation and selfish distrust, ultimately leading to unrest and violence.

Professor Dunham-Jones of Georgia Tech, co-author of *Retrofitting Suburbia*, has proposed a typology of urban public space: Civic, Everyday, Green Space, Infrastructure, Spectacle and Sprawl Space. These six types cover the gamut, from commemorative, symbolic places to everyday sidewalks, to parks and greens, train stations and airports to tourist meccas and arterial strip malls. It's a rich panoply, which varies from culture to culture. In traditional Arab cities, there is much less public space, although many private realms have given way to the public realm, often including mosques themselves. In this and other cultures, spiritual space could be included in the Civic category, or it might be added as a seventh type. It includes sacred and symbolic spaces, such as religious shrines, cemeteries and temporary encampments. These can be small: a tiny shrine or cemetery, a plaza attached to a church, temple, mosque or pagoda, or huge, like India's amazing Kumbh Mela, a temporary Hindu city for 30 million people that happens every 12 years.[6]

Public functions often require and benefit from large plazas. However, outdoor public spaces that are more human-scaled and spatially contained to engender the feel of outdoor living rooms are usually more popular and beloved than over-sized ones. Eye-to-eye, auditory and even olfactory contact, whether with friends or strangers, is enhanced in smaller public spaces. Well-proportioned plazas and streets, often populated with trees and greenery, lend a greater sense of place and of comfort than the windswept and agoraphobic expanses of many Modernist plazas and streets. Attractive and thermally cool public space can have the knock-on effect of improving the social milieu and economic life of a city, by promoting walking, socializing, outdoor art and activities that add to a collective sense of well-being. Mutual tolerance of each other's views – tolerating "the other" – is encouraged and nurtured by casual visual or speaking encounters. As Jacobs pointed out over 50 years ago, it's not so much about knowing, much less liking or interacting with strangers, as it is about respecting them.

On another axis of cosmopolitanism, there's nothing more interesting and compelling for many people than to visit and interact with different cultures and places. It leads them to travel the world, often to distant destinations that are as different and exotic as possible, making global tourism a massive international industry. Tourism is both positive and negative arguably. In spite of tending to commercialize, overrun and fetishize local places and indigenous cultures, it does voluntarily distribute wealth from richer to poorer people. And if done with the right economic and educational agenda, it can promote mutual understanding of difference, even celebrate it. But the educational benefits are typically one-way – from the locals to the visitors. The considerable economic benefits of tourist spending need to be spread locally, and not, like cruise ships that overwhelm ports-of-call, accrue primarily to the travel industry. And when the onslaught of tourism is too great – congesting urban sites and ruining pristine environments – it can destroy the very qualities that made the place worth visiting or residing in. National and international exchange programs, typically for individuals and for longer durations, tend to be more mutually beneficial.

With well over a billion visits per year, global tourism is a $1.2 trillion industry, and growing every year. Previous estimates of the tourism industry's carbon footprint put it at between 2.5 percent and 3 percent of total global CO_2 emissions. But a recent year-and-a-half-study that includes the many supply chains for the goods and services that support tourism, concludes it's more like 8 percent. The United States topped the list, with U.S. travelers responsible for over 1,000 metric tons of emissions, with almost equal emissions generated by foreign travelers to the U.S. China was second with roughly half the total American footprint, and Germany third, with about a third.[7] Because tourism takes place to a large extent in cities, often in hot developing countries, heat islands threaten both local residents and their economic dependence on tourism.

Tourism may be pleasant, interesting and educational for visitors and profitable for local residents, but getting disparate peoples to live together long term can be another matter. The happy and peaceful co-existence of different ethnic, racial and religious groups within the same community or society is one of the great geopolitical challenges, even enigmas, of this unprecedentedly international era. Almost inexplicably, different ethnic and religious groups that have peacefully lived side-by-side for decades suddenly erupt in hateful conflict. It remains difficult to predict when and where these eruptions might happen. Tribal, ethnic and religious fault lines and adverse reaction to newcomers have no doubt been a social problem since the dawn of civilization, but they are heightened now by the ease of mobility and the high and growing number of global immigrants and refugees. Conflict is inevitable in cities, perhaps aggravated by public and social media; the question is how to reshape and channel it in constructive ways.[8]

Some observers of contemporary life might argue that social media have undermined the physical public realm. Cell phones, with seemingly endless communication apps, preoccupy so many people so much of the time in public spaces. As overpowering as that trend may seem, there are some countervailing findings from recent 24/7 videos of the public realm – the same ones William Whyte famously filmed a half century ago. Across the board, the researcher

> found that the story of public spaces in the last 30 years has not been aloneness, or digital distraction, but gender equity. Females now *linger* in public places, not just move through them going from destination to destination. He also found that when people use cell phones outside, they tend to be alone, not interrupting companions.[9]

It could be argued that "modern technology gives us a kind of intersection of urban spaces and cyberspace, which we think could be a platform for a much more inclusive and efficient society."[10]

Stewart Brand points out that the public spaces of cities continue to cultivate a cosmopolitan culture, one that is "multi-cultural, multi-racial, global, worldly-wise, well-traveled, experienced, un-provincial, cultured, sophisticated, suave, urbane."[11] Cities entail a diversity that, in Benjamin Barber's eloquent words

> mandates tolerance; their openness invites immigration from without and mobility from within; their interdependence makes their borders porous and their behavior interactional and transactional; their friction-inducing density ignites imagination and creativity; their anonymity and liberty inspire innovation and entrepreneurship. In sum, their defining features constitute a recipe for democratic civility – whether or not it is formalized in a democratic governing system . . . the city is intrinsically democratic.[12]

The Seattle provocateur Dan Savage has a more basic, hortatory take on urban life:

> Urban life is good for your social life. It's good for your emotional life. It pulls you out of yourself. You can walk down the street and turn a corner and meet someone . . . Cities have a way of funneling people through spaces where you're going to encounter people you know or like or meet people you might know or like. That can be social, that can be professional, that can also be sexual.[13]

It could be argued, as MIT Professors Paulo Ferraro and John Fernandez do, that the

> urban world is really nothing more, and nothing less, than the accumulated and intertwined web of mutual self-interest . . . Transactions of every kind abound in the urban space, and their results lead to enterprise and affluence, cultural inspiration and production, knowledge creation and inventiveness, and consumption as never before.[14]

This view of the city as a primarily transactional network is worth some elaboration, as some experts feel cities have become too commercial in nature. Professor Julian Agyeman writes "We need to reinvent and recreate the urban commons as a place where humans interact in a much more relational way, not just in a transactional way."[15]

The Sharing City: A Way to Prosperity without Growth

> There used to be a romanticism about ownership, because it meant you were free, you were empowered . . . I think now, for the younger generation, ownership is viewed as a burden. Young people will only want to own what they want responsibility for. And a lot of people my age don't want responsibility for a car and a house and to have a lot of stuff everywhere.

So writes David Chesky, co-founder of Airbnb. The widely-read *New York Times* columnist and book author Tom Friedman elaborates:

> Airbnb understood that the world was becoming hyperconnected . . . And if someone created the *trust* platform to bring them together, huge value could be created for both parties. That was Airbnb's real innovation – a platform of "trust" – where everyone could not only see everyone else's identity but also rate them as good, bad or indifferent hosts or guests . . . a relevant "reputation" visible to everyone else in the system.[16]

A whole new language has suddenly emerged to describe a shared and sharing culture: peer economy, collaborative economy, crowdsourcing, collaborative consumption, the maker movement, co-creation, co-housing, co-living, Twitter, wiki – plus the exploding list of commercial names like Facebook, Instagram, LinkedIn, Airbnb, Uber, Lyft, Pandora, Zillow, Dropbox, WhatsApp and WeWork. It's been a fast and heady pace for many young inventors and entrepreneurs. Nothing short of a revolution, it is brought on by the confluence of new digital technology and a younger generation eager to try new paradigms after growing up in the Great Recession – much as their grandparents changed the world after the Great Depression and World War II.

Before dissecting the shared/sharing economy, a quick look at the notion of cooperation is in order. Yuval Noah Harari has made some interesting observations about cooperation in the animal kingdom. He points out that vast numbers of ants can cooperate with each other, but they do so rigidly; they can't change their genetically controlled patterns to deal with new circumstances or conditions. Chimpanzees, on the other hand, can cooperate flexibly, with the ability to adapt to new circumstances, but not in large numbers, because they need to personally be familiar with every other chimp. Only humans can cooperate both flexibly and in large numbers, because they don't have to personally know everyone in their complex human webs and systems. (For instance, I don't know you, the reader, or the person who designed the computer keyboard on which I'm typing this, any more than you knew the pilot of your last flight or the check-out clerk for your last grocery purchase.) Hence humans have developed cities, monetary systems, judicial systems, religions, etc. to our great advantage as we evolved to dominate the world.[17]

A heavily changed or post-capitalist system will no doubt include the sharing of assets and services. A definitive contemporary book on the phenomenon of sharing and cooperation is McLaren and Agyeman's *Sharing Cities*. They make a compelling case to expand the current commercial notion of a sharing economy to a broader conception of a sharing paradigm or sharing culture. They start with dictionary definitions, which describe sharing as dividing something between multiple users, allowing others to consume a portion of, or take a turn in using things that are ours, or which we use. Sharing includes occupying or enjoying a facility, space or resource jointly with one or more other people. In economic terms of owned goods, it includes the "voluntary lending, pooling, allocation of resources, and authorized use of public property, but excluding contractual renting, leasing or unauthorized use of property (squatting)."[18]

The authors conclude that too much of the sharing economy is *commercially* driven, involving money and sometimes a formal contract. They see a much wider, more egalitarian sharing, not just sharing of things (such as cars, bikes, tools, books), services and places (for meetings or sleeping), but also activities and experiences (political and leisure activities). In their inclusive model, sharing can be material in nature or virtual, tangible or intangible, consumptive or productive, simultaneous or sequential, and rivalrous or shared, like open source software. It reflects their belief that sharing could potentially be the basis for a post-capitalist economy and society, and is about well-being as much as commerce. They refer to the "solidarity or social economy," which includes a host of entities, such as community crowdfunding, credit unions, participatory budgeting, co-working, co-housing and community land trusts. Their conception is less about reciprocity and trade, and more about cooperation and community.[19] Other entities include tenement syndicates, mutual aid housing cooperatives and limited equity cooperatives where joint ownership is democratic – all of which also increase housing affordability.

> Common spaces are popping up in new development projects across Europe. Many new buildings offer guest rooms, lounge areas for working and socialising, terraces with outdoor kitchens, drying rooms for laundry – all shared by the owners of the flats. Such shared facilities could increase utility for households at an affordable cost and encourage a more community-based lifestyle.[20]

In America, the waste in the ubiquitous single-family house is excessive – rooms that get little or no use, and individual ownership of equipment that could be shared. New concepts are bringing much more flexibility into housing, as it copes with elderly people having difficulty downsizing, or "swing rooms" that can be detached from one apartment and attached to the one next door as needs change. Flexible seating, desk-sharing, office hoteling, tele-working, and audio and video conferencing are major trends in the marketplace. In the commercial sector, there's shared office space where individuals and corporations rent as much space as they need for as long as they need it.

The tension is thick between more idealistic, altruistic sharing and commercial sharing.

> Sharing can help us achieve economic *degrowth* in consumption and production – and the wastes that come with them, like carbon emissions – while maintaining quality of life, or even improving it with more social interactions and stronger community relationships . . . [or] The sharing economy is a nice way for rapacious capitalists to monetize the desperation of people in the post-crisis economy while sounding generous, and to evoke a fantasy of community in an atomized population.[21]

Matt Yglesias of the Vox Media website goes further to argue that commercially mediated sharing is not sharing at all, but simply short-term rentals or secondary markets.[22] The jury is still out on which type of sharing will prevail. We'll no doubt see the idealistic, socially just, cooperative model *and* the more rapacious, business-as-usual, commercial model. The net impact of the two models is very likely to be positive, given the fact that even commercial sharing distributes new income and other forms of wealth to more diverse and less-moneyed strata of the populace. It's more bottom-up than the current economic system, and collectively it more efficiently utilizes a city's physical assets. This efficiency obviously helps fight CC and UHIs by reducing both carbon and waste heat footprints.

The Smart City is a more controversial manifestation of sharing. It's mainly about managing a city's assets and operations by collecting and sharing data in real-time with information and communication technology (ICT) and the Internet of Things (IoT). The sophisticated and pervasive electronic monitoring of countless variables in urban existence is about tackling inefficiency. Appropriately, it's Wikipedia that tells us "ICT is used to enhance the quality, performance and interactivity of urban services, to reduce costs and resource consumption and to improve contact between citizens and government."[23] Smart Cities utilize the IoT primarily to regulate and operate the physical infrastructure. Sociologists like Richard Sennett criticize the system as too prescriptive and squelches self-organization. He writes that

> once basic services are in place people don't value efficiency above all; they want quality of life . . . If they have a choice, people want a more open, indeterminate city in which to make their way; this is how they can come to take ownership of their lives.[24]

This more flexible, open-ended model is arguably more efficient in the long run, and certainly more resilient.

There are other critiques of the Smart City, including one by Professor Shannon Mattern of The New School:

> Instead of more gratuitous parametric modeling, we need to think about urban epistemologies that embrace memory and history; that recognize spatial intelligence as sensory and experiential; that consider other species' ways of knowing; that appreciate the wisdom of local crowds and communities; that acknowledge the information embedded in the city's facades, flora, statuary, and stairways . . . We must also recognize the shortcomings in models that presume the objectivity of urban data and conveniently delegate critical, often ethical decisions to the machine.[25]

It's true that things like dance, ritual, cooking and sports, not to mention physical experience of things like shadows, wind and rust are lost in data. Computerizing the city may be appealing, as it rationally frames and simplifies its messiness, but much of the messiness is what makes cities creative, productive, dynamic, exciting and fun.

Another media maven, the founder of *Mask Magazine* Hanna Hurr, observes that computers are starting to program themselves, designing algorithms that are too complex for human understanding.

> That is, they are becoming like cities themselves, whose complexity has defied efforts at urban planning . . . no less than nine tech company proposals for smart cities . . . ooze with the same kind of bold optimism you see in modernist architectural manifestos. Not only do these tech companies consider the city a problem for them to solve rather than a public institution to participate in, but they also, like certain Bible verses, predict apocalypse only to offer redemption. They pledge their intelligent, automated, big data-driven supervision of the "smart city" will solve everything from climate change to resource depletion.[26]

It is clear that the computerized smart city has much to offer, but it's not the salvation for urban problems that some of its proponents frothily predict.

Why is sharing important to our civilization, our cities and the earth? It's critical, even essential to our survival, because without it, we will overconsume the planet's resources and overheat it. At this point in our evolution, two things seem inevitable. The first is that world population will continue to grow, before leveling off, as the U.N. predicts. Pandemics and violent strife may slow or even reverse this predicted growth, but there will still likely be too many human beings to sustain themselves. The second inevitability is that as rural migrants continue to move to cities, their consumption will increase, and along with it, humanity's footprint. Urban efficiencies and synergies, as well as lower birth rates, will help compensate, as will expected technological breakthroughs. But overall, it seems to be increasingly apparent that these countermeasures will not be enough to sufficiently lower humanity's footprint to avoid tipping points in the climate. Sharing our assets, our services and places, even our activities and experiences may be our best hope to reduce the human ecological, energy and carbon footprints.

Humans are not about to give up their pursuit of a high quality of life. Some would argue it needs to be an *ever-higher* quality of life to satisfy our seemingly insatiable appetite for pleasure and happiness. In either case, economic growth has traditionally provided the means for the rise in our physical standard of living and the presumed improvement in the quality of life. Increasing per capita growth will continue to drive this pursuit, but the historic rate of 2 percent or more per year of compounding personal or national GDP is not endlessly sustainable. For instance, a continuous 3 percent annual growth rate would mean that the economy would double every 25 years, grow 16-fold every century, 250 times every two centuries, which is hardly sustainable.

Free markets are known to be brilliant at producing and distributing goods and services, but idiotic when it comes to dealing with externalities. This why they need to be regulated by themselves or the public sector. The Global North's market economies *have* produced astounding wealth, although its equitable distribution has gone from pathetic to bathetic within some societies. Clair Brown describes a more interdependent local and global economy in *Buddhist Economics*:

> The free market model, in which each person is assumed to have independent and well-defined desires, evaporates. Social welfare is no longer the simple addition of everyone's consumption, because your well-being adds to my well-being, and our well-being depends on much more than our income. Well-being ripples outward as we share resources globally . . . Sustainable shared prosperity requires that people in rich countries develop simpler, sustainable lifestyles so that people in poor countries can live comfortably.[27]

It is of paramount importance that we find ways to increase prosperity without economic growth, or better yet, to achieve degrowth. In the meantime, society needs to provide both individual and collective prosperity and happiness to satisfy human desires and needs. Some people may find it in religion or spiritual practices, such as meditation and mindfulness, while others may find it through voluntary simplicity in their lives. Cities need to foster or at least make possible such practices. Many will want and need other methods and means, which the sharing paradigm could provide for both local and global communities. Sharing assets and services could help satisfy our physical needs, and sharing activities and experiences could help satisfy our social and psychological needs. It may be the best, if not the only way, to provide prosperity without growth – arguably market capitalism's greatest, perhaps insurmountable challenge.

New, more humane metrics have been developed around the world by various organizations and governments to encourage prosperity and well-being without economic growth. In addition to Bhutan's celebrated Gross National Happiness Index, there is the U.N.'s Human Development Index, OECD's Better Life Index (BLI), the Genuine Progress Indicator (GPI), the Happy Planet Index (HPI) and others. These dashboards focus on a different gamut of variables, ranging from harder economic and health data to softer estimations of well-being and happiness. No single system satisfies everyone, including cool-eyed econometricians, evolutionary ecologists, CEOs, compassionate Buddhists, devout Christians, frugal homemakers and the many, many other walks of life

To review the key role of sharing in cities and in societies worldwide, let us return to McLaren and Agyeman, who synthesize the case for sharing cities with six concluding points that offer further hope for the future:[28]

1   Humans are natural socio-cultural sharers, but as a result of consumerism and commercialization, these traits have taken a back seat to our competitive, individualized selves.
2   The future of humanity is urban, which necessitates sharing: of resources, goods, services, experiences and capabilities.
3   New opportunities for sharing will give new opportunities to enhance trust and rebuild social capital.
4   Sharing with equity and justice can naturally shift cultural values and norms toward trust and collaboration.
5   An enhanced public realm or urban commons establishes a precondition and motivation for collective political debate that recognizes the city as a shared system.
6   "Sharing the whole city" should become the guiding purpose of the future city. The city should not be structured into two exclusive tiers, a central zone tied into elite global markets and a periphery of surplus and casual labor. Sharing offers both a sustainable platform for participatory urban democracy and a transformative approach to urban futures.

These very idealized goals for open, equitable and sharing cities will not come easily or quickly in commercialized, materialist societies. Nor will the idea of no growth, as Tim Jackson elaborates in *Prosperity without Growth*:

> Questioning growth is deemed to be the act of lunatics, idealists and revolutionaries. But question it we must . . . The idea of a non-growing economy may be an anathema to an economist. But the idea of a continually growing economy is an anathema to an ecologist . . . Economics – macro-economics in particular – is ecologically illiterate . . . If we keep growing GDP, then we fail to cut greenhouse gases deeply. This means we stoke destruction of prosperity beyond the short-term horizons – "next quarter's growth figures" and all the rest – on which we routinely put such emphasis today.[29]

No-growth economies do offer prosperity without growth. However, this admirable and necessary goal will take more than a sharing economy.

As Jackson says, three macro-economic interventions are needed to achieve ecological and economic stability in a new economy:[30]

1 more serviced-based activities and jobs and less industry
2 investment in ecological assets, activities and jobs
3 workday and workweek policies and practices to spread and lower over-productivity.

Whether a reformed version of capitalism or a fundamentally new economy, the sharing city and no growth ethic form a large, profound and open question. In any case, from an energy use and emissions point of view, doubling energy and technological efficiency or doubling the intensity of asset use though sharing have much the same impact – whether it's cars, transit, homes, equipment, offices or workshops. This realization opens up a huge new opportunity for reforming or replacing neoliberal capitalism with longer-term thinking and more humane economics.

Notes

1 Kwame Anthony Appiah, personal email, 10/5/18
2 Doug Kelbaugh, *Repairing the American Metropolis*, University of Washington Press, 2002, p. 8
3 "Key Findings," Briefing Paper 1, Conflict in Cities, www.conflictincities.org
4 D. Kelbaugh, R. Adams, P. Elmlund et al., *Key Messages from Future of Places*, UN Habitat III, 2015
5 David Brooks, "How would Jesus drive?" *The New York Times*, 1/4/18
6 Rahul Mehrotra et al., *Kumbh Mela: Mapping the Ephemeral Megacity*, South Asia Institute, Harvard University, 2013
7 Kate Wheeling, "Tourism's climate footprint is much larger than previously thought," *citylab*, 5/9/18
8 For data on fragile cities, visit https://igarape.org.br/en/apps/fragile-cities-data-visualization/ and www.conflictincities.org
9 Mark Oppenheimer, "Technology is not driving us apart after all," *The New York Times*, 1/17/14
10 Julian Agyeman, interview on *Grist*, 4/7/17
11 Stewart Brand, *Whole Earth Discipline*, Viking, 2009, p. 73
12 Benjamin Barber, *Jihad vs. McWorld*, Times Books, 1995
13 Ben Crowther, "Interview with Dan Savage, Part I: Why cities" *The Urbanist*, 8/1/17
14 Paulo Ferraro and John Fernandez, *Sustainable Urban Metabolism*, MIT Press, 2013
15 Juilan Agyeman, co-author of *Sharing Cities*, interview on *Grist*, 4/7/17
16 Tom Friedman, "And now for a bit of good news . . .," *The New York Times*, 7/19/14
17 Noah Yuval Harari, "Why humans rule the world," TED talk, 7/24/15
18 Richard Belk, "Why not share rather than own," *Annals of the American Academy of Political and Social Sciences*, 611, 2007, pp. 126–140
19 Duncan McLaren and Julian Agyeman, *Sharing Cities*, MIT Press, 2015
20 Lloyd Alter, "Six ways to transform the built environment," *Treehugger*, 8/17/18

21 Sam Bliss, "The sharing economy is bullsh!t: here's how we can take it back," *Grist*, 3/9/15
22 Matthew Yglesias, "There is no 'sharing economy,'" *Slate*, 12/26/13
23 "Smart City," Wikipedia, 4/15/17
24 Richard Sennett, "No one likes a city that's too smart," *The Guardian*, 12/4/12
25 Shannon Mattern, "A city is not a computer," *Places*, February, 2017
26 Hanna Hurr, "Panic city," *reallifemag.com*, 8/30/17
27 Clair Brown, *Buddhist Economics*, Bloomsbury, 2017, p. 85
28 Duncan McLaren and Julian Agyeman, *Sharing Cities*, p. 85
29 Jeremy Leggett, "Prosperity without growth," *The Guardian*, 1/22/10
30 Tim Jackson, *Prosperity without Growth*, Earthscan, 2009, p. 200

8 Cities
Our Last, Best Hope

Mitigation or Adaptation?

The four strategies to address UHIs – especially enhancing albedo and reducing waste heat – also help *mitigate* CC. More specifically, albedo enhancement mitigates CC by reducing solar heat gain on earth, and reducing waste heat reduces GHGs. And diminishing the depth and dark colors of urban street canyons helps mitigate CC by decreasing solar heat gain. But urban canyon and cool micro-climate strategies only modestly address CC, the latter by sequestering carbon in foliage and shading buildings to reduce air conditioning. The primary benefit of cool micro-climates is *adapting* to hotter temperatures brought on by CC. In fact, all four strategies *adapt* to CC by tempering the additional heat that it brings. Because all of them both mitigate and adapt, they could also be described as *adaptive mitigation* or *mitigative adaptation*. They all offer understandable, proven, efficacious and actionable ways to simultaneously cool both the city and the planet. None of them are radical, new or exotic, although the necessary scale of their implementation is dramatic enough to change the form and feel of the city.

The adaptation vs. mitigation discussion itself can heat up, escalating into a hot debate. In the end, most parties agree that we need both, but there can be vehement debate about their relative priority. Adaptation has been gaining ground, as the full mitigation of CC becomes seen as a future whose time has passed. Environmentalists and urban planners are now embracing adaptation, provoked by extreme weather events like recent hurricanes. Not that long ago, it was a taboo subject, seen as an admission of early defeat in the face of CC. The mitigation advocates retort that solely or primarily adapting to flooding, sea level rise, drought, etc. may be essential, but without mitigation, these problems will only become worse and costlier over time. It not like there's one cliff to fall off, but many cliffs in our carbon-intensive world. Environmental analyst Jeff Howards strikingly likens adaptation responses that do not also mitigate to "learning that the house is on fire but, instead of fighting the fire, trying to devise methods to live in the flaming structure."[1] Or, as urbanism advocate Michael Mehaffy puts it:

CC is not a "one and done" kind of thing. There is not a binary condition of "too late" or "not too late." There is "later" and there is "much later" and "much much later." The first is bad, and then they get really bad, and then really really bad.[2]

The judicious balancing of the two positions needs to account for local and regional differences. Clearly mitigation that also adapts – or vice versa – is more resilient, and should be pursued, given the rapidity of CC. From sea walls to "rolling easements" that gradually move residents from threatened areas, strategies need to be augmented by building community capacity in ways like Ahmedabad, India has pioneered. "As of 2016, more than 40 U.S. communities have created standalone climate adaptation plans, with potentially hundreds more embedding climate considerations into other planning approaches. However, the thoroughness and consistency of these plans vary wildly."[3] As former New York City Mayor Bloomberg has repeated, most adaptation takes place at scales beneath the national level, in a devolution of power called subsidiarity. For example, the Mississippi River Cities and Towns Initiative, with 85 mayors along the river, has developed a Climate/ Disaster Resilience and Adaptation program because they recognize the need for their communities, many of which are smaller, to deal with the reality of a changing climate.[4] There is no one-size-fits-all approach, which is why "community-based adaptation" (CBA) is taking hold as an alternative to top-down, government-driven and sponsored initiatives. The grassroots activism of CBA also appeals to both sides of the ideological spectrum, no small matter in today's polarized politics. It also appeals to the human preference and proclivity for taking action against threats.

Cities are already taking an aggressive lead in reducing carbon footprints. Over 500 cities worldwide were reporting their greenhouse gas emissions by 2016, a 70 percent increase in reporting since the Paris Agreement a year earlier. About a third of these cities and over half those in North America have GHG emissions reduction targets, with many committing to zero emissions, or an 80 percent reduction by 2050 or earlier.[5] The C40 global network of 91 large cities representing 650 million urban citizens and more than a quarter of the global economy[6] reported in late 2016: "U.S. cities can account for a third of the emissions reductions necessary to hit the country's climate goal under the Paris Agreement by 2025. U.S. members have already taken 2,400 individual climate-related actions in the last decade."[7] The sense of urgency was accelerated in September of 2017 by the alarmingly rapid succession of Hurricanes Harvey, Irma and Maria, as well as simultaneous flooding in South Asia. A sadly prophetic moment of extreme heat occurred when Irma knocked out electrical air conditioners, and 14 residents at a Florida nursing home died from the stifling heat.

A dozen global cities in the C40 coalition have pledged to take major steps toward cutting transportation emissions, promising a future of cities where walking, cycling and shared transport are how the majority of citizens move around. In late 2017, signatories pledged to purchase only zero-emissions buses beginning in 2025, and that a major area of their city be zero emission in effect banning internal combustion engines in certain districts by 2030.[8] Singapore, one of the most expensive places in the world to buy a vehicle, announced it will freeze the number of private cars on its roads from 2018, while vowing to expand public transit. It's costly to buy a vehicle, as ten-year "certificates of entitlement" cost on average US$37,000![9]

Many mayors are committed to squeezing carbon out of their cities by investing in and promoting renewable energy, electric cars, LED street lights, more energy-efficient buildings, automated rapid transit, mobility-on-demand services, etc. For the first time, municipal governments have a formal role within the U.N.'s Intergovernmental Panel on Climate Change (IPCC), the scientific body that advises national governments. The panel recently adopted an urban lens in its research and reports, and convened the first #CitiesIPCC conference to prepare a research agenda.[10]

> In these contested times, a slow realization is taking hold in national capitals, regions and cities across the world of the potential for public awareness of sustainable urbanization to accelerate the implementation of sustainable development. Simultaneously, the United Nations is shifting from a fragmented 20th-century orientation to a more integrated 21st-century response to urbanization.[11]

Cities are estimated to account for more than 70 percent of total global greenhouse gas emissions,[12] as well as being the locus of UHIs. With a very high percentage built in coastal areas, cities will also be the likeliest victims of flooding, permanent inundation and soil salinization. The first wave – literally – is from extreme storm surges, followed by ongoing sea level rise.

> Barring a radical reduction of emissions, we will see at least four feet of sea-level rise and possibly ten by the end of the century. A third of the world's major cities are on the coast, not to mention its power plants, ports, navy bases, farmlands, fisheries, river deltas, marshlands and rice-paddy empires, and even those above ten feet will flood much more easily, and much more regularly, if the water gets that high. At least 600 million people live within ten meters of sea level today.[13]

A recent report authored by the U.K.'s Special Representative for Climate Change noted how with just one metre of global sea level rise, what is today a "100-year flood" will become about 40 times more likely in Shanghai, 200 times more likely in New York and 1,000 times more likely in Kolkata . . . with some estimates even predicting that current modeled losses could be undervalued by as much as 50%, should recent weather trends prove indicative of the new normal.[14]

And as costly as flooding has been to date, the new normal will continue to escalate as both coastal cities grow and the oceans rise. The U.N. reckons that between 1995 and 2015, storms and floods caused $1.7 trillion of destruction, and that losses in Europe will increase fivefold by 2050.[15] As the sea level rises and with the freshwater flooding seen in recent years in places like Houston, there will be wholesale population shifts to higher ground. The Congress for the New Urbanism is now addressing the migration of whole towns and cities to upland locations, particularly to cities in stress that need people and businesses. A team from Tufts University, Rutgers University and the Potsdam Institute for Climate Impact Research in Germany found that if countries manage to keep the rise in global temperature to 1.5°C (2.7°F), sea level rise would be about seven inches less than under a 2°C (3.6°F) increase by 2050.[16] Seven inches may sound trivial, but it represents large economic and social costs.

Because cities are the prime, disproportionate cause and victim of UHIs and CC, it is appropriate that they are in a position to act on both. Michael Bloomberg, the official U.N. envoy on CC, has stated,

> climate change may be the first global problem where success will depend on how municipal services such as energy, water, and transportation are delivered to citizens. Cities have only just begun to seize the opportunities they have to make changes that can produce both local and global benefits.[17]

As Benjamin Barber ardently urged, cities should throw their considerable weight behind the transnational Global Parliament of Mayors, ICLEI (International Council for Local Environmental Initiatives) and C40. Through them, cities can participate in high-level international processes and have a more formal voice in climate negotiations within international forums like the U.N.[18]

These networks also facilitate cities' entrepreneurialism, as mayors and city officials learn about practical, low-cost solutions to their own problems. From booming bike-share systems to participatory budgeting, ideas disseminate rapidly and widely through the city networks. Barber also believed that the biggest cities, especially in the Global North, bear a special responsibility both to be at the forefront of these efforts and also to help their poorer counterparts. These goals are not easy to reach, especially given the reluctance of nations to relinquish power to lower levels of government. This downward distribution of power, i.e., subsidiarity, is about devolving decision making to the lowest level of a government, organization or institution that is sufficiently competent to deal with the issue at hand. This level is increasingly the city or metro area, but both face a battle to be taken seriously in international affairs and to compete for funding and relevance.[19]

Brookings Institution's Bruce Katz writes

> We are about to witness a burst of institutional innovation that both connects cities to cities (enabling them to share and replicate best innovations), as well as connects consortia of cities to global capital and corporations (enabling them to invent new financial instruments that can routinize investments). Some of this is already occurring through new city networks like C-40, which focuses on climate change, and the Rockefeller Foundation's 100 Resilient Cities, which enables cities to tackle natural shocks and socio-economic stresses. More institutional innovation is on the way as cities and capital start working together on making investments in innovative, sustainable, and inclusive growth the norm rather than the exception. The architecture of the global order is changing. The city-state and the nation-state are now linked in intricate and complex ways.[20]

The U.N. adopted its Millennium Development Goals in 2000 as its major 15-year initiative to improve extreme poverty, through the sharing of rich countries' resources with poor countries. The goals tended to address rural rather than urban problems, but many of the gains happened in cities, because of increased migration to and sharing in cities. The drive was a staggering success on many levels: People living in extreme poverty fell from almost 2 billion people, sadly 43 percent of the population of the developing world in 1990, to just under 900 million people, 17 percent of the developing world in 2012. Enrollment in primary schools rose to 91 percent, and women's positions have improved, with more employment available to women outside of agriculture and more women in elected national positions. The child mortality rate declined by half, down to 43 deaths per 1,000 live births. Nonetheless, 16,000 children died each day from preventable pneumonia, diarrhea and malaria, made more acute by malnutrition. The number of people with access to safe drinking water grew dramatically around the world, from 663 million people in 1990 to 2.6 billion in 2012. However, sanitation lags far behind; one in three people were still without adequate sanitation facilities.[21] "More people have cell phones than a toilet. You lose a kid under the age of five every 90 seconds because of lack of access to clean water and sanitation."[22] And, sadly, fewer than 1 in 20 girls from poor rural families in sub-Saharan Africa can be expected to finish secondary school.[23]

The United Nation's New Urban Agenda

The Millennium Development Goals were replaced in late 2016 by the Sustainable Development Goals (SDG), which include 17 interrelated goals for 2015 through 2030. They changed the lens and focus from rural to urban, prompted by the fact that the world population was already over half urban and expected to reach 60 percent by 2030, including over one billion people in squatter settlements within urbanized areas. That's nearly one in seven humans living in slums. In late 2016 at Habitat III in Quito, Ecuador, the U.N. officially adopted the New Urban Agenda (NUA), which is based on the SDG. The new U.N. goals include sustainable production, services and infrastructure, all of which are about doing more with less while addressing welfare and poverty worldwide. Importantly, Goal 11 is about more equitable, accessible and livable cities, including a robust public realm. It commits to making "cities and human settlements inclusive, safe, resilient and sustainable." The year 2018 was officially the Year of SDG 11. This and other objectives of the NUA make cities the centerline of U.N. global activities – a sea change in their approach to assessing and addressing the world's pressing problems.

The NUA is an important and relevant U.N. initiative that was unanimously and enthusiastically adopted. Its "cities for all" theme implies equity, inclusion, high quality public space, open institutions, etc. It subtly excludes the walled fortification or survivalist mentality, as well as informal latte-sippers in an over-heated tech bubble. It includes precise physical urban planning and development goals, such as promoting open space of 45 percent, with 30 percent for street circulation and 15 percent for public space, parks and public facilities.[24] This far exceeds the prevailing norms in informal settlements throughout the Global South, which typically have 2 percent open space, consisting of left-over spaces for public circulation and gathering.[25] Hong Kong has only 25 square feet of green recreational space per capita; Mumbai has only 12 square feet per capita – the size of a toilet stall – compared to about 200 square feet per capita in my city of Ann Arbor, Michigan.

The agenda's goals also "envisage cities and human settlements that are participatory, promote civic engagement, engender a sense of belonging and ownership among all their inhabitants, prioritize safe, inclusive, accessible, green and quality public spaces."[26] Unlike earlier U.N. policy and programs, and perhaps most importantly, *the NUA sees slums, squatter settlements, favelas, barrios, etc., as fully worthy investment, no longer considering them non-permanent, illegitimate or hopeless.* As difficult as it will be to retrofit squatter settlements with more and better public space, it is essential. Without adequate streets, plazas and infrastructure, as well as more secure land tenure, these communities will not be able to mature into healthy, permanent urban neighborhoods.

Improving existing informal settlements as opposed to building new top-down government projects is essential, simply because there are far too many informal settlements to replace whole cloth.

Although it focuses on cities, the NUA cannot afford to ignore rural dwellers. A 2017 U.N. report states

> 85% of the world's poor are in rural areas . . . The development gap between urban and rural areas is still large and urgently needs to be bridged . . . It is widely acknowledged that urban growth has a positive impact on economic development, but still most of the world's poor live in rural areas . . . the urban–rural divide needs to be reimagined as a harmonious continuum, where policies and programmes aimed at helping people on one side can help people on the other side as well.[27]

Clearly, regional policies and programs for energy, water, transportation, economic growth and tourism can be better coordinated across the rural–urban transect. And creating and overhauling laws can safeguard the rights of ethnic groups, slum dwellers and women while clamping down on bribes and other forms of crime and corruption.

In 2017 Habitat for Humanity published a small book on the NUA, the *Quito Declaration on Sustainable Cities and Human Settlements for All*. It was generated by over 40 U.N. agencies, thousands of subnational governments, more than 1,100 organizations and 58,000 networks, and endorsed by 197 countries. Several of the many goals and objectives are about public space, including one that specifically mentions UHIs, as well as one that includes heat waves:

> We commit ourselves to promoting the creation and maintenance of well-connected and well-distributed networks of open, multi-purpose, safe, inclusive, green and quality public spaces, to improving the resilience of cities to climate change, including floods, drought risks and heat waves, improving . . . household and ambient air quality, to reducing noise and promoting attractive and livable cities, human settlements and urban landscapes.[28]

Among many other declarations, it is adamant about sustainability and resilience:

> We commit ourselves to promoting the development of urban spatial frameworks, including urban planning and design instruments that support sustainable management and use of natural resources and land, appropriate compactness and density, polycentrism and mixed uses, through infill or planned urban extension strategies, as applicable, to trigger economies of scale and agglomeration, strengthen

food system planning and enhance resource efficiency, urban resilience and environmental sustainability.[29]

Another excerpt:

> We recognize that urban form, infrastructure and building design are among the greatest drivers of cost and resource efficiencies, through the benefits of economy of scale and agglomeration by fostering energy efficiency, renewable energy, resilience, productivity, environmental protection and sustainable growth in the urban economy.[30]

One could hardly come up with a more succinct synopsis of this book.

Andrew Rudd of U.N. Habitat's NUA staff has noted the four most common development models that are plaguing the planet, especially in the developing world:

1   greenfield developments
2   inefficient sprawl developments
3   obsolete development models (e.g., China's superblock and super arterial/ring road, or the American cul-de-sac subdivision)
4   unplanned, informal, squatter settlements (which lack amenities and infrastructure).

The NUA recognizes the need to deploy UHI strategies to cool hot cities, while simultaneously addressing CC. It is against greenfield developments that leap-frog into and destroy virgin forests and agricultural lands, highlighting the need for mixed-use, mixed-income, walkable, bike-able, transit-oriented towns, cities and metro areas. As New Urbanist architect/builder Seth Harry says, "While the suburban consumer market is determined by the size of the arterial road, the urban consumer market is determined by density and proximity."[31] The NUA promotes smaller arterials and dense urban proximities to promote walking, biking and transit.

Since the Quito Declaration, the U.N. has been pushing hard for implementing the NUA, with more emphasis on public–private collaboration and possibly more oversight of U.N. Habitat from a broader, more powerful Urban Forum to promote national urban policies. About one-third of the countries have some kind of existing national strategy for urban development, and they aim to raise it to half by 2025. Their formal definition of such a strategy is "a coherent set of decisions derived through a deliberate government-led process of coordinating and rallying various actors for a common vision and goal that will promote more transformative, productive, inclusive and resilient urban development for the long term."[32] The former top-down, national policies are yielding to a more balanced approach today, with a growing sense that mayors and local governments should play a bigger role.

Implementation was the focus of the Ninth World Urban Forum in Kuala Lumpur in 2018, the first since the adoption of the New Urban Agenda. The implementation obstacles are daunting. "Business as usual" – often sprawl – still prevails in many places, despite the well-known human benefits of urbanization. New Urbanist Michael Mehaffy offered five takeaways from the forum:

1   The world is urbanizing at a blistering pace. At present rates – and there's currently no sign this will change – the world's urban population will more than *double* in the next 40 years. "Essentially we will create more urban fabric than has ever been created *in all of human history* up to now."
2   Much of this urbanization is sprawling and resource-inefficient.
3   Growing numbers of people recognize that we must change business as usual.
4   Many people are still addicted to the short-term profits from sprawling, resource-intensive urbanization, and too many places look like they could have been designed for 1940 (with updated avant-garde art packaging) instead of 2020.
5   The New Urban Agenda represents a hopeful way forward for all. The world now has a landmark agreement by 193 countries to move in a new direction – a new paradigm.[33]

As mentioned earlier, no one is more emphatic about reform than former New York City Mayor Michael Bloomberg, who co-authored the popular book *Climate of Hope*. "More than any national law or policy, devolving power to cities is the single best step that nations can take to improve their ability to fight climate change."[34] He proclaims that cities

> can't wait for national governments to act . . . Most representative democracies have voting systems weighted – some might say rigged – to give more power to rural areas than population warrants . . . This tradition is being challenged by the reality of the twenty-century-economies . . . Cities, not rural areas, are the nexus of this new economy – and cities . . . also have enormous incentives to take action on climate change. Since markets are centered in urban areas, it makes sense for them to lead the way in addressing market failures. And, fortunately, cities are uniquely equipped to do it.

Reconfronting Sprawl: Still Paved with Good Intentions, If Less Asphalt

No one better reveals the problems of sprawl than David Owen in his precocious, now classic 2004 article "Green Manhattan" in *The New Yorker*. "If you made all eight million New Yorkers live at a density of my town, they would require a space equivalent to land area of the six New England states, plus Delaware and New Jersey." Edward Glaeser follows up in *Triumph of the City*: "We are a destructive species, and if you love nature, stay away from it. The best means of protecting the environment is to live in the heart of a city."[35]

Suburbia first manifested itself in London in the nineteenth century, but the modern suburb as we know it started in the U.S. after World War II. It has spread like a virus ever since, especially in North America, Australia and parts of Europe. With the private automobile promising independence for every household, it was an unspoken assumption that American cities would spawn suburbs, and that the public sector would provide the infrastructure while industry provided the cars. There were not only federal subsidies for roads and sewers, but federal mortgage programs for returning war veterans that subsidized ownership of single-family homes, rather than rental apartments. Because rental units were much more common in cities than suburbs, the programs heavily favored what soon spread into concentric rings of leap-frog sprawl. Indeed, the suburban home surrounded by a private yard and with a car or two parked in the driveway or garage became the American Dream.[36] In addition to tax breaks for mortgages and farm land, gasoline was directly and indirectly subsidized by government tax policies. Racial discrimination and better suburban schools added to the "white flight" to these bedroom communities.

No one has been more damning of the American suburb than Jane Jacobs, who over a half century ago savaged the often saccharin attitude toward the natural land that surrounds our cities:

> It is no accident that we Americans, probably the world's champion sentimentalizers about nature, are at one and the same time probably the world's most voracious and disrespectful destroyers of wild and rural countryside . . . It is neither love for nature nor respect for nature that leads us to this schizophrenic attitude. Instead, it is a sentimental desire to toy, rather patronizingly, with some insipid, standardized, suburbanized shadow of nature . . . And so, each day, several thousand more acres of our countryside are eaten by the bulldozers, covered by pavement, dotted with suburbanites who killed the thing they thought they came to find.[37]

And Austrian-born architect Victor Gruen, the inventor of the modern shopping mall, quickly came to condemn its impact in 1978 as "land-wasting seas of parking."[38] These two defects have only gotten worse since their frank and harsh pronouncements. It is tragic that America not only smeared the suburban compromise of town and country across its 50 states, but it also exported it to a world only too happy to embrace the seemingly happy lifestyle they'd seen in the movies and on TV.

Figure 8.1 Sprawl American style, with its over-equipped McMansions on cul-de-sac plumes, single-use zoning, dispersed road and utility infrastructure, with frustratingly long red lights because the gargantuan intersections are spaced too far apart in a coarse network that requires signalized left-turn lanes. Some clever archeologist in the future will dig up a suburban intersection and realize that this civilization was plagued by too few places to turn left. As urbanist Leon Krier has said, "The very great challenge of the future . . . will be the urbanization of suburbia, the redevelopment of sprawl."[1] (image collage by M. Mehaffy)

1 Nikos Salingaros, "The future of cities: the absurdity of modernism," *Planetizen*, 11/5/01

These policies and practices have continued into the twenty-first century. As real estate developer and fellow student of Buddhism Jonathan Rose points out in *The Well-Tempered City*: "From 1970 to 2015 the size of the average home in the U.S. doubled, as did the number of cars, and its number of televisions has tripled, all this while the number of occupants per home halved!"[39] And even these ballooning houses were not big enough for the consumptive lifestyle that suburbia allowed and encouraged: Americans on average now rent over 5 square feet in a storage unit on some forlorn arterial strip. The typical house in the contemporary American suburb "is estimated over a forty-year life cycle to use a staggering 15,455 GJ (Gigajoules) of energy. That amount of energy is enough to traverse the U.S. by automobile more than a thousand times."[40] Immense suburban lawns are both the pride and the burden of McMansions, surrounded by fenced backyards, generally useless side yards and manicured front yards. "In suburbia, you see no one doing anything in their yard other than working on it . . . its purpose is to be taken care of."[41] As the author Michael Pollan says "Lawns are the largest irrigated crop in America . . . the area in lawn in this country is three times as big as the corn crop."[42] Other than mowing it, Americans spend no time in the front yard, which is beautifully maintained as a symbolic space, but too exposed to public view for relaxation. Pollan goes on to say that a Martian would wonder why no one spends time in their expansive front yard, while squeezing their outdoor activities into the back yard?

The U.S. has more shopping malls than high schools, and retail consumption accounts for 80 percent of its economy.[43] No longer just machines of consumption or bedroom communities, suburbs now have numerous workplaces, most notably office parks. The famous architect Rem Koolhaas describes these campuses as "a bland suburban environment that is becoming increasingly exclusive, its tech bubbles insulated from the public sphere."[44] These commercial islands of free-standing office blocks surrounded by parking are connected by rivers of asphalt with oceanic intersections, to allow multiple left-turn lanes, which make the red lights seemingly interminable.

It's estimated that there are three nonresidential parking spaces for every car in the United States. That adds up to almost 800 million parking spaces, covering about 4,360 square miles, an area larger than Puerto Rico. In some cities, like Orlando and Los Angeles, parking lots are estimated to cover at least one-third of the land area, making them one of the most salient landscape features of the built world.[45]

This is the land of big asphalt, which absorbs solar radiation and creates heat islands even in low-density suburbia.

The preferences of transit-inclined Millennials, who were born between 1980 and roughly 2000, are causing angst in traditionally car-dominated suburbia.

> Suburbs nationwide have long lured companies – and the high-skilled workers they seek to attract – with good schools, relatively low crime and spacious corporate campuses surrounded by vast parking lots near major highways. A realization is growing among those communities' business and civic leaders that the traditional suburban brand needs an overhaul.[46]

For instance, the inescapable suburban shopping mall is finally being retrofitted or displaced by street-oriented retail shops, but only after killing many stores in the host city and spawning nearby bottom-feeding outlets, all floating within a sea of parking.

> Drenched in cafe-au-lait stucco, the mall was bordered by an example of America's most unique architectural contribution to the world, a parking lot. Some bemoan the brutalism of socialist architecture, but was the blandness of capitalist architecture any better? One could drive for miles along a boulevard and see nothing but parking lots and the kudzu of strip malls catering to every need . . . each one an advertisement for the pursuit of happiness.[47]

Nonetheless, some Millennials are starting to leave cities for suburbs, where housing is usually more affordable and there are yards for their kids. But according to MIT's Alan Berger, they want a different kind of suburbia:

> They want breathing room but disdain the energy wastefulness, visual monotony and social conformity of postwar manufactured neighborhoods. If new suburbs can hit the sweet spot that accommodates the priorities of that generation, Millennial habitats will redefine everyday life for all suburbanites, which is 70% of Americans . . . Climate will determine how environmental goals can be achieved in a given place: solar in the Sunbelt, say, or advanced water management in the rainy regions like the Pacific Northwest . . . In sustainable new suburbs, house and lot sizes are smaller – in part because driveways and garages are eliminated – paving is reduced up to 50% and landscapes are more flexible. The plant-to-pavement ratio of the contemporary suburb is much higher than that of cities, but the next generation of suburbs can be even better at absorbing water.[48]

Drone deliveries, ride-sharing, car-sharing, AVs that park themselves and connect to house lights and thermostats will be commonplace, as will up to a 50 percent reduction in paved area. Less hardscape won't be difficult, given the absurdly wide streets in contemporary subdivisions. There will be fewer fences and more common land for recreation, gardens, ponds, woods and wetlands.

These new suburbs will also tend to have more welcome, summer air temperatures than cities, but they will still consume land, resources and energy at a faster per capita rate, although there will be fewer trips by gasoline-powered vehicles. In a study of urban spatial structure and heat waves across more than 50 large U.S. cities, Brian Stone found the frequency of extreme heat events to be rising faster in sprawling cities than in compact cities.[49] Nonetheless, suburbs' carbon contribution per person remains worse than cities: With over half of its residents living in suburbs, 5 percent of the world population and 30 percent of the automobiles, the U.S. astoundingly emits 45 percent of global transportation CO_2 emissions.[50] This amounts to nine times its share! Because the auto-dependence in suburbia is acute and pervasive, it tends to cancel any climate benefits that accrue in the core city. "Dominated by emissions from cars, trucks and other forms of transportation, suburbs account for about half of all household GHG emissions in the United States."[51] Cars are the biggest culprit in the dispersion and fragmentation of our cities. To quote David Owen again, "cars have defined our culture and our lives, car is speed and sex and power and emancipation. It makes its driver a self-sufficient nation of one. It is everything a city is not."[52]

Suburb's egregious contribution to both UHIs and CC is precisely why suburban development – that agonizing American compromise between urban and rural – should be stubbornly resisted in developing countries. Unfortunately, cities are exploding in population and area, usually leading inadvertently toward huge metro areas. These megalopolises often struggle to keep up with infrastructure and services for economic productivity, quality of life and self-fulfillment for their residents.

> For LUS (Large Urban Systems) development, the financial, political, environmental and social costs, challenges and implications are increasingly prohibitive for cities. Cities must devise innovative ways to collaborate on LUS by taking advantage of economies of scale, resource and institutional capacity-leveraging and other regional assets and opportunities.[53]

The huge conurbations of the Global South – from Mexico City, Lagos, Cairo, New Delhi to Bangkok and Shanghai – are spreading out into their hinterlands at an alarming speed. High land costs and ensuing gentrification are forcing workers to live up to three hours from the central cores of the cities, with onerous commutes that require multiple transit legs. Long commute times are not unknown in the U.S.

In a large, continuing study of upward mobility based at Harvard, commuting time has emerged as the single strongest factor in the odds of escaping poverty. The longer an average commute in a given county, the worse the chances of low-income families there moving up the ladder . . . The relationship between transportation and social mobility is stronger than . . . crime, elementary-school test scores or the percentage of two-parent families in a community.[54]

This finding would likely surprise many an urban planner, municipal official and politician.

Humans may be living in a world that is over 50 percent urban and Americans in a country that is 80 percent urban, but in fact much of the urbanized area is actually suburban. Despite seeing a return of residents and offices to central cities in the U.S., especially older ones with a surplus of housing stock, "most of the population growth in the U.S. is again happening on the fringes of fast-growing metro areas in the South and West."[55] The growth is in both land area and population. Even though metro areas make up just 3.6 percent of the total size of the 48 contiguous states, 80 percent of Americans reside there. The metro areas are expanding by an average of about 1 million additional acres a year – the equivalent of adding the area of Los Angeles, Houston and Phoenix combined. U.S. metro areas have grown fourfold since World War II. On a percentage basis, urban creep outpaces growth in all other land-use categories combined.[56] While many large cities in the U.S. grew faster than their suburbs between 2000 and 2015, in the subsequent two years the suburbs outgrew cities in two-thirds of America's large metropolitan areas, according to demographer William Frey of the Brookings Institution. "Fourteen big cities lost population in 2015 –16 compared with just five in 2011–12, with Chicago, the nation's third-largest city, hemorrhaging the most people."[57] Once again, American suburbs are growing, leaving open the question of whether sprawl or urbanism will be the dominant paradigm.

According to MIT's Center for Advanced Urbanism,

While statistics demonstrate that the world population in metropolitan areas is rapidly increasing, rarely is it understood that the bulk of this growth occurs in the suburbanized peripheries of cities. By 2030, an estimated half a million square miles of land worldwide will become suburban.[58]

Major metro areas in the developing world are now spreading out and decentralizing. In the last decade, population densities in Chinese cities have declined by a quarter on average.[59] If rural migrants to cities end up in suburban settlements, their carbon footprints will climb higher than if they had moved to a dense city. City dwelling must be planned and made more attractive and affordable, or environmental gains will be lost as more people move to the suburbs to live more consumptive life-styles. The environmental paradox of cities – namely walkability, transit and smaller, multi-family and shared dwellings – will disintegrate in this case. The developing world needs to beware the ever-tantalizing appeal of suburbia.

The Metropolitan Regional Containment Index, published by London's Philipp Rode in 2012, shows cities tend to spread out less if they are denser to begin with. For instance, Stockholm, Brussels and Helsinki have contained sprawl more effectively than Dallas, Washington, Houston and Prague.[60] And cities with strong green belts, like London, or Urban Growth Boundaries, like Portland, have also better resisted the spread of sprawl. However, the typical low-density American pattern is resistant to densifying and retrofitting. Nonetheless, Ellen Dunham-Jones' and June Williamson's ongoing research and seminal book *Retrofitting Suburbia* show more and more examples of "grayfield" redevelopment. Marginal malls have been converted into mixed-use, bus-served and sometimes rail-served centers, often open-air. Though urbanizing a suburban mall is usually a positive step, it may just become

> an al fresco pedestrian treadmill where visitors can window-shop and stroll in circles – constrained on all sides by parking lots, malls, and an eight-lane road. This, like other developments scattered across our suburbs, may boast a "Live, Work, Play" lifestyle, but the reality is more in line with "Commute, Work, Netflix."[61]

And the typical self-contained, cul-de-sac subdivision is even more physically resistant to both densification and connection to the larger circulation network.

As big cities in the developing world spread out and suburbanize, residents with long commutes spew more CO_2, because jobs – especially for the middle and upper classes – remain in the central city, including service jobs for poor commuters to support the rich. There are excep-tions to this trend: In countries like Bangladesh the garment industry is opening factories on the periphery. Although the poor try to move to where the jobs are, jobs sometimes move to where the workers are. Sprawl is not the only societal problem: As more rural residents leave the farms for employment in the city, there is also the potential danger that food supply might decrease below the growing demand for it. This danger particularly threatens low-lying countries like Bangladesh, where rising sea level, amplified by stronger monsoons, makes the soil salty. Indeed, food shortages, even famine is potentially a problem throughout the developing world.

In addition to emission costs, there are the well-known health costs of the automobile, particularly injuries and deaths in auto-dominated sprawl. Americans are over 500 times as likely to die in an automobile collision than in a terrorist attack.[62] These fatalities make living in suburbia on average more dangerous than living in the American inner city – even when homicides of strangers are included – because suburbanites drive more miles and drive faster. This means that the generation that took their families to suburbia actually exposed them to more danger than in the city! There are also respiratory ailments associated with automobile pollution, most notably asthma. A less-dissected cost of vehicles is the spatial one. When compared to a pedestrian, *the typical car takes up about 20 times as much space, weighs about 20 times as much, and likes to move at about 20 times as fast on streets that are much wider than sidewalks.* It's simply not spatially possible to make good urbanism when there are so many of these mechanical behemoths roaming and parking in a city.

A less direct but also disturbing cost is the increase in obesity and diabetes among suburbanites whose every trip is by car, not infrequently to a fast-food outlet for a high-calorie meal. Obesity rates in the U.S. are among the world's highest, and climbing to perhaps as high as 50 percent. Sugar is now a greater danger than gunpowder, because it causes more deaths than guns.[63] The nation currently spends as much on treating obesity and related health problems as it does on national defense![64] A study by Oxford University and the University of Hong Kong showed that areas with about seven homes per acre had the greatest rates of obesity and lowest rates of exercise, and the best health came in areas with more than 14 units/acre. It also found in over 20 British cities that people living in built-up residential areas had lower levels of obesity and exercised more than residents in scattered homes.[65] The study goes on to note that the densities of the popular London neighborhoods of Georgian townhouses are about four times that dense, enough to support trams and subways, while 14 units/acre is barely enough to support a bus service. Jane Jacobs recommends densities considerably higher, at least 100 units/acre and even up to 200, in her Manhattan, the densest of American urban centers.

There are other costs of sprawl worth mentioning. For starters, it gobbles up open space, destroying farm land and habitat for plants and animals. The superhighways that empty the central city every evening rush hour allow low-density development to leap-frog into the countryside. This carpet of sprawl requires expensive infrastructure to build and maintain, increasingly more than the local governments can afford. Tax revenue

at low suburban densities isn't nearly enough to pay the bills . . . property taxes at suburban densities bring in anywhere from 4 cents to 65 cents for every dollar of liability. Most suburban municipalities . . . are therefore unable to pay the maintenance costs of their infrastructure, let alone replace things when they inevitably wear out after 20–25 years. The only way to survive is to keep growing or take on more debt, or both.[66]

It seems likely that the next round of municipal bankruptcies will be in suburbia.

And the suburbs are getting poorer as low-income urban residents move out to first-ring suburbs, which have become less expensive as middle-class incomes and employment have stagnated due to automation and offshoring of jobs. What Yuval Noah Harari has labeled the economically "useless class" tends to settle there. Scott Allard points out in his new book *Places in Need: The Changing Geography of Poverty*,

> there are more poor people living in suburbs today than in cities. What's worse is that suburbs don't have the government and non-profit infrastructure to deliver assistance to those in need. Without the appropriate fiscal policy tools, suburbs will continue to struggle just as central cities did 30 years ago.[67]

Professor Dunham-Jones corroborates the point: "Since 2005 more Americans in poverty live in suburbs than in cities and they have less access to social networks and cushions."[68] One can easily imagine extensive suburban slums of the future, with subdivided McMansions poorly maintained by absentee landlords and with their large lawns strewn with broken down cars and appliances. With warped wood studs and sagging sheetrock, they will not age as well as the old brick and plaster urban mansions that were once subdivided to accommodate poor residents in declining cities. As well as decayed, crowded houses, there will also be abandoned areas, which will be a cheap, blank slate for redevelopment, with much less political opposition and NIMBYism seen in more desirable locations.

The true and full cost of sprawl is as approximate as it is immense. According to a 2015 report by the London School of Economics and the Victoria Transport Policy Institute, the annual cost in the U.S. is about $1 trillion![69] The economic and fiscal disadvantages of sprawl have become more and more apparent. It's verging on a sort of unintended Ponzi Scheme that requires ongoing growth to cover the high cost of servicing an extensive area with sewer, utilities, garbage collection and fire and police protection. Worth proclaiming again: The whole suburban experiment is a conspiracy of good intentions – government policy-makers, planning officials, bankers, transportation engineers, traffic engineers, fire marshals, code officials all trying to make it a better, safer, more affordable, more convenient place to live, but adding up to compounding costs that have often been hidden.

Another cost of sprawl has come to light more recently, one that is very relevant to CC. It has to do with combustion at a much larger scale – forest fires. These calamitous events happen more and more at the "wilderness-urban-interface" (WUI), where suburbs are developed on the previously unbuilt edges of cities. This development makes for a volatile mix of buildings and flammable vegetation. As combustible as the suburban–exurban edge is, when developments leap-frog into exurbia and are completely surrounded by nature, this "intermix" version of WUI is even more fiery than "interface" WUI. In the U.S., almost four in ten houses in the country are located in these zones, and 10 million new housing units were built in them during the decade leading to 2010. A report from the Center for Insurance Policy and Research reports that approximately two million, or 15 percent of California homes are in WUIs, followed by Texas and Colorado.[70]

Wildfire has been an under-appreciated if episodic aspect of sprawl that directly contributes to UHIs when the wind pushes the extra heat into the city. It also contributes to and is exacerbated by CC: the slow increase in ambient temperature, which in turn dries out vegetation, making it more flammable; and there is less rainfall due to the warmer temperatures during the CC-revved-up dry season that further desiccate vegetation, making all the more fuel for wildfires. Then more rainfall in the CC-induced wet season often over-corrects for the preceding drought with additional precipitation that tends to increase vegetative growth, amplifying the next cycle. This classic case of positive feedback is anything but positive for the humans, not to mention plant and animal species that are ravaged by wildfires. Nowhere is this trend more obvious than in California since 1980, with spring and summer temperatures warming by 5.4°F[71] and larger wildfires burning hotter.

Last, there is the architectural and landscape mediocrity of sprawl. The suburban arterial strip has become an aesthetic blight, especially during daylight. The strips look better at night, when they are simplified to a sea of glowing electric signs and look less visually chaotic. If modern cities have skylines with tall, free-standing buildings competing for attention like so many perfume bottles on a shelf, the suburbs have second- and third-rate low-rise boxes with aggressive signage fighting for attention. New Urbanist James Kunstler has colorfully described the suburban detritus as having the architectural presence of a collection of "muffler shops," even criticizing them as a place for which American soldiers may not continue to want to proudly lay down their lives.[72]

It is fair to say that in the country of origin as well as many others, the American "suburban experiment" has generally been an environmental failure. On top of the fiscal issues of low tax revenue per acre, sprawling infrastructure is more expensive to construct and maintain. Roads are wider, with more paving to install and maintain. Water and sewage capital and service costs are higher. Emergency services are costlier because more fire stations and police stations are needed per capita to keep response times down. Children's busing distances to school are further, as are most trips in suburbia.

One study by the Denver Regional Council of Governments found that conventional suburban development would cost local governments $4.3 billion more in infrastructure costs than compact, "smart growth" through 2020, only counting capital construction costs for sewer, water, and road infrastructure. A 2008 report by the University of Utah's Arthur Nelson estimated that municipal service costs in low-density, sprawling locations can be as much as 2.5 times those in compact, higher-density locations.[73]

There are exceptions, like the older, more compact and walkable railroad suburbs radiating out from what were once the country's four largest cities – New York, Philadelphia, Boston and Chicago.

A major overhaul of suburbia is needed. The basic geometric pattern is dendritic, meaning the circulation network is too hierarchical, with cul-de-sacs and collector roads feeding into arterials and limited-access freeways. This branching, tree-like geometry leads to bottle necks and very wide arterials, which are unfriendly to pedestrians and bicycles. With too few intersections, there aren't enough places to turn left, necessitating left turn lanes and signals, which essentially double the time sitting at intersections. The mostly low-rise buildings on arterials are set back to provide convenient customer-friendly parking in front, diluting any sense of spatial containment or human scale. Parking lots dominate all the suburban pods, whether retail, office or institutional. It's an auto-dominated, sprawling and endless carpet of architectural and urban mediocrity. We need a paradigm shift like the City Beautiful Movement, which American cities embraced a century ago. The popular reform movement

> turned the centers of many American cities from muddy cow towns and squalid factory towns into places with picturesque parks, public plazas, and grand boulevards. These civic spaces were dotted with elegant, neoclassical government buildings, as well as museums, libraries, pavilions and band shells, all artfully sited in public gardens and among fountains, lakes, and lagoons.[74]

We need not revive neoclassical architecture, but attention to high quality design and construction is essential.

Climate Refugees

There are two types of migration: domestic and international. Some is voluntary and some is forced. Domestic migration tends to be voluntary, often moving from rural areas to urban areas in search of jobs and better economic opportunity. Although this farm-to-city shift is as old as civilization, it has accelerated in recent decades. In fact, the largest migration in human history is the one taking place right now within the borders of

China.[75] Migration between countries, which has historically been about people in poor countries moving to rich ones, has also been on the rise in recent decades. According to the 2015 International Migration Report, the number of international migrants worldwide has grown rapidly over the past 15 years, reaching 244 million in 2015. That's up from 173 million in 2000.

> Migration is a top urban concern. At least 75 percent of the migrants settle in cities . . . The reasons are obvious. Cities offer better work opportunities; they provide better public services – schools, health-care, housing. Domestic migrants worldwide number nearly 750 million, according to the U.N. . . . "One in seven people in this world is a migrant."[76]

Most global migration is forced, either by war, political turmoil, social or religious unrest and intolerance, lack of employment, seismic or meteorological disaster or drought and famine. Voluntary migration often is about seeking better jobs or more freedom. In a world of growing nationalism, this cross-border movement is becoming more difficult and often involves asylum. A 2017 study in *Science* magazine of 103 countries examined voluntary migration involving asylum, which is much less frequent than forced migration. It found that CC impacted migrant requests, increasing when hotter countries get hotter, and dropping when cold countries get warmer. Under one scenario, in which GHG emissions decline, the researchers predict there could be 98,000 more asylum applications to the EU each year by 2100. If emissions continue to rise, it could lead to up to 660,000 additional applications.[77] These numbers are likely to continue to grow, as both the climate and related unrest heat up, although border controls are getting tighter.

The Buddhist economist Clair Brown writes "In an era marked by vast economic disparities and the threat of environmental collapse, with opulent living for a few, comfortable living for many, and deprivation with suffering for most, something is clearly wrong."[78] Cities attract and concentrate most of these impoverished people, but arguably they don't cause or create poverty. In fact, they provide ways to escape it, with opportunities for men and women alike. The first to articulate this urban paradox of poverty, Edward Glaeser contends "Cities aren't full of poor people because cities *make* people poor, but because cities *attract* poor people with the prospect of improving their lot in life . . . a favela beats stultifying rural poverty . . . cities, not farms, will save the developing world."[79] This assumes that the favela is not afflicted with drugs or dominated by organized crime, which unfortunately is not infrequent. And as the Dutch-American sociologist Saskia Sassen writes, this migration to cities is not as voluntary as often claimed.

[S]urvival has become a major challenge for local residents, even for the relatively small proportion able to get a job in the plantations and mines. Migrating to the cities is one major option. When politicians drone on mindlessly about more than half the world's population becoming urbanised, they rarely bring up the diverse ways in which people are being pushed off their land. Where else can they go but cities? These new migrations are a key marker of our epoch.[80]

And job opportunities for women can be overstated: in the 36 million jobs that India has created since 2005, 90 percent went to men.[81]

Coping with climate refugees or "environmental migrants" will continue to escalate as a geopolitical problem. In a 2018 annual report, the U.N. Refugee Agency announced a record-high 68.5 million migrants, including 25 million refugees, wandering the world.[82] Because there is no internationally recognized legal definition for CC victims, there is no formal reckoning of how many have migrated due to CC making their lives or livelihoods untenable. In a 2010 Gallup World Poll, "about 12 percent of respondents – representing a total of 500 million adults – said severe environmental problems would require them to move within the next five years."[83] Other estimates are much higher, some expecting hundreds of millions by mid-century, far more than the huge number of refugees unleashed by World War II. Ironically, in an age when barriers to the movement of goods, capital and communication have been disappearing, the physical defenses between countries have been literally mounting. According to research that confirms Ai Weiwei on refugee migration,

> in 1990 just 15 states had walls or fences at their borders; by 2016 nearly 70 did. In the past such defences were set up principally between neighboring states (North Korea and South Korea, for instance), but today's border defences are primarily focused on civilians, aimed at stopping unwanted or 'irregular' migration . . . According to the International Organization for Immigration, forty thousand people died attempting to cross a border, between 2005 and 2014.[84]

Rural migration to cities is happening in most countries. Its pace and magnitude vary within and between countries, and every dynamic is not fully understood. Overall it has helped alleviate poverty, but it is by no means a story of unalloyed benefits. Among other debits, the depopulation of rural areas is threatening the erasure of the ecological and cultural balance of whole regions.

> Nowadays, people from all over the world have a right to expect a better life, more comfort, better housing and services as they can see it in the best parts of major cities. The past is the past, and there is

no lost paradise. But the built heritage is, very often, the expression of strong folk art, part of genuine cultures which have demonstrated deep knowledges in local resources: treasures of skills, experiences and know-hows that have be passed down through the generations and run the risk of disappearing in the short term.[85]

There are also heightening socio-political divisions and polarizations between big cities and small towns, between urban and rural regions, and between "blue" and "red" states in the U.S. The friction, distrust and disconnect do not bode well.

Historic rural areas and towns are experiencing the loss of centuries of conscious and unconscious knowledge encoded into them. The dumbing down of culture is an undeniable and tragic collateral cost of migration to cities, and it is not limited to the developing world. In parts of the Americas and Europe many houses, shops and schools sit empty, fields fallow. These rural communities were once intricately tied to the land, with farmers, shepherds, merchants and crafts-persons. When they are depleted or die, unique skills and traditions are also erased. Small towns in countries like the United States or Italy – to name but two – are left behind by new technologies and economies that make them obsolete, forcing migration to cities. "One picturesque medieval hamlet in Tuscany . . . sold itself on eBay for $3.1 million. Another . . . tried to follow, offering itself for only $330,000, listing the item's condition as 'used.'"[86] A few of the more fetching towns have survived on tourism, but as shells of themselves with few residents, often older folks and few if any children.

There is another dimension to sustaining rural communities. As pundit-practitioner Koolhaas and his two firms have recently researched, there are some radical changes to rural environments currently underway. In looking at 15–20 rural areas around the world, they found some unusual developments. In Russia, for example,

> agriculture has migrated northward as permafrost melts . . . while farming communities have become increasingly isolated by hundreds of airport closings around the country. And in the United States, the Californian–Nevada border near Reno has been turned into "Silicon Valley's back of house. You could say it's not a city yet (although) the scale of development is definitely kind of urban. But it is a new kind of urban, because it will be inhabited by machines and robots, and few people."[87]

Koolhaas has also written: "in order to feed, maintain and entertain ever-growing cities, the countryside is becoming a colossal back-of-house, organised with relentless Cartesian rigour. That system, not always pleasant, is proliferating on an unprecedented scale. The resulting transformation is radical and ubiquitous."[88] It is becoming more obvious, if under-reported, that as urbanism morphs in the twenty-first century, the countryside is also changing in new, unexpected and often unfavorable ways.

On balance, however, it must be said that migration to cities has improved the lives of hundreds of millions of people all over the world. Sound practices and policies must be developed to sustain migration to the cities in a manner that can be a positive step toward reducing CC, while continuing to improve migrants' physical standard of living and quality of life.

> Since the 1990s more than one billion people have been lifted out of extreme poverty, six million fewer children die every year from disease, tens of millions of girls are in school, millions more people have access to clean water, and democracy – though often fragile and imperfect – has become the norm in the developing countries around the world.[89]

The migration to cities has played a major role in this happy story. There's always the chance that this dynamic could slow or end, even reverse per occasional outlying predictions, but urban migration doesn't seem likely to end in the foreseeable future. And even it does reverse, large cities will continue to exist, with their benefits tending to outweigh their deficits.

However, if there is a slowdown or reversal in migration, extreme heat – along with other impacts of CC, such as flooding – will likely have played a major role. If we allow cities to become much hotter in summer, urban residents will leave for the suburban fringe or exurban hinterland, wherever there are jobs and affordable shelter. This reverse migration would very likely lower their standard of living and increase their footprint. Therefore, it's wise to address UHI and keep cities intact and growing in the right way, especially second-tier cities, which are likely to grow at an increasingly fast rate, as the overcrowded and ever-hotter megacities tend to attract fewer migrants or start to shed or repel them. And even as the carbon footprints of migrants grow because of increased consumption, they do not grow as fast in cities that are walkable, bike-able, mixed-use and transit-oriented. Sound, sustainable urbanism works for rural migrants as well as for longtime urban residents.

"We are already seeing the impact of mass migration on global politics but, if you believe these projections, it hasn't even started to take hold."[90] Currently, it is generally estimated that about 1 percent of the world's population has been displaced by violence and disaster, and that it could rise to approximately 3 percent by mid-century and as high as 7 percent by 2100, with some 500 million refugees.

More than 140 million people in Africa, Latin America and South
Asia could move to another part of their country by 2050 to escape
the worsening impacts of climate change – unless urgent action is
taken to curb global warming and help people adapt, (according to)
the World Bank.[91]

Surely, this level of climate dislocation will profoundly change the world
order if not civilization itself.

The indefatigable, incomparable Chinese artist Ai Weiwei claims in his
movie *Human Flow* that 65 million people – 34,000 per day – have been
forcibly displaced from their homes in our era. Fleeing their homes to
escape war, famine and poverty, these refugees worldwide spend on average 26 years displaced from their home. Many are never able to return to
their homeland. It's difficult to know how many of them are directly or
indirectly CC refugees, but it's clearly a growing trend. As soon as 2020,
CC will aggravate drought, hunger and disease for 250 million people in
Africa alone, forcing migration within and beyond the fastest growing
continent. The film points out that when the Berlin Wall came down in
1989, there were 11 countries in the world that had border walls and
fences; 70 countries had them by 2016.[92]

Just to physically accommodate these refugees is a Herculean task.
Worldwide, approximately 30 million people currently live in camps, a
number set to rise to 40 or even 45 million if current military/political
trends continue.[93] These camps need to be quickly designed and built in
unpredictable places at an accelerating rate. How much better to sometimes conceive of and plan them not as temporary settlements, but as
semi-permanent or even permanent towns and cities, aspiring to have
productive, inclusive urban and social fabrics. Rahul Mehrotra, an
architect/urban designer and Harvard professor, has explored and written on what he calls "ephemeral urbanism." His multiple publications
illustrate remarkable examples of temporary settlements, some of which
are repeated cyclically, for example, the previously touted Kumbh Mela
with many millions of visitors. These short-lived cities are religious, cel-
ebratory, transactional, extractive, disaster-related, military and places
of refuge. The largest refugee camps range in size from those in Jordan
and Lebanon to a cluster in Sri Lanka that collectively house 300,000
residents to those in Dabaad, Kenya, with 500,000 residents.[94] Rohingya
refugee camps in Bangladesh for Muslims fleeing Myanmar house over
a million people.[95] Camps in some conflicted parts of the world have
been occupied for two decades, which strongly suggests they need to be
accepted and developed as more permanent cities.

Among these political and cultural challenges, it's time that the related
professions of architecture, engineering, urban design and planning, ecology and surveying work together more closely. They need to effectively
shape and develop new settlements that would otherwise continue to

236 Cities: Our Last, Best Hope

happen without formal structures and formats in place. It runs against the grain of current, neoliberal architectural exuberance, with its unending thirst for sensational, iconic buildings that amaze as much or more than they address function and need. It's necessary for our society, architects and their patrons/clients to give up some of their often self-centered and sometimes super-profitable projects for these less glamorous but weighty necessities. Better urban fabric is needed more than architectural wonders, which should punctuate cities as exceptional statements. Retrofitting sprawl with well-designed and re-designed buildings is essential, as it's too big and indelible an investment to abandon. These problems can and should be seen and promoted as a global practice, as well as major design opportunity.

New Urbanism(s)

New Urbanism (NU) has been a major player in the debate about sprawl over the last quarter century, and a strong voice for livable and sustainable urban design and planning. Its parent organization, the Congress for the New Urbanism, has convened 28 large annual conferences and many symposia and workshops for a broad membership of design and planning professionals, developers, government officials, academicians, community activists, students and citizens. The movement counts scores of books and countless design charrettes, and it is well known for popularizing transit-oriented development and the Urban Transect, among other urban development concepts and initiatives. The 27 principles in its Charter of the New Urbanism are devoted to the Region, the Neighborhood, the Block and the Building. Its Sustainability Canons promote environmental sensitivity, ecological resilience, renewable energy and energy-conserving architecture and urban design. It is a forward-looking, progressive movement, but with respect for past achievements in the urban design and planning of traditional towns and cities.

> It is possible to verify the connection with many traditional principles of urban design, and to recognize for instance the legacy of Kevin Lynch, Jane Jacobs, Jan Gehl, Gordon Cullen . . . and also of Ebenezer Howard, Frank Lloyd Wright, together with the teaching of traffic calming and environmental sustainability practices and theories. The NU refers to the model of the European old city, a compact city made by districts and blocks. This movement recalls the values of community, democracy, identity, but it is market oriented too.[96]

It also loosely aligns with the Project for Public Spaces, whose slogan – "It takes a place to create a community and a community to create a place" – captures the public idealism of both organizations. After three decades, NU's broad, deep and continuous debate continue to keep the movement alive and vibrant.

In most architecture schools and in the upper echelons of the profession, NU is discredited because of its neo-traditional architecture. However, its championing of mixed-use, walkable, bike-able, transit-friendly and street-oriented urbanism has been widely influential in the private and public planning and development communities in the developed world. While it tended to focus for the first half of its history on greenfield development, which was more compact and more mixed-use than conventional sprawl, it has spent the last decade concentrating more on mixed-income, sustainable urban infill and redevelopment. More recently some of its adherents have developed Tactical Urbanism (TU) and Lean Urbanism (LeanU). And the movement is delving deeper into UHIs and CC, including adaptation measures, such as moving communities from flood-prone areas and developing nomenclature. They have suggested four categories of adaptation, acknowledging that there is always overlap, including with mitigation: Defensive (e.g., levees to reduce flooding), Palliative/Ameliorative (e.g., trees for shade), Resilient (e.g., local food sheds), and Conceding/Yielding (e.g., mobile housing).

TU and LeanU deserve some explanation, as they indirectly deal with CC, UHIs and sprawl. The former is for acting first, asking for permission second and seeking code and/or policy changes later. Words like fast, small, temporary and do-it-yourself come to mind. It activates streets and plazas with pop-up cafes, food trucks, community dinners, chair-bombing public spaces, guerilla gardening and other local interventions that build social capital and hope to trigger bigger, more permanent changes. This pop-up, try-it-before-you-buy-it approach has become popular in many cities, often driven by local residents in an effort to improve their neighborhoods, especially in empty derelict spaces. They include retailers who launch temporary shops in stalls or shipping containers to revitalize flagging main streets or food trucks gathered in empty parking lots or cycling activists who paint bike lanes without government approval. "Tactical Urbanism is a city, organizational, and/or citizen-led approach to neighborhood building, using *short-term*, low-cost, and scalable interventions intended to catalyze *long-term* change."[97] The Project for Public Spaces, another effective group that has promoted placemaking in the public realm, has a similar initiative called Lighter, Quicker, Cheaper. These movements are timely in the world's fastest growing cities, because public space is both shrinking and getting too crowded.[98]

If TU focuses on the small and temporary and NU deals with large-scale projects and policy, LeanU is in between. It builds more permanently than TU, but develops smaller projects than NU. It addresses the widely needed attempt to provide low-cost housing without government subsidies. Its motto is "making small possible." A signature strategy is the Pink Zone, which relaxes bureaucratic red tape to a lighter shade of regulation, for example less required off-street parking. It encourages legal "code workarounds" to build more affordable housing: three-story, walk-up apartments and condos that don't require elevators and two fire stairs, shorter Environmental Impact Statements, and pre-approved architecture plans and architects. Live–work units that allow residents to live above their workplace are also encouraged, as it offers the convenient and low-footprint opportunity for a zero-commute. Also encouraged are self-build units, as well as co-living units, where several bedroom/bathroom suites share a kitchen and living area, and the building shares a gym and workshop.

New Urbanist architect Robert Orr waxes eloquent on both New Urbanism and LeanU:

> [C]ities are their streets. Streets are not a city's veins but its neurology, its accumulated intelligence . . . Lean Urbanism identifies problems spawned by large, unaffordable, and out-of-touch systems, and constructs systems for removing the "fat." Removing the fat recognizes the advantages of small over large, manifest in: decentralized instead of centralized, disassembled property instead of assembled property, separated instead of consolidated, slow instead of fast, compact instead of diffuse, neighborhood and block instead of city . . . unique instead of ubiquitous, affordable instead of unaffordable, unsubsidized instead of subsidized, authentic instead of artificial, messy human instead of predictable algorithm, vulnerable instead of invulnerable, one step for a man instead of one giant leap for mankind . . . "community" and "communication" both mean "to make common." Parenthetically, with its dependence on resources within close communication, authentic human habitat eliminates the highest percentage of carbon emissions, cements the most stable relationships, and applies the most viable brakes on resource depletion and on population growth.[99]

Both TU and LeanU are meant to empower local citizens to develop their neighborhoods and to build small projects in simpler, more modest and affordable ways. Sometimes they touch on a raw nerve in many parts of the U.S. by making a basic, decent life possible and respectable. Along with New Urbanism, these two initiatives also directly address UHIs and CC. For instance, the bottom-up, low-tech nature of albedo enhancement, which can be as easy as applying white paint to rooftops, is consistent with both TU and LeanU. In other cases, community volunteers have painted crosswalks at dangerous intersections, only to have the municipality follow up with official striping. Planting and watering street trees and other vegetation along sidewalks and in median strips – so called guerilla gardening – has been done with volunteer labor. LeanU's lower-cost housing can help residents deal with the gentrification in cities within both developing and developed countries. Under the right circumstances it can provide affordable new housing to residents with below-the-median income with little if any government or institutional subsidy. Higher height bonuses can require affordable housing to be included. Local governments must do their share, with increases in allowable densities, especially around transit stops. The time has come for municipalities to be more proactive, including higher density overlay zones, despite neighborhood residence.

An alternate, competing model to New Urbanism is Landscape Urbanism, sometimes called Ecological Urbanism, which has also spawned multiple conferences and publications. According to its promoters, the landscape, rather than buildings, is more capable of organizing the city and enhancing the urban experience. This movement considers the centrality of landscape and ecological flows, including the landscape in between buildings. It's often superbly designed, environmentally sensitive, large-scale landscape architecture, but rarely has it included much actual urbanism, other than tower-in-the-park Modernist structures in the distance in elegant perspective drawings. Because it focuses more on hydrology than energy, Landscape Urbanism's projects are thermally – and artistically – cooler than both conventional urbanism and New Urbanism. Its flowing water and landforms, as well as lush plantings, are visually seductive.

To briefly delve into architectural theory, this humanist optimism is contrary to the relativist, post-structural and often dystopian strains of theory that dominated design and art in the last quarter of the twentieth century. This post-humanist, post-structuralist philosophy culminated in a subjective view that saw reality as narrative rather than fact. It resulted in a fragmented, titillating and dramatic architecture and urbanism that often bombastically shouted for attention with striking buildings that shouted "look-mom-no-hands." This mania to stand out is fundamentally at odds with the conception of nature as an integral, interdependent whole. In the meantime, novelty-hungry media lapped it up, with academicians also championing the exotica with obtuse prose and fantastic digital imagery. It has been a late phase in a Modernist epoch that has long delighted in big, bold, free-standing, sculptural architecture. Abstract at all scales, it often has too little detail to hold the attention of viewers at closer distances. In any case, "starchitects" have become celebrities, as have their wealthy developer-clients.

Recently esoteric academic theory has swung back into smaller, hands-on, built digital creations, all provocative and often stunningly beautiful, but too infrequently addressing pressing practical problems. It's all part of a post-Modernist thirst to express the zeitgeist – whether unified or fragmented, pure or eclectic, historically inspired or repelled – while trying to avoid historical clichés. In general, it has been part of ongoing play in a giant sandbox of forms. In the meantime, NU has fought for more realizable, on-the-ground design and development that can be profitably built by speculative developers for middle- and upper-middle-class households. This pragmatic movement, coupled with a middle America of conventional, typically traditional architectural taste, has resulted too often in an architecture that can be cloyingly neo-traditional and even banal. To its credit, NU protagonists were the first to change the national conversation on suburbia. Now, its spin-offs LeanU and TU strive to do the same with affordable housing, as well as to make public realms livelier and more responsive to a more diverse demographic. It also reaches out to design and planning professionals and developers in other countries.

Another urban sustainability movement is called Transition Town. Its grassroots community projects seek to increase self-sufficiency in order to reduce the impacts of fossil fuels, climate change and economic turmoil. Its initiatives aim to build resilient communities able to withstand severe energy, climate or economic shocks, while fostering a better quality of life. In 2013 there were over 1,100 community initiatives recognized as official Transition Towns in the United Kingdom, Ireland, Canada, Australia, New Zealand, Italy and Chile. In the U.S., their initiatives have been started in many communities, with the stated vision

> that every community in the United States will have engaged its collective creativity to unleash an extraordinary and historic transition to a future beyond fossil fuels; a future that is more vibrant, abundant and resilient; one that is ultimately preferable to the present.[100]

Gentrification

On a related front, authors Edward Glaeser and Richard Florida have prominently promoted the economic power of city cores. Florida's "creative class" and concepts like "innovation districts" are designed to attract a critical mass of talent to interact in a knowledge-based economy. However, Florida is now backpedaling, now bemoaning gentrification that is caused largely by this creative class bidding up real estate values beyond the reach of most renters and buyers, and displacing existing residents. Glaeser extols the environmental and economic efficiencies of density and compact living, inspired by the urban economics of Jane Jacobs, who did indeed champion the capacities of cities as creative engines of human development. But she warned against the kind of "silver bullet" thinking that imagines an innovation district or a downtown creative class is going to generate benefits that will automatically trickle down to the rest of the city. On the contrary, she pointed to the dangers of any form of monoculture, including the monoculture of an innovation district or creative class. Instead, Jacobs argued for a more diverse kind of city – diverse in population, diverse in kinds of activities and diverse in geographic distribution. Her's was a polycentric city, with lots of affordable pockets full of old buildings and opportunities waiting to be targeted.[101]

The supply of walkable, transit-friendly neighborhoods in the U.S. is limited. Demand outstrips supply. And spatial and political hurdles make it difficult to further densify them or build more of them. Urban infill and redevelopment is almost always politically charged, if not dead on arrival. Developed countries, especially in North America and Europe, are building very few new cities. Creating a dense, walkable area almost always means increasing the density of a built environment that already exists and often has been developed around the automobile. Infill development often steps on the toes of existing residents and so frequently arouses the NIMBYism that arises because of fears of higher density, with more cars to park, more traffic and shadow-casting buildings. In other cases, it's fears of an unwelcome change in demographics – often the influx of low-income residents – or in neighborhood character and real estate values, which may go down or up. The latter leads to gentrification that threatens displacement of existing residents of modest means, especially renters who don't profit from inflated real estate values. The reason cities often become too expensive is simple arithmetic – lots of people want to live there, resulting in demand exceeding supply. The U.S. needs more good urbanism.

Dense, walkable areas tend to be buzzy, vibrant, diverse and multicultural. In some cases, the simple but basic fear of change and of difference often manifests itself in the form of NIMBYs, or more extreme BANANAs – Build Absolutely Nothing Anywhere Near Anybody. The "Advocacy Planning" movement in the 1960s and '70s started the trend of public input and community meetings, which are now a standard expectation. Public participation is still intact, but it has increasingly been replaced by citizen zeal to "preserve" and "protect" their communities from any change, especially a decline in real estate values. As public input has become de rigueur, it has too often tended to devolve into blatant self-interest and obstructionism. Whatever the motive, it has become the punishment, if not the undoing of real estate developers.

Densifying often means up-zoning to allow greater height and bulk in existing urbanized areas, by allowing duplexes, triplexes or mid- and high-rise apartment and condominium buildings in formerly single-family areas. It can mean adding shops on the ground floor of new or existing residential buildings, as well as live–work units that allow people to live above a commercial or work space, yielding the shortest possible commute. It can mean allowing an Accessory Dwelling Unit (ADU), a.k.a. granny flat, backyard cottage, mother-in-law suite or carriage house, either attached to the home or detached along back alleys above garages. They are very popular in Vancouver, Canada, where roughly a third of all single-family homes – about 26,000 houses – have an ADU on the property. Roughly half a million backyards in L.A. could potentially be put to this additional use, without dramatically changing neighborhood character. After barriers were removed in 2017, the number of permits for backyard ADUs increased 1,851 percent in one year! These relatively inexpensive units are meaningful in L.A., where homelessness is growing and nearly a third of its residents spend more than half of their income on rent.[102] Densifying can also mean extending transit to new areas that include dense nodes. Fortunately, there are countless examples of successful densification of existing cities and suburbs, including retrofitting of "grayfield" malls, office parks and subdivisions.

As the many different costs of suburbia mount and become better known, the appeal of the city will keep growing, particularly for young professionals and empty-nesters. Up-zoning and retrofitting will continue to flourish. Young adults who grew up in their parents' suburbs and are attracted to the liveliness, opportunities and conveniences of urban lifestyles, will find new ways to populate cities. It's not consciously about reducing energy footprints per se. To quote another work by David Owen,

> [I]n a dense city the truly important environmental issues are less likely to be things like the carbon footprints of apartment buildings than they are to be old-fashioned quality-of-life concerns like education, culture, crime, street noise, bad smells, resources for the elderly, and the availability of recreation facilities – all of which affect the willingness of people to live in efficient urban cores rather than packing up their children and fleeing to the suburbs.[103]

The appeal of the city to Americans aged 65 and older is already strong, with 80 percent of this cohort now living in metro areas. Life expectancy for this group has increased, as lifetimes in the U.S. have gone from 47 years in 1900 to 79 years in little more than a century.[104] While many of these elderly citizens may live in the suburban fringes, they are attracted to the abundance and convenience of good health systems, continued learning opportunities, public transportation and arts and culture. GLAM – Galleries, Libraries, Archives and Museums – have special appeal for both young professionals and empty-nesters.

High housing costs are often the biggest deterrent to migrating to central cities in developed countries, where there is runaway gentrification and unrelenting displacement of the poor. Ever-higher land costs make development of new or renovated affordable housing evermore more difficult. Without government subsidies, affordable housing is often not feasible. Over-focusing on the wealthy cores of cities, with their empty luxury towers, can stoke this inequity, and at the same time make the urban cores more socially monocultural. Gentrification in central cities is a worldwide problem, and may in numerous cases rival or exceed

UHI as a prohibitive factor in people's decision to move to or to stay in cities. A new kind of homesteading in New York City shows promise of helping to crack this hard nut: Community Land Trusts (CLT) are a model of collective ownership of housing on community-owned land, designed to encourage long-term stability and foster neighborhood self-determination. They develop property through community-run organizations, sometimes along with the local government and private sector, but independent of conventional government funding streams or commercial financing.

Another approach to gentrification and the real estate speculation is to tax vacant land more heavily. The logic, famously promoted by Henry George at the beginning of the twentieth century, is that land speculation yields an unearned windfall profit which can and should be heavily taxed. And much of the value added is because of public investment in infrastructure, such as transit, parks, airports, etc., which tends to benefit a small land-owning slice of the urban population. Vancouver, Canada is considering taxing what it calls the "land-lift" that accrues to these property owners, and using that money to support affordable housing for the 20 percent of their residents for whom housing costs are well beyond reach.

California passed 15 bills in 2017 that attack the growing housing affordability problem in different ways. The U.S. needs to fund the construction of below-market-rate housing, while making all housing development faster and more afforadable by smoothing notoriously lengthy and unpredictable government-approval processes that have been blamed for the housing shortage. These and other such initiatives, policies, laws and practices are desperately needed in the increasingly winner-take-all world, which tends to concentrate inequities in global cities. Indeed, increasing gentrification is a structural problem in market capitalism, one beyond the book's scope, other than how the strategies and policies mentioned can help, plus the earlier-mentioned benefits of a sharing economy. There is one ironic benefit of gentrification: it reduces birth rates, which is so necessary in developing countries. To what extent this trend applies in the Global South needs to be studied, but in the U.S., counties that saw some of the steepest increases in home values also saw some of the steepest declines in birth rates.[105]

Some Dangling Issues and Wicked Problems

There is much unfinished business, both urban and climatic. As Barke Engels states "The city is never completed. It has a beginning but it has no end. It is a work in progress."[106] Pittsburgh Mayor Bill Peduto emphasizes the climatic business: "If you are a Mayor and not preparing for the impacts of climate change, you aren't doing your job."[107] There are numerous unresolved environmental, geopolitical and cultural issues associated with CC. It's not entirely clear in what climate zones the extreme heat of UHIs and heat waves will most effectively mobilize action, and where other issues will be more pressing. In much of Asia, air and water pollution are very visible and salient motivators. China and India are fighting air pollution with vigorous initiatives in renewable energy. In Central and South American cities, as well as in Africa, both dirty water and flooding are major stimulants for reform, as well as extreme heat. A recent landmark study found that "traditional" pollution deaths – from contaminated water and wood cooking fires – are falling as massive efforts in the developing world bear fruit. However, current pollution of air, water, soils and workplaces accounts for at least 9 million premature deaths per year, which is 15 times as many as war and other violent deaths![108] The report found that pollution is annually responsible for diseases that kill one in every six people around the world, with a more accurate total likely to be millions higher because the impacts of many pollutants are poorly understood.

> The deaths attributed to dirty air and water are triple those from AIDS, malaria and tuberculosis combined, not to mention road accidents, war and murder . . . the vast majority of these deaths still happen in poor nations and in some, such as India, Chad and Madagascar, pollution causes a quarter of all deaths . . . air pollution deaths in south-east Asia are on track to double by 2050 . . . The researchers estimated the welfare losses from pollution at \$4.6T a year, equivalent to more than 6% of global GDP.[109]

This ongoing environmental threat is in and of itself a major problem, sometimes independent of CC.

Reasons to mobilize are legion. In arid areas, drought, soil salinization and famine can mobilize action. In Europe, it can be the influx of unwanted climate refugees that precipitates action. In North America, extremely wet and windy weather events, like New York's Superstorm Sandy, or devastating dust bowls and droughts can be the local game changers. Any coastal metropolis with low-lying areas, from Miami to Shanghai, is likely to be preoccupied with sea level rise, as well as by sinking land. Hydrologists say Jakarta has only a decade to halt its sinking before most of its 30 million residents will be underwater.[110] A hopeful aside: As sea level rises, it would be a welcome and productive twist of fate if the residents, institutions and businesses were to move to and help densify declining cities and underdeveloped suburbs that are situated on higher ground. If nothing else, leafy suburbs are better able to absorb the increasingly heavy rain that is falling on much of the urbanized world.

There are also thermal counter-currents: cities at high latitudes and high elevations with harsh winters may appreciate warmer temperatures from UHIs and CC. However, a Brown University study looked at cold-related deaths under two CC scenarios and with and without population growth. Overall the authors found that while rising temperatures reduced the risk of dying from cold, the reduced threat of cold was overwhelmed in eight of ten metro areas by the much greater increased risk from heat, leading to a net increase in the number of temperature-related deaths under climate change overall.[111] Many cities – from Chicago, Detroit and New York to London, Moscow and Beijing – also have hot summers with increasingly frequent heat waves. Cities with cool summers in areas such as North America's Pacific Northwest and northern Europe tend to welcome warmer summer temperatures, unless the heat waves become too intense over time. Cities that are not bothered by UHIs or see them as beneficial, may need to find other ways to rally their citizens to address CC. But there is no shortage of other problems affecting them, from extreme weather and flooding to sea level rise, epidemics and the influx of climate refugees.

There remain some technical issues of climate science that need further study. Some of the direct and indirect relationships between UHI and CC are not yet fully understood. For instance, the role of water vapor in the air and resulting formation of clouds in and around cities is a complex and bedeviling issue: It's the equivalent of a very potent but very short-lived GHG; condensed vapor results in rainfall that cools urban surfaces, and cloud cover increases albedo. It's well known that the air's capacity to absorb moisture goes up at an exponential rate, how fast air temperatures will rise in real time is uncertain. Humidity makes cities less comfortable, and is worsening as heavier rainfall and fiercer storm events result in more flooding. Add to this the fact that hotter air temperatures near the ground tend to further increase the level of UHIs due to ozone depletion, which also exacerbates CC. Nor has the *quantitative* extent to which air temperature can be lowered by the four UHI antidotes been widely measured. And there may emerge other UHI strategies and techniques – such as radiant cooling panels on roofs – that will be more effective or less expensive or both. More research is needed, as well as more media attention, which has been surprisingly thin to date for such a pervasive, unavoidable problem.

Mitigating heat waves will continue to be extremely critical for cities in hot, humid climate zones, as outdoor activity becomes more and more uncomfortable, or even prohibitively hot and unhealthy for outdoor physical activity. "Simulations in the NASA-funded research suggest that the number of 'high heat stress' days in Houston will more than double by mid-century . . . In some areas, the number could triple."[112] A long list of American cities – Baltimore, Birmingham (AL), Charleston (SC), Charlotte, Denver, Memphis, Nashville, Richmond, St. Louis and Washington – are estimated to see five to nine times as many heat-stress days (above 90° or 100°F, depending on the climate zone) by 2050, and 18 to 33 times as many by 2100.[113] Climatic conditions could overwhelm the human body's ability to cool itself through perspiration and ventilation.

> By the end of this century, areas of the Persian Gulf region could be hit by waves of heat and humidity so severe that simply being outside for several hours could threaten human life, according to a recent study . . . (some cities in the Middle East) are likely to experience temperature levels that are intolerable to humans.[114]

Cities and metropolitan areas the world over will need to step up to these challenges, as some of them already have. Consolidating public works, water, sewerage, utility and environmental departments into a super green agency often makes sense. Cities also need to be given more control and power from their central governments, which are usually reluctant to devolve power to municipal and regional governmental units. Fortunately,

> they are doing so with greater frequency as they recognize the national benefits that can come with local control. That trend will only accelerate as the world becomes increasingly urbanized and cities become increasingly connected to one another, promoting the spread of best practices across national borders.[115]

We may even see the emergence of city-states or nation hybrids that allow even more localized autonomy and agency.

More Urban Resilience

Cities are extremely complex systems with many moving parts that can break down in times of crisis. Given their extreme complexity, it has always amazed me they are as functional as they are, and that there are not *more* breakdowns, even chaos from time to time. They do tend to be more fragile and less resilient in times of disaster than rural communities, which have their own food production and other means of local self-reliance. The terms "resilient urbanism" and "urban resilience" are gradually coming more to the forefront than the urban efficiency that has been touted throughout the book. For some, the term has more currency than "sustainability," which like all popular, overused words inevitably becomes tired and clichéd over time. The term "resilience" can have two quite disparate meanings. The first is the ability to elastically bounce *back* to the status quo after setbacks and crises, or "the capacity of a system to survive, adapt and grow in the face of unforeseen changes, even catastrophic incidents."[116] The second meaning is "transformation to create an alternative equilibrium,"[117] or the ability to bounce *forward* into a better state than the former one.

A conceptual sea change from sustainability to resilience is happening more quickly as UHIs and CC lurch forward into more extreme weather events. The U.S. declares a federal disaster every five days on average, with the frequency increasing.[118] At considerable cost to the efficiencies, the economies and the paradoxes of cities, there is the need for more *redundancy* in physical and institutional infrastructure. All things being equal, resilience is therefore costlier than sustainability in terms of capital investment, maintenance and stockpiling of goods and resources. And the costs of both will escalate if CC mitigation and adaptation are not pursued concurrently with resilience. The longer-term economics are more salutary. For every $1 that the U.S. government spends on resiliency projects, such as elevating buildings in flood zones and improving water management systems, society saves $6 on the future costs of natural disasters, according to a 2018 report by the National Institute of Building Sciences. Although no doubt overly precise, that's higher than the 4-to-1 savings the institute originally reported in a 2005 report, due in large measure to the growing impacts of CC.[119]

Unfortunately, the investments in resiliency tend to compete with investments in efficiency. If overdone or misplaced, resiliency expenditures could jeopardize the long-term war against CC, by leading to premature bankruptcy and a downward spiral. In short, resilience is both increasingly costly and increasingly crucial. It needs to be balanced with efficiency, much the same way as adaptation must be balanced with mitigation. Luckily, as noted before, the antidotes to UHIs are typically "adaptive mitigation" and "mitigative adaption," simultaneously helping to balance both of these competing but complementary pairs. Neither combination may come soon enough or be resilient enough to plug the holes in the global ship that CC is sinking, but they make the holes smaller and buy more time.

The efficient use and recycling of energy and resources is a cornerstone of resilience. It should advance integrated mitigation and adaptation, if used along with other climate management strategies. This suggests two levels of integrated mitigation and adaptation: passive and active. Passive integrated mitigation and adaptation (PIMA) includes climate-responsive design such as plantings, reflective ground surface, natural ventilation and solar orientation. PIMA represents good design practice and should underlie the basic design strategies for buildings and cities, as outlined in "The 7 Principles of Passive Energy-efficient Buildings" in Chapter 3. In high-density urban districts, however, active integrated mitigation and adaptation (AIMA) may be required. AIMA deploys more advanced building systems and district infrastructure, such as building energy management, active renewable energy systems, energy storage, district energy systems, water recycling and on-site wastewater treatment, that actively reduce energy and climate impacts.[120]

Cities are beset with other difficult issues. They are often grid-locked with congestion and are usually more polluted. With tightly packed neighborhoods and more residents frequenting public places, communicable diseases tend to spread more quickly than in rural areas, although cities have more doctors, clinics and hospitals, and ambulances (which were originally developed in cities). In developing countries cities usually offer economic opportunity, but they often require greater reliance on cash income than the countryside, and they collect more taxes. And there is a higher percentage of residents living on illegally occupied land, who are subject to sudden eviction. Over two million Americans were touched by eviction in 2016.[121] Indeed, cities in wealthy countries like the U.S. can be difficult places to overcome poverty, because the poor tend to live separately from the rich, with substandard schools, infrastructure and services. And racial and ethnic segregation is often forced rather than voluntary. Organized crime and street gangs tend to be higher in cities, including homicide rates, although as noted earlier, stranger homicides kill considerably fewer people than automobile collisions over the metro area, especially in auto-dependent sprawl.

Health and Aesthetics

> Living among millions of strangers is a very unnatural state of affairs for a human being . . . One of the jobs of a city is to accommodate that problem. How do you build a society where people treat each other kindly in that kind of setting? That is more likely to happen when people feel good. If you feel positive you're more likely to speak to a stranger.[122]

Canadian researcher Colin Ellard goes on to write that a person's state of mind is strongly affected by architecture and urban design, especially building façades along street walls. If a façade is complex and interesting at multiple scales, it affects a pedestrian's frame of mind positively, not negatively as when it is simple and monotonous, such as Modernist façades that are formally simple and abstract. The lack of complexity in relatively blank street walls does not reward closer viewing, leaving the passer-by less stimulated, even lost on long, blank stretches.

The role of good urban design goes beyond aesthetic pleasure. Some researchers have shown that "growing up in a city doubles the chances of someone developing schizophrenia, and increases the risk for other mental disorders such as depression and chronic anxiety."[123] A main trigger seems to be "social stress" – a lack of social bonding and neighborhood cohesion. A researcher at the University of Heidelberg has found that urban living can change the actual brain biology in some people. Comfortable, lively public spaces will not cure loneliness or stress in cities, but they can help by making residents feel more engaged and comfortable with their surroundings.[124] Others assert that repetitive parallel lines in architecture stress the brain, prompting increased blood flow to the visual cortex, giving people headaches.[125] A sense of place seems essential to both personal and social health, and there is a deficit of it in many Modernist cities.

Despite the stress, pressures and even anonymity of urban living, suicide rates tend to be significantly lower in cities. Recent statistics from Centers for Disease Control and Prevention show an increasing gap between suicide rates in the central areas of metro areas with more than a million people and suicide rates in rural areas. In 2000 the ratio of rural to urban suicides was about three to two, but by 2015 the ratio had spread to almost two to one, with less of a spread for suburbanites.[126] Nonetheless, cities "are associated with higher rates of most mental health problems compared to rural areas. City dwellers have an

Figure 8.2 Urban scenes tend to feature regular, repetitive patterns in windows, staircases and railings. Regular patterns of this kind are rarely found in nature. Because the repetitive patterns of urban architecture break this rule of nature, it is more difficult for the human brain to process them efficiently, making them less comfortable to look at. With monotonous patterns of straight lines as far as the eye can see, there's nowhere pleasant to rest your gaze, with some relentless façades triggering headaches and even epileptic seizures.[1] (LAIF/Redux)

1 "Looking at buildings can actually give people headaches: here's why," *CNN Style*, 7/5/18

almost 40% higher risk of depression, over 20% more anxiety . . . in addition to more loneliness, isolation and stress."[127] These disorders may partially explain why cities have higher murder rates: city dwellers take out their woes more on others than themselves; they commit suicide less frequently, but murder other people more frequently than country folk.

To reinforce earlier points, cities must alleviate psychological stress by providing accessible green spaces that allow relaxation, exercise and social interaction. Exposure to trees and other vegetation can decrease mental fatigue, and reduce stress as well as feelings of anger, depression or anxiety. Indeed, urban greenery directly promotes physical and mental well-being. After adjusting for other relevant factors, a study in London

> found a clear correlation between street trees and well-being: those areas with fewest street trees had the highest number of residents taking anti-depressant prescription drugs. Parks and park activities also help create the social cohesion that not only has significant health benefits, but also leads to reduced costs for police and fire protection, prisons and counseling, and rehabilitation.[128]

Another study in England found that "the health effects of inequality, which tends to increase the risk of circulatory disease among those lower down the socioeconomic scale, are far less pronounced in greener areas."[129] The visual richness of natural environments acts as a kind of mental balm.

To moderate the stress that leads to conflict and violence, parks and playgrounds can be woven into the daily lives of everyone. These places of relaxation and convivial exchange can welcome everyone, from rich to poor, young to old, natives to immigrants. Representatives of these groups, when and where possible, should also be involved in their design and development. These green spaces need to be safe and feel safe, especially for the risk-averse citizens who feel insecure in more dangerous zones. Not only can urban open spaces be inclusive, they can be neutral zones, where radically different socio-economic, ethnic and racial groups can co-exist peacefully, often picnicking and recreating together or in close proximity. No place happily embodies and freely celebrates a polyglot culture more than a green park on a pleasant day.

Likewise, city parks also work to alleviate physiological ailments. As described in the chapter on trees,

> The more trees on a block, the less likely people are to be obese or have diabetes or heart disease. They're also more likely to report feeling healthier . . . Being around more trees is the health and well-being equivalent to making $10,000 more at your job.[130]

There is the widely-accepted understanding that people exercise more if they live within a short walk or bike ride of a park. As noted earlier, urbanites in general walk more than suburbanites, even though many people ironically choose to live in suburbia to spend more time outdoors. As a consequence of their habitual walking, it's a well-established fact that urban dwellers weigh less on average. Transit requires walking, but it seems more like getting to work than exercise per se. "Taking the bus or train usually means walking to your final destination, thus providing an automatic period of pound-shedding daily exercise."[131] The authors of a study in *Preventative Medicine* noted a 1 percent increase in usage of public transit is associated with a 0.2 percent decrease in the obesity rate.[132]

Last but not least, to help overcome various psychological and physiological drawbacks, the city needs to appeal to the senses and be enjoyable, engaging and continually refreshing and invigorating. It needs a public realm of lively streets lined with trees and intensified by vibrant public plazas and parks. In the best of all worlds, these public outdoor rooms are spatially well defined, with tree canopies and good architecture providing enclosure, with free-standing objects occasionally punctuating the spaces. To address these and other challenges, the means and the outcomes that feel comfortable and natural, if not delightful, fun, lovable are necessary. The role of beauty in enriching our lives is not to be underestimated. For sustainability itself to be sustained, it wants to be aesthetically attractive, even beautiful and endlessly captivating. As one of the founders of the Congress for New Urbanism (CNU) Daniel Solomon writes in his short book *Cosmopolis*:

> Sustainability alone is not sustainable . . . We are obliged to be interesting; it is a duty. No one will pay the slightest attention to us otherwise . . . We actually have very little chance of doing good or being good, if all we offer the world is the dreary salvation of non-consumption.[133]

If a building is lovable enough to be maintained for centuries, it stretches its carbon impact over a long time and is far superior to an unlovable building that is quickly razed. Esthetics is arguably the fourth "E" of sustainability (if we spell it with an "e"), along with the "Three Es of Environment, Economics and Equity/Ethics."

Cities: Our Last, Best Hope

Let me close with two telling quotes. The first is by architect Charles Correa, the 2017 RIBA Gold Medalist: "At this moment, we are going to shape the city for generations to come. People need to realize this is an opportunity which will never come again."[134] Joan Clos, Secretary

General of U.N. Habitat said this at the 2016 Venice Biennale: "Too much architecture, too little urbanism." Both quotations reinforce points made repeatedly in this book. Indeed, cities are arguably the greatest of human accomplishments and the most human of great accomplishments.

They have been the birthplace, engine and repository of civilization, as well as its collective soul. Of the many virtues of cities, a number are particularly relevant to rescuing civilization from the ever-larger jaws of CC: economic productivity, social opportunity, creativity, commerce, community, arts and culture. These are the fertile mix, mash-ups and entanglements of healthy, robust cities. Without them, society would not be able to rise to the climate challenge. It would not have the talent, economic wherewithal and sufficient socio-economic-political resilience to summon up for this profound problem of our time. We also want to be sure not to throw the proverbial baby out with the bath water. The city, especially the democratic polis, has produced too many flowers and fruits to be put at risk, much less jettisoned, in our rush to accommodate the endless goal of growth. Humanity cannot afford to let our cities be made unbearably hot by UHIs and CC. Density, agglomeration economics and innovation do make a serious difference. As does democracy, although it "is at once the most serious obstacle those who would address climate change must overcome, and their indispensable vehicle for achieving success."[135]

The city is also politically instrumental in stabilizing the nation-state.

> Failing cities lead to failing states . . . If the governability of cities, their planners and architects cannot successfully adjust to the changing conditions of the twenty-first century, there is the risk that human culture, and with it the nation state, will die out in the wilderness of future megacities.[136]

It is one thing if countries devolve into clusters of dense, coherent city-states, but a very different thing if countries slide into miasmic smears across quasi-urban landscapes. Placeless conurbations of vehicle-dependent, mega-sprawl would be the worst physical outcome, a drag on further human development and a sad ending to what has been the wonderfully rich evolution of the city. If "urban agglomeration" – the unflattering coinage for the sprawling megacity – swallows and homogenizes suburbs and nearby smaller cities to create a single, undifferentiated urban mass-cum-mess, the magic of cities will be sacrificed.

Cities are huge economic investments, no doubt humanity's largest. The built environment is the biggest economic asset class, worth more than all the stocks, bonds and other instruments in the world's financial markets.[137] Long-lived, it embodies both local and international culture, making connections across the past, present and future. The twentieth-century Modernists thought of the city as a machine or a system. Then it was seen as an organism, like an individual animal, plant or cell. Interestingly, animals all have about the same number of heart beats over the course of their life. For the vast majority of animals, the larger the body mass, the slower the metabolism and longer the life. If their weight was plotted against their metabolic rate on a logarithmic scale, Kleiber's Law tells us that it results in very close to a straight line, from mice to dogs to cows to elephants. Physicist Geoffrey West of the Santa Fe Institute discovered from big data that if an elephant is a scaled-up mouse, then a city is a scaled-up elephant. Double the size and intensity of a city, and its metabolism – measured in energy consumption and carbon produced – goes up about 85 percent, not 100 percent. Infrastructure – such as the number of gas stations, the area of roads, the length of electric cables – also scales at the same sublinear rate.[138] This inherent efficiency is a basic, intrinsic reason that cities combat CC, and it explains much of the environmental paradox of cities. There is an important distinction between organisms and ecosystems: the former all die and the latter survive for many generations, even millennia. The city is an ecosystem.

West's team also found that Kleiber's law is reversed to superlinearity when it comes to creativity and invention. As measured in patents per capita, a metropolis that is ten times bigger and denser in population than its neighbor is roughly 12 times more innovative.[139] Indeed, the largest metros in the U.S. produce a very high share of the nation's new patents, as well as successful new businesses, because of the *economies of agglomeration.*

> [J]ust 20 metros produce 63 percent of all patents. In biotechnology, for example, just three metro areas – Boston, San Diego and San Francisco – produce a majority of new biotech firms. Dispersing these researchers – who rely on critical mass and close and serendipitous interaction – would reduce the flow of new ideas that drive economic growth . . . Since the economic peak of the last expansion, large metro areas have accounted for about 87% of net new jobs in the U.S. economy.[140]

Other socio-economic phenomena that are also not analogous to physiology behave in the same superlinear way. Not only patents but also wages and local GDP grow with city size, but unfortunately so do crime, number of police, aids cases, etc. The combination of urban size and intensity is a double-edged sword.

The robust economic impact of urbanization continues to obtain worldwide. The Director of the Indian Institute for Human Settlements states that "cities represent an immense emergent economic opportunity, and are the largest site of incremental employment globally."[141] The economic output of China further corroborates the role of cities: "Already the 90 largest Chinese cities account for around $6 trillion – the size

City GDP vs. Population

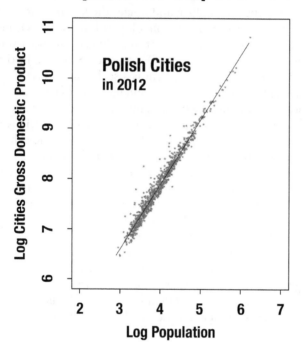

Figure 8.3 As a city grows in population and accompanying density, its
economic productivity, a.k.a. its GDP, goes up at a noticeably
faster rate due to inherent urban efficiencies and economy
of agglomeration. Creativity and innovation also go up at a
superlinear rate. (K. Cebrat and M. Sobczyński, "Scaling Laws in
City Growth: Setting Limitations with Self-Organizing Maps,"
PLoS ONE, 11(12) (2016): e0168753)

of the national economies of Germany and France combined."[142] As is
frequently proclaimed, more than half the human race now live in cities, but it might come as more of a surprise to learn that the largest 300
metropolises account for nearly half of world economic output with only
a fifth of world population.[143] At two-and-a-half times their per capita
share, cities box well above their weight.

While the economy of agglomeration is associated with cities, it's not
clear that it still adds to national wealth. As automation and AI replace
more and more jobs, as they very clearly are starting to, that won't necessarily curtail economic activity or a country's wealth. But it means that
economic activity will be determined less by the size of a country's population than in the past, and increasingly by the quality of its technology

and infrastructure.[144] The large and growing populations in developing countries like India and Nigeria may not necessarily translate into the large global economic powerhouses that have been historically associated with a large national populace.

The incessant interaction of people and their ideas, the cultural fertility and the creative chemistry of the arts all thrive in cities. They are well worth the ecological compromise and physical harm cities do to the natural environment. In the larger sense, they perform an essential ecological role by providing compact habitat for humans, and preserving natural habitat for other species. Most people who have spent time in Venice would agree that it was well worth giving up a marsh in this Adriatic lagoon. If it represents an ecological sacrifice zone, its extraordinary human achievements and delights far outweigh its environmental costs. With respect to towns and cities, this trade-off brings up the distinction between *ecocentric* and *anthropocentric*, which is helpful in describing cities, including their environmental paradox.

If cities are acts of ecological compromise, many animals in cities and suburbs are genetically evolving to deal with the ubiquitous presence of humans through fast-paced natural selection.

Examples abound. Urban populations of some birds, adjusting to traffic noise, are becoming hard-wired to sing at a higher pitch than their country cousins. White-footed mice in Central Park are evolving to better deal with the fatty foods that New Yorkers serendipitously drop their way. Caribbean lizards are undergoing epigenetically driven physical changes to better maneuver along urban surfaces that are far smoother than the rough bark of trees.[145]

While remarkable, this resilient ability of some species to adapt to city life in no way lessens the urgent need to preserve the earth's remaining natural areas. Nor should it undermine the anthropocentric view of cities.

Unlike organisms, ecosystems are more complex biological communities that are much longer-lived, able to span many generations of their member organisms. Cities can be equally long-lived; some have been with us for millennia. Think of Cairo, Athens, Istanbul, Beijing, Paris. It's a long list. As noted above, there is a difference between analogy and reality in this case. *The city is not analogous to an ecosystem; it is* one. As Jane Jacobs pointed out, human settlements are just as natural as colonies of prairie dogs or beds of oysters, or hives of bees. People-watching in sit-able urban places is as much about nature as bird-watching is in the countryside, and a more commonplace activity at that.

Cities are intrinsically lively and exciting. They're stimulating places to reside and/or work, full of life and surprises. As Jacobs wrote,

> Cities have always had a magnetic pull . . . Anyone not living in the
> city feels like a second-class citizen . . . People living in cities have
> always enjoyed more freedom and possibilities for development than
> those living outside them. Cities have the capability of providing
> something for everybody, only because, and only when, they are cre-
> ated by everybody.[146]

Indeed, cities are places of economic opportunity and productivity. Migrants to cities on average experience more job opportunities,
higher incomes and more personal freedom than in the rural areas they
left behind. As noted earlier, Glaeser contends that "Cities don't make
people poor; they attract poor people."[147] Wages and productivity rise;
the bigger and denser, the greater the creation of wealth and higher the
wages. Density plays a surprisingly significant role: Some studies suggest
that doubling the density raises productivity by at least 6 percent and up
to 28 percent. Some economists have concluded that more than half the
variation in output per worker in the U.S. is explained by density alone. It
explains more of the productivity gap across the country than education
levels, tax policies or industry concentrations.[148]

The intricate pattern of urbanism is complex, but it's far from random. As Jacobs argued, it exhibits a high degree of order among many
interconnected variables – what has come to be called "organized complexity." This is opposed to the "disorganized complexity," which
describes equally complex patterns of *unconnected* variables, such as
actuarial tables. And there is "simplicity," which has a limited number of
variables, as in classic Newtonian science. This pattern of productivity is
rooted in physical connectivity, starting at the scale of the sidewalk, and
encompassing all the other movements and connections of urban activity.
"Sidewalk contacts are the small change from which a city's wealth of
public life may grow,"[149] she wrote.

Since Jane Jacobs wrote this over a half century ago, society has
become plugged in electronically with mobile phones and the internet.
But, as research by Robert Putnam and others is showing,

> the root of the system is the *physical* proximity with the people. This
> pattern of physical connections generates remarkable efficiencies,
> forming a kind of "urban metabolism." Simply put, it's the idea that
> within a city, if you are making x, and I am making y, then our
> combined knowledge might allow us to make z together – but only if
> we are physically close enough that our knowledge can "spill over"
> from one sort of enterprise to another. Jacobs has since been credited
> for observing highly local "knowledge spillovers," casual transfers of
> knowledge about a job or a new tool, that help to grow new enter-
> prises and new economic activities.

Her insight, now called a "Jacobs Externality" by respectful economists, helps explain how a city generates wealth.[150]

New Urbanist and Jacobs devotee Michael Mehaffy goes on to speculate:

> In the same vein, the brain scientists offer some other important insights. For one thing, it is not just that density (neurons or people) per se is important but that the *patterns of connections* are important. So, we have to be able to ensure that the "neural pathways" can form – in the case of a person's brain, that the person is healthy and well-nourished enough to remember, and learn. In the case of cities, we have to ensure that we have well-connected, walkable cities, facilitating a lot of cross-connection. The brain scientists even believe now that this pattern of neural cross-connection is key to the formation of consciousness. In effect, the different parts of the brain are joined up into a larger system, and the result is that the system self-organizes into a state that is smarter and more aware. Something similar might be going on with well-connected cities: they can self-organize to become "smarter" in their ability to generate great urban vitality with fewer resources. But this is true only if their "neurons" (the people) are able to be connected, especially physically connected, in this way.[151]

Given all these advantages, it might be argued that cities must unfairly hoard resources and monopolize wealth. This conjecture misses the point that cities actually *create* wealth and value through inherent efficiencies that produce increasing returns on the investment of capital and human resources. Urbanites are more productive, more innovative and have higher skills, and can search over a wider range of job opportunities, and move from one firm to another at will, typically improving their productive contribution. Glaeser also emphasizes how cities enable the spread of ideas and new information by being around other intelligent people. He also notes that density generates other positive externalities, such as the easier movement of goods over shorter distances.

On the UHI and CC front, it's been shown that air temperature impacts productivity. When temperatures rise above 84°F (29°C), worker productivity declines sharply, particularly for outdoor jobs.[152] Other studies suggest that the reduction in total factory productivity in response to hot temperatures is the primary driver behind losses in output. A medium-term CC prediction suggests that it will reduce production by 3 to 5 percent, and result in losses of 4.5 to 7 percent. This corresponds to $25–40 billion losses, in 2013 values.[153] Beyond its obvious impacts on agricultural production, CC effects human production in cities. A 2015 study published in *Nature* shows that peak economic productivity occurs at 55°F (13°C) and that it declines sharply as it gets hotter.

This pattern is observed around the world for both agricultural and nonagricultural activities, in both rich and poor countries. The result is that already global warming hurts production in tropical countries that have warm temperatures, and slightly improves productivity in cooler countries as they become warmer. If the world does not reduce global warming, average global production will fall 23%, resulting in even more global income inequality, because the rich countries are mostly in cooler climates.[154]

Arguably a principal reason that they are more productive and richer is simply they do not have as much sweltering heat as the Global South.
If personal income is a measure of productivity, then cities today look good, even compared to their affluent suburbs. A recent study at the University of Virginia showed that the trajectories of income have recently diverged quite markedly between inner city and suburb, underscoring the growing wealth of cities.

In 1990, per capita incomes at the city center in Phoenix were about $1,500 less than in communities at 30 miles. Now, in inflation-adjusted dollars, per capita incomes at the city center are $25,000 more. In Denver, per capita incomes were lower at the city center than 30 miles out in 1990; now they are more than one-third higher at the city center. In Charlotte, per capita incomes in 1990 were slightly higher 30 miles out than at the city center; now incomes are more than twice as high in the city.[155]

This urban advantage has attracted more college graduates to the center of the nation's 50 largest metro areas – soaring from less than a quarter to just over half since 1990, compared to less than a third in suburbs only 30 miles away.[156] The 21-point gap indicates how much the appetite for urban living has overtaken suburban living.

To leave no stone unturned, there's a final externality of extreme heat: its impact on aviation. Heat hampers on-the-ground airport workers, loading and unloading luggage and servicing planes, and the hotter, less dense air provides less lift on the wings of airplanes. In Phoenix, when hot temperatures forced the cancellation of more than 40 flights in 2017,

American Airlines set up cooling stations – air-conditioned tents on the tarmac – for its employees. As global temperatures continue to rise, some of the heaviest planes on the longest flights may eventually be unable to depart during the hottest part of summer days. Like an ocean liner waiting for the right tide to leave port, airplanes may be grounded until the air is cool and dense enough for takeoff at full capacity.[157]

Runways will need to be lengthened and made of materials that don't soften at higher temperatures, and airlines will have to institute tighter weight restrictions. Also, airplanes need more robust electronics at especially hot airports. And, of course, the many airports built at low elevations, often on landfill, are vulnerable to sea level rise. These limitations will no doubt grow in importance and frequency with intensifying heat.

As we've seen already, cities also generate outright negative externalities, including higher levels of crime and congestion, the spread of infectious disease and less resilience in crises. However, cities have historically reduced these negatives through greater wealth, education and stronger institutions, from sanitary infrastructure to hospitals and universities to garbage collection and policing. A vivid example is the now commonplace ambulance, which was invented to deal with the rise and concentration of disease and mishaps in cities. There is usually less of a safety net and less health care in cities of the developing world, with the greater national rates of poverty and corruption, but these cities are likely to follow the same upward trajectory.

Before the final chapter, let's pause and remember why cities are so important for the survival and flourishing of civilization. Along with agriculture they are surely one of human civilization's two most enabling accomplishments, exceeded only by the pre-historic development of spoken language. Suffice it to say that cities have allowed humans to flourish, but very much because the benign climate since the end of the last Ice Age about 20,000 years ago allowed humans to develop farming and cities some 8,000 years later. As that favorable climate changes, let's hope advanced civilization does not abandon its many hard-won fruits. As English philosopher Bertrand Russell once wrote "Strange how one values civilization – more than all one's friends or anything – the slow achievement of men emerging from the brute – it seems the ultimate thing one lives for."[158]

Notes

1 Rich Bunnell, "Urban climate adaptation and resisting the urge to panic," *Agora*, p. 20
2 Personal email from Mehaffy, 11/24/17
3 Rich Bunnell, "Urban climate adaptation and resisting the urge to panic," p. 20
4 Tonya Graham, "Building climate resilience in America's smaller cities and towns," *Meeting of the Minds*, 8/9/18
5 Ed Mazria, "Life during Trump: progress on climate change will come from the bottom up," *Common/Edge*, 11/13/16
6 Mark Watts, "Cities can defend us against climate change," London Essays, *centreforlondon.org*, 9/28/17
7 Gregory Scruggs, "In Mexico City for climate talks, U.S. mayors get advice on how to deal with Donald Trump," *citiscope*, 12/6/16

8 Ibid.
9 "Singapore: no more cars allowed on the road, government says," *Agence France-Presse*, 10/24/17
10 Gregory Scruggs, "Explainer: what is the Paris Agreement on climate change and what does it mean for cities?" *citiscope*, 3/30/17
11 Aromar Revi, "Next month, a key opportunity to re-imagine the global response to an urban world," *citiscope*, 8/22/17
12 Michael Bloomberg, "City century: why municipalities are the key to fighting climate change," *Foreign Affairs*, September–October, 2015
13 David Wallace Wells, "Climate change will make Earth too hot for humans," *New York Magazine*, 7/9/1
14 Tom Herbstein, "Climate change: now's the time to look outside, to take action inside," News and Blog, Cambridge Institute of Climate Leadership, 9/14/16
15 "How government policy exacerbates hurricanes like Harvey," *The Economist*, 9/2/17
16 "For coastal communities, the 1.5c climate goal is a matter of life or death," *Futurism*, 1/14/18
17 Michael Bloomberg, "City century: why municipalities are the key to fighting climate change"
18 "On Benjamin Barber: cities, democracy, and global governance," *citiscope*, 5/19/17
19 Ibid.
20 Bruce Katz, "The city state meets the nation state," *Updates from Bruce Katz*, 7/15/17
21 Clair Brown, *Buddhist Economics*, Bloomsbury, 2017, p. 91
22 Susan Goldberg, "Talking toilets with Matt Damon," *National Geographic*, August, 2017
23 "Universal lessons," *The Economist*, 7/7/18
24 Habitat III Issue Papers, No. 11, Public Space, 5/31/15
25 Andrew Rudd, "The U.N. New Urban Agenda," ROWE/ROME conference, Rome, 6/21/17
26 *New Urban Agenda*, Habitat III Secretariat, 2017
27 David Hatch, "'Urban–rural continuum' essential to achieving New Urban Agenda," *citiscope*, 10/18/17
28 Ibid.
29 Ibid.
30 Ibid.
31 Listserv email from Seth Harry
32 Gregory Scruggs, "Explainer: what is a national urban policy?" *citiscope*, 9/19/17
33 Michael Mehaffy, "Five key takeaways from the 2018 World Urban Forum," *City Square*, 3/19/18
34 Michael Bloomberg and Carl Pope, *Climate of Hope*, St. Martin's Press, 2017, pp. 234, 254–255, 257
35 Edward Glaeser, *Triumph of the City*, Macmillan, 2011
36 David Owen, "Green Manhattan," *The New Yorker*, 10/18/04
37 Jane Jacobs, *Life and Death of Great American Cities*, Random House, 1961, p. 445
38 Leigh Gallagher, *The End of the Suburbs*, Portfolio/Penguin, 2013, p. 48
39 Jonathan Rose, *The Well-Tempered City*, Harper Wave, 2016, p. 341
40 Steve Kieran, "Scaling regionalism," *Energy Accounts*, 2017
41 David Owen, "Green Manhattan"

42 Michael Pollan, "An odd and completely unnatural institution: why is the front lawn so beloved by Americans?" video on *Aeon*, 2017
43 Kennedy Smith, oral plenary presentation, CNU27, Savannah, GA, 2018
44 Rem Koolhaas, "My thoughts on the smart city" (an edited transcript of a talk given at the High Level Group meeting on Smart Cities, Brussels, 9/24/14), *Digital Minds for a New Europe*, European Commission, 3/11/14
45 Eran Ben-Joseph, "When a parking lot is so much more," *The New York Times*, 3/25/12
46 Katharine Shaver and Bill Turque, "Suburbs such as Montgomery County rethink transit to court millennials," *Washington Post*, 3/29/15
47 Viet Thanh Nguyen, *The Sympathizer*, Corsair, 2015
48 Alan Berger, "The suburb of the future: almost here," *The New York Times*, 9/15/17
49 Alan Berger, "The suburb of the future: almost here," *The New York Times*, 9/15/17
50 Conor K. Gately, Lucy R. Hutyra, Ian Sue Wing, "Cities, traffic, and CO_2," in Susan Hanson (ed.), *Proceedings of the National Academy of Sciences*, 3/13/15
51 Urban design studio report, University of California, Berkeley, 2014
52 David Owen, "Green Manhattan"
53 Jerry Kolo, "Lessons from cities in the United Arab Emirates for the development of large urban systems," *Iglus Quarterly*, July, 2017
54 M. Bouchard, "Transportation emerges as crucial to escaping poverty," *The New York Times*, 5/7/15
55 Ben Bolgar, "Train architects to help resolve the great crises of mass migration," *The Architects' Journal*, 7/18/17
56 Dave Merrill and Lauren Leatherby, "Here's how America uses its land," *Bloomberg*, 7/31/18
57 Richard Florida, "The urban revival is over," *The New York Times*, 9/1/17
58 Center for Advanced Urbanism, MIT, 2/11/16
59 *New Climate Economy*, World Resources Institute, 2014
60 J. Raven et al., "Urban planning and urban design," in C. Rosenzweig et al. (eds), *Climate Change and Cities: Second Assessment Report of the Urban Climate Change Research Network*, Cambridge University Press, 2018, p. 149
61 Robert Steuteville, quoting Daniel Harris in "Genuine change or lipstick on a pig?" *Public Square*, 9/22/17
62 Jeff Speck, plenary talk, CNU27, Savannah, GA, 2018
63 Yuval Noah Harari, "Nationalism in the 21st century," YouTube, 2018
64 Doug Farr, "Sustainable nation," plenary talk, CNU 25, Seattle, WA, 2017
65 "Inner-city living makes for healthier, happier people, study finds," *The Guardian*, 10/5/17
66 Leigh Gallagher, "The suburbs will die: one man's fight to fix the American dream," *Time*, 7/28/14
67 Justin Marlow, "Tax battle lines shift in cities and suburbs," *Governing*, October, 2017
68 Ellen Dunham-Jones (with June Williamson), *Retrofitting Suburbia*, John Wiley & Sons, 2008
69 Steve Gleydura, "Lands' end," *Cleveland Magazine*, 10/16/17
70 Adam Rogers, "The west is on fire: blame the housing crisis," *Science*, 7/18/17
71 Ben Geman, "Generate," *Axios*, 8/15/18
72 James Kunstler, *The Geography of Nowhere*, Touchstone, 1993; *Home from Nowhere*, Touchstone, 1996

73 Leigh Gallagher, quoting Charles Marohn in *The End of the Suburbs*, p. 60
74 Doug Kelbaugh, "City Limits," *Architecture*, 2008, p. 363
75 Daniel Trilling, "Should we build a wall around North Wales?" *London Review of Books*, 7/13/17
76 Patralekha Chatterjee, "'Migrants are agents of development', says UN migration chief William Lacey," *citiscope*, 10/20/16
77 Alison Snyder, "Faced with rising temperatures, people may seek asylum," *Axios*, 12/22/17
78 Clair Brown, *Buddhist Economics*, p. ix
79 Edward Glaeser, *Triumph of the City*, 2011, p. 70
80 Saskia Sassen, "Migration is expulsion by another name in world of foreign land deals," *The Guardian*, 5/29/13
81 "How India fails its women," *The Economist*, 7/7/18
82 Thomas Friedman, Opinion, *The New York Times*, 6/26/18
83 Jessica Benko, "How a warming planet drives human migration," *The New York Times*, 4/19/17
84 Daniel Trilling, "Should we build a wall around North Wales?"
85 Alain Hays, "'Eco-cultural' perspectives for green building design and built heritage," *Chinese Academy of Sciences*, 2017
86 Deborah Needleman, "Who will save this town?" *The New York Times Style Magazine*, 9/10/17
87 Joshua Barone, "Rem Koolhaas looks at the countryside," Arts Briefly, *The New York Times*, 11/30/17
88 "Rem Koolhaas sees the future in the countryside," The World in 2018, *The Economist*, 11/7/17
89 Steve Radelet, *The Big Surge*, Simon & Schuster, 2015
90 Ben Bolgar, "Train architects to help resolve the great crises of mass migration"
91 Ben Geman, "Generate"
92 Ai Weiwei, *Human Flow*, Amazon Studios, 2017
93 Rahul Mehrotra and Jose Mayoral, *Ephemeral Urbanism*, ListLab, 2017, p. 6
94 Ibid., p. 232
95 Morning newscast, NPR, 8/11/18
96 Patrizia Gabellini, "Urban design intentions: urbanism into the change," ROWE/ROME conference, Rome, June, 2017
97 Mike Lydon, "Should MoMA tout tactical urbanism(s) as a solution to uneven growth?" *Planetizen*, 12/20/14
98 Gregory Scruggs, "Can pop-ups pave the way to thriving public space in world's cities?" *Place*, 3/13/18
99 Robert Orr, personal email, 9/2/17
100 http://transitionus.org/our-story
101 Michael Mehaffy, "Beware of 'voodoo urbanism,'" *Livable Portland*, 6/14/17
102 Adele Peters, "This new tool tells you if you can build a house in your L.A. backyard," *Fast Company*, 3/2/18
103 David Owen, *Green Metropolis*, Riverhead Books, 2009
104 J. Kruger and A. Sifferlin, "The surprising secrets of living longer – and better," *Time*, 2/15/18
105 Stef W. Kight, "Fertility rates are falling faster in areas with higher home values," *Axios*, 7/6/18
106 Genevieve Goh, "Architecture and sustainable design," *perxeption.wordpress.com*, 3/19/17
107 Maureen Groppe, "Mayors take the lead on fighting climate change," *USA Today*, 6/2/17

108 Dean Jonathan Overpeck, 2017 Graham Lecture and Dean's Installation, University of Michigan, 11/25/17
109 Damian Carrington, "Global pollution kills 9m a year and threatens 'survival of human societies,'" *The Guardian*, 10/20/17
110 Michael Kimmelman, "Jakarta is sinking so fast, it could end up underwater," *The New York Times*, 12/21/17
111 "Study projects deaths from heat and cold for 10 U.S. metros through 2090," *Brown University News*, 7/25/17
112 Carol Christian, "Houston's high heat stress days could double by mid-century," *Houston Chronicle*, 6/10/15
113 Ibid.
114 J.S. Pal and E.A.B. Eltahir, "Future temperature in southwest Asia projected to exceed a threshold for human adaptability," *Nature: Climate Change*, 10/25/15
115 Michael Bloomberg, "City century: why municipalities are the key to fighting climate change"
116 Kim O'Connell, "Preparedness beyond the coast," *Architect*, April, 2017
117 Patrizia Gabellini, "Urban design intentions: urbanism into the change"
118 Laura Clemons, oral presentation, CNU26, Savannah, GA, 2018
119 "Federal resiliency efforts pay off six times their investment, new report finds," *E360 DIGEST* (Yale University), 1/22/18
120 J. Raven et al., "Urban planning and urban design," p. 149
121 Deane Madsen, "Evicted opens at the National Building Museum in D.C.," *Architectural Record*, May, 2018
122 Colin Allard, as quoted in Michael Bond, "The hidden ways that architecture affects how you feel," Future, *BBC*, 6/6/17, www.bbc.com/future/story/20170605-the-psychology-behind-your-citys-design
123 Colin Allard, ibid.
124 Colin Allard, ibid.
125 Ann Sussman and Justin Hollander, "Three foundational errors in architectural thinking and how to fix them," *Common/Edge*, 7/16/18
126 S. Kiegler et al., "Trends in suicide by level of urbanization, 1999–2015," *Medscape*, 4/5/17
127 "The impact of urban design on mental health and wellbeing," The Center for Urban Design and Health, May, 2016
128 Jonathan Rose, *The Well-Tempered City*, p. 231
129 Michael Bond, "The hidden ways that architecture affects how you feel"
130 "Living near a lot of trees makes you feel 7 years younger (and $10,000 richer)," *Fast Company*, 7/17/15
131 Philip Rojc, "Study: transit really does reduce obesity," *Planetizen*, 5/21/17
132 Ibid.
133 Daniel Solomon, *Cosmopolis*, The University of Michigan, 2007, p. 14
134 As quoted in *Citizen Jane: The Battle for the City*, dir. Matt Tyrnaurer, 2017
135 Benjamin Barber, *Cool Cities: Urban Sovereignty and the Fix for Climate Change*, Yale University Press, 2017, p. 8
136 Wolfgang Nowak, Foreword, in Ricky Burdett and Deyan Sudjic (eds), *The Endless City*, Phaidon Press, 2010, p. 6
137 The case has been made by Professor Chris Leinberger of the Brookings Institution and George Washington University.
138 Geoffrey West, Santa Fe Institute, "The surprising math of cities and corporations," *TED talk*, July, 2011
139 Ibid.

140 Joe Cartwright, "Breaking bad: why breaking up big cities would hurt America," *City Observatory*, 3/28/17

141 Aromar Revi, as quoted in Gregory Scruggs "Panel formation marks turning point in confusion over New Urban Agenda monitoring," *citiscope*, 4/13/17

142 *New Climate Economy*, World Resources Institute, 2014

143 Ibid.

144 "A contrarian theory about Chinese power," The Interpreter, *The New York Times*, 4/4/18

145 Diane Toomey, "Urban Darwinism: how species are evolving to survive in cities," *Yale Environment 360*, 4/5/18

146 Wolfgang Nowak, Foreword, *The Endless City*, p. 5

147 Edward Glaeser, *Triumph of the City*, p.9

148 Ryan Avent, *The Gated City* (Kindle Single), 2011

149 Jane Jacobs, *Life and Death of Great American Cities*

150 Michael Mehaffy, *On Resilient Settlement*, blog, 2/27/12

151 Michael Mehaffy, *On Resilient Settlement*, blog, 1/4/17

152 B. Plumer and N. Popovich, "95-degree days: how extreme heat could spread across the world," *The New York Times*, 6/22/17

153 Peng Zhang, "Temperature and economic growth: new evidence from total factor productivity, *SSRN*, 8/25/15

154 Clair Brown, *Buddhist Economics*, pp. 79–80

155 Ronald Brownstein, "This is the new 'giant sucking sound' you hear: it's changing the economy and disrupting politics," *CNN*, 10/24/17

156 Ibid.

157 Zach Wickter, "Too hot to fly? Climate change may take a toll on air travel," *The New York Times*, 6/20/17

158 Bertrand Russell, a letter written from Cambridge, 1915, as seen in Grantchester, UK, April, 2017

9   Time to Act

We are compelled to act on CC for many reasons. Our own survival certainly compels us, but there is also the moral imperative to protect fellow humans and other species. In the words of Danish architect Bjarke Ingels, "Sustainbility can't be like some sort of moral sacrifice or political dilemma or a philanthropical cause. It has to be a design challenge." CC is also moral movement that demands activism.[1] Ironically, the most effective way to act often is to change our fixations. "So many aspects of life depend on fossil fuels, except for music and love and education and happiness. These things, which hardly use fossil fuels, are what we must focus on."[2] It's true that these and other such positive foci and activities will tend to diminish our febrile consumption of energy and resources. Often an indirect angle is more effective and enabling than mounting an outright, frontal assault. A middle way that balances both active and passive action is often superior, as Buddhists and other spiritual traditions seek to embody and promote. We need to keep it powerfully simple and straightforward.

> After a century of urban confusion, of wrongly placed energy, of seduction by over complicated technology, it's time to clean up. To return to a spirit of *mater atrium necessitas* – necessity is the mother of invention. We need to act in order to save our cities – and us – from ourselves. To fix a century of broken with a tool that fixes.[3]

And because there's

> no crowned, vengeful Nature frowning in judgment. We have an awesome responsibility that we have to approach with humility and caution. We should preserve whatever we can, but we also have to grow up . . . Basically, it's a you-break-it-you-own-it situation, and we broke it.[4]

Before advocating specific ways forward, here's a short review of what typically motivates people to change their behavior and ultimately the status quo. A case could be made that the best, most effective and non-manipulative way to promote sustained behavior change is to provide

information about the problem and how it can be addressed. An understandable menu of reasonable steps to taking meaningful action is plainly
helpful. It needs to resonate with people on an emotional level and in
a practical way, mobilizing a *desire* to do something about it, rather
than mandating a plan. Bertrand Russell pointed out in his 1950 Nobel
Prize acceptance speech that all human activity is prompted by desire,
and points to four of them – acquisitiveness, rivalry, vanity and love of
power. The last one, power, he claims to be infinite, although the other
three also seem quite unquenchable.

There are other axes in what seems to be a limited number of basic
human drivers of behavior and its modification. Pleasure and love, fear
and anxiety, and guilt and remorse certainly figure among the leading
ones. Sometimes called carrots, sticks and hot potatoes, these three pairs
need to be briefly parsed. Pleasure includes an especially wide range of
feelings, from enjoyment and satisfaction, delight, amusement to comfort, beauty, fun, novelty and love. Fear focuses on worry about the dire
consequences of our thoughts and actions, from angst, anxiety and awe
to distress, nightmare and panic. And guilt is a complex emotion that
includes remorse, self-blame and disgrace that sometimes begets repent-
ance and reform. It has arguably been a central motivating factor in
the social construction of modern Western civilization. The Catholic,
Protestant and Jewish religions have flourished for 2,000 years or longer
by promising redemption from the guilt of sin, which they believe is an
unavoidable aspect of the human condition. In Alan Lightman's words
"being connected to something larger than ourselves, to feeling some
unseen order or truth in the world" may be the most powerful evidence
of a spiritual realm.[5]

Last, as noted in the first chapter, love is arguably the greatest human
motivator. It includes love of self, or self-interest, which most often
induces behavioral change, as opposed to self-sacrifice. We have an altruistic and a selfish gene, with a wide spectrum in between. It is important
to underscore that emotions and feelings lead to actions; facts and figures
can startle and open eyes and minds, but gut instincts more often drive
action. There are other, less dramatic emotions and feelings that also
move us to act: freedom, safety, comfort, health and both physical and
psychological security. These tend to form the wide base of Maslow's
hierarchy of needs pyramid, with the issues of social conformity, respect
and self-actualization higher on the pyramid.

And there are the perennial pocketbook issues. They seem important
to rich and poor consumers alike when it comes to their own money –
regardless of whether they are for fiscal restraint or heavy spending in
government. For a relative instance, one of the first domestic financial
issues is rising insurance rates in areas threatened by sea level rise, such as
Miami Beach. For better or worse and whether premature or timely, sudden and steep rate increases could bring on real estate panic that could

precipitate a mass sell-off.[6] The right economic policies and incentives can push and pull individuals and organizations to allow self-interest to be in the best collective interest of society and the earth.

There is no doubt in this capitalistic age of *homo economicus* that maximizing economic gain – both savings for consumers and profits for producers – is a commonplace if not universal driver. CC and UHIs will have an increasingly major economic impact, which will vary from climate to climate. In the U.S. the most grievous cost

> will come from a projected increase in heat wave deaths . . . Higher temperatures could also lead to steep increases in energy costs in parts of the country, as utilities may need to overbuild their grids to compensate for heavier air-conditioning use in hot months. Labor productivity in many regions is projected to suffer, especially for outdoor workers in sweltering summer heat. And higher sea levels along the coasts would make flooding from future hurricanes far more destructive.[7]

It will not be pretty as these changes unfold.

It's painfully obvious how great the economic impacts of CC will grow to be at the global scale over the next decades. What's harder to gauge is how the hotter temperatures will affect people on the ground.

> "No one lives at the national level – people live at the local level," says Bob Kopp, a climate scientist at Rutgers University-New Brunswick . . . "If you look at the impacts at too aggregated a scale, you miss a lot of the story" . . . In a paper published in *Science* (July, 2017), they . . . found a huge discrepancy in the effects of climate change on economic activity depending on where people live.[8]

The ten authors examined impacts in the U.S., such as heat- and cold-related deaths, the ability of people to work in the heat, crop yields, energy demand, coastal storms and crime. While some areas in the far north and parts of the Rockies, may be spared net harm – or may even benefit from modestly higher temperatures – areas in the south are especially likely to experience economic harm.

There will be a net transfer of wealth from the south to the north, and from poorer to wealthier people, which has multiple political repercussions. The Southeast U.S. could see economic losses of 25 percent or more. The losses are almost entirely driven by increases in temperature, the researchers found. Areas like northern Michigan and Maine could benefit from GDP bumps of 10 percent or more, due to fewer cold-weather deaths, lower energy costs and longer growing seasons. Despite fallout from high-profile weather events such as Hurricanes Harvey and Irma, those hardships pale in comparison to the effects of excess heat

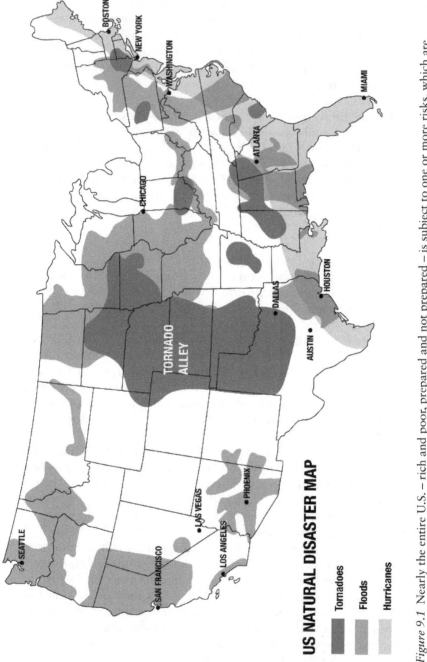

US NATURAL DISASTER MAP

- Tornadoes
- Floods
- Hurricanes

Figure 9.1 Nearly the entire U.S. – rich and poor, prepared and not prepared – is subject to one or more risks, which are increasing in frequency and intensity. Increasing scientific evidence corroborates that floods, hurricanes and tornadoes are amplified by CC (Red Cross.org, NOAA.gov; image redrawn by author)

at a national scale. One of the study's authors states "'The silent killer is the increase in temperature,' explaining that hotter temperatures will cause crops to wither, violent crime to increase, and people to die from heat exposure."[9] This dire prognosis is a vivid reminder of how game-changing extreme heat is, especially in cities.

People can feel conflicted by the push and the pull of contradictory emotional and personal economic issues. Conflicting impulses in the face of menacing information can render people indecisive or irrational, like those who ignore evacuation orders in extreme weather events. Upton Sinclair once insightfully penned "It is difficult to get a man to understand something when his salary depends on his not understanding it."[10] People can be illogical and inconsistent about pocketbook issues. The U.S. federal government estimates the combined social cost of carbon pollution from a typical household's electricity consumption is about $20 per month. A national poll found that over 40 percent of Americans were unwilling to pay an additional $1 per month in their electricity bill to combat CC, and almost 30 percent of respondents said they'd be willing to pay that much or more.[11] That response is despite the fact that 77 percent said they think CC is happening. On the other hand, in China

> an innovative analysis . . . examined how much consumers were willing to pay for cleaner air through their buying habits of air purifiers. The study's analysis suggests that residents of northern China would be willing to pay about $491 over five years to bring their air quality in line with national standards.[12]

On the personal axis, *patience* – something the fast-pace of city-dwelling can deplete – will be needed more than ever. Interpersonal conflict – resulting in mental breakdown, injury and even death – is likely to increase exponentially with CC. High urban temperatures, jacked higher by UHIs, are exacerbating the link between heat and physical strife. Terms like "hot-tempered," "hotheaded," "hot under the collar" and "hot-blooded" illustrate the general perception that there is a link between temperature and violence. Common sense tells us that the increase in temperatures will lead to more violence – interpersonal and intergroup, and even intrapersonal, with more suicides. There's evidence that even people used to living in very not climates will not necessarily have more patience with each other and themselves as ambient temperatures and/or humidity rise. Writers like Charles Mann and Steven Pinker have made a compelling case that human-on-human physical violence has fallen very dramatically. Up to 25 percent of males in hunter-gatherer and tribal societies died violently, or roughly 500 times Europe's current rate.[13] Is this long-term positive trend now jeopardized by more stifling and irritating islands and waves of extreme heat in cities?

Such change will require vast reserves of *both patience* and *compassion*. As Jonathan Rose also points out, compassion is a necessary ingredient in dealing with these human challenges. Even the most egalitarian, generous and democratic societies have underlying social, racial and economic injustices and unrest, most of which seem to be a constant in the human condition. And there's the sheer poverty of countless people on the planet, including an increasing global cohort of urban dwellers. We can't forget the mental and physical pain and suffering that accompanies the raw lack of decent housing, infrastructure, health care and services that is endemic for over a billion residents of informal settlements throughout the Global South. Indeed, "the huge scale of premature death, illness, injury and impoverishment . . . (is) much more serious . . . in most informal settlements."[14] The migrants' economic and education prospects may be better than in the rural villages they left behind, but it's an arduous life in slums. Rising temperatures make it all the more punishing, which begs more compassion, which like discord, fortunately can also be contagious.[15]

We also know there are different social and political persuasions with different reasons and modes for dealing with the threats of CC. New Urbanism co-founder Andrés Duany has classified Americans, dividing them into a half dozen CC cohorts.[16] There are the *Ethicists*, who are moralists and activists who want to proactively save the environment; the *Trendsetters*, including urban hipsters tuned into the "urban cool" factor, who will conspicuously live greener lives if it isn't too onerous; the *Opportunists*, who are pragmatic and entrepreneurial about the business investment opportunities with good paybacks; the *Survivalists*, who are "anarcho-libertarians" pessimistic enough to circle the wagons for family and friends, and even retreat to armed, survivalist compounds or floating "sea-steads" in international waters; the *Apathetics*, who are ignorant, skeptical or indifferent, but will come along if and when their climate changes too much; last, there are the *Denialists*, who simply refuse to admit there's a problem and who believe CC is bad science, a conspiracy or fabrication of scientists, even a hoax.

Nowhere is humankind's simultaneous mix of grand vision and tunnel vision more apparent than in how the U.S. is planning for a warmer world. Politically conservative skeptics and denialists have issued messages that try to perpetuate a black-and-white political debate, which doesn't exist in the scientific community. Contrary to the belief of most scientists that denial of CC is a product of scientific illiteracy, it's almost perfectly aligned with left-wing versus right-wing ideology and politics. The denialists' arguments have become so strained that even oil and coal companies have distanced themselves publicly, though some still help to finance the campaigns of politicians who espouse skepticism and denial.[17] The U.S. debate on CC is unusual in international terms. The conservative position has been anchored in denial, the liberal position has been associated with policy response, with a more radical emergent position calling for the abolition of fossil fuel usage as soon as possible. That is not the typical ideological landscape of CC debate in most countries.

> The U.S. Republican Party is the only major political party in the developed world that denies CC – and rejects all attempts at solutions – as a matter of party orthodoxy. The "do something, anything" attitude is coded as "liberal." "Keep it in the ground" is radical anywhere, but it appears unusually radical in the US.[18]

This denial flies in the face of the fact that 17 of the 18 warmest years since modern record-keeping began have occurred since 2001.[19]

It might be said that the denialists have taken the case from the Greenhouse Effect to Madhouse Effect

> "Too often, we allow contrarians in the CC debate to frame themselves as modern day Galileos railing at the scientific establishment," said Michael Mann, Professor of Atmospheric Science at Penn State University. "The indiscriminate rejection of overwhelmingly established scientific findings is not skepticism . . . It's a denial of basic science."[20]

One of Mann's pet peeves is the way the connection between climate change and extreme weather events is publicly discussed.

> "The question whether we can prove that CC caused some particular storm is the wrong question . . . The relevant question is, are the impacts of these storms being made worse by CC, are they becoming more common?" . . . He disagrees with the notion that it's a coincidence the planet's waters have become warmer at the same time we've witnessed some of the worst natural disasters on record . . . [a] "massive misinformation campaign intended to confuse both the public and policymakers about climate science . . . denial has several stages, including claiming it does not exist, that it's natural or self-correcting, or that it's possibly 'a good thing.'"[21]

This denial flies in the face of the fact that the six warmest years on record have all occurred since 2010.

Personal wealth plays an abashed role in CC beliefs and behaviors. An article published in the journal *Environment and Behaviour* finds that

> those who identify themselves as conscious consumers use more energy and carbon than those who do not. Why? Because, environmental awareness tends to be higher among wealthy people. It is not attitudes that govern our impacts on the planet, but income. The richer we are, the bigger the footprint, regardless of our good

intentions. Research by Oxfam suggests that the world's richest 1% (households with an income of $100,000 or more) produce around 175 times as much carbon as the poorest 10%.[22]

This unconscionable inequity begs radical reform.

It is true that technological advances and unprecedented wealth have raised living standards and enabled

> a new global elite to enjoy lifestyles more lavish in energy consumption and environmental impact than those enjoyed by any aristocracy in the past . . . if our current tax systems don't penalize damage to the planet and can be side-stepped by the nomadic, hybrid lifestyles unlocked by technology, one solution could be to shift from disconnected national taxation systems to a collaborative global regime, whereby individuals are charged on the basis of their personal energy footprint.[23]

Those who eat and live locally, who rarely travel on airplanes, and use recycled or multi-purpose materials would be taxed less than the high-living jetsetters lavishing their lifestyle with imported products. Equally, those whose work requires frequent travel would pass the tax bill on to their employers, compelling companies to more responsibly weigh eco-logical impacts on their ledger and bottom line.

Major aspects of the U.S. economic and political systems need to change, and to change soon. It will take a loud wakeup call, a "Pearl Harbor" or "911." All six of Duany's CC groups, with the possible exception of the proactive Ethicists, will otherwise be proverbial frogs in slow-to-boil water. As popularized by Al Gore's groundbreaking 2007 movie *An Inconvenient Truth*, it is a vivid metaphor for the numbness of humans to dangers that arise too slowly. Gore's *An Inconvenient Sequel* a decade later takes on the political quagmire that has since devel-oped around CC. It's taken the growing toll of climate disruptions and extreme weather to wake up many people. Fortunately, many Apathetics are becoming less skeptical, and more Denialists are rethinking their position, increasingly persuaded by the unfolding reality of CC.

> Signatories to the "We Are Still In" campaign to signal the inter-national world that America's state and local governments are still committed to the Paris Agreement, bear this out. Among the signers are Dallas, TX; Atlanta, GA; Charlotte, NC; Houston, TX; Little Rock, AR; Anchorage, AK; Salt Lake City, UT; and Phoenix, AZ – all red states, but with major cities standing in opposition on the issue of climate change.[24]

Some of these cities are less than 250,000 population, where most Americans live and where CC denial tends to live.

All the cohorts are subject to universal human instincts and genetic hard-wiring. They will be motivated by similar emotions to change their values and lifestyles, if in different ways and at different times. It's helpful to distinguish between experiential learning and analytically learning. Seeing daffodils bloom early because of warmer temperatures is a type of experience that is likely to have a lasting impact on a person's mindset. In contrast, the analytical learning people experience of a talking-head scientist on TV is less likely to leave an impact, because it takes more thinking and faith.[25] Skeptics and denialists that are hard to convince with facts, would no doubt respond better if their religious leaders were outspoken about addressing CC. A case in point is that people are not persuaded to embrace urbanism simply because it will lower GHG emissions. For most people that's a fringe benefit. They become convinced because it's nice to walk, to live in a neighborhood with lots of things to do, friends to see, ability to get to resources and work without being stuck in traffic. *Fostering change will take clever, effective public education, strong leadership and rapid adoption of new practices, regulations, policies, norms and values.*

As Amory Lovins and others have noted, we don't need a consensus of motives; we don't have to agree *why* we need to address this cauldron of challenges. At least for the time being, it doesn't matter whether one is mobilized by concerns about environment, health, flood insurance, national security, or by simply saving or making money, even by being cool, fashionable or opportunistic. In the global picture, the *impacts* of one's lifestyle, intentions and actions are more important than the underlying beliefs or motives, which are elusive in any case. The principle that impacts are more important than beliefs and motives applies to government policies as well. According to *The Economist*, the single biggest reduction in global GHG emissions has resulted from the Montreal Protocol, which was adopted to address the ozone problem, not CC. It has had roughly twice the impact as #2 hydropower worldwide and almost three times the impact of nuclear power. Even more ironically, the magazine's research – which they state is approximate – indicates that China's One Child Policy ranks #4, right behind nuclear power worldwide and ahead of all worldwide renewable energy use other than hydro. The positive unintended consequences of policies such as these examples are often greater than the intended ones. On the other hand, policies to manage population growth can have decisive, intended impacts:

> [I]f the world's population reached only 7.5B people by mid-century, rather than more than 9B, in 2050 we would be spewing 5B to 9B fewer tons of carbon dioxide into the air. This alone . . . would keep the global temperature from rising more than 2°C above that of the late 19th century.[26]

These policies should encourage migration to cities, as well as access to education and modern birth control, as an effective, non-coercive ways to lower birth rates.

Many potential motivators are triggered by urban challenges around the world – from air pollution, congestion and housing shortages to health problems, gentrification and infrastructure failure, not to mention the equally global phenomenon of sea level rise, extreme weather, flooding, drought, famine, etc. The particular concerns will vary from climate to climate, culture to culture and economy to economy. In metro-Detroit, a dominant environmental issue is storm water flooding, accompanied by sanitary sewer overflow, or CSOs, which are due to combined sanitary and storm water systems. But summer heatwaves may soon overtake flooding as the preeminent issue here and elsewhere. Arguably, extreme heat is a more pervasive problem than sea level rise, or hurricanes, tornadoes and the other climate extremes that threaten more limited areas more episodically. Heat waves can also persist longer than more intense extreme storms, even if they are more sporadic and less predictable.

For most urbanized places, especially those in hot and in temperate climates, rising local temperatures from UHIs are making trouble sooner than CC. Deadly heat waves kill more and more people, not just in poor and marginal areas, but in all areas of the metropolis. Indeed, the loss of air-conditioning in a Middle Eastern city during a horrendous heat wave in the summer of 2015 is reputed to have triggered civil unrest at least as intense as the geopolitical violence in this war-torn area. Generally natural disasters and climate disruptions are more devastating in the poorer Global South than in the richer Global North, because the lack of physical and institutional infrastructure makes it more vulnerable.[27] And the lack of financial resources makes recovery slower and less complete.

To briefly review some of the fundamentals that have been presented: because the cooling of our cities emphasizes quicker-term adaptation more than longer-term mitigation, it appeals to the universal human tendency for short-term thinking and prompt action in times of crisis. Concrete UHI initiatives provide a proactive sense of progress during the vagaries and uncertain unfurling of the bigger challenge of CC. Adaptation is also more local in its execution, reducing requests for permissions from higher levels of government. Much to our good fortune, the four UHI antidotes – albedo enhancement, reduction in waste heat, urban ventilation and cool microclimates – also frontally address global CC, even though the benefits take longer to manifest. Urban cooling is essential for cities to continue to thrive, retain residents and attract and accommodate new residents. It must be remembered that as metropolises in developing countries mushroom with suburbs, the result is higher consumption and carbon footprints. These outcomes aggravate CC and make *both* cities and suburbs even hotter and less healthy. Lower birthrates help offset larger per capita urban consumption in cities of the *developing* world, much as lower per capita energy consumption in cities reduces urban carbon footprints in the *developed* world.

Joe Walston of the Wildlife Conservation Society summarizes the current situation succinctly with "the four pillars" of conservation in the modern era – a stabilized human population, increasingly concentrated in urban areas, able to escape extreme poverty, and with a shared understanding of nature and the environment. He singles out the trend *toward urbanization as the biggest driver of environmental progress, bigger perhaps than all the conservation efforts undertaken by governments and environmental groups alike.* New arrivals from the countryside have better access to medical care, with decreased child mortality that in time leads to fewer children, who go on to better schooling and potentially more rewarding work lives. And physically contained urbanization retains habitat for wildlife in abandoned rural areas, as is already happening in Europe, where wolves, bears, lynx, bison and other species are re-wilding a densely populated, highly urban continent.[28]

Moving Forward

CC begs the cultivation of a sense of common cause to deal with its costly and varied impacts. Climatologists tell us we have no time to waste. Leaders of the international business sector agree: a 2016 report from the World Economic Forum stated the #1 global risk in the next ten years is the water crisis, with failing to adapt to CC and extreme weather ranked as the two next greatest risks.[29] While water does pose an immediate threat, other groups would rank CC as the top risk, in some cases by a wide margin. Cities, as should now be more evident, can play a bigger-than-expected role in addressing these problems. Two sobering quotes, the first from noted journalist Thomas Friedman and the second from Lord Nicholas Stern of the London School of Economics, underscore the global magnitude of the problem:

> [T]he chief economist of the International Energy Agency has declared that "about two-thirds of all proven reserves of oil, gas and coal will have to be left undeveloped if the world is to achieve the goal of limiting global warming at two degrees Celsius."[30] If we burn all current reserves of fossil fuels, we will emit enough CO_2 to create a prehistoric climate, with Earth's temperature elevated to levels not experienced for millions of years.[31]

As for the magnitude of the American challenge, the U.S. continues to lead major Western powers in per capita carbon emissions, emitting more than twice as much GHGs per person as France or the European Union as a whole.[32] It has cumulatively pumped more GHGs into the atmosphere than any other country, as much as China, Russia, Germany and the UK combined. Accordingly, Americans should be taking the global lead, with new, muscular public policies, taxes, incentives and codes to deal with this emergency, as well as effective national leadership. Many salutary policies already in place throughout the world need to be embraced by the U.S. government.

Although China has stepped up to a "leadership" role in implementing the Paris Agreement and has cancelled or postponed many coal-fired power plants, it is still building them at home and especially abroad.

> Chinese corporations are building or planning to build more than 700 new coal plants at home and around the world, some in countries that today burn little or no coal . . . Overall, 1,600 coal plants are planned or under construction in 62 countries . . . The new plants would expand the world's coal-fired power capacity by 43% . . . [and would] make it virtually impossible to meet the goals set in the Paris climate accord.[33]

In many countries, including the two biggest GHG emitters China and the U.S., environmental and energy regulations are often seen as contrary to economic growth.

Because coal emissions contribute so heavily to both air pollution and CC, it's worth elaborating on what's happening to curtail the use of coal globally. China has the most coal-fired power plants, with some 4,000 in operation, but it has shelved or cancelled over 2,500 new ones. India is #3 in both global GHG emissions and coal-fired plants, with roughly a quarter as many as China. It has shelved and cancelled more than twice as many as the number currently operating there. The U.S. has the second most coal plants, about 600, but had only four new plants in the pipeline as of July, 2017.[34] In my region of Michigan, two-thirds of our electricity is generated with coal, barely higher than the Chinese average. Ohio and Kentucky depend even more heavily on dirty electricity. Clearly the U.S. needs to cancel coal plants, while the fast-growing Global South needs to shelve them. The Paris COP Climate Agreement of 2015, a.k.a. Paris Accord, has little if any chance of achieving its limit of a 2°C global temperature rise if coal-fired plants aren't dramatically removed from the equation.

Also, existing coal plants can be radically improved with technically feasible but very expensive technology that captures their emissions. In late 2017, only 17 such capture projects existed around the world, according to the Carbon Capture and Sequestration Institute, which was founded in 2009 and funded by fossil fuel companies and others to more widely deploy the technology. Just *two* of those projects are capturing carbon from coal-fired plants, despite all the recent American hoopla about safely reviving coal's use. By 2017 over 15 nations announced plans to phase out coal by 2030, and that number is growing. But as long as the world's biggest coal-consuming nations – China, the U.S. and India – are not part of the initiative, its impact will be limited.[35]

It comes as no surprise that in the realm of politics, short-term thinking tends to override long-term thinking and distant needs. Roger Pielke, Jr., the University of Colorado professor who has sometimes been described as a CC skeptic, has taken some caustic jabs at decarbonizing. He calls this his ironclad law of carbon policy:

When there's a conflict between policies promoting economic growth and policies restricting CO_2, growth wins every time . . . Burning fewer fossil fuels is the most obvious way to counteract GHG and CC, and the notion has a universally virtuous appeal . . . as long as it's being done by someone else![36]

These sentiments pungently portray the human tendency to avoid difficult decisions and to push responsibility and blame onto others, making policy and laws that have real teeth all the less likely. Roy Scranton echoes these sentiments when he writes "No population on the planet today is going to willingly trade economic growth for lower carbon emissions, especially since economic power remains the key index of global status."[37]

A surprising historical footnote on CC public policy: neither UHIs nor albedo enhancement were mentioned in the Kyoto Protocol, which focused entirely on GHG mitigation. Also, there has been no international mandate or enforceable framework that builds a multi-lateral incentive to fight global CC, including the otherwise monumental Paris Accord. The U.N.'s New Urban Agenda briefly mentions UHIs but gives them no specific attention. With no UHI standards, or even common metrics, there has been no multi-lateral policy or incentive to invest in *local* urban heat management. International agreements need to include UHIs as well as CC in their calculus and their mandates if a healthy local as well as global thermal commons is to be saved.

Although it lacks mandatory targets, the Paris Accord is nonetheless a long stride forward on CC. Since then, the U.N.'s follow-up statement Mission 2020 describes its goals "'to fully decarbonize buildings and infrastructure by 2050.' As for transport, the campaign calls for zero-emissions vehicles to be 'the preferred form of all mobility in the world's major cities and transport routes.'"[38] Think how much and how fast cities and their metro areas changed to accommodate the automobile, radically altering land-use patterns and infrastructure during the twentieth century. Can humanity rally to make equally large and rapid changes in the opposite direction?

City mayors and their municipal administrations have been more attuned to action than national governments. Cities better know how to de-carbonize, and if they act collectively, they can do it on a scale that makes a difference in the global climate. We shouldn't forget that they are our most enduring civic and political bodies. In the late Benjamin Barber's words,

> Rome is much older than Italy, Istanbul older than Turkey, Boston older than the United States, Damascus older than Syria . . . Concrete and palpable, they draw their existence from their concrete, organic growth, rather than from boundaries drawn on a map; from the art of communal life rather than the science of public administration. Cities define our essential communitarian habitat in a way nation-states cannot . . . Cities are closer to us, more human in scale, more trusted by citizens.[39]

Cities often are aggressively proactive and responsive to CC and UHI issues. As former Mayor of New York City Bloomberg states, "We're the level of government closest to the majority of the world's people. While nations talk, but too often drag their heels – cities act."[40] Many American cities now have chief resilience officers, and have formally committed to 100 percent renewable energy. Six American cities run on 100 percent renewable energy as of 2017.[41] In 2016, a coterie of mayors announced the Global Covenant of Mayors for Climate and Energy. Within a year, a remarkable number of cities had signed on – about 7,500 cities representing some 675 million people – nearly 10 percent of the world's population.[42] Two years after the signing of the 2015 Paris Accord, Mayor Bloomberg and California Governor Jerry Brown upped the ante with America's Pledge, a 127-page statement that enthusiastically supports the original American pledge on climate action. As of the Bonn meeting in 2017, this network of non-federal U.S. leaders had swelled and included more than 2,300 states, tribal nations, counties, cities, businesses, non-profits, universities, and colleges. These efforts constitute a new era of American climate action.[43]

In the institutional and NGO sector, there are far too many organizations to mention. In America alone, there are numerous green codes and standards, from ASHRAE, LEED and Architecture2030 to Vision California and the Living Building Challenge. The Charter of the Congress for the New Urbanism and its 1,500 members should be credited with changing the national discourse on suburbia, specifically densifying and mixing land uses in real estate development on urban peripheries. As noted, recently its members and adherents have been focusing much more on urban infill and suburban retrofit. They have spawned parallel initiatives like Tactical Urbanism and Lean Urbanism, which focus on very modest, local problems and opportunities, while New Urbanism continues to focus on larger developments and state, national and international public policy. CNU has also begun a direct focus on CC and UHIs, working with collateral organizations in North America and internationally.

There are scores of other organizations, initiatives and programs that promote the ideas presented throughout the book. The Project for Public Spaces, an effective group similar in purpose to CNU, has promoted place making in the public realm and has an initiative similar to LeanU called Lighter, Quicker, Cheaper. Another organization is Friends of the Earth, whose Big Ideas Project was led by Mike Child, who has eloquently summarized the softer advantages of cities, especially the sharing revolution:

> A revolution that builds on the digital world of the 21st century that utilizes the ingenuity and imagination that springs from the cross-fertilization of ideas from the diversity of people living in cities; that builds empathy and understanding between people rather than fear and loathing; that leads to much greater levels of sharing of stuff and much greater resource efficiency; that takes naturally evolved cultural traditions of sharing within families and local communities, and re-invents them to enable sharing between citizens and strangers; and that fundamentally transforms the dominant world view that individualism and material possessions are central to what it is to be human.[44]

When coupled with addressing CC and overpopulation, there could hardly be a more humane and inspiring agenda for the balance of this century.

The number of organizations, institutions and NGOs dealing with CC and/or social justice is overwhelming. Paul Hawken, the author of several popular books on sustainability, set out to count the total number of organizations in the world dedicated to sustainability and social justice for his best-selling book *Blessed Unrest*. He gave up, estimating that it was between one and two million, making it what he claims to be the largest organized social movement ever! In a memorable quote, he writes

> If you look at the science that describes what is happening on the earth today and are not pessimistic, you don't have the correct data. If you meet the people in this unnamed movement and aren't optimistic, you haven't got a heart.[45]

His later book, *Drawdown*, shows the most consequential paths forward, as covered in the next section.

What Next?

Paul Hawken's *Drawdown* offers the most complete menu of how not only to address and stop climate change but also to reverse it. Reversal will require a total reduction of over one billion tons of GHGs by 2050, but even that mind-numbing number is a moving goalpost. His team developed three scenarios – Plausible, Drawdown and Optimum. The Plausible scenario is described as reasonable yet optimistic in its assumptions about a 30-year solution that would avoid and sequester enough carbon to stop its further build-up. But it would take the more stringent scenario to fully stop and reverse CC by 2050, achieving a net decrease in GHGs by 2050. The Optimum scenario might achieve reversal and a significant net reduction by 2045. Although the modeled solutions are costly – $440 per capita per year – the *net* cost is much lower. By subtracting the cost of business-as-usual, it drops the price tag to about 20 percent of the estimated $139 trillion total cost. And overall savings over the lifetimes of the investments is close to $74 billion. It's a price we can't afford *not* to pay.[46]

The 80 strategies outlined in the book are divided into the following categories: Buildings and Cites, Energy, Food, Land Use, Materials, Transport, and Women and Girls. If fully implemented, the *urban* and *architectural* strategies within Buildings and Cites, Materials, Transport and Energy can get over one-third of the way to reversing CC. In short, the built environment can play a major role in getting to zero carbon. The balance can be made up by systemic changes in the production of energy and food, which together account for over half the total GHG reductions. Family planning and educating girls account for over a tenth, much of which is associated with the migration to cities previously highlighted.[47] Indeed, the education and empowerment of females is a socio-cultural virtue of cities, and their role in reducing birth rates is an environmental benefit.

There are some unexpected findings reported in the book. Within the top ten solutions of the Plausible scenario, it might surprise you that preserving and expanding "Tropical Forests" would reduce total carbon more than all solar electric and solar thermal systems that can be reasonably deployed on the planet. If Educating Girls and Family Planning were combined, they would be at the top of the list, well ahead of the combined renewable energy sources of Wind Turbines, Solar Farms and Rooftop Solar. And if you combined Food Waste and Plant-Rich Diet, which are arguably connected, the pair would top the list. "[T]he World Bank projects, by mid-century Europeans and North Americans will produce a quarter more waste than they do today. In the same period, volumes will grow by half in East Asia, double in South Asia and triple in sub-Saharan Africa."[48] A 2017 study by NRDC found that residents in three American cities tossed away 2.5 pounds of edible food per day, and that 68 million potential meals from the cities' grocery stores, restaurants and institutions go uneaten each year.[49]

What you eat is more important than where it comes from. Eating only locally grown food for one year would save the greenhouse gas equivalent of driving 1,000 miles, but eating just one vegetarian meal a week for a year saves 160 miles more than that.[50] So, it's important to reiterate in this final chapter that addressing such diverse issues as overpopulation, food waste and diet are among the most effective things that can be done to combat CC, including all the architectural and urban strategies to cool the city. Most importantly, it will require *all* 80 strategies to sufficiently negate and reverse all the impacts of CC.[51]

In general, the Plausible Scenario opts for cautious assumptions about costs and emissions savings. The economic modeling of costs is conservative and barely bakes in historic trends of falling prices for many items, some of which will surely get cheaper in the future, some radically so. For instance, the 50 percent drop in battery costs between 2015 and 2017 suggests an ongoing trend.[52] Other promising techniques were not included, such as converting ambient CO_2 into nano-fibers at a lower than current cost in medical and other technological applications. The important "rebound effect" of cost reductions proved too hard to predict to be factored in, although the book's website (www.drawdown.org) addresses this elusive economic aspect of human behavior. No carbon cap-and-trade policies were assumed, nor any radical new technologies, some of which are sure to come. And the future capacity of oceans, trees and soils as carbon sinks are treated as an unknown, despite recent evidence that suggests that these giant natural sponges may be depleting faster than expected. Even with stabilizing and likely peaking global carbon emissions, the ppm of carbon in the atmosphere continues to climb to new historic highs.[53]

There are also surprise findings on economic payback, or return on investment. These savings are important to know in advance to prevent going bankrupt before the many solutions are exhausted. The solution with the highest economic payback, as opposed to total GHG drawdown potential, is Solar Farms, at $80 billion per year with lifetime savings of $5 trillion. Nuclear is also cost effective, with lifetime savings of about $1.7 trillion, which represents almost a 2,000-fold return by 2050! And it has a total drawdown potential of 16 gigatons of CO_2E, which squeaks it into the top 20 solutions. LED domestic and commercial lighting are very cost effective, with extremely high savings. Solar water heaters could return their capital investment over 250-fold by 2050. Other solutions with good paybacks are Geothermal, Bike Infrastructure, Conservation Agriculture (no-till or low-till) and Smart Thermostats. Many of these solutions fall within the topics covered in this book.

As perfunctory as "Refrigerant Management" sounds, it's ranked #1, with the drawdown potential of almost 90 gigatons. Although the 1987 Montreal Protocol successfully banned chlorofluorocarbons (CFCs) to close the ozone holes, their replacement was hydrofluorocarbons (HFCs), which represent only a small part of GHG emissions but have 1,000 times as much greenhouse effect as CO_2. Impressively, 170 nations adopted the Kigali amendment, which has specific timetables and targets to replace HFCs with cleaner alternatives. The 2016 agreement also has trade penalties to punish non-compliers, and an arrangement for rich countries to help poor countries fulfill their commitments. This is precisely the binding type of international agreement that is needed on CC.

One category that Hawken does not utilize is urban albedo, which the IPCC estimates would offset 44 gigatons of CO_2 emissions,[54] earning 8th place in the rankings. In fact, if there is one fault in the team's exhaustive study, it would be that their categories underplay the role of urbanism in drawing down carbon from the atmosphere. As pointed out in the last chapter, sprawling urbanism may account for about 30 percent of all GHGs. In Hawken's home state of California, Governor Brown championed the passage of the strictest emission laws of any state. But expensive urban housing is forcing more residents to sprawl further out in search of affordable housing. Transportation accounts for more GHG emissions than any other sector in California, almost 40 percent, compared with 27 percent nationwide.[55] Add in the emissions from heating, cooling and lighting suburban homes, as well as their embodied, construction and maintenance energy, and the percentage goes even higher. Other metro regions in heavily suburbanized states are not far behind, underscoring that detached single family houses should no longer be indirectly and directly subsidized by government programs and policies.

Political and environmental leaders have long backed renewable energy, often too quick to ignore or dismiss technologies that economic modeling shows will be necessary to combat CC. This oversight includes carbon capture – or better yet carbon reuse – from power plants and industrial facilities, and nuclear power. Nuclear energy is essentially carbon-free, if fraught with more immediately lethal substances. But it is essential, as most experts agree that renewables can't answer all our electricity needs in the foreseeable future. Because it would take building 12,000 new nuclear power plants over the next 35 years – one coming on line just about every day – to keep CO_2 below 450 ppm,[56] it obviously needs to be part of a more comprehensive strategy. But to remove nuclear from the table, as has more or less happened since the Three Mile Island, Chernobyl and Fukushima disasters, is short-sighted if not irresponsible, especially with recent safety improvements.

What Next, More Literally?

Two major thrusts – convincingly framed and vigorously promoted around the world – are urgently needed to act on the issues that have been raised in this book.

1   More research is required to fill significant gaps in knowledge about cooling cities. For instance, the spatial extent and morphology of urban areas remain relatively simplistic in contemporary modeling approaches. Waste heat resulting from energy use in building heating,

ventilation and air-conditioning systems is also crudely accounted for in current data. These examples highlight the importance of cooperation between planners, urban designers, architects, engineers and climatologists. Another important research topic is how to deal with the potential doubling of global cities' physical footprints within the next 15 years. This expansion shouldn't be ignored because it offers a very significant opportunity for mitigating future CC at the global scale. Another need is refining urban climate modeling to improve its ability to examine the adaptive capacity of "what-if" growth scenarios and strategies to inform the planning and design process prior to development and construction.

There are examples of progress in current abilities to predict the performance of new development or redevelopment in a timely manner. Hong Kong's Planning Department has an Urban Climatic Map System, including advice on building density, site coverage, building height, building permeability, and greening. It allows policy advisors and physical designers and planners to balance various needs and requirements before making their final decisions. Proper urban design and planning are critical, because once built, a city's overall layout and morphology are relatively fixed and difficult to change. With existing urban fabric, the immediate emphasis should focus on lightening surface colors and using appropriate construction materials. Where change is possible, design goals should seek to ensure access to the sun for solar electric and solar thermal, and provide shade, wind protection and ventilation by breezes. Urban areas not yet built, such as the many new cities in developing countries, have the advantage of being able to incorporate these strategies in advance of their construction.

2   The major sectors of society – government, commerce, religion, the academy, the military, charitable/not-for-profit/NGOs and the media – need to cooperate to develop more vigorous and better integrated CC and UHI strategies, policies and practices. This mandate should take front-row priority at all levels of government. What most cities need is a coherent climate plan, which addresses interrelated environmental issues including flooding and air quality, as well as surface and air temperatures. It should permeate the culture and practice of the architecture, urban design, urban planning and engineering professions. While the public sector incentivizes and codifies this kind of urbanism, the not-for-profit sector and the private sector must also aggressively pursue sustainable, resilient design and development. It will take concerted action by these three parties, as well as bottom-up citizen participation and initiative. It may be easier to galvanize all the parties if the emphasis is on adaptation, as it is less about the cause of or blame for CC, and more about concrete steps that address its impacts and yield a satisfying sense of progress and

accomplishment. And new terminology can help: "climate-proofing" implies that CC, flooding and other environmental risks are primarily technical problems, with straightforward solutions that avoid political controversy.

The urban planning, architecture, landscape architecture and civil engineering professions must also redouble their efforts, reforming their university and continuing education, as well as growing their numbers. This group, along with real estate developers, is critically important because decisions on urban form have long-term consequences – more than 50 years. We need more urban designers and planners, because "although cities are developing at a rapid pace, the number of people that are involved in city planning is very small."[57] This is especially true in the fast-growing cities of the developing world, which are too often unplanned, under-planned or poorly planned. In 2013, there were only 194 registered urban planners in Nairobi, which is less than half a planner per 100,000 people.[58] In the UK, there were almost 38 planners per 100,000 people. Guest professionals hired by developing countries are not always sufficiently knowledgeable about the local culture to understand the multiple, contested concepts of local adaptation and resilience. For instance, these professions have come to recognize the errors of mid-century freeway construction, urban renewal and suburban sprawl, and have accepted that they were to a large extent responsible. Now they need to avoid similar shortcomings in climate mitigation and adaptation, especially in the rapidly developing Global South.

Mitigation strategies that simultaneously yield adaptive benefits should be prioritized.

> Consideration needs to be given to how regional decisions may affect neighborhoods or individual parcels and vice versa, and tools are needed that assess conditions in the urban environment at city block or neighborhood scale. There is a growing consensus around integrating urban planning and urban design, climate science, and policy to bring about desirable microclimates within compact, pedestrian-friendly built environments that address both mitigation and adaptation . . . [and] reach across physical scales, jurisdictions, and electoral timeframes. These activities need to deliver a higher quality of life for urban citizens as the key performance outcome, as well as climate change benefits.[59]

Fortunately, powerful new tools are emerging for planning and design professionals. Calthorpe Analytics' "Urban Footprint" is the most advanced computer software that makes clear to officials and citizens the future implications of urban planning and design decisions. It is fast, accessible and precise in presenting and comparing the impacts for a menu of various scenarios for future development. It draws on immense data at all scales, from individual land parcel and household census data for the entire U.S. to multiple metrics for all its regions. Other game-changing applications include similar analysis of proposed changes in agricultural and wilderness areas. The program's analytics and graphics can help local communities and their officials – as well as not-for-profits, foundations and community organizations – build consensus.[60]

Jeffrey Raven and his co-authors succinctly conclude their chapter in *Climate Change and Cities* with a cogent summary of the strategies and paradoxes presented in previous chapters:

> Cities shaped by integrated mitigation and adaptation principles can reduce energy consumption in the built environment, strengthen community adaptability to CC, and enhance the quality of the public realm. Through energy-efficient planning and urban design, compact morphology can work synergistically with high-performance construction and landscape configuration to create interconnected, protective, and attractive microclimates. The long-term benefits are also significant, ranging from economic savings and risk reduction through reduced energy consumption to the improved ability of communities to thrive despite climate-related impacts. And a community's capacity to cope with adversity, adapt to future challenges, and transform in anticipation of future crises yields wider social resilience with particularly positive benefits for poor and marginalized.[61]

Reducing the global birth rate is a positive trend, because the 2018 total world population required over 1.7 earths to support the consumption of resources and to absorb the waste of some 7.6 billion human beings. As individual carbon, resource and pollution footprints are reduced, global population needs to also diminish. And it's becoming more obvious that the enlarging footprints of people in the fast-growing developing world, on top of the already large footprints in the developed world, are seriously and irreversibly disrupting our global climate. This threat means that extreme population is as serious as extreme heat, and that urbanization is, ironically, a way to reduce it.

The other non-climatic virtue of cities is their sponsorship of multiple economic, social, cultural and other benefits. They are the incubators of ingenuity, the purveyors of productivity, the engines of efficiency, the arena of the arts, communities of culture, and the social condensers and blenders of our many personal and collective differences. To the extent its citizens want it, the city provides public stimulation, exchange and excitement, as well as private shelter, sanctuary and retreat. The full transect of work, retail, recreation, institution and religion is expressed and somehow sorted out. The rich mashup is sometimes seamlessly pleasurable and other times painfully awkward. In any case, the city is continuously trying to resolve its facts and fictions – the miraculous urban ballet that Jane Jacobs championed and the complex physical artifact that she loved. It is human culture made manifest and its history made live.

A city is a face-to-face cauldron, which used to be called a "melting pot" in America. "Salad bowl" seems to better describe the diverse cultures that cities now tend to accommodate rather than merge or integrate with earlier immigrants. Cities have lifted billions of people out of poverty over the centuries. They offer opportunity and freedom. However, they *do* tend to encourage commercial consumption, even as they increase transportation and heating efficiencies. It's ironic that one of our greatest successes – bringing so many people out of poverty – now presents an equally big challenge: how to keep these people satisfied as their consumption appetites inevitably rise along with their incomes. Along with achieving prosperity without growth, it's perhaps society's greatest socio-economic-political conundrum.

Scientists tend to agree that we will reach dangerous tipping points in the planet's climate sometime between 2050 and 2100, unless there's a *quick* and *dramatic* decrease in GHG emissions. CC has not a single tipping point but multiple ones – such as the melting of the Greenland ice sheet, the thawing of the tundra or the collapse of a major ecosystem or a biome. The accumulation of tipping points could be totally devastating to homo sapiens. As Hawken's 80 strategies indicate, it will take very muscular efforts to get to zero carbon emissions and to take carbon out of the atmosphere. More experts are beginning to feel their climate models are under-estimating the speed of CC. A temperature bump of 2°C (3.6°F) will be reached much sooner than predicted according to a report authored by seven leading climate scientists, including Sir Robert Watson, the former chair of the Intergovernmental Panel on Climate Change. *The Truth about Climate Change* report states, "The 1.5°C target could be reached by the early 2030s and the 2°C target by 2050."[62] These estimates and predictions are sure to change over time, for better or worse, but it's clear that big changes are in store sooner than once expected. Indeed, a Fall 2018 report from the Intergovernmental Panel on Climate Change, compiled by hundreds of scientists from around the world, warns that

> dangers are no longer remote or hypothetical. Nations have delayed curbing their greenhouse gas emissions for so long that warming of 1.5°C (2.7°F) is now all but inevitable. At current rates of warming, the world will likely cross the 1.5°C threshold between 2030 and 2052, well within the lifetime of most adults and children alive today.[63]

Pope Francis's encyclical *Laudato Si': On Care for Our Common Home* on climate justice is beautifully crafted: "climate change and justice go hand in hand and . . . the stewards of God's bounty have misread a bounteous earth as an invitation to excess."[64] He gets more concrete and exacting:

> The warming caused by huge consumption on the part of some rich countries has repercussions on the poorest areas of the world, especially Africa, where a rise in temperature, together with drought, has proved devastating for farming . . . By itself, the market cannot guarantee integral human development and social inclusion.[65]

The pope's questioning of the ability of market capitalism to fully address CC raises a timely and profound issue. Avoiding the pervasive damage, a 2018 report by the IPCC asserts, "requires transforming the world economy at a speed and scale that has 'no documented historic precedent.'"[66]

The Mother of All Challenges

Could the case for CC be false or overstated? Are its magnitude and speed being exaggerated? The short answer is No. If anyone studies the science, they will find that it is exceedingly unlikely that CC's basic physical explanation, recent trends and grave impacts are false. The evidence clearly supports that humans *are* powerful enough to cause CC, or at the very least speed up and amplify it. Because it's intangible and complicated, CC is an easy target for our era of fake news. But no political movement, no army or navy can back up fictional narratives about CC. There are deeper, more essential questions to ask: Are we too successful for our own good? Humanity has sufficient science to predict our potential end, but do we have the imagination, willpower and means to avoid it? No species has ever had to predict and plan its existential future so far in advance. It's both a privilege and an anxiety-ridden burden. Are we up to it?

In a high-rise in Malaysia's capital in 1999, a group of scientists "convened to designate '100 of the World's Worst Invasive Alien Species' . . . Every single person in the room agreed, humans are the worst invasive species."[67] Do humans need to accelerate their evolution – for their sake and the sake of the earth? Arguably, it is already happening: Alan Lightman writes that the homo sapiens species is already transitioning to homo techno: "We are modifying our evolution by our own hand. We are remaking ourselves . . . part animate, part inanimate, hybrid of living animal and machine."[68] He goes on to point out that life expectancy for Americans has increased from 47 to 79 years since 1900, primarily because of improved medicine to fight deadly diseases. Perhaps this remarkable progress suggests that refocusing and redoubling efforts to achieve comparable success is possible in the war against CC.

Nothing in the last 800,000 years compares to what we are confronting today. It is a shattering of an eon-measured rhythm, accelerating into an unprecedented challenge. Our species has never faced a crisis as pervasively disastrous as CC, and with so little time to address it. This is a challenge that is possible to overcome, but it isn't going to be easy. Humans have bet the bank on endless resources and new ones to replace the ones that become exhausted; perpetual economic growth; extreme urban growth in the developing world; and faith in seemingly inevitable technological solutions. All sails have been set for a following wind. But the downwind course is getting turbulent, as the weather shifts into a strong headwind. Global CC is caused by a tiny change in the chemistry of the planet's upper atmosphere. It is more fundamental and lasting than the changing weather patterns in the lower atmospheric layer, as violent as they can be.

Any way you massage or slice the current challenges and opportunities, major changes in our civilization are needed. And they are needed *as soon as possible.* As Michael Oppenheimer, a climate scientist at Princeton University, who testitified with James Hansen in 1988, warns: "The clock has run out in terms of avoiding damaging changes – they have already begun. At this point, we are into damage control."[69] Even though the International Energy Agency estimates that global energy needs will increase more slowly than in the past, they will still grow by 30 percent between 2017 and 2040. It argues for a very aggressive agenda as

> low-carbon sources double their share in the energy mix to 40% in 2040, all avenues to improve efficiency are pursued, coal demand goes into an immediate decline and oil consumption peaks soon thereafter. Power generation is all but decarbonised, relying by 2040 on generation from renewables (over 60%), nuclear power (15%) as well as a contribution from carbon capture and storage (6%) – a technology that plays an equally significant role in cutting emissions from the industry sector. Electric cars move into the mainstream quickly, but decarbonising the transport sector also requires much more stringent efficiency measures across the board, notably for road freight . . . Renewables and efficiency are the key mechanisms to drive forward the low-carbon transition.[70]

The planet no longer affords the luxury of making mega-mistakes. Humans, pressed together as they are by globalization and the traditional search for security and opportunity, have no choice but to better learn how to live with increasing diversity and density. The arithmetic of the growth and mixing of our species is obvious. The stakes have never been higher. So, a critical question is whether an economic, social and political shift of this type and of this magnitude ever happened before in human history? In her provocative book *This Changes Everything: Capitalism vs. The Climate,*

Naomi Klein directly takes on this urgent question. She relates how several historians and commentators have suggested that the abolition of slavery was of a similar magnitude. The economic dependence in the U.S. on slave labor was comparable to the modern global economy's reliance on fossil fuels. Moreover, the loss to slave owners was "a stunning $10 trillion . . . roughly similar to the value of the carbon reserves that must be left in the ground worldwide if we are to have a good chance of keeping warming below two degrees Celsius."[71]

Klein explains that the analogy is not perfect, or morally equivalent. There were unjust economic extortions and reverse reparations to slave owners, plus the profitability of the rising industrial economy to cushion the financial blow to slave owners. There is much less of a consolation prize for the oil, gas and coal industries, as decentralized solar and wind will supply neither the concentrated energy nor the high profits to which the fossil fuel corporations are all too accustomed.

> In other words, the economic costs to our elites will be real – not only because of the carbon left in the ground, but also because of the regulations, taxes and social programs needed to make the required transformation. Indeed, these new demands on the ultra-rich could effectively bring the era of the footloose Davos oligarchs to a close.[72]

Accordingly, Klein goes on to assert with Jane Jacobs directness that

> any attempt to rise to the challenge will be fruitless unless it is understood as part of a much broader battle of world views, a process of rebuilding and reinventing the very idea of the collective, the commons, the civil and the civic after so many decades of attack and neglect . . . Because the hot and stormy future we have already made inevitable through our past emissions, an unshakeable belief in the equal rights of all people and a capacity for deep compassion will be the only thing standing between civilization and barbarism.[73]

What is needed, she concludes, is nothing less than an alternative world view and set of policies to replace the one that underlies the very heartbeat of the current ecological and climate crisis – one that replaces hyper-individualism and hyper-competition with interdependence and cooperation.

In *Learning to Die in the Anthropocene*, Roy Scranton hurls much harsher criticism at our existing "carbon-fueled capitalism and its promises of infinite economic growth,"[74] and its voracious commodification and assimilation of everything that has quantifiable value. He unabashedly points out that capitalism needs to produce profit in order to attract investors, and that profit requires growth. Others might argue that increases in efficiency play the same role as growth. In any case, economic stability requires some kind of cheap, efficient energy that fossil fuels have amply provided civilization since the Industrial Revolution fired up its first furnaces He points out five reasons that switching from oil and gas to non-fossil fuels will be

> much more difficult than is commonly realized: the scale of the shift; lower energy-intensity of replacement fuels; substantially lower power density of the renewable energy extractions; intermittence of renewable flows; and uneven distribution of renewable energy sources. It would take decades to develop and implement new systems of carbon-free or carbon-minimal infrastructure, if it's even possible, and we don't have decades.[75]

His sobering but inspirational little book goes on to suggest ways to calmly deal with the inevitability of CC. It's sanguine about geoengineering, because it sets up the planet for sudden runaway global warming if it were to be discontinued. He describes global warning as a "wicked problem," that is, one that doesn't offer clear answers, only better and less bad responses. It can't be solved by one country or by a single continent, which means the whole world has to work together, which is entirely unprecedented. It could be argued that an extra-terrestrial threat might provoke such planetary unity, and in fact CC *is* such a threat – from a sun 93 million miles away. The irony that Scranton painfully points out is that carbon powers the world's political and economic systems, and indirectly but assuredly, configures the collective consciousness of human civilization.

> It's coal and oil we have to thank for connecting the many nations of the world into one tight, integrated economy. Without the information, energy and transportation infrastructures built and sustained with carbon, there wouldn't be any global civilization to try to save.[76]

Stewart Brand and his cohorts take a more middling position in the *EcoModernist Manifesto*. This statement emphasizes the decoupling of human production and consumption from nature, i.e., satisfying our needs with as little imposition as possible on and interference with natural systems and ecologies. With increased efficiency in all aspects of civilization and with energy systems that rely on solar, wind, geothermal, nuclear fission and fusion, humans can separate and withdraw into a more self-contained world. It's less about Klein's and Scranton's social and economic transformation, even scuttling, of capitalism, and more about technological salvation. It is more sanguine about reforming rather than rejecting the current economic system. The ending quote of the manifesto is an inspiring way to sum up much of this book: "We value the liberal principles of democracy, tolerance, and pluralism in themselves, even as we affirm them as keys to achieving a great Anthropocene."[77]

Some random, excruciating observations about humanity's current state of affairs: Something is basically afoul in a civilization where every 90 seconds a young child dies from lack of access to drinkable water and sanitation. It's even more painful when you realize that Americans use about 50 billion plastic water bottles and that all humans collectively spend $60 billion each year on bottled water – over $100,000 per minute![78] That expenditure is estimated to be over 25 times greater than the annual sum needed to bring clean water to the planet's population that currently lacks it. Another distressing observation: Worldwide nearly 13 million tons of plastic are dumped into the ocean each year, and at the current pace there could be more plastic than fish in the oceans by 2050.[79] While fertilizer run-off can cause 16–60 times more damage than plastic litter, up to US$800 per year.[80] Even more odious is our world economy: The two men at the top of an inhumanely steep economic pyramid had a 2017 annual income equal to the entire bottom half of humanity. In the U.S. the bottom half has captured only 3 percent of total economic growth since 1980.[81] Since then the average income before taxes of the top 1 percent of Americans has increased more than threefold, while the top hundredth of the top 1 percent has risen more than sevenfold.[82]

If any government charged a blue-ribbon task force to design a permanent colony on another planet, they would not in their wildest imagination, much less in any scenario planning, consider setting up such an obscenely unequal society. It's also unthinkable they would plan a society unable to provide clean, potable water to everyone. Water, it is worth remembering, is more than a natural *resource* – it's a *source* of nature and of life itself. Nor would islands of plastic be gathering in the oceans. And CEO salaries wouldn't be hundreds if not thousands of times higher than the corporation's lowest-paid worker, especially when that differential was a fifth or even a tenth of that just a generation ago.[83] It's not hard to list other examples of the world's staggering socio-economic dislocations and inequities that would be unspeakable, even unthinkable, in any such plan for a new colony or society. The task force would be condemned for its heartless, mindless thinking and short horizon.

We are stuck with an inequitable global civilization that is facing a challenge that is far more threatening to our survival than widespread poverty. CC is a global problem that individual countries cannot arrest and reverse by themselves. Only by everyone working together can the international community address it. The historian-cum-futurist Harari raises the stakes: he questions whether the nation-state can rise above the fundamental purpose of coalescing and defending its territory to collaborate on a global challenge of this magnitude. He goes on to say that allegiance to one's country is fine, but only if citizens realize their country is unique but not supreme, as is loyalty to family, profession and community.[84] *There must be allegiance to the planet.* A better system of worldwide loyalty, cooperation and problem-solving is needed, one that has yet to emerge.

While Naomi Klein's argument, Roy Scranton's critique and Stewart Brand's manifesto may seem hyperbolic, in the longer run their positions do not over-dramatize the situation. Our challenge is every bit that colossal. The good news is that the means are both mutually reinforcing and at hand – extremely daunting yes, but not impossible. We are fortunate that so many issues align. As Gwynne Dwyer has wisely written,

> [H]ere is the little miracle that shows we still have more than our share of good luck: at exactly the same time when it became clear that we have to stop burning fossil fuels, a wide variety of other technologies for generating energy became available. We are truly blessed.[85]

Resource depletion, ecological destruction, toxic emissions, habitat-loss, sprawl, etc. are more or less tackled the same way as CC and UHIs – by building good urbanism, producing clean energy, stewarding the environment and minding the community. We will not be excused by future generations for not taking advantage of this confluence of good luck at the moment of our greatest challenge. If we come up short, we will not be blameless, as future generations will curse and lament.

Our children and their children have reason to be worried, even depressed and angry. There's a new field – eco-psychology – that has emerged to deal with this understandable condition. Recent developments in the international geopolitics of addressing CC are not encouraging. Although the Paris Accord was a giant step forward, it no longer appears to be the long stride that is so needed. Even if we think countries will live up to their Paris pledges, many, if not most scientists think it will fall short of its goal There's mounting evidence that we are headed for a 3°C rise, both because countries are likely to be lax on follow-through and the commitments may not have been sufficient in the first place. And, as Al Gore pointed out in his second movie, there's little chance of holding warming to 2°C unless we come up with "negative emissions" technologies and policies that allow us to actively and widely withdraw CO_2 from the atmosphere. A colleague Bruce Donnelly thinks that we need get a handle on two things: new energy technology, including fusion, and sequestering and extracting massive amounts of CO_2.

If a 3°C rise is in store for the earth, the repercussions from sea level rise alone are very daunting. Recent predictions are for roughly 3 feet of sea level rise this century, but new assessments of the disintegration of glaciers, and more data from deep in the Earth's past, have convinced many scientists that we could be looking at double or triple that . . . Which may take what would have been a major problem and turn it into a largely insoluble new reality.[86]

To belabor this one impact of CC:

Many experts believe that even if emissions stopped tomorrow, 15 or 20 feet of sea level rise is already inevitable, enough to flood many cities unless trillions of dollars are spent protecting them. How long it will take is unclear. But if emissions continue apace, the ultimate rise could be 80 or 100 feet.[87]

Other devastating impacts – on everything from agriculture in Alabama to zoology in Zanzibar – are easy to imagine. We're in a war that nature, as always, will win. More literally, we are now at war with the sun, as atmospheric gases trap too much of its otherwise beneficent gift to the planet, reminding us that there is no room for complacency. And yet, after a three-year plateau, global emissions were up 2 percent in 2017.

It should not be forgotten that meeting the Paris Accord goal of "zero emissions by 2050" doesn't result in quick drawdown of the current high ppm of GHGs. The atmospheric pool stops *filling* if and when we turn the hose off, but then we need to *drain* the pool. We should also remember the global 2°C temperature target masks a lot of regional variation: land warms faster than oceans, high-latitude areas faster than the tropics, and inland areas faster than coastal regions. And the global population is concentrated in specific regions of the planet, increasingly in cities. In the worst-case scenario of continued growth in emissions, about 44 percent of the population will experience warming over 9°F (5°C), and 7 percent to about 11°F (6°C) – in 2100. These temperature increases pose grave health risks, on top of very widespread discomfort.

To untangle the climatic hairball, there is a stark choice: either act now, right-size our economy and lives, and manage the transition in a carefully aggressive way – or CC will do it for us. If we slouch into the latter option it will be unimaginably destructive and chaotic. We can't afford to be the least bit naive or sluggish even for a decade; climate has more momentum and a longer tail that most other societal problems. We can't recover from several years of inaction and lapsed policy on CC mitigation as easily as we can from ignoring crime, corruption, waste and other social problems.

What definitely won't suffice is a climate strategy built out of wishful thinking, the proposition that countries can be cajoled and prodded into increasing their ambition to cut emissions further, and that laggards can be named and shamed into falling into line . . . There is no momentum for investing in carbon capture and storage, since it could be seen as condoning the continued use of fossil fuels. Nuclear energy, the only source of low-carbon power ever deployed at the needed scale, is also anathema. Geoengineering, like pumping aerosols into the atmosphere to reflect the sun's heat back into space, is another taboo. But eventually, these options will most likely be on the table, as the consequences of CC come more sharply into focus.[88]

To end on more positive notes: There are sure to be unexpected techno-breakthroughs, as there always have been and always will be. In fact, the science and technology is accelerating. Many of the favorable facts and promising predictions presented in the previous pages can be placed into seven promising trends that offer hope. One of them, surprisingly, concerns food. Because of the methane production associated with the belching and manure of cattle, new plant-based products, mimicking meat and dairy items, are coming out monthly. Major investors like Bill Gates, Tyson, Danone and Nestlé, are putting forward major funds. The most advanced megatrend is renewable energy. The prices of solar panels and wind turbines have plunged by 90 percent in the last decade, and are still falling, triggering exponential growth in renewables. The third bright spot has to do with the filthiest of the fossil fuels: coal. It appears to have peaked in 2013, with many cancelled power plants and many fewer planned. In parts of the country, wind and solar now offer the cheapest power available, even counting coal, which was long seen as unbeatable.[89] And as these renewable systems become cheaper, there's another tipping point: electric vehicles, with China leading the way and virtually every major carmaker in the world following suit. If current trends continue, it's estimated that most new cars will be electric by 2030. Batteries – the fifth big trend – crushed prices by 60 percent between 2011 and 2017, and promise to drop markedly by 2030. A smaller but interesting positive note is that between 2009 and 2015 "the number of biogas plants in the EU grew from 6,000 to 17,700 – heating houses with old banana skins and uneaten porridge."[90]

As pointed out in the 7 Principles of Energy Efficient Buildings in Chapter 3, defensive strategies are the sixth of the seven CC and UHI antidotes. These include unsexy things like better building insulation and more efficient heating and cooling equipment, with higher standards for household appliances particularly helpful. The seventh and last major trend addresses what might be the biggest negative megatrend – literally failing to see the forest for the trees. The destruction of forests around the world for ranching and farming accounts for 10 percent of global carbon emissions, and annual tree losses have roughly doubled since 2000. Urban areas lose an estimated 36 million trees annually, according to a study from the U.S. Forest Service. Tree cover in urban areas has declined at a rate of around 175,000 acres per year, while impervious cover – such as roads and buildings – has grown by an estimated 40 percent, often in areas where trees used to grow.[91]

Slowing deforestation and restoring damaged forests could deliver a quarter or more of the carbon reductions needed by 2030 to avert dangerous CC.[92] Offering carbon offsets can prevent the vast deforestation of tropical rainforests such as in the Amazon basin. As inexpensive as it is to plant trees, reforestation can be one of the least costly and fastest ways to cut emissions. Yet according to experts, funding to replant trees is less than 1 percent of the money spent on the commodities that drive deforestation – palm oil, soy, beef and timber. The good news, they say, is that proper land management could deliver up to a third of the carbon cuts the planet needs. In the past two decades, tree-planting in China, India and South Korea has removed three times the annual emissions of the entire European Union. Although the reforestation is often driven by fears of flooding, CC is increasingly seen as the crucial factor.[93]

Will these trends be in the "too-little-too-late" category, or will they accelerate to keep us from the more worrisome tipping points that lay in our current trajectory? Some say we need not only to aggressively pursue renewable energy and more sustainable cities and towns, but also must close down the fossil fuel industry. As Lord Stern opines, "the two key words are 'start' and 'might' . . . There is no long-run high-carbon growth story, because it creates an environment so hostile that it turns development backwards."[94] The stakes no longer allow incrementalism. Transformation is needed, as in change that is *radical*, in the true sense of the word – going to the roots.

No one wants a hotter, more stressed planet, but everyone wants the modern lifestyle that cheap energy has enabled. To switch to carbon neutrality, much less to carbon capture, is expensive, very expensive. Progress is complicated by the extreme social diversity and inequality, which means there is no one-size-fits-all strategy or single optimal solution. Scientific input is essential, but there are always disagreements about which scientists to trust. We need to come together over

> opportunities for collective betterment . . . In the end, it is people, and their institutions – not science – that will decide our future . . . we must focus on strategies for working more effectively across all of our diverse and unequal social worlds . . . Collectively, we have the potential to create a much better planet than the one we are creating now.[95]

Somehow we need to balance limits and hope, while providing a realistic but diligent sense of progress without technological hubris and false optimism. We must be industrious and dogged in the specific ways outlined in this book and others of similar message.

296 Time to Act

Let us close with two powerful quotations, the first from a favorite book, *A Short History of Progress*, by the Canadian historian Ronald Wright:

> The vessel we are now aboard is not merely the biggest of all time; it is the only one left. The future of everything we have accomplished . . . will depend on the wisdom of our actions over the next few years. Like all creatures, humans have made their way in the world so far by *trial and error*; unlike other creatures, we have a presence so colossal that error is a luxury we can no longer afford. The world has grown too small to forgive us any big mistakes.[96]

The second quote is from Bill McKibben, a strong and articulate international voice on CC:

> We're used to metaphors: the war on drugs, the war on poverty. But in the case of carbon and methane — without malice but also without mercy – we are waging a war on the civilization that emitted them . . . we've lost huge swaths of the world's coral; vast sheets of ice disappear daily. Our adversary is taking territory. It's high time we stop these killers, even take back lost ground.[97]

We must humbly acknowledge, as mentioned in Chapter 2, that more carbon has been released since Dr. Hansen's congressional hearing in 1988 than had been released in the entire history of civilization prior to his astonishing but unheeded testimony. As unintentional and perhaps overstated as this acceleration may have been, we have no choice but to arrest and reverse it as soon as possible.

Whether it's Klein's post-capitalist society, Brand's *EcoModernist Manifesto*, Rifkin's 3rd Industrial Revolution, Glaeser's triumphant city, Brown's Buddhist economy, Mann's moral progress, Barber's cool cities, Hawken's drawdown, or Scranton's Anthropocene, a sustainable economy must be something more than the sum of its carbon-neutral parts. Its goal is to provide a peaceful prosperity, without blind growth and escalating competition, as well as to outgrow novelty and consumption for their own sake. It strives to replace inequality with equity, attachment and greed with compassion and wisdom. It believes that ultimately synergy and optimization can supplant maximization; balance can beat bloat; mindfulness can instill moderation and modesty; cooperation can beget community; and economic and social justice can improve – all of which mean that common cause can prevail over self-centered gain.

Within this mighty, idealistic context, addressing urban CC and UHIs sits on the right side of multiple ledgers. It nests deeply in the "no regrets" category, as it brings environmental and ecological co-benefits and helps sustain and improve civilization. It also benefits other plant and animal species, ones that we depend on, as well as delight in. As a persistent and pervasive incentive to address our warming cities and planet, UHIs and CC can positively shape and motivate society. We are fighting our biggest battles against the increasingly dystopian disruptions of changing local and global climates, as well as overpopulation and over-consumption. Cooler, greener cities can render our civilization more sustainable, while enhancing the quality of human lives now and for generations to come. And as we deal with heat, health and habitat in the Anthropocene, maintaining our cool – literally and figuratively – will help us to navigate the coming storm, as we embrace resilient cities. "The Urban Fix," in all of its many dimensions, makes us more efficient, effective and collaborative, while enhancing and saving countless current and future lives. It's our last, best hope.

Notes

1 Bjarke Ingels, *Brainy Quote*, 1/4/19
2 Mayer Hillman, Policy Studies Institute, U.K.
3 Mikael Colville-Andersen, *Copenhagenize*, Island Press, 2018
4 Bruce F. Donnelly, personal email, April, 2018
5 Alan Lightman, *Searching for Stars on an Island in Maine*, Corsair, 2018
6 Andrés Duany, "The principles of New Urbanism," Core Session, CNU 25, Seattle, May, 2017
7 B. Plumer and N. Popovich, "As climate changes, southern states will suffer more than others," *The New York Times*, 6/29/17
8 Michael Blanding, "Feeling the heat," *Princeton Alumni Weekly*, 11/8/17, p. 21
9 Ibid., p. 22
10 Upton Sinclair, *I, Candidate for Governor: And How I Got Licked*, Farrar & Rinehart, 1935
11 Sam Ori, "How much will Americans pay to battle climate change? Not much," *The Wall Street Journal*, 5/23/17
12 Ibid.
13 Book review of *Progress: Ten Reasons to Look Forward to the Future*, by Johan Norberg, *The Economist*, 9/1/16
14 David Satterthwaite, "Urban risks: what are the five biggest blind spots?" *citiscope*, 4/24/17
15 Vice President Joe Biden, plenary talk at ULI annual meeting, Seattle, May, 2017
16 Andrés Duany, lecture, University of Michigan, April, 2013, and in *Agrarian Urbanism*, Prince's Federation, 2011, pp. 66–68 (later retitled *Garden Cities*)
17 Philip Galanes, "The mind meld of Bill Gates and Steven Pinker," *The New York Times*, 1/28/18
18 David Roberts, "The McKibben effect: a case study in how radical environmentalism can work. Extreme proposals can shift polarized debates," *Vox*, 9/29/17
19 Somini Sengupta, "2018 is shaping up to be the fourth-hottest year: yet we're still not prepared for global warming," *The New York Times*, 8/9/18
20 Jared Wadley, "Academic Freedom Lecture to consider politics of climate change," *University Record*, Michigan News, 9/14/17

21 Michael Mann, 27th Annual University Senate Lecture on Academic and Intellectual Freedom, University of Michigan, 10/3/17

22 George Monbiot, "Everything must go," blog at www.monbiot.com/2017/11/24/everything-must-go/, 11/24/17

23 Iason Athanasiadas, "Everyone in the world should be taxed on their energy footprint," *Aeon*, 12/6/17

24 Tonya Graham, "Building climate resilience in America's smaller cities and towns," *Meeting of the Minds*, 8/9/18

25 Amy Harder, "Harvey and climate change: why it won't change minds," *Axios/Harder Line*, 9/6/17

26 Eduardo Porter, "Reducing carbon by curbing population," *The New York Times*, 8/6/14

27 Professor Elizabeth Diller, lecture, Taubman College, University of Michigan, 10/28/16

28 Richard Connif, "Despairing on Earth Day? Read this," *The New York Times*, 4/21/18

29 Moises Velaquez-Manoff, "Cashing in on climate change," *The New York Times*, 12/4/16

30 Thomas Friedman, *The New York Times*, 3/25/14

31 Lord Stern, "Foreword," in *Unburnable Carbon 2013: Wasted Capital and Stranded Assets*, Carbon Tracker and the Grantham Research Institute, LSE, 2013

32 Kaid Benfied, Senior Counsel, Placemakers, citing the World Bank, email exchange, 3/23/17

33 Hiroko Tabuchi, "As Beijing joins climate fight, Chinese companies build coal plants, *The New York Times*, 7/1/17

34 "Global coal plant tracker," *endcoal*, endcoal.org, July, 2017

35 Elizabeth Kolbert, "Can carbon removal save the world?" *The New Yorker*, 11/20/17

36 John Tierney, "Climate proposal puts practicality ahead of science," *The New York Times*, 1/16/12

37 Roy Scranton, *Learning to Die in the Anthropocene*, City Lights Books, 2015, p. 43

38 Gregory Scruggs, "Buildings, energy must help insure emissions turning point by 2020 new initiative warns," *citiscope*, 4/11/17

39 Benjamin Barber, *Cool Cities: Urban Sovereignty and the Fix for Climate Change*, Yale University Press, 2017, p. 67

40 Michael Bloomberg, "City century: why municipalities are the key to fighting climate change," *Foreign Affairs*, September–October, 2015

41 Walter Einenkel, "Here are the 6 cities in the U.S. running on 100 percent renewable energy," *Daily Kos*, 10/26/17

42 Gary Scruggs, "Explainer: what is the Paris Agreement on climate change and what does it mean for cities?" *citiscope*, 3/30/17

43 Numerous authors, "America's pledge," Bloomberg Philanthropies, November, 2017

44 Mike Davis, as quoted in Duncan McLaren and Julian Agyeman, *Sharing Cities: A Case for Truly Smart and Sustainable Cities*, MIT Press, 2015

45 Paul Hawken, *Blessed Unrest: How the Largest Movement in the World Came into Being and Why No One Saw It Coming*, Viking Penguin, 2007

46 Paul Hawken, *Drawdown: The Most Comprehensive Plan Ever Proposed To Reverse Global Warming*, Penguin, 2017, p. 220

47 Ibid., p. 221

48 "A load of rubbish," *The Economist*, 9/29/18

49 Dana Gunders and Devon Klatell, "New research to help waste less food in America's cities," NRDC, 10/25/17

50 World Energy Outlook 2017, Executive Summary, IEA, 11/14/17
51 Paul Hawken, *Drawdown*, pp. 221–225
52 Rajan Chudgar and Dan Gabaldon, "What you need to know about energy storage," *Power Engineering*, 4/18/17
53 Justin Gillis, "Carbon in the atmosphere is rising, even as emissions stabilize," *The New York Times*, 6/26/17
54 Karen Seto and Shobhakar Dhakal, "Human settlements, infrastructure and spatial planning," *IPCC 2014 Mitigation*
55 Ezmé e Deprez, "California's housing policy is holding back its climate policy," *Bloomberg Business Week*, 11/15/17
56 Roy Scranton, *Learning to Die in the Anthropocene*, p. 47
57 Martin Dubbeling, "Urban planning: linchpin for sustainable urban development?" interviewed by Gregory Scruggs, *citiscope*, 7/19/17
58 Richard Sennett et al., *The Quito Papers and the New Urban Agenda*, Routledge, 2018, p. 59
59 Raven et al., "Urban planning and urban design," in C. Rosenzweig et al. (eds), *Climate Change and Cities: Second Assessment Report of the Urban Climate Change Research Network*, Cambridge University Press, 2018, p. 140
60 Peter Calthorpe, "Urban footprint," CNU Climate Change Summit, Alexandria, VA, September 29–30, 2017
61 J. Raven et al., "Urban planning and urban design," p. 168
62 "Scientists say temperatures will pass critical 2°C threshold by 2050 and that was before the election of Trump," *Real News Network*, http://therealnews.com/t2/index.php?option=com_content&task=view&id=2940
63 "A dire forecast of warming temperatures," *The New York Times*, 10/8/18
64 Benjamin Barber, *Cool Cities: Urban Sovereignty and the Fix for Climate Change*, pp. 4–5
65 Pope Francis, "*Laudato si': care for our common home*," Encyclical on Climate Change and Inequality, Melville House, 2015
66 "A dire forecast of warming temperatures," *The New York Times*, 10/8/18
67 Livia Albeck-Ripka, "Are we an invasive species?" Climate Fwd., *The New York Times*, 12/6/17
68 Alan Lightman, *Searching for Stars on an Island in Maine*, 2018
69 Michael Oppenheimer, quoted in Mike Allen, "1 big thing . . . 30-year alarm: climate change reality," *Axios*, 1/5/19
70 World Energy Outlook 2017, Executive Summary, IEA, 11/14/17
71 Naomi Klein, *This Changes Everything: Capitalism vs. The Climate*, Simon and Schuster, 2014, p. 456
72 Ibid., p. 457
73 Ibid., p. 462
74 Roy Scranton, *Learning to Die in the Anthropocene*, p. 26
75 Ibid., pp. 44–45
76 Ibid., p. 53
77 Stewart Brand et al., *The EcoModernist Manifesto*, www.ecomodernism.org/reading/
78 George Monbiot, "Everything must go"
79 "Has the environment reached peak plastic," *Research*, Morgan Stanley, 5/11/18
80 "Clearing the waves," *The Economist*, 9/29/18
81 Eduardo Porter and Karl Russell, citing the *2018 World Inequality Report* in "It's an unequal world: it doesn't have to be," *The New York Times*, 12/14/17
82 Anand Giridharadas, "Merchants of fake change," *The New York Times*, 8/26/18

83 Amie Tsang, "Britain to 'name and shame' firms with outsize executive compensation," *The New York Times*, 8/30/17
84 Yuval Noah Harari, "Nationalism in the 21st century," YouTube, 2018
85 Gwynne Dyer, *Climate Wars*, Oneworld, 2009
86 Bill McKibben, "We're not even close to being prepared for the rising waters," *The Washington Post*, 11/10/17
87 "Climate change," *The New York Times*, 9/19/17
88 Eduardo Porter, "Fighting climate change? We're not even landing a punch," *The New York Times*, 1/23/18
89 Justin Gillis and Hal Harvey, "Why a big utility is embracing wind and solar," *The New York Times*, 2/6/18
90 "Modern day alchemy: businesses are trying to reduce, reuse and recycle," *The Economist*, 9/29/18
91 Naomi Larsson, "US cities losing 36 million trees a year, researchers find," *The Guardian*, 5/10/18
92 Michael Oppenheimer and Steve Schwartzman, "How California can save the Amazon," *The New York Times*, 8/29/18
93 These two paragraphs are based on Damian Carrington's "The seven megatrends that could beat global warming: 'There is reason for hope,'" *The Guardian*, 11/8/17
94 Ibid.
95 Erle C. Ellis, "What kind of planet do we want?" Sunday Review, *The New York Times*, 8/12/18
96 Ronald Wright, *A Short History of Progress*, Canongate, 2005
97 Bill McKibben, "A world at war," *The New Republic*, 8/15/16

Index

Page numbers in *italics* refer to figures.

accessibility versus mobility 107–108
Accessory Dwelling Units (ADUs)
  241–242
active design strategies 134
active integrated mitigation and
  adaptation (AIMA) 246
adaptation xiii–xiv, 4, 211–212, 246,
  255, 274
aesthetics xviii, 248–251, *249*
agglomeration, economies of 27,
  253–254, *254*
agriculture 6–7, 40, 44, 50
Agyeman, Julian 202, 203–204, 208
Ahmedabad, India 193–196, *195*
Ai Weiwei 232, 235
air conditioning: aggravating effect of
  58–59; demand for 129, *130*, *131*,
  132; dependence on 134–135; human
  health and 52–53; improvements to
  78, 128–129, 133
air pollution 31, 101–102, 158, 244
air quality requirements 178
Airbnb 202
albedo 6, 84–97, *87*, *95*, 211, 282
Allard, Scott 228
ambient noise 31
America's Pledge 278
Anthony, Susan B. 111
Apathetics 270
Appiah, Kwame Anthony 198
architectural strategies for waste heat
  127–141
Architecture 2030 initiative 134, 137
Automated Rapid Transit (ART) 119
automation 27–28
automobile dependency *see* car use
aviation 258–259
awards 175

Barber, Benjamin xxii, 32–33, 201,
  214, 278, 296
Berger, Alan 223
Bernstein, Scott 19
bicycling and bike-sharing 110–115,
  112, 187
biochar 6
bio-energy with carbon capture and
  storage (BECCS) 7–8
birth rates: reducing 15–17, 69,
  273–274, 280, 285; urbanization
  and 16, 20–21, 75–78; *see also*
  population growth
Black, Joseph 41
Blessed Unrest (Hawken) 279
Bloomberg, Michael 212, 214,
  219, 278
brain interface, partial 27
Brand, Stewart xxii, xxiii, 40, 201,
  290, 292, 296
Brown, Clair xxii, 207, 231, 296
Brown, Jerry 278, 282
Buddhism xviii
Buddhist Economics (Brown) xxii, 207
building codes 177–178
building materials 135, 138
building size, reducing 133

C40 196, 212–213, 214
Calthorpe, Peter xxiii, 183
Campbell, Scott 53–54
car use 26–27, 64, 68, 213, 224,
  226–227; *see also* motorized space;
  parking; pavement; vehicular miles
  travelled (VMT) per capita
carbon, pools of 6
Carbon Capture and Sequestration
  Institute 276

carbon capture and sequestration/ storage (CCS) 7–8
carbon cycle 6
carbon dioxide 41, 42
carbon emissions: Atlanta/Barcelona comparison of 67; country comparison of 66; rate of 41; *see also* greenhouse gases (GHGs)
carbon farming 6
carbon mineralization 8
carbon sinks 7
Carrier, Willis 128
Carson, Rachel xix
case studies 173–196
Chakrabarti, Vishaan xxiii
Chambers, Jeffrey 160
Chesky, David 202
Chessboard and the Web, The (Slaughter) 32
Chicago case study 179–182, *180*
Chicago Climate Change Action plan 181
Child, Mike 279
child mortality rates 215
childlessness 16
children's health 62; *see also* health, human
Childs, Mark xi
City and the Coming Climate, The (Stone) xxii, 46
climate change: challenges of 41–46; compounding impacts of xii–xiii; connecting dots and 3; economic impact of 266–267, 269; overview of xi–xii, 3–4; strategies to address 4–5; as term 4; as threat multiplier 1; UHIs and 12, 14
Climate Change and Cities (Rosenzweig et al.) xxiii, 285
climate models 5
Climate of Hope (Pope and Bloomberg) 219
Climate Positive 2040 183
climate refugees 230–236
climate science 4
Clos, Joan 251–252
coal 276–277, 294
cobra effect 7
Coffee, Joyce 173
Community Land Trusts (CLT) 243
community-based adaptation (CBA) 212
commuting times 224–225
compassion 270

comprehensive plans 177
concrete, steel versus 96–97
Conflict in Cities (CinC) 198–199
Congress for New Urbanism 26, 236
connections 256–257
connectivity 108
conservation movement xix, 275
consumption 4–5
Continuous City, The (Lerup) 184
conventional suburban development (CSD) 108, 109
Cool Cities (Barber) xxii, 32–33
cool pavement 92
cooling centers 56
cooperation 203
Correa, Charles 251
cosmopolis 198–202
Cosmopolis (Solomon) 251
crime: air pollution and 31; health and 31; trees and 161–162
Crowther, Thomas 159

Dalai Lama xiv
deadhead trips 119
deaths from heat waves xii, 14, 22, 52, 56–57, 59
decarbonization 6
defensive strategies 136
deforestation 166–168
demonstration projects 174
Denialists 270–273
design guidelines 177
direct air capture 7
disease ecology 53
displacement 30
disturbance regime 160
Dittmar, Hank 19
DMS (dimethyl sulfide) 8
Donnelly, Bruce 292
Doyle, Arthur Conan 113
Drawdown (Hawken) xxii, 89, 133, 279
driverless/autonomous vehicles 118–124
drones 126–127
Duany, Andrés 270, 272
Dunham-Jones, Ellen xxiii, 121, 199, 226, 228
Dwyer, Gwynne 292

eco-gentrification 166
ecological footprints 19
Ecological Urbanism 239
EcoModernist Manifesto 290, 296

economic impact: of climate change 266–267, 269; of urban trees 156–158
economics of agglomeration 27, 253–254, *254*
eco-psychology 292
ecosystems 50–51, 253, 255
edge cities 64
education 215, 280
electric vehicles 124–127
electrical power production 141–144
Ellard, Colin 248
emotions 21
energy crisis xx
energy demand of buildings 136
energy intensity 143
energy-efficient buildings 135
environmental paradox of cities 19–20, *20*, 33, 63–68, *65*, *67*, 226
ephemeral urbanism 235
Ethicists 270
evapotranspiration 159–160, 167
extinctions 39

Farr, Douglas xxiii
fear 266
Fernandez, John 202
Ferraro, Paulo 202
fertility decline *see* birth rates
First Law of Thermodynamics 135
flooding 5–6, 23, 44, 53, 96, 164, 185–186, 213–214; *see also* sea-level rise
Floor-Area-Ratio (F.A.R.) 64
Florida, Richard 240
food waste 280–281
Ford, Henry 111
forest bathing 162
forest fires 166, 228–229
Fossil-Fuel-Free Streets Declaration 126
fountains 153
Fowles, John 151
Fraker, Harrison xxiii, 103
Francis, Pope 199, 286–287
free market model 207
Frey, Thomas 126
Frey, William 225
Friedman, Thomas 202, 275
Friends of the Earth 279

Garcetti, Eric 92
gateway effect 145
Gehl, Jan 190
gentrification 29–30, 166, 240–243

geoengineering 62–63, 294
George, Henry 243
Giamatti, Bart 198
glaciers xiii
Gladwell, Malcolm 9–10
Glaeser, Edward xxii, 27, 145, 220, 231, 240, 256, 257, *296*
glass buildings 128
Global Covenant of Mayors for Climate and Energy 278
Global Parliament of Mayors 214
global population growth xii
Good Practice Guides 196
Gore, Al xx, 53, 272, 292
government insurance 178
government subsidies 178–179
grants 174
grayfield redevelopment 109, 226
Green Alley initiative 175, 181
green buildings 134, 177
"Green Manhattan" (Owen) 219
green roofs 85–86, 89–90, 101, 153, *154*
green walls 100–101, 153
greenfield developments 109, 121, 218, 237
greenhouse effect, description of 12, 14, 50
greenhouse gases (GHGs): autonomous vehicles and 120; city emissions of 212–213; sources of 42; trees and 167; *see also* carbon emissions
Grimshaw, Jackie 19
Gruen, Victor 220
guerilla gardening 238
guilt 266
Gulf Coast Institute 185
Guo 75

Hanks, Tom xxii
Hansen, James 57, 288
Harari, Yuval Noah 11, 203, 228, 291–292
Harry, Seth 218
Hawken, Paul xxii, 4, 89, 133, 279–280, 282, 286, *296*
health, human 51–54, 62, 114, 116, 162, 226–227, 248–251
Heat Action Plan (Ahmedabad, India) 194–196
heat cramps 52
heat exhaustion 52
heat from dark surfaces 14, 18

heat rash 52
heat stroke 52
heat vulnerability 193–194
heat waves xii, 22, 46, 54–62, 181–182, 193–194, 224, 244–246, 274
Hemingway, Ernest xiv
high-rise sprawl 68
historic preservation movement xix–xx
housing subsidies 30
Houston Advanced Research Center (HARC) 185
Houston case study 184–188
Howards, Jeff 211–212
Human Flow 235
humidity 245
Hurr, Hanna 206
Hurricane Harvey 185–187
hypothalamus 51

ice sheets, melting of xiii, 5–6
immigration 28
incentive grants and rebates 174
Inconvenient Sequel, An 272
Inconvenient Truth, An 272
Industrial Revolution (IR) 141
inequality xv, 291
infill development 241, 278
informal settlements 217
Ingels, Bjarke 106, 243, 265
insulation 138
insurance 178, 266–267
Intergovernmental Panel on Climate Change (IPCC) 7, 213, 286, 287
international case studies 188–196
International Council for Local Environmental Initiatives (ICLEI) 214
International Migration Report 231
interstitial greenery 164

Jackson, Tim xxiii, 208–209
Jacobs, Jane xix, 162, 199, 200, 220, 227, 240–241, 255–257, 286, 289
Jevons Complimentary Corollary 145
Jevons Paradox 144–145
Jouzel, Jean 59

Katz, Bruce 215
Kigali amendment 281–282
Kimmelman, Michael 3, 25
Kleiber's Law 253
Klein, Naomi xxii, 288–289, 292, 296
Kolbert, Elizabeth 39

Koolhaas, Rem 222, 233–234
Kopp, Bob 267
Krugman, Paul 72–73
Kunstler, James 229
Kyoto Protocol 277

land surface temperature *49*
landscape ordinances 176–177
Landscape Urbanism 239
latent heat 14
Laudato Si' (Pope Francis) 286–287
lawns 222
Leakey, Richard 39
Lean Urbanism (LeanU) 237–239, 278
Learning to Die in the Anthropocene (Scranton) xxiii, 289–290
LED bulbs 23, 144–145
Lerup, Lars 184
liberal values 28–29
lighting 23, 136, 144–145
Lightman, Alan 266, 287
Lister, Nina-Marie 51
Litman, Todd 122
love 21, 266
Lovins, Amory 273

Man Who Planted Trees, The (Robbins) 150–151
Mann, Charles 40, 269, 296
Mann, Michael 271
Maslow's hierarchy of needs 266
Mattern, Shannon 205
Mazria, Ed 134
McKibben, Bill 1, 296
McLaren, Duncan 203–204, 208
megacities 69, 73
Mehaffy, Michael 212, 219, 257
Mehrotra, Rahul 72, 235
mental health 248–250
methane 42–43
Metropolitan Regional Containment Index 226
micro-cities 71
micro-climates 18, 150–169
Mies van der Rohe 106
migration 230–236
Millennium Development Goals 215, 216
mini-grids 143
Mission 2020 277
mitigation strategies 4, 211–212, 246, 284–285
Mobike 110
mobility hubs 119

mobility versus accessibility 107–108
Montreal Protocol 132, 273, 281
mosquitoes 53
motorized space 92, 93; *see also*
    car use
Mouzon, Steve 21
municipal finances 32
Muscat, Oman 190–193
Musk, Elon 27

National Flood Insurance Program 178
natural disaster map 268
natural ventilation 9, 23, 47, 59, 102,
    140, 190, 192, 247
negative emissions technologies
    (NETS) 7, 62
Nelson, Arthur 230
New Urban Agenda (NUA) 32,
    216–219, 277
New Urbanism (NU) 236–240
Ng, Edward 54, 76
nitrous oxide (N₂O) 50
no-growth economies 208–209
noise pollution 31
nuclear power 281, 282, 294

obesity rates 227, 251
oceans 8–9
offensive strategies 136
office parks 222
Ofo 110
old-growth forests 166
olivine 8
On Beauty and Being (Scarry) xviii
One Child Policy 273
One Million Acres and No Zoning
    (Lerup) 184
Oppenheimer, Michael 288
Opportunists 270
optimism bias 10
organized complexity 256
Orr, Robert 238
overpopulation, challenges of 68–79
Owen, David 219, 224, 242
ozone 158

Paris Climate Accord 9, 32, 78, 212,
    272, 276, 277, 292, 293
parking 91–92, 93, 94, 108, 122, 222;
    see also car use
particulate air pollution 101–102
partisanship 29
passive, energy-efficient buildings
    137–141

passive design strategies 134, 135–136,
    137–141
passive integrated mitigation and
    adaptation (PIMA) 246
passive solar heating 136, 138–139
pavement 91–97, 95
Peduto, Bill 243
pets 117
photosynthesis 6, 8, 159
photovoltaic panels 136, 143; *see also*
    solar industry
phytoplankton 8
Pielke, Roger, Jr. 277
Pink Zone 237–238
Pinker, Steven 269
Places in Need (Allard) 228
plants 6–7
Plato xi
Plausible scenario 280–281
pleasure 266
policy initiatives 175–179
Pollan, Michael 222
polycultural navigation 29
pools 153
population growth: connecting dots
    and 2, 3; in developing countries
    14–15; *see also* birth rates
population paradox of cities 20–21,
    33–34, 76–79
positive feedback, as term 9–10
poverty xv, 22–23, 27, 215, 217,
    228, 231
private sector initiatives, voluntary
    174–175
procurement 175
productivity, air temperature and
    257–258
Project for Public Spaces 236, 237, 279
Prosperity without Growth (Jackson)
    xxiii, 208
public education 175
public space 199–201
Putnam, Robert 256

Quality of Life Coalition (Houston)
    185
*Quito Declaration on Sustainable
    Cities and Human Settlements for
    All* (Habitat for Humanity) 217

Rathi, Akshat 63
Raven, Jeffrey 285
real estate values 151, 157, 161, 240,
    241, 243

rebates 174
rebound effect 144–145
recarbonization 6
redundancy 246
Reed, Chris 51
refrigerant management 133, 281–282
refugee camps 235
renewable energy systems 143
resilience xx, 45, 217–218, 246–247
resolutions 175
Retrofitting Suburbia (Dunham-Jones and Williamson) 199, 226
Revi, Aromar xvi
rideshare services 122–123
Rifkin, Jeremy xxiii, 141–142, 296
Robbins, Jim 150–151
Rode, Philipp 226
rooftops 85–91, *87*, *95*, *96*, 101, 153, *154*, 178, 180–181, 194–195, *195*
Rose, Jonathan xxii, 222, 270
Rosenzweig, Cynthia xxiii
Rudd Andrew 218
Russell, Bertrand 259, 266

Salt Lake City case study 182–183
Sassen, Saskia 73, 231–232
Savage, Dan 202
Scarry, Elaine xviii
Scranton, Roy xxiii, 277, 289–290, 292, 296
sea-level rise 213–214, 293; *see also* flooding
Second Law of Thermodynamics 135
secondary cities 72–73
Sennett, Richard 205
sensible heat 14
Shared-Use Mobility Center 115
Sharing Cities (McLaren and Agyeman) xi, 203–204
sharing culture 202–209
shopping malls 60, 120, 199, 220, 222, 223, 226
Short History of Progress, A (Wright) xxii, 296
Shoup, Donald 91
sick building syndrome (SBS) 53
sidewalks 117
Sinclair, Upton 269
singularity xiv
Sivaram, Varun 89
Sixth Extinction, The (Kolbert) 39
Slaughter, Anne-Marie 32
slavery 289
slums *70*, 71, 216–217

Smart Cities 205–206
snow removal 117
social engineering 122–123
social equity *54*–55
social stress 249
solar industry 136–137, 143, 145, 281, 294
solar reflectance (SR) 85
Solar Reflectivity Index (SRI) 85, 96
solar thermal systems 88–89
Solomon, Daniel 251
Speck, Jeff xxiii
sprawl 219–230, *221*, 252, 282
steel, concrete versus 96–97
Stern, Nicholas 275, 295
Stiglitz, Joseph xv
Stone, Brian xxii, 46, 55, 153, 160, 224
Stuttgart, Germany 188–190
subsidiarity 212, 215
subsidies 178–179
suburbs 219–230
suicide rates 249
sun 84–85
Sun Also Rises, The (Hemingway) xiv
Survivalists 270
sustainability xx, xxii, 217–218, 251, 265
Sustainable Development Goals (SDG) 216
sustainable drainage systems (SUDS) 96
swamp coolers 153

Tactical Urbanism (TU) 237, 238, 278
taxation 272
temperature maps *13*
thermal diffusivity 94, 96
thermal paradox of cities 24
thermoregulation, human 51–52
Thich Nhat Hanh xviii
Third Industrial Revolution, The (Rifkin) 141–142
This Changes Everything (Klein) xxii, 288–289
three-degree warming xix, 292–293
Tipping Point, The (Gladwell) 9–10
tipping points xiv, 9–10, 286
tourism 200–201
Transition Town 240
transit-oriented development (TOD) 26–27, 107, 109
transpiration 159–160, 167
transportation: CO_2 from 42; waste heat and 107–127; *see also* aviation; car use

Tree, The (Fowles) 151
tree protection ordinances 176–177
trees 26, 150–169, *152, 165, 176,*
179–180, 250, *294–295*
Trees for Houston 185
Trendsetters 270
Triumph of the City (Glaeser)
xxii, 220
Truth about Climate Change, The 286

unmanned aerial vehicles (UAVs)
126–127
urban canyons, ventilating 97–103,
99, 100, 102
urban density xv, 64
urban heat islands (UHIs): causes of
47; challenges of 46–68; connecting
dots and 2, 3; description of 11–12,
12, 14; in developing countries 25;
extension of 23–24; heat waves
and 54–62; mitigation strategies
for 18–19; outdoor activities and
22–23; social equity and 54–55;
summary of 34; trees and 26; urban
design and 97–98, *99;* waste heat
and 106–107
urban planning 284–285
urban poverty paradox 27
urban residents, ecological footprints
of 19–20, *20*
urban resilience xx, 246–248
urbanization: birth rates and 75–78;
in developing countries 74; rate of
69, 71–72
U.S. case studies 173–188

vehicular miles travelled (VMT) per
capita 64, 107, 108, 144; *see also*
car use
violence, heat and 25–26, 269

volcanos 9
voluntary private sector initiatives
174–175
voluntary/demonstration efforts
174–175

Walk Score 118
walking 115–118
Walston, Joe 275
waste heat 11, 14, 18, 26, 47–48,
106–145, 282–283
water runoff 96
water stress 44–45, 291
Watson, Robert xix, 286
Watt, James 41
weather events, increasingly severe
43–44
Wellenius, Gregory 51
Well-Tempered City, The (Rose)
xxii, 222
West, Geoffrey 253
white roofs 86–87, *87,* 89–90, 101
Whole Earth Discipline (Brand)
xxii, 40
Whyte, William 201
wilderness-urban-interface (WUI)
228–229
Williamson, June xxiii, 226
Wilson, E.O. 39
wind conditions, trees and 153, 155
wind power 143, 294
Wohlleben, Peter 168–169
work capacity losses 56
Wright, Ronald xxii, 296
Wright Brothers 111

Yglesias, Matt 205

zero-occupancy vehicle (ZOV) 119
zoning codes 177

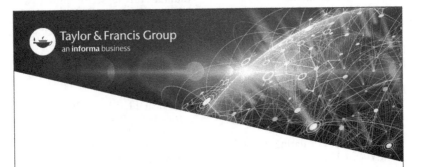